THE NEW ANTHOLOGY OF AMERICAN POETRY

The New Anthology
of American Poetry

VOLUME THREE

Postmodernisms
1950–Present

* * * * * * * * * * * * *

EDITED BY

Steven Gould Axelrod

Camille Roman

Thomas Travisano

RUTGERS UNIVERSITY PRESS
NEW BRUNSWICK, NEW JERSEY, AND LONDON

Visit our Web site: http://rutgerspress.rutgers.edu

Produced by BookComp, Incorporated

Library of Congress Cataloging-in-Publication Data

The new anthology of American poetry / edited by Steven Gould Axelrod,
    Camille Roman, and Thomas Travisano.
        p. cm.
    Vol. 3.
    Includes bibliographical references and index.
    Contents: v. 3. Postmodernisms, 1950–Present.
    ISBN 0-8135-5155-5 (cloth : alk. paper)—ISBN 0-8135-5156-2 (pbk. : alk. paper)
    1. American poetry. I. Axelrod, Steven Gould, 1944–   II. Roman, Camille,
    1948–   III. Travisano, Thomas J., 1951–
    PS586.N49 2003
    811.008—dc21   2002070502

A British Cataloging-in-Publication record for this book is available from the
British Library.

To Our Families and Students

CONTENTS

xviii ✦ Contents

PREFACE

WE ARE HAPPY TO INVITE YOU into the world of postmodern poetry and culture. The poetry is notable for its fluidity of outlook and expression—its chameleon-like ability to change color. Some of the poems, for example, are deeply personal. Elizabeth Bishop writes to herself (in "In the Waiting Room"): "But I felt: you are an *I*, / you are an *Elizabeth*." Robert Lowell *seems* to be making a personal statement when he writes (in "Skunk Hour"), "I myself am hell," though he is actually echoing John Milton in *Paradise Lost*, thus complicating any simple notion of confession. Even George Oppen, often the most impersonal of poets, asks (in "Birthplace: New Rochelle"), "I am this?" Alternatively, many poems of the period are transfixed with others—with individuals or communities—rather than with their author's identity. Gwendolyn Brooks (in "The Life of Lincoln West") focuses on her young protagonist, fighting his way through a tangle of racism. Adrienne Rich (in "Power") similarly focuses on Marie Curie, sedimented in layers of power, "living in the earth-deposits of our history." Yet other poets concentrate on the intensities and voids of language itself. Lyn Hejinian (in "[It is the writer's object]") subverts the very idea of a cohesive, common-sense "I": "It is the writer's object / to supply the hollow green / and yellow life of the / human I." Rae Armantrout does the same to "you" when she writes (in "Attention"), "The 'you' / in the heart of / molecule and ridicule."

The poetry of 1950 to the present has emerged as a medium of exploration, and postmodernism appears not only as a condition of this writing but also as a condition of living. Lowell writes (in "Dolphin"), "my eyes have seen what my hand did," suggesting the mutual enmeshment of experience and writing. Lorna Dee Cervantes echoes that notion when she asks (in "Drawings"), "Is there some library where you'll find me, smashed / on the page of some paper?" As the poets of this anthology enter the institution of poetry, they grapple with both life and language—that is, the essential slipperiness of both life and language, which is only made more obvious by poetry's proclivity for indirection and condensation. Yet while snared in this frustrating but exhilarating thicket of words, the poets strive to say something—about themselves, about others, about the world, or about the mysteries of language itself. If each poem is an account of its struggle to come into being, perhaps as we read we will want to say with Frank Bidart (in

"Lament for the Masters"), "Teach me, masters who by making were / remade, your art."

Overviews are difficult to achieve in a poetry so contradictory and so near to us. Yet three general trends might be discerned, though they tend to overlap. One would be a poetics of subjectivity, employing methods of introspection and what critic Harold Bloom has called a trope of vulnerability. Selected poems by Robert Lowell, Sylvia Plath, Anne Sexton, Frank Bidart, and Marilyn Chin might exemplify this trend. Another trend would be a poetics of linguistic de-centering, employing a method of language play and a trope of irony. Poems by George Oppen, John Ashbery, Charles Bernstein, Rae Armantrout, and Har-ryette Mullen might exemplify this trend. And a third trend would be a poetics of social critique, employing methods of identification, empathy, and advocacy and a trope of cultural awareness. Certain poems by Gwendolyn Brooks, Lorna Dee Cervantes, Bob Dylan, Cherríe Moraga, and Sherman Alexie might exem-plify this trend.

As soon as one invents such categories, however, they begin to crumble. Frank O'Hara is vulnerable, ironic, and culturally aware at the same time. Nathaniel Mackey combines linguistic decentering with a specifically African-American consciousness. Lyn Hejinian both implies and subverts notions of a phenom-enon one can meaningfully call "my life." Most of the poets in this anthology have moved back and forth among the trends outlined there. They generated, and still generate, unstable discursive fields, capable of being seen in many ways from many different viewpoints. They reflect and respect the fluidity of history—the powerhouse of change—and to some degree their poetry helps channel that change. Perhaps the most one can say of the period from 1950 to the present is that it is confusing and unstable. The poetries of postmodernism, like the period itself, are not nailed down, and perhaps never will be. The vitality of this work beckons to us now.

Although you will be introduced to a range of ideas about the poems in this volume, you will more importantly make contact with the poems themselves, and with their gloriously rich and mysterious verbal details. You will embark on the kind of experience Allen Ginsberg (at the end of "Howl") called "a sea-journey on the highway across America." It is also a sea-journey into the English language and into a time that is our own, or very nearly our own.

ACKNOWLEDGMENTS AND A NOTE
ON THE COVER ART

AS IN THE EARLIER VOLUMES of this anthology, we are deeply indebted to numerous literary scholars, poets, librarians, historians, and anthologists, many of whose names appear in our notes and "Further Reading" selections. We also thank our students at the University of California, Riverside, Washington State University, and Hartwick College for their eagerness to explore the poetry with us. We are grateful to our colleagues as well for their support and encouragement.

As always, our most heartfelt thanks go to Leslie Mitchner, our wonderful editor at Rutgers, for her enthusiasm, professionalism, imagination, wisdom, and patience. We have reason to be especially grateful for that last quality this time around. We are also grateful to the rest of the staff at the press, particularly Katie Keeran and Bryce Schimanski. For their great and generous help in arranging for our use of Pierre Daura's painting *The Love of the 3 Oranges* (1953–60) as our cover art, we especially thank Martha Daura and Tom Mapp as well as Lisa Fischman, director of the Davis Art Museum at Wellesley College, and the talented Sandra Hachey of the museum staff who discovered that Daura had painted more than one version of the cover art. We are grateful, as always, to Melody Lacina for her expert copy-editing. We also thank Carol Bifulco of BookComp.

Steven Gould Axelrod thanks his remarkable research assistant, Anthony Randall, who solved many a riddle and shared with him the experience of permissions dilemmas and victories. He thanks Hong Jig Rim, who performed expert research assistance at an earlier stage of composition. He is grateful to the librarians at the Tomás Rivera Library and the computer specialists at the University of California, Riverside, for their wise counsel, and he thanks the university's Research Committee for financial support. He thanks the following poets, scholars, and lovers of the arts for their invaluable advice and help: Elmaz Abinader, Rae Armantrout, Doris Awad, Charles Bernstein, Frank Bidart, Alicia Contreras, Liam Corley, Fred Courtright, Catherine Cucinella, Amy Gerstler, Callie Gladman, Jeffrey Gray, Bill Ehrhart, the late Emory Elliott, Lyn Hejinian, Tim Hunt, Frank Kearful, Lisette Ordorica Lasater, Gerald McCarthy, Bill Mohr, the late Kathryn O'Rourke, Marjorie Perloff, Amy Moorman Robbins, Jan Roselle, Maurya Simon, Cathy Song, Elizabeth Spies, Kathleen Spivack,

Craig Svonkin, Paul Tayyar, Mitsuye Yamada, Guojing Yang, and John Yau. Finally, he thanks Rise B. Axelrod, Jeremiah B. C. Axelrod, Melissa Axelrod, and Lil Delcampo for intellectual stimulation, emotional support, and more; and he welcomes Amalia and Sophie Axelrod-Delcampo into the world.

Camille Roman wishes to acknowledge Washington State University's timely financial support from Douglas Epperson, dean of the College of Liberal Arts, and George Kennedy, chair of the Department of English as well as the assistance of Annette Bednar and Assistant Dean Paul Phillip. Erich Lear, former dean of the College of Liberal Arts, and Victor Villaneuva, former chair of the Department of English, also have been supportive. Roman thanks her university colleagues for their collegiality and hospitality—especially Nic and Karen Kiessling. Also, for their support, Jana Argersinger, Susan Armitage, David Barnes, Ann Berry, Paul Brians, Joan Burbick, Donna Campbell, Peter Chilson, Paula Coomer, Richard Domey, Paula Elliott, Diane Gillespie, Lynn Gordon, Alex Hammond, Barbara Hammond, Elwood Hartman, Polly Hartman, Desiree Hellegers, Tim Hunt, Virginia Hyde, Linda Kittel, Alex Kuo, Buddy Levi, Cami Levi, Stan Linden, Luci Linden, Allison Llevenseller, Michael Llevenseller, Susan McLeod, Rory Ong, Leonard Orr, T.V. Reed, Augusta Rohrbach, Marian Sciachitano, Carol Siegel, Elizabeth Siler, Jerrie Sinclair, Barbara Sitko, Jan Slaybaugh, Richard Slaybaugh, Susan Spurlock, Noel Sturgeon, Al von Frank, Jane von Frank, and Mary Wack. She is grateful to Meghan Wiley as well as Allison Llevenseller and the staff at the Holiday Inn Express in Pullman, Washington, who gave her a cherished space for working on this volume—as well as Debra Royer, at the Crumpacher Family Library, Portland (Oregon) Art Museum, for her inspiring reading room there and archival talents.

For their energizing research support, she thanks her former students, especially Laura Gruber, but also Naomi Allen, Mary Anderson, Christy Kord, Lee Maguire, Jason Miller, Drew Piper, and Patti Ver Straat as well as her poetry and culture classes at Washington State University from 2000 to 2008.

Roman expresses her deep gratitude to Brown University, especially Kevin McLaughlin, dean of the faculty, and Carolyn Deane, senior associate dean of the faculty, for offering her a visiting scholar appointment. She also wishes to thank the Department of English, especially the generous Acting Chair Stephen Foley and its excellent staff members Marilyn Netter and Lorraine Mazza, as well as the talented Rosemary Cullen of the John Hay Library staff.

Roman is grateful to Filipino-American Studies scholar Jane Sarmiento Schwab, who worked with great patience and knowledge alongside her as an assistant editor on the Filipino and Filipino-American cultural and poetry scholarship. Both Roman and Schwab wish to acknowledge the following for their invaluable contributions to this volume. We are deeply grateful to Tom Bolling, Odegaard Undergraduate Library, University of Washington; James Stack,

Special Collections Division, University of Washington; Morgen MacIntosh Hodgetts, DePaul University; and David Pavelich, University of Chicago. We are also especially indebted to an extraordinary circle of scholars, writers, and poets at the University of Hawaii at Manoa that includes, but is not limited to, Teresita Ramos, founder of the Filipino and Phillipine Literature Program, Ruth Mabanglo, coordinator, Amy Agbayani, Nina Agbayani, Richard and the late Nena Benton, and Aleli and the late Stan Starosta. Equally important are the following: Delia Aguilar, Nick Carbo, Jonathan Chua, John Cowen, Isagani R. Cruz, Reme Grefalda, Luisa Igloria, Fatima Lim-Wilson, Linda Nietes, Lorena O'English, David Romtvedt, E. San Juan, Jr., Eileen Tobias, Timothy Yu, and Nelly and Cesar Zamora.

For their remarkable assistance in the annotations for "The Ghost of Soul-making," Roman wishes to thank Michael Harper and Ruth Heimann Oppenheim for their generosity and wisdom—and Claudia Oppenheim Cameron, Jeffrey Oppenheim, and Selma Moss-Ward for their support.

For sharing their talents and interests in the arts generously as she worked on volume three, Roman wishes to thank her husband Chris D. Frigon with great affection first and foremost. She also is grateful to Roger Allen and Marie Jones, Sandra Barry, Scott Berg, Daria Bessom, Roger Bessom, Jamie Bhatty, Mutlu Blasing, Courtney Carter, Dottie Chidester, Martha Cutter, Suzanne del Gizzo, Scott Donaldson, Cheryll Faust, Richard Flynn, the late Gerald Frigon and family, Jay and Adrian Glasson, Laura Glenn and family, Lorrie Goldenssohn, Greta and the late Doris Gustafson, Philip Hansen, Hillard Howard, Andi John and family, Dorothy and Bob Johnson and family, Connie Kirk, Nick Kreofsky, Alexia, Jim, and Rick Liebenow, Freddi Lipstein, Eleanor and the late Bob Lowry, the late Bill Maloof, Rajamma Matheu, June and Jim May and family, Jerry McCubbin and Judi McGavin, George Monteiro, Mary Nichols, Pat O'Brien and family, Annette O'Donnell, the late Walter Oppenheim, Peter Papulis and family, Allison Reeves and family, the Jeff Reingolds, the late Harold Reisner, Julie Richie, Donna Riley and family, Bob and Betsy Roman and the Sherricks, Nikki Roman-Bhatty and the Viventis, Marilyn Roman and family, Mary Roman and family, Richard Romiti and family, Karen Skoog, Tori Smith, Frank and Michael Suchomel, the late Darryl Thierse, the late (Elizabeth) Ann (Roper) (Hart) Whitsell, Phyllis Wojciechowski, Susanne Woods, Patricia Yeager, and Ellie Zuckow.

Thomas Travisano wishes to thank research assistants Stevens Van Duzer and Zachary Tilfer, his students at Hartwick College, for their dedicated and enthusiastic work in support of this project. He thanks the reference department at the Hartwick College Library. He is also grateful to the Board of Trustees of Hartwick College and the Office of Academic Affairs for their generous and ongoing support, particularly through a Faculty Research Grant and a Wandersee

xxvi   ◆   Acknowledgments

Scholar in Residence Award that supported work on this volume. He thanks his Hartwick classes, particularly in Contemporary American Literature and Four Modern American Poets, for their excellent questions and inquiring attitude. Most of all, he thanks his wife, Elsa Travisano, for her computer expertise and literary judgment as well as for her resilience, patience, good humor, and good counsel.

The cover art of this volume is a reproduction of *The Love of the 3 Oranges*, painted by Pierre Daura between 1953 and 1960. Daura (1896–1976) was born on the Spanish island of Minorca, grew up in Barcelona, Catalonia (a region of Spain), and lived for many years in Paris. His Spanish citizenship was revoked after he fought with the anti-fascist forces in the Spanish Civil War. While he and his family were visiting Virginia in 1939, World War II broke out, preventing their return to France. Daura lived the rest of his life in Virginia and became an American citizen. *The Love of the 3 Oranges*, painted in oils, is notable for its fluidity, motion, and color—qualities that can be inferred in many of the poems in this anthology. The oranges in the painting are abstracted, and they appear to resemble human figures. Their ambiguity also seems appropriate to the poetry of this period. Daura's daughter Martha has told us that her father worked on his art while listening to music. He painted this piece, for example, while listening to the Sergei Prokofiev opera, *The Love for Three Oranges*. The painting, therefore, includes qualities of musicality, visuality, and intertextuality, as do the poems in this volume.

PART ONE

✦

Mid-Twentieth-Century Poetry

INTRODUCTION

Mid-twentieth-century American poetry witnessed revolutions in form and content that were as sweeping as the modernist revolutions of the earlier twentieth century. Whereas many modernist poets had emphasized impersonality, many midcentury poets brought a seemingly autobiographical speaker into their texts. While earlier high modernist poets, such as T. S. Eliot, Ezra Pound, and Allen Tate, had often expressed anxiety about social change, repugnance toward mass culture, and nostalgia for an idealized past, the midcentury poets were more likely to celebrate change, to display ambivalence toward the past, and to reveal a keen fascination with mass culture. Perhaps this new generation of poets was learning to live in and resonate with the conditions of their rapidly altering universe, even though they usually confronted those conditions with complicated feelings. Their modernist predecessors continued to have an impact on the midcentury generation, whom Randall Jarrell was among the first to label "postmodernist." But the new poets, often after serving an informal apprenticeship under one or more members of the elder generation, moved ahead on their own terms, building on their mentors' formal experiments while transforming the sometimes conservative ethos of those older poets into something rich, unpredictable, and fresh.

Midcentury was a complicated and contradictory time. Although many Americans increased their wealth in the 1950s, the gap between rich and poor was widening, and the apparent general prosperity was interrupted and threatened by intermittent recessions. Thrilled at their triumph in World War II, and buoyed by material advances, numerous Americans experienced what one historian, William O'Neill, has called an "American high." But this era of good feeling came at a price: social conformity, persistent racial and gender iniquities, foreign crises, an expanding "military-industrial complex" (as President Eisenhower called it), and, over all, a dread of nuclear annihilation. The 1960s ushered in a mixed period of social progress and social conflict, culminating in the Vietnam War, in which more than fifty-eight thousand Americans and many times more Vietnamese and others lost their lives.

It was a complex fate being an American poet at midcentury. Most of these poets grew increasingly wary about key elements of American domestic and foreign policy while at the same time they engaged in fruitful efforts to reinvent American poetry for the post–World War II era. They were estranged, but they were also increasingly entrenched, as more and more of them found positions teaching in the nation's schools and universities. American poetry of the 1950s and 1960s participated in Cold War culture. The ways of seeing instilled by the rivalry between the United States and the Soviet Union and by the ever-present threat of nuclear war filtered subtly into poetic and everyday consciousness. Containment policy, which stipulated that the United States try to "contain" Soviet power and influence, fostered a reliance on dualisms of "us" and "them" that affected nearly all cultural projects. Middle-class women and families were in effect "contained" in newly built suburbs, while many poor people, single people, immigrants, and people of color were left stranded in urban areas that suffered from a loss of jobs, a contracting tax base, worsening schools, and a rising crime rate. These conditions were complexly mirrored and critiqued in the poetry of the period. Although African-American advocacy groups succeeded in dismantling the legal foundations of racial segregation, these hard-won political changes were not necessarily accompanied by social or economic improvement. By the mid- and late 1960s, American culture was in crisis. Assassinations claimed the lives of President John F. Kennedy, Martin Luther King, Jr., Robert Kennedy, and Malcolm X. The Vietnam War raged. Many American poets opposed the war, and a large and visible body of them actively resisted it. The placid conformity and the patina of progress that had marked 1950s culture came crashing down, and poetry was at the center of the social conflict.

While it is impossible to categorize all the important trends in mid-twentieth-century American poetry—because this body of work was so various and dynamic—we can roughly divide the poets into four distinct, yet interrelated groups, which will be discussed in more detail below. The mainstream poets were a loosely affiliated assemblage that included but was not limited to the "confessional," "introspective," or "domestic" poets who made such an impact in their time. Although sometimes viewed as less aesthetically adventurous than their artistic rivals, these poets explored personal experience with unprecedented candor, keenly dramatizing the ways that experience diverged from normative stories of happy families and happy endings. These poets worked sometimes in free verse and sometimes in traditional poetic forms, though when they utilized traditional forms they often subverted them. A second distinct camp comprised the Beat poets, who engaged in vigorous self-expression and radically opposed bourgeois social standards while employing free verse and other open forms almost exclusively. A third group included poets of color, especially African-American poets who focused on black culture and the civil rights movement, but also other poets from socially marginalized backgrounds. These poets participated in a complex interaction with traditional and modernist forms that were themselves to some degree emblematic of a dominant, exclusionary culture in need of critique and change. A fourth group was composed of various experimental movements, including the Objectivist poets, the Black Mountain poets, and the New York poets—all of whom in some way carried further the experiments of earlier avant-garde poets. All four of these camps, as different from each other as they were, shared an antipathy to conventional norms and in particular to the social conformity that prevailed in the 1950s and early 1960s. They devoted their lives to creative discovery. They resisted trends in American culture while also sharing in and shaping them.

Mainstream poets looked closely at the world around them and often responded in a manner that appeared intensely personal. Some of them were thought of as "confessional" poets, and as such they challenged an early-twentieth-century preference for impersonality that had been advocated by their modernist mentors. These poets were "self-analytic," as scholar Alan Williamson asserted in *Introspection and Contemporary Poetry*. They gazed inward, bringing to light their memories and secrets, in a way that was meant to *seem* real even within the intricate design of poetic form. These poets often found their center of gravity in their family relations, friendships, and love relationships. Robert Lowell published poems that dwelt on material that earlier generations might have kept hidden, such as family conflicts and mental illness. Lowell's students Anne Sexton and Sylvia Plath published self-exploratory poems as well, and they would soon be followed by Lowell's friends Randall Jarrell, John Berryman, and even the characteristically reticent Elizabeth Bishop. Such works broadened the range of lyric poetry to include elements of plot and character usually associated with fiction, memoir, and film. The poems were often written in free verse, which in itself signaled an emotional openness. At the same time, they were highly nuanced in their linguistic and formal properties. Writing in a less "confessional" vein, Muriel Rukeyser addressed both personal and political issues through the lens of woman-centered myth, and Adrienne Rich combined formal elegance with a highly theorized and revolutionary gender awareness. Mid-twentieth-century culture was invested in issues of home and family, personal identity and the textures of personal life, as a method to both escape and deal with troubling political issues and social conflicts of race and gender. Mainstream poems by Bishop, Lowell, Rich, and Plath—and by poets of color such as Gwendolyn Brooks and Mitsuye Yamada—satisfied those interests by focusing on the heretofore private household as well as the always exposed public sphere.

Beat poets more overtly challenged established social and artistic norms. If Lowell and Plath destabilized norms from within, by illustrating how fractured self and family actually were, Beat poets such as Allen Ginsberg, Diane di Prima, and to some extent Gary Snyder and Amiri Baraka assailed those norms from without. They showed what an alternative social and artistic arrangement might look like, as they rebuffed the social conformity of the 1950s and encouraged the countercultural projects of the 1960s. Beat poets called for the overthrow of conventional standards of behavior, belief, and poetic practice. But their connection to other poetic groups was often palpable. Amiri Baraka, for example, began as a Beat poet and evolved into an advocate for Black Arts who showed some affinities with the New York school as well. Ginsberg and Lowell were rivals, but they knew, interested, and influenced each other. Ginsberg would grandly assert, "I saw the best minds of my generation destroyed by madness" in 1956, only to be echoed by Lowell's confession, "My mind's not right," in 1959. Di Prima's gender awareness can be seen as complementary to that of Rukeyser, Brooks, Rich, and Plath. Ginsberg's use of dreamlike language, surprising juxtapositions, and silences and repetitions can be compared to similar verbal practices by experimental poets of the Objectivist and Black Mountain schools.

African-American poets such as Robert Hayden, Gwendolyn Brooks, Derek Walcott, and Amiri Baraka explored the personal and political existences of black America, focusing on ordinary people as well as heroes and artists. Their poems became increasingly political as time went on and as racial frustration, conflict, and progress became more pronounced. By the 1960s, Baraka and Brooks were identifying themselves with a more assertive form of racial expression that Baraka called the "Black Arts" movement, which to some degree grew out of his earlier affinity with the Beats. Brooks argued that to be black was inherently to be political in a land where racial inequality was so pervasive. But then she added, quite powerfully, that "to be *anything* is to be political." Poems by African Americans engaged in a cultural decentering, moving readers toward multicultural perspectives on poetry and culture. This decentering was reinforced by the poetry of other previously marginalized social groups, who were similarly engaging in a process of self-exploration and self-presentation. Important voices that arose included Latina/o poets Julia de Burgos (herself partly of African descent) and Tino Villareal and Asian-American poets Carlos Bulosan and Mitsuye Yamada. In the context of social marginalization, one might also consider the many gifted lesbian, gay, and bisexual poets who came to the fore during this period: Elizabeth Bishop, Muriel Rukeyser, Robert Duncan, Allen Ginsberg, James Merrill, Frank O'Hara, John Ashbery, and Adrienne Rich. Through such poets a variety of new experiences, forms, and vocabularies entered into and affected the texture of American poetry.

Experimental poets also predominated in the post–World War II era. Like the Beats, with whom they shared an affinity, the experimentalists were a band of rebels, or rather several different bands of rebels. One band was the Objectivist group, which arose in the 1930s. George Oppen was its youngest member, and he flourished in the late 1950s and 1960s. Oppen carried further the innovative project of such modernists as Ezra Pound, William Carlos Williams, and Charles

Reznikoff, while infusing it with his personal idiosyncrasies and his passion for social justice. A related experimentalist movement was the Black Mountain school of poets, which included Charles Olson, Robert Duncan, Denise Levertov, and Robert Creeley. In 1950 Charles Olson called for a new style of "open field" composition, in which the content should generate an improvised form. Instead of resembling a straight line going from point A to point B, the poem would enact a wandering movement within an open discursive space, aiming at no particular end point. Like the other experimentalists, the Black Mountain poets wanted a poetry in which one perception led immediately to another, without cohering around a stable, centralized "I." Finally, the New York school poets such as James Merrill, Frank O'Hara, and John Ashbery combined both realistic and dreamlike images in an improvisational style, producing jaunty poems with an urban sensibility, a basis in popular culture, and an off-the-cuff good humor. Because the New York poets were closely attuned to vanguard developments in the visual and musical arts, their poems often have strongly visual and musical elements as well. These experimental poets attempted to push the modernist innovations even further and, in so doing, fostered a new postmodernist avant-garde.

All of these mid-century poets reacted inventively and proactively to the social, political, and cultural conditions they encountered and, in fact, were helping to create. Although contradictory in many of their aims and procedures, the poets reveal a common desire to make something new and valuable in a time when identity confusion, increased social regulation, glaring public inequity, and nuclear dread led frequently to bleak or unsettling cultural conditions. We often find these poets engaged in a struggle to make their poems matter in a world that no longer seemed to have time for poetry. That the poems did come to matter, and that they seem to matter more with every passing year, is perhaps the most astonishing thing about this astonishing era.

GEORGE OPPEN
1908–1984

GEORGE OPPEN, a great innovator in American poetry, combined social awareness with an interrogation of language and a developing spiritual sense. He sought
to discover what he called (in "Anniversary Poem") the "paradise of the real." He
believed that in the act of perceiving one's self and the world—and one's self *in*
the world—one comes into being. His poems enacted philosopher Jacques Mari-
tain's comment that "we awake in the same moment to ourselves and to things."
The poems evoke those moments of reality-making perception at the same time
as they critique social inequality and as they rupture language itself, so that words
are revealed as a dense, foregrounded medium and not a transparent, invisible
one. Oppen's poetry challenges and entices. It raises questions and possibilities.
It sets realizations into motion and rarely sees them through to closure. To enter
into his work is to enter into the world and language with new eyes.

Oppen's experimental work functions as a vital bridge connecting such modernist poets as Ezra Pound, William Carlos Williams, and Charles Reznikoff
(included in Volume Two) with such midcentury poets as Robert Duncan and
Robert Creeley and such present-day poets as Lyn Hejinian and Charles Bernstein (all included in this volume). Oppen was the youngest member of the
Objectivist group, which came to attention in the 1930s and included Louis
Zukofsky and Lorine Niedecker (included in Volume Two). He wrote poems
that emphasized the objects of the world and the human beings with whom
he interacted. Oppen obsessed over each word he used, as he laboriously constructed, pruned, and revised his lines, often pasting one word over another until
the poem was thick with words, most of them discarded in favor of the alternative
pasted on the very top. The surviving sentences are often baffling. Oppen tore
syntax apart to reveal the holes in language. In the resulting tension between
words and emptiness, meanings and silence, the dynamism of the poetic process
emerges. Oppen's poetry includes a vision of the power and limits of language
and, even more deeply, of the value of perception, connection, and articulation.

Oppen was born to a middle-class Jewish family in New Rochelle, a suburb
of New York City. When he was four, his mother, who had suffered a mental breakdown, committed suicide. This tragic loss interrupted Oppen's childhood and haunted his existence for the rest of his days. When he was seven,
his father remarried, but (according to Michael Davidson in his introduction
to Oppen's *New Collected Poems*) "the boy's relationship with his stepmother
was traumatic," involving "forms of psychological and physical abuse." When
Oppen was ten, the family moved to San Francisco, where he grew up alongside

an older sister and a younger half-sister, with whom he remained close through-out his life. Going away to college at Oregon State University, he met his future wife, Mary, in a modern poetry course. On their first date, they stayed out all night, causing Mary to be expelled and George suspended. They immediately left Oregon together and began a fifty-year relationship that became one of the happiest marriages in American poetic history.

After four years of hitchhiking and temporary work, the couple landed in New York, where they became friends and allies of the older experimental poets William Carlos Williams and Charles Reznikoff as well as the younger innovator Louis Zukofsky. All of these poets felt like cultural outsiders. They identified with the working class and wanted to discover new poetic forms and vocabularies. George and Mary Oppen founded the Objectivist Press, a name that reflected Zukofsky's poetic program of objectivity and sincerity (and which had nothing to do with novelist Ayn Rand's "objectivist ethics," which stressed individualism over community). The press published books by Williams and Reznikoff and also Oppen's own first book, *Discrete Series*, which included *Tug against the river* and *She lies, hip high*, printed below.

Oppen's poems were intended to comment on the suffering of workers dur-ing the Great Depression and at the same time to seek what Williams called an "irreducible minimum" of words in the achievement of the poems' purpose. Fol-lowing the book's publication in 1934, George and Mary joined the Communist Party in an effort to fight inequality and fascism, then on the rise throughout the western world. They participated in protests and in relief efforts for the poor. In the hubbub of political work and the effort to support a family through manual labor (they soon had a daughter named Linda), Oppen stopped writing poetry. The hiatus continued through World War II, in which he saw active combat and was ultimately severely injured. Lying wounded in a foxhole, surrounded by injured and dying soldiers, he buried his dog tags, which would have identified him as Jewish to the nearby Nazi enemies.

Awarded a Purple Heart after the war, he returned to New York in late 1945. Although he and Mary had left the Communist Party years before, they moved to Mexico City in the early 1950s to avoid questioning about their politics and possible imprisonment. Oppen supported his family by working as a furniture maker. After twenty-five years of silence, he began to write poems again in the late 1950s. When he later tried to explain his complex political reasons behind the long interruption, critic Hugh Kenner summed up, "In brief, it took twenty-five years for you to write the next poem." By 1961, the Oppens were back in New York, and Oppen's poems were receiving a degree of attention and praise that his earlier poems had not. In 1966, the couple moved to San Francisco, the cityscape where Oppen had grown up. He continued to write poetry, and the couple remained involved in progressive causes, especially in opposing the

Vietnam War. Oppen's volume *Of Being Numerous* appeared in 1968, becoming his best-known book and winning the Pulitzer Prize. These later poems contemplated what Oppen called (in "Of Being Numerous #7") "the meaning of being numerous," which included for him the multiplicity of both meaning and being. In the 1970s, Oppen received more awards, but he gradually drifted into forgetfulness. He died in a nursing home in 1984 at the age of seventy-six. According to Michael Davidson, the poet had left a final note to himself in his study: "I think I have written what I set out to say."

FURTHER READING

Rachel Blau DuPlessis and Peter Quartermain, eds. *Objectivist Nexus: Essays in Cultural Poetics.* Tuscaloosa: University of Alabama Press, 1999.

Burton Hatlen, ed. *George Oppen: Man and Poet.* Orono, Maine: National Poetry Foundation, 1981.

Michael Heller. *Speaking of the Estranged: Essays on the Work of George Oppen.* Cambridge, Eng.: Salt, 2008.

George Oppen. *New Collected Poems.* Ed. Michael Davidson. New York: New Directions: 2002.

———. *Selected Letters.* Ed. Rachel Blau DuPlessis. Durham, N.C.: Duke University Press, 1990.

Mary Oppen. *Meaning a Life: An Autobiography.* Santa Barbara: Black Sparrow Press, 1978.

Steve Shoemaker, ed. *Thinking Poetics: Essays on George Oppen.* Tuscaloosa: University of Alabama Press, 2009.

[Tug against the river]

Tug[1] against the river——
Motor turning, lights
In the fast water off the bow-wave:[2]
Passes slowly.

1934

This brief poem records an observer's perceptions of a tugboat moving slowly against the current in a river harbor. Oppen's editor, Michael Davidson, states that the poet "refined his poems into tough, recalcitrant lyrics that would endure the test of time." Perhaps this little tugboat has some of those same "tough, recalcitrant" qualities. This poem and the next appeared in Oppen's first volume, *Discrete Series*, published when he was twenty-six. Each poem was printed on a page of its own, with no title. The poet later commented that in these early poems he was "attempting to construct a meaning by empirical statements, by imagist statements."

1. A strongly built boat used for towing and pushing larger ships in harbors.
2. The wave that forms at the bow, or front, of a boat as it moves through water. Beyond or "off" the bow-wave is water unaffected by the boat's movement.

[She lies, hip high]

She lies, hip high,
On a flat bed
While the after-
Sun passes.

Plant, I breathe——
                    O Clearly,
Eyes legs arms hands fingers,
Simple legs in silk.

                    1934

This erotic and spiritual poem evokes the poet's wife, Mary Oppen.

Eclogue

The men talking
Near the room's center. They have said
More than they had intended.

Pinpointing in the uproar
Of the living room

An assault
On the quiet continent.

Beyond the window
Flesh and rock and hunger

Loose in the night sky
Hardened into soil

Tilting of itself to the sun once more, small
Vegetative leaves
And stems taking place

Outside—— O small ones,
To be born!

                    1962

An eclogue is a bucolic poem in which shepherds often speak. The form, popularized
by the classical poet Virgil, reached heights in Latin poetry and the Renaissance. In an

interview with L. S. Dembo reprinted in Hatlen's *George Oppen: Man and Poet*, Oppen commented, "The title because—it's almost ironic—my version of a bucolic poem, a rural scene, looking out the window. . . . The humans talking of deals and triumphs as a kind of artillery bombardment against that indestructible natural world."

Birthplace: New Rochelle

Returning to that house
And the rounded rocks of childhood——They have lasted well.

A world of things.

An aging man,
The knuckles of my hand
So jointed! I am this?

       The house
My father's once, and the ground. There is a color of his times
In the sun's light

A generation's mark.
It intervenes. My child,
Not now a child, our child
Not altogether lone in a lone universe that suffers time
Like stones in sun. For we do not.

1962

Like a poem by Robert Lowell or Sylvia Plath, though very different in tone and method, this poem returns to the scene of childhood and ponders generational change. Oppen was born in suburban New Rochelle and lived there until the age of four, shortly after his mother's suicide. His daughter, Linda, was about twenty when he wrote the poem. The last lines suggest Oppen's belief in the interconnectedness of human beings and generations.

Time of the Missile

I remember a square of New York's Hudson River glinting between warehouses.
Difficult to approach the water below the pier
Swirling, covered with oil the ship at the pier
A steel wall: tons in the water,

   ❊   ❊   ❊

Width.
The hand for holding,
Legs for walking,
The eye *sees!* It floods in on us from here to Jersey tangled in the grey bright air

Become the realm of nations.

My love, my love,
We are endangered
Totally at last. Look
Anywhere to the sight's limit: space
Which is viviparous:[1]

Place of the mind
And eye. Which can destroy us,
Re-arrange itself, assert
Its own stone chain reaction.

1962

In a letter to a friend, Oppen pondered the degree to which "Time of the Missile" pertains to the Cold War: "You suggest that it isn't really the missile—that it could have been said at any time that 'This is the way the world ends' etc. Sure you're right. I didn't really mean to disguise it as a political or topical poem—I just meant that I thought these things must be in everyone's mind with the threat of the missile right there. I did go on to say that we can never be free of this immediate fear—Suppose we do make an agreement on atomic weapons—do we really then feel assured that it 'will never be broken'?" Oppen also commented that the poem begins with praise for "human vision which creates the human universe" but that it also "describes something like despair because destruction by the missile would indeed be total defeat and meaninglessness in the future perfect."

O Western Wind

A world around her like a shadow
She moves a chair
Something is being made—
Prepared
Clear in front of her as open air

✴   ✴   ✴

1. Producing living young instead of eggs from within the body, in the manner of nearly all mammals; or, botanically, germinating while still attached to the parent plant.

The space a woman makes and fills
After these years
I write again
Naturally, about your face

Beautiful and wide
Blue eyes
Across all my vision but the glint of flesh
Blue eyes
In the subway routes, in the small rains
The profiles.

1962

The title of this love poem alludes to an anonymous fifteenth-century English song: "O western wind, when wilt thou blow / That the small rain down can rain? / Christ, that my love were in my arms / And I in my bed again!"

Squall

coming about
When the squall knocked her[1]
Flat on the water. When she came
Upright, her rig was gone
And her crew clinging to her. The water in her cabins,
Washing thru companionways and hatches
And the deep ribs
Had in that mid-passage
No kinship with any sea.

1962

In "Squall," as Burton Hatlen has commented, "the human collectivity confronts the sea."

Still Life

(From a poem by Buddhadeva Bose)[1]

What *are* you, apple! There are men
Who, biting an apple, blind themselves to bowl, basket

1. A sailboat.
1. Buddhadeva Bose (1908–1974) was a poet and friend who wrote in the Bengali language. Born in what is now Bangladesh, he lived as an adult in Calcutta, India.

Or whatever and in a strange spell feel themselves
Like you outdoors and make us wish
We too were in the sun and night alive with sap.

1962

Of Being Numerous #7

Obsessed, bewildered

By the shipwreck
Of the singular

We have chosen the meaning
Of being numerous.

1968

"Of Being Numerous," the chief text in Oppen's Pulitzer Prize–winning volume, *Of Being Numerous*, is a sequence of forty numbered poems. According to Michael Davidson, "the title refers to Oppen's lifelong concern with unity in diversity, with achieving autonomy while living among others. In the title poem, the problem is expressed as 'the shipwreck of the singular' represented by Robinson Crusoe on his island." In a letter written in 1969, Oppen observed: "and then the construction of 'Humanity'—a single figure. A monster Well, it's been tried We've SEEN it fail in our own lifetimes Because really each one has his own life—."

Anniversary Poem

'the picturesque
common lot' the unwarranted light
Where everyone has been

The very ground of the path
And the litter grow ancient

A shovel's scratched edge
So like any other man's

We are troubled by incredulity
We are troubled by scratched things

Becoming familiar
Becoming extreme

✳ ✳ ✳

Let grief
Be
So it be ours

Nor hide one's eyes
As tides drop along the beaches in the thin wash of
    breakers

And so desert each other

——lest there be nothing

      The Indian girl walking across the desert,[1] the
sunfish under the boat

How shall we say how this happened, these stories, our
    stories

Scope, mere size, a kind of redemption

Exposed still and jagged on the San Francisco hills[2]

Time and depth before us, paradise of the real, we
      know what it is

To find now depth, not time, since we cannot, but depth

To come out safe,   to end well

We have begun to say good bye
To each other
And cannot say it

                              1969

Referring to "Anniversary Poem" in a letter to a friend, Oppen wrote; "Either Mary or I
soon must face the question of whether any life can come out well alone. Whether a life
can end well I try to face it."

1. According to Davidson, this is a reference to Oppen's wife, Mary.
2. Oppen commented in a letter, "I'm not sure I ever visualize anything but depth . . . Or a point, a detail so sharply defined that I'm shaken by the implication of space."

Till Other Voices Wake Us

the generations

and the solace

of flight memory

of adolescence with my father
in France[1] we stared
at monuments as tho we treaded

water stony

waters of the monuments and so turned
then hurriedly

on our course
before we might grow tired
and so drown and writing

thru the night (a young man,
Brooklyn, 1929) I named the book

series empirical[2]
series all force
in events the myriad

lights have entered
us it is a music more powerful

than music

till other voices wake
us or we drown[3]

1978

In his late poem "Till Other Voices Wake Us," Oppen crucially revises T. S. Eliot's "The Love Song of J. Alfred Prufrock." For Prufrock, the voice of the other is what drowns us, by rousing us from our isolated perfection. For Oppen's speaker, precisely the opposite occurs. The voice of the other wakes us from our solipsistic dream and thereby prevents us from drowning in it.

1. Oppen went on a trip to Europe with his father and stepmother before entering college.
2. Oppen ultimately called his first book *Discrete Series* (1934).

3. A variation on T. S. Eliot's famous last line of "The Love Song of J. Alfred Prufrock": "Till human voices wake us, and we drown."

THEODORE ROETHKE
1908–1963

Born in Saginaw, Michigan, to German-American parents, Theodore Roethke spent his childhood and youth surrounded by growing plants while working for his father, Otto, a market-gardener who owned an extensive local greenhouse. His bond with his powerful but undemonstrative father was both intense and difficult, as is reflected in such poems as "My Papa's Waltz." Roethke's father died in 1923, when the aspiring poet was fifteen, and by then the core elements of Roethke's mature poetry had already taken root: an identification with small growing things, a keen awareness of isolation and loss, and an absorption in the mysteries of personal and psychological growth. Such preoccupations would find expression in such early poems as "Cuttings" and "Cuttings (later)" and in later poems such as "In a Dark Time."

Throughout his life, Roethke struggled with alcoholism and with bouts of depression that sometimes placed him in mental institutions, yet he maintained an active career as a teacher and publishing poet. Having served at various teaching posts, in 1947 Roethke joined the faculty of the University of Washington in Seattle, where he became an influential teacher of future poets. Roethke died of a heart attack in 1963.

Roethke's work is marked from beginning to end by an affinity for romanticism, by a surrealism grounded in a deep knowledge of and sensitivity to biological processes, and by a pervasive lyricism. Using these elements, he strove to speak through his poetry in what he called "the wild, disordered language of the natural heart." Even when working within traditional poetic forms, as in his villanelle "The Waking," Roethke's diction is natural, even conversational, although the conversation may be an internal discourse with the self. Roethke's friend and fellow poet John Berryman (also included in this anthology) aptly described Roethke's poetry as "Teutonic, irregular, delicate, botanical, and psychological, irreligious, personal." A large man physically, Roethke wrote verse that often reflects a curiously lumbering gracefulness combined with passionate intensity and an extraordinary sense of flow.

FURTHER READING

Theodore Roethke. *The Collected Poems.* New York: Anchor Books, 1974.
———. *On Poetry and Craft.* Ed. Ralph J. Mills. Port Townsend, Wash.: Copper Canyon Press, 2001.
———. *Selected Letters.* Ed. Ralph J. Mills. Seattle: University of Washington Press, 1968.

————. *Straw for the Fire: From the Notebooks of Theodore Roethke*. Ed. David Wagoner. Port Townsend, Wash.: Copper Canyon Press, 2006.
Allan Seager. *The Glass House: The Life of Theodore Roethke*. Ann Arbor: University of Michigan Press, 1991.

Cuttings

Sticks-in-a-drowse[1] droop over sugary loam,
Their intricate stem-fur dries;
But still the delicate slips keep coaxing up water;
The small cells bulge;

One nub of growth
Nudges a sand-crumb loose,
Pokes through a musty sheath
Its pale tendrilous horn.[2]

1948

"Cuttings" and its sequel, "Cuttings (later)," contemplate the process by which new plants are propagated not from seed but by cuttings. The stem (or "slip") is cut from an established plant and placed in water to develop new roots, then transplanted into soil. Roethke often used images from his childhood experience of his father's greenhouse to explore his adult sense of his body and being—his hopes, fears, and desires.

Cuttings
(later)

This urge, wrestle, resurrection of dry sticks,
Cut stems struggling to put down feet,[1]
What saint strained so much,
Rose on such lopped limbs to a new life?

I can hear, underground, that sucking and sobbing,
In my veins, in my bones I feel it—

1. Early in the propagation process, the stems appear dormant. Loam: fine, rich soil into which the new cuttings have been transplanted.

2. Slender, spiraling extension (or tendril) used by a climbing plant to grasp a support.
1. That is, roots.

The small waters seeping upward,[2]
The tight grains parting at last.
When sprouts break out,
Slippery as fish,
I quail, lean to beginnings, sheath-wet.

1948

My Papa's Waltz

The whiskey on your breath
Could make a small boy dizzy;
But I hung on like death:
Such waltzing was not easy.

We romped until the pans
Slid from the kitchen shelf;
My mother's countenance
Could not unfrown itself.

The hand that held my wrist
Was battered on one knuckle;
At every step you missed
My right ear scraped a buckle.

You beat time on my head
With a palm caked hard by dirt,
Then waltzed me off to bed
Still clinging to your shirt.

1948

"My Papa's Waltz" is itself composed in waltz time, with a sometimes irregular three-beat (iambic trimeter) measure. This bittersweet recollection is one of the earliest instances of a memory poem about child and parent, a genre that would become hugely significant in the 1950s and 1960s in works by such poets as Robert Lowell and Sylvia Plath. The genre continues today in the work of such poets as Gary Soto, Marilyn Chin, and Li-Young Lee.

2. Capillary action by which plants draw water and nutrients up through their roots.

The Waking

I wake to sleep, and take my waking slow.
I feel my fate in what I cannot fear.
I learn by going where I have to go.

We think by feeling. What is there to know?
I hear my being dance from ear to ear.
I wake to sleep, and take my waking slow.

Of those so close beside me, which are you?
God bless the Ground! I shall walk softly there,
And learn by going where I have to go.

Light takes the Tree; but who can tell us how?
The lowly worm climbs up a winding stair;
I wake to sleep, and take my waking slow.

Great Nature has another thing to do
To you and me; so take the lively air,
And, lovely, learn by going where to go.

This shaking keeps me steady. I should know.
What falls away is always. And is near.
I wake to sleep, and take my waking slow.
I learn by going where I have to go.

1953

"The Waking" is a villanelle, a highly structured form composed of nineteen lines, with two repeating rhymes and two refrains. The first and third lines of the opening tercet (three line stanza) are alternately repeated as the last lines of the succeeding tercets, and then together they compose the concluding couple of the final quatrain. The form dates from Jean Passerat's sixteenth-century poem "Villanelle." Elizabeth Bishop uses the form as well in "One Art."

In a Dark Time

In a dark time, the eye begins to see,
I meet my shadow in the deepening shade;
I hear my echo in the echoing wood—
A lord of nature weeping to a tree.
I live between the heron and the wren,

Beasts of the hill and serpents of the den.
What's madness but nobility of soul
At odds with circumstance? The day's on fire!
I know the purity of pure despair,
My shadow pinned against a sweating wall.
That place among the rocks—is it a cave,
Or a winding path? The edge is what I have.

A steady storm of correspondences![1]
A night flowing with birds, a ragged moon,
And in broad day the midnight come again!
A man goes far to find out what he is—
Death of the self in a long, tearless night,
All natural shapes blazing unnatural light.

Dark, dark my light, and darker my desire.
My soul, like some heat-maddened summer fly,
Keeps buzzing at the sill. Which I is I?
A fallen man, I climb out of my fear.
The mind enters itself, and God the mind,
And one is One, free in the tearing wind.

1964

CHARLES OLSON
1910–1970

CHARLES OLSON brought epic ambitions, comprehensive intelligence, and rugged intensity to his work as a poet, as a literary critic and theorist, as a teacher, and as a mentor to younger poets. His signal accomplishments in all of these fields mark him as one of the leaders of the influential Black Mountain school of poetry and as one of American poetry's most forceful and important midcentury figures. Olson was born in Worcester, Massachusetts—also the birthplace of his fellow poets and close contemporaries Elizabeth Bishop and Stanley Kunitz—and received a B.A. and M.A. from Wesleyan University. He began work on a

1. Sensory links connecting nature with human thought and emotion. See French poet Charles Baudelaire's nineteenth-century sonnet "Correspondences."

Ph.D. in the brand-new program in American studies at Harvard University in 1936, but he left in 1938 without completing the degree. His graduate school research on Herman Melville, though, later resulted in the remarkable critical volume *Call Me Ishmael* (1947), the first publication to bring Olson significant literary attention.

In the early 1940s, Olson became involved in campaign work for Franklin Delano Roosevelt and served, during World War II, as assistant chief of the Foreign Language Division of the Office of War Information. Olson left Washington in 1945 over objections to the more conservative turn he felt the Democratic Party was taking under Roosevelt's successor, Harry Truman. In 1948, Olson took a position at the innovative Black Mountain College, which attracted such major artists and intellects as Josef Albers, John Cage, Franz Kline, Merce Cunningham, and Buckminster Fuller. There Olson met and worked with various poets, including Robert Creeley and Robert Duncan. Olson served as rector of Black Mountain College from 1951 to 1956, when the college closed.

Olson's influential 1950 essay "Projective Verse" helped to define the core concepts of the Black Mountain school, including the principles of "OPEN verse" and what he termed "COMPOSITION BY FIELD," which he defined as being "opposed to inherited line, stanza, over-all form, what is the 'old' base of the nonprojective." Olson was deeply concerned with associating the poetic line with the breath of the poet and reader, and he noted, "It is the advantage of the typewriter that, due to its rigidity and its space precisions, it can, for a poet, indicate exactly the breath, the pauses, the suspensions even of syllables, the juxtapositions even of parts of phrases, which he intends. For the first time, the poet has the stave and bar a musician has had." Olson's own work reveals an ongoing fascination with the interaction between syllable and line as they register and articulate the fluid interplay between feeling and thought.

While studying Mayan ruins in the Yucatán in the early 1950s, Olson engaged in an extensive correspondence with Robert Creeley while continuing to develop the principles outlined in "Projective Verse." This correspondence was published in 1953 as *Mayan Letters*. During this period, Olson also reached full maturity as a poet, creating such distinctive lyrics as the powerful "As the Dead Prey Upon Us," a poem based on a series of vivid dreams involving the apparent return to life of Olson's deceased mother. Poems like "The Distances" explore the haunting contemporary presence of mythic and historic figures of the ancient past, such as Zeus, Galatea, Pygmalion, and the Roman emperor Augustus.

At the same time as he was crafting these innovative lyrics, Olson was working on his contemporary epic, *The Maximus Poems*, a work centered on his adoptive home, the small seaport town of Gloucester, Massachusetts. The poem's central figure, Maximus, resembles Olson himself. Even the name "Maximus" appears to refer to the author—Olson, at six foot eight, was a bulky and towering figure. Although Olson denied a direct connection, *The Maximus Poems*—represented here by "The Songs of Maximus"—seem modeled in significant ways on Ezra Pound's *Cantos* and William Carlos Williams's *Paterson*, particularly in their concern with the poet as a potentially legendary figure and in their preoccupation with the importance of history and locality as they interact with myth and personality.

After spending some years quietly in Gloucester, Olson began to teach at the University of New York at Buffalo, where he emerged again as an influential teacher. In his last years, he struggled with alcoholism and died of liver cancer in 1970, yet not before he had completed the third and final volume of the *Maximus Poems*. Olson remains a crucial figure in American letters—a poet, teacher, and critic who inspired many poets of his own generation and who has continued to inspire poets up to the present day.

FURTHER READING

Robert J. Berthoff. "Charles Olson (1910–1970)." In *The Greenwood Encyclopedia of Poets and Poetry*, vol. 4, ed. Jeffrey Gray, James McCorkle, and Mary McAllen Balkum, 1174–78. Westport, Conn.: Greenwood Press, 2006.
Tom Clark. *Charles Olson: The Allegory of a Poet's Life*. New York: Norton, 1991.
Ralph Maud. *Charles Olson's Reading: A Biography*. Carbondale: Southern Illinois University Press, 1996.
Charles Olson. *Collected Poems*. Ed. George Butterick. Berkeley: University of California Press, 1987.
———. *Collected Prose*. Ed. Donald Allen and Benjamin Friedlander. Berkeley: University of California Press, 1997.
———. *The Maximus Poems*. Ed. George Butterick. Berkeley: University of California Press, 1985.
Robert von Hallberg. *Charles Olson: The Scholar's Art*. Cambridge, Mass.: Harvard University Press, 1978.

As the Dead Prey Upon Us

As the dead prey upon us,
they are the dead in ourselves,
awake, my sleeping ones, I cry out to you,
disentangle the nets of being!

I pushed my car, it had been sitting so long unused.
I thought the tires looked as though they only needed air.
But suddenly the huge underbody was above me, and the rear tires
were masses of rubber and thread variously clinging together

※　※　※

as were the dead souls in the living room, gathered
about my mother, some of them taking care to pass
beneath the beam of the movie projector, some record
playing on the victrola,[1] and all of them
desperate with the tawdriness of their life in hell

I turned to the young man on my right and asked, "How is it,
there?" And he begged me protestingly don't ask, we are poor
poor. And the whole room was suddenly posters and presentations
of brake linings and other automotive accessories, cardboard
displays, the dead roaming from one to another
as bored back in life as they are in hell, poor and doomed
to mere equipments.

      my mother, as alive as ever she was, asleep
when I entered the house as often I found her in a rocker
under the lamp, and awaking, as I came up to her, as she ever had

I found out she returns to the house once a week, and with her
the throng of the unknown young who enter on her as much in death
as other like suited and dressed people did in life

O the dead!

    and the Indian woman and I
    enabled the blue deer
    to walk

    and the blue deer talked,
    in the next room,
    a Negro talk

    it was like walking a jackass,
    and its talk
    was the pressing gabber of gammers[2]
    of old women

    and we helped walk it around the room
    because it was seeking socks

1. An early record player, often cranked by hand. 2. Idle talk of old country women.

or shoes for its hooves
now that it was acquiring

human possibilities

In the five hindrances[3] men and angels
stay caught in the net, in the immense nets
which spread out across each plane of being, the multiple nets
which hamper at each step of the ladders as the angels
and the demons
and men
go up and down

> Walk the jackass
> Hear the victrola
> Let the automobile
> be tucked into a corner of the white fence
> when it is a white chair. Purity

is only an instant of being, the trammels

recur

In the five hindrances, perfection
is hidden

> I shall get
> to the place
> 10 minutes late.

> It will be 20 minutes
> of 9. And I don't know,

> without the car,

> how I shall get there

O peace, my mother, I do not know
how differently I could have done
what I did or did not do.

> That you are back each week
> that you fall asleep
> with your face to the right

3. In Buddhism, negative mental states that impede successful meditation.

*   *   *

that you are as present there
when I come in as you were
when you were alive

that you are as solid, and your flesh
is as I knew it, that you have the company
I am used to your having

but o, that you all find it
such a cheapness!

o peace, mother, for the mammothness
of the comings and goings
of the ladders of life

The nets we are entangled in. Awake,
my soul, let the power into the last wrinkle
of being, let none of the threads and rubber of the tires
be left upon the earth. Let even your mother
go. Let there be only paradise

The desperateness is, that the instant
which is also paradise (paradise
is happiness) dissolves
into the next instant, and power
flows to meet the next occurrence

Is it any wonder
my mother comes back?
Do not that throng
rightly seek the room
where they might expect
happiness? They did not complain
of life, they obviously wanted
the movie, each other, merely to pass
among each other there,
where the real is, even to the display cards,
to be out of hell

The poverty
of hell

*   *   *

O souls, in life and in death,
awake, even as you sleep, even in sleep
know that wind
even under the crankcase of the ugly automobile
lifts it away, clears the sodden weights of goods,
equipment, entertainment, the foods the Indian woman,
the filthy blue deer, the 4 by 3 foot 'Viewbook,'
the heaviness of the old house, the stuffed inner room
lifts the sodden nets

> and they disappear as ghosts do,
> as spider webs, nothing
> before the hand of man
>
> The vent! You must have the vent,
> or you shall die. Which means
> never to die, the ghastliness
>
> of going, and forever
> coming back, returning
> to the instants which were not lived
>
> O mother, this I could not have done,
> I could not have lived what you didn't,
> I am myself netted in my own being
>
> I want to die. I want to make that instant, too,
> perfect
>
> O my soul, slip
> the cog

II
The death in life (death itself)
is endless, eternity
is the false cause

The knot is otherwise, each topological[4] corner
presents itself, and no sword
cuts it, each knot is itself its fire

          *   *   *

4. Topology: the study of the topography of a given place, especially as it reflects its history.

each knot of which the net is made
is for the hands to untake
the knot's making. And touch alone

can turn the knot into its own flame

(o mother, if you had once touched me

o mother, if I had once touched you)

The car did not burn. Its underside
was not presented to me
a grotesque corpse. The old man

merely removed it as I looked up at it,
and put it in a corner of the picket fence
like it was my mother's dog?

or a child's chair

The woman,
playing on the grass,
with her son (the woman next door)

was angry with me whatever it was
slipped across the playpen or whatever
she had out there on the grass

And I was quite flip in reply
that anyone who used plastic
had to expect things to skid

and break, that I couldn't worry
that her son might have been hurt
by whatever it was I sent skidding

down on them.

It was just then I went into my house
and to my utter astonishment
found my mother sitting there

as she always had sat, as must she always
forever sit there her head lolling
into sleep? Awake, awake my mother

*   *   *

what wind will lift you too
forever from the tawdriness,
make you rich as all those souls

crave crave crave
to be rich?

They are right. We must have
what we want. We cannot afford
not to. We have only one course:

the nets which entangle us are flames

O souls, burn
alive, burn now

that you may forever
have peace, have

what you crave

O souls,
go into everything,
let not one knot pass
through your fingers

let not any they tell you
you must sleep as the net
comes through your authentic hands

What passes
is what is, what shall be, what has
been, what hell and heaven is
is earth to be rent, to shoot you
through the screen of flame which each knot
hides as all knots are a wall ready
to be shot open by you

the nets of being
are only eternal if you sleep as your hands
ought to be busy. Method, method

I too call on you to come
to the aid of all men, to women most

who know most, to woman to tell
men to awake. Awake, men
awake

I ask my mother
to sleep. I ask her
to stay in the chair.

My chair
is in the corner of the fence.
She sits by the fireplace made of paving stones. The blue deer
need not trouble either of us

And if she sits in happiness the souls
who trouble her and me
will also rest. The automobile

has been hauled away.

1957

Robert J. Bertholf comments: "'As the Dead Prey Upon Us' is the first of several poems
whose sources were literal dreams. A visitation occurs, an appearance by the poet's deceased mother. . . . The poem seems to confirm all the primitive senses of the restlessness
of departed souls. The poet's mother returns in the life of his sleep, and the poem is filled
with unsought images and the elasticity of dream. Strands of dream matter are interwoven like the automobile tires presented in the dream, 'masses of rubber and thread
variously clinging together.' The strands, the entangling nets of dream, which at first had
seemed so extraneous to the main burden of the poem, are actually quite useful in resolv-
ing it at the end, when the poet flatly announces that the automobile—source of much
trouble and uncertainty (dreamed strangeness)—has been hauled away."

The Distances

So the distances are Galatea[1]
          and one does fall in love and desires
mastery
          old Zeus[2]—young Augustus
Love knows no distance, no place

---

1. The traditional name for the statue in the form
of a beautiful woman—carved by the sculptor
Pygmalion—which, in answer to the artist's
prayers, comes to life through the powers of the
goddess Aphrodite.
2. Ruler of the ancient Greek gods. Augustus (63
B.C.E.—14 A.D.): the first Roman emperor.

                                    is that far away or heat changes
into signals, and control
                          old Zeus—young Augustus
Death is a loving matter, then, a horror
                                    we cannot bide, and avoid
by greedy life

                    we think all living things are precious
                    —Pygmalions
                                    a German inventor in Key West
who had a Cuban girl, and kept her, after her death
in his bed
                                    after her family retrieved her
he stole the body again from the vault

Torso on torso in either direction,
                    young Augustus
                                    out via nothing where messages
are
          or in, down La Cluny's[3] steps to the old man sitting
a god throned on torsoes,

                    old Zeus

Sons go there hopefully as though there was a secret, the object
to undo distance?
                                    They huddle there, at the bottom
of the shaft, against one young bum
                                    or two loving cheeks,
                    Augustus?
You can teach the young nothing
                                    all of them go away, Aphrodite[4]
tricks it out,
                    old Zeus—young Augustus

You have love, and no object
                                    or you have all pressed to your nose
which is too close,
                    old Zeus hiding in your chin your young
                    Galatea

3. The National Museum of the Middle Ages,   4. Ancient Greek goddess of love.
in Paris.

*   *   *

the girl who makes you weep, and you keep the corpse live by all
your arts

                    whose cheek do you stroke when you stroke the stone face
                    of young Augustus, made for bed in a military camp,
                    o Caesar?

O love who places all where each is, as they are, for every moment,
yield

                   to this man

                            that the impossible distance
be healed,

                   that young Augustus
                   and old Zeus
be enclosed

                   "I will wake you,
stone. Love this man."

                                       1960

The Songs of Maximus

Song 1

           colored pictures
of all things to eat: dirty
postcards
           And words, words, words
all over everything
                No eyes or ears left
to do their own doings (all

invaded, appropriated, outraged, all senses

including the mind, that worker on what is
                        And that other sense
made to give even the most wretched, or any of us, wretched,
that consolation (greased
                 lulled
even the street-cars

song

      *   *   *

Song 2

> all
wrong
> And I am asked—ask myself (I, too, covered
with the gurry[1] of it) where
shall we go from here, what can we do
when even the public conveyances
sing?
> how can we go anywhere,
even cross-town
> how get out of anywhere (the bodies
all buried
in shallow graves?

Song 3

> This morning of the small snow
I count the blessings, the leak in the faucet
which makes of the sink time, the drop
of the water on water as sweet
as the Seth Thomas[2]
in the old kitchen
my father stood in his drawers to wind (always
he forgot the 30th day, as I don't want to remember
the rent
> a house these days
so much somebody else's,
especially,
Congoleum's:[3]

> Or the plumbing
that doesn't work, this I like, have even used paper clips
as well as string to hold the ball up   And flush it
with my hand
> But that the car doesn't, that no moving thing moves
without that song I'd void my ear of, the musickracket
of all ownership . . .

1. Fish entrails.
2. A famous nineteenth-century American maker
of clocks.

3. Manufacturer of linoleum and vinyl flooring.

Holes
in my shoes, that's all right, my fly
gaping, me out
at the elbows, the blessing
                    that difficulties are once more

"In the midst of plenty, walk
as close to
bare
            In the face of sweetness,
piss
                In the time of goodness
go side, go
smashing, beat them, go as
(as near as you can

tear

In the land of plenty, have
nothing to do with it
                    take the way of
the lowest,
including
your legs, go
contrary, go

sing

Song 4

I know a house made of mud & wattles[4]
I know a dress just sewed
                    (saw the wind
blow its cotton
against her body
from the ankle
                so!
it was Nike[5]

            ✳   ✳   ✳

4. Alludes to the small cabin, made of "clay and wattles," built by the speaker in William Butler Yeats's poem "The Lake Isle of Innisfree."   5. Greek goddess who personified victory.

And her feet: such bones
I could have had the tears
that lovely pedant had
who couldn't unwrap it himself, had to ask them to,
          on the schooner's deck

and he looked,
the first human eyes to look again
at the start of human motion (just last week
300,000,000 years ago
          She
was going fast
across the square, the water
this time of year, that
scarce

And the fish

Song 5

I have seen faces of want,
and have not wanted the FAO: Appleseed
's gone back to
what any of us
New England

Song 6

you sing, you

who also

wants
1960

ELIZABETH BISHOP
1911–1979

Elizabeth bishop has emerged as one of the most important and widely discussed American poets of the twentieth century. Bishop published comparatively little in her lifetime, and our image of her as a writer and as a person has undergone continuous revision since her death. This revision results from the publication of additional poems, prose writings and letters but also from the intense critical activity her work has generated, which has revealed the deeply yet subtly self-exploratory nature of a body of work that once was widely considered to be precisely observed but coolly impersonal. During Bishop's lifetime, she tended to be pegged as a shy and almost reclusive figure—an adept minor poet who pursued a curiously isolated career, disconnected from the major currents of contemporary history, culture, and thought. But Bishop is now being widely and more acutely read as a poet of audacious and masterly skills and of considerable emotional power—and as a poet who was crucially engaged with such vital cultural and political issues as gender, sexuality, social marginality, national identity, class, war, the environment, power relations, and family intimacy and conflict.

Bishop is also recognized as a deeply influential poet and as a cultural figure who was engaged in significant dialogue with an extraordinary spectrum of important writers, artists, and composers of many nations. She had considerable roots not only in New England but also in Canada and Brazil, and she is now often studied as a poet of the border-grounds, a cosmopolitan poet, and a transnational prose writer and correspondent. Her global importance and her influence over younger poets appear to be continually expanding.

Bishop was born in Worcester, Massachusetts, in 1911. Her father, Thomas Bishop, a prosperous building contractor, died eight months later of the still-incurable Bright's disease. Bishop's mother, Gertrude Bulmer Bishop, never recovered from the loss. Instead, she suffered a series of mental breakdowns. Following her return to her native Great Village, Nova Scotia, with her child in 1915, Gertrude experienced a major breakdown and was permanently institutionalized the following year, when the poet was five. After her mother's collapse, Bishop was passed around among various maternal and paternal relatives in both the United States and Canada. During this formative time she suffered from severe autoimmune disorders—chiefly asthma and eczema—which nearly killed her when she was six and which prevented her from taking part in formal schooling until 1926, when she was fifteen years old. Bishop wrote extensively and with understated wit, beauty, and poignancy about her childhood. Indeed, these early experiences haunted her with feelings of homelessness and loss and confirmed her as a lifelong reader and traveler. They also gave her a multinational perspective, while conditioning her to observe the world, in Adrienne Rich's phrase, with "the eye of the outsider."

When her health permitted her to return to formal studies, attending North Shore Country Day School and then Walnut Hill School from 1926 to 1930, she published a brilliant series of essays, reviews, stories, and poems in her school magazines. Supported by a trust fund from her late father, she attended Vassar College from 1930 to 1934 and continued to produce remarkable work in college publications while forming friendships with classmates such as Mary McCarthy, Louise Crane, and Eleanor Clark. In 1934, Bishop met the poet Marianne Moore, who became her mentor. Following college graduation, Bishop traveled extensively in Europe, North Africa, and Florida. From 1938, Bishop settled for part of each year in Key West while maintaining an apartment in New York City. Bishop thus established the geographical poles that would be articulated in the title of her first book, *North & South* (1946), and that would recur throughout her later work. A surrealistic dream landscape of New York, typical of her earliest mature work, appears in "The Man-Moth," while the southern pole is represented in such Florida-centered poems as "The Fish."

In 1947, Bishop met Robert Lowell (who also appears in this anthology). Lowell soon became her favorite poet and closest friend. The extensive body of letters they exchanged over the next thirty years, exploring all aspects of their lives and art, has been published as *Words in Air: The Complete Correspondence Between Elizabeth Bishop and Robert Lowell*. In just his second letter to her, Lowell praised the recently published "At the Fishhouses," confessing that "I felt very envious reading it—I'm a fisherman myself, but all my fish become symbols, alas! The description has great splendor, and the human part, tone, etc., is just right." Such a poem-by-poem interchange would continue between them until Lowell's death in 1977.

However, the late 1940s was a troubled period for Bishop (as suggested in the poem "Insomnia"), and in 1951, Bishop resettled in Brazil. There she lived with her partner Lota de Macedo Soares, sharing an apartment in Rio de Janeiro and Lota's mountain estate, Samambaia, where Soares, a self-taught architect, designed and built a house according to advanced modernist principles as well as a separate writer's studio for Bishop. Brazil soon emerged as an important subject for Bishop, as evident in such poems as "Questions of Travel" and "The Armadillo," but Bishop also found herself returning to her early experiences as a child in Great Village, as reflected in such poems as "First Death in Nova Scotia." Bishop's initial years in Brazil were the happiest of her life, but gradually her relationship with Soares became strained and then broke down completely, and—on a doctor's advice—they separated. Lota died of an overdose of tranquilizers while visiting Bishop in New York in 1967.

With the help of Lowell, Bishop found a teaching post in 1970 at Harvard, where she met Alice Methfessel, who would become the partner of her later years. Bishop's anxiety about losing Methfessel's love became the focal point of one of her most famous poems, "One Art," though ultimately Bishop and Methfessel remained together. In her final years at Harvard, Bishop produced a brilliant series of late retrospective poems, some of which—including "One Art," "Poem," and "In the Waiting Room"—are featured in her remarkable last book, *Geography III* (1976). Others, such as "Pink Dog" and "Sonnet," appeared separately in the years before her sudden death, at the height of her powers, from a cerebral aneurysm in 1979. Over the course of a career spanning more than forty years, Bishop produced a body of work in poetry, prose, and correspondence that is all but unparalleled in terms of its freshness, precision of observation, subtle emotional depth, keen self-exploration, and understated formal invention.

FURTHER READING

Steven Gould Axelrod. "Heterotropic Desire in Elizabeth Bishop's 'Pink Dog.'" *Arizona Quarterly* 60.3 (Autumn 2004): 62–81.

Elizabeth Bishop. *Collected Prose*. Ed. Robert Giroux. New York: Farrar, Straus & Giroux, 1984.

———. *Complete Poems: 1927–1979*. New York: Farrar, Straus & Giroux, 1983.

———. *One Art: Letters*. Ed. Robert Giroux. New York: Farrar, Straus & Giroux, 1994.

———. *Edgar Allan Poe & the Juke-Box: Uncollected Poems, Drafts, and Fragments*. Ed. Alice Quinn. New York: Farrar, Straus & Giroux, 2006.

———. *Poems, Prose, and Letters*. Ed. Robert Giroux and Lloyd Schwartz. New York: Library of America, 2008.

——— and Robert Lowell. *Words in Air: The Complete Correspondence Between Elizabeth Bishop and Robert Lowell*. Ed. Thomas Travisano with Saskia Hamilton. New York: Farrar, Straus & Giroux, 2008.

Bonnie Costello. *Elizabeth Bishop: Questions of Mastery*. Cambridge, Mass.: Harvard University Press, 1991.

Gary Fountain. *Remembering Elizabeth Bishop: An Oral Biography*. Amherst: University of Massachusetts Press, 1994.

Lorrie Goldensohn. *Elizabeth Bishop: The Biography of a Poetry*. New York: Columbia University Press, 1991.

David Kalstone. *Becoming a Poet: Elizabeth Bishop with Marianne Moore and Robert Lowell*. New York: Farrar, Straus & Giroux, 1989.

Susan McCabe. *Elizabeth Bishop: Her Poetics of Loss*. University Park: Pennsylvania University Press, 1994.

Brett C. Millier. *Elizabeth Bishop: Life and the Memory of It*. Berkeley: University of California Press, 1993.

Adrienne Rich. "The Eye of the Outsider: The Poetry of Elizabeth Bishop," *Boston Review* 8 (April 1983): 15–17.

Camille Roman. *Elizabeth Bishop's World War II–Cold War View*. New York: Macmillan-Palgrave, 2001.

Thomas Travisano. *Elizabeth Bishop: Her Artistic Development*. Charlottesville: University Press of Virginia, 1988.

———. *Midcentury Quartet: Bishop, Lowell, Jarrell, Berryman, and the Making of a Postmodern Aesthetic*. Charlottesville: University of Virginia Press, 1999.

The Man-Moth

Here, above,
cracks in the buildings are filled with battered moonlight.
The whole shadow of Man is only as big as his hat.
It lies at his feet like a circle for a doll to stand on,
and he makes an inverted pin, the point magnetized to the moon.
He does not see the moon; he observes only her vast properties,
feeling the queer light on his hands, neither warm nor cold,
of a temperature impossible to record in thermometers.

But when the Man-Moth
pays his rare, although occasional, visits to the surface,
the moon looks rather different to him. He emerges
from an opening under the edge of one of the sidewalks
and nervously begins to scale the faces of the buildings.
He thinks the moon is a small hole at the top of the sky,
proving the sky quite useless for protection.
He trembles, but must investigate as high as he can climb.

Up the façades,
his shadow dragging like a photographer's cloth behind him,
he climbs fearfully, thinking that this time he will manage
to push his small head through that round clean opening
and be forced through, as from a tube, in black scrolls on the light.
(Man, standing below him, has no such illusions.)
But what the Man-Moth fears most he must do, although
he fails, of course, and falls back scared but quite unhurt.

Then he returns
to the pale subways of cement he calls his home. He flits,
he flutters, and cannot get aboard the silent trains
fast enough to suit him. The doors close swiftly.
The Man-Moth always seats himself facing the wrong way
and the train starts at once at its full, terrible speed,
without a shift in gears or a gradation of any sort.
He cannot tell the rate at which he travels backwards.

*   *   *

Each night he must
be carried through artificial tunnels and dream recurrent dreams.
Just as the ties recur beneath his train, these underlie
his rushing brain. He does not dare look out the window,
for the third rail,[1] the unbroken draught of poison,
runs there beside him. He regards it as a disease
he has inherited the susceptibility to. He has to keep
his hands in his pockets, as others must wear mufflers.

If you catch him,
hold up a flashlight to his eye. It's all dark pupil,
an entire night itself, whose haired horizon tightens
as he stares back, and closes up the eye. Then from the lids
one tear, his only possession, like the bee's sting, slips.
Slyly he palms it, and if you're not paying attention
he'll swallow it. However, if you watch, he'll hand it over,
cool as from underground springs and pure enough to drink.

                                                            1936

Bishop's note on the poem's title reads, "Newspaper misprint for 'mammoth.'"

The Fish

I caught a tremendous fish
and held him beside the boat
half out of water, with my hook
fast in a corner of his mouth.
He didn't fight.
He hadn't fought at all.
He hung a grunting weight,
battered and venerable
and homely. Here and there
his brown skin hung in strips
like ancient wallpaper,
and its pattern of darker brown
was like wallpaper:
shapes like full-blown roses
stained and lost through age.

1. An extra rail from which a subway train derives the electric current that makes it run.

He was speckled with barnacles,
fine rosettes of lime,
and infested
with tiny white sea-lice,
and underneath two or three
rags of green weed hung down.
While his gills were breathing in
the terrible oxygen
—the frightening gills,
fresh and crisp with blood,
that can cut so badly—
I thought of the coarse white flesh
packed in like feathers,
the big bones and the little bones,
the dramatic reds and blacks
of his shiny entrails,
and the pink swim-bladder
like a big peony.
I looked into his eyes
which were far larger than mine
but shallower, and yellowed,
the irises backed and packed
with tarnished tinfoil
seen through the lenses
of old scratched isinglass.[1]
They shifted a little, but not
to return my stare.
—It was more like the tipping
of an object toward the light.
I admired his sullen face,
the mechanism of his jaw,
and then I saw
that from his lower lip
—if you could call it a lip—
grim, wet, and weaponlike,
hung five old pieces of fish-line,
or four and a wire leader
with the swivel still attached,
with all their five big hooks

1. A thin, transparent sheet of mica.

grown firmly in his mouth.
A green line, frayed at the end
where he broke it, two heavier lines,
and a fine black thread
still crimped from the strain and snap
when it broke and he got away.
Like medals with their ribbons
frayed and wavering,
a five-haired beard of wisdom
trailing from his aching jaw.
I stared and stared
and victory filled up
the little rented boat,
from the pool of bilge
where oil had spread a rainbow
around the rusted engine
to the bailer rusted orange,
the sun-cracked thwarts,
the oarlocks on their strings,
the gunnels—until everything
was rainbow, rainbow, rainbow!
And I let the fish go.

1940

At the Fishhouses

Although it is a cold evening,
down by one of the fishhouses
an old man sits netting,
his net, in the gloaming[1] almost invisible,
a dark purple-brown,
and his shuttle worn and polished.
The air smells so strong of codfish
it makes one's nose run and one's eyes water.
The five fishhouses have steeply peaked roofs
and narrow, cleated gangplanks slant up
to storerooms in the gables
for the wheelbarrows to be pushed up and down on.

1. Twilight; dusk.

All is silver: the heavy surface of the sea,
swelling slowly as if considering spilling over,
is opaque, but the silver of the benches,
the lobster pots, and masts, scattered
among the wild jagged rocks,
is of an apparent translucence
like the small old buildings with an emerald moss
growing on their shoreward walls.
The big fish tubs are completely lined
with layers of beautiful herring scales
and the wheelbarrows are similarly plastered
with creamy iridescent coats of mail,
with small iridescent flies crawling on them.
Up on the little slope behind the houses,
set in the sparse bright sprinkle of grass,
is an ancient wooden capstan,[2]
cracked, with two long bleached handles
and some melancholy stains, like dried blood,
where the ironwork has rusted.
The old man accepts a Lucky Strike.
He was a friend of my grandfather.
We talk of the decline in the population
and of codfish and herring
while he waits for a herring boat to come in.
There are sequins on his vest and on his thumb.
He has scraped the scales, the principal beauty,
from unnumbered fish with that black old knife,
the blade of which is almost worn away.

Down at the water's edge, at the place
where they haul up the boats, up the long ramp
descending into the water, thin silver
tree trunks are laid horizontally
across the gray stones, down and down
at intervals of four or five feet.

Cold dark deep and absolutely clear,
element bearable to no mortal,
to fish and to seals . . . One seal particularly

---

2. A windlass, used for winding in ropes or cables.

I have seen here evening after evening.
He was curious about me. He was interested in music;
like me a believer in total immersion,
so I used to sing him Baptist hymns.
I also sang "A Mighty Fortress Is Our God."[3]
He stood up in the water and regarded me
steadily, moving his head a little.
Then he would disappear, then suddenly emerge
almost in the same spot, with a sort of shrug
as if it were against his better judgment.
Cold dark deep and absolutely clear,
the clear gray icy water . . . Back, behind us,
the dignified tall firs begin.
Bluish, associating with their shadows,
a million Christmas trees stand
waiting for Christmas. The water seems suspended
above the rounded gray and blue-gray stones.
I have seen it over and over, the same sea, the same,
slightly, indifferently swinging above the stones,
icily free above the stones,
above the stones and then the world.
If you should dip your hand in,
your wrist would ache immediately,
your bones would begin to ache and your hand would burn
as if the water were a transmutation of fire
that feeds on stones and burns with a dark gray flame.
If you tasted it, it would first taste bitter,
then briny, then surely burn your tongue.
It is like what we imagine knowledge to be:
dark, salt, clear, moving, utterly free,
drawn from the cold hard mouth
of the world, derived from the rocky breasts
forever, flowing and drawn, and since
our knowledge is historical, flowing, and flown.

1947

---

3. Well-known hymn composed by Martin Luther (1531).

Insomnia

The moon in the bureau mirror
Looks out a million miles
(and perhaps with pride, at herself,
but she never, never smiles)
far away beyond sleep, or
perhaps she's a daytime sleeper.

By the universe deserted,
she'd tell it to go to hell,
and she'd find a body of water,
or a mirror, on which to dwell.
So wrap up care in a cobweb
and drop it down the well

into that world inverted
where left is always right,
where the shadows are really the body,
where we stay awake all night,
where the heavens are shallow as the sea
is now deep, and you love me.

1951

Questions of Travel

There are too many waterfalls here;[1] the crowded streams
hurry too rapidly down to the sea,
and the pressure of so many clouds on the mountaintops
makes them spill over the sides in soft slow-motion,
turning to waterfalls under our very eyes.
—For if those streaks, those mile-long, shiny, tearstains,
aren't waterfalls yet,
in a quick age or so, as ages go here,
they probably will be.
But if the streams and clouds keep travelling, travelling,
the mountains look like the hulls of capsized ships,
slime-hung and barnacled.

       ✳   ✳   ✳

---

1. Bishop had settled in Brazil in 1951.

Think of the long trip home.
Should we have stayed at home and thought of here?
Where should we be today?
Is it right to be watching strangers in a play
in this strangest of theatres?
What childishness is it that while there's a breath of life
in our bodies, we are determined to rush
to see the sun the other way around?
The tiniest green hummingbird in the world?
To stare at some inexplicable old stonework,
inexplicable and impenetrable,
at any view,
instantly seen and always, always delightful?
Oh, must we dream our dreams
and have them, too?
And have we room
for one more folded sunset, still quite warm?

But surely it would have been a pity
not to have seen the trees along this road,
really exaggerated in their beauty,
not to have seen them gesturing
like noble pantomimists, robed in pink.
—Not to have had to stop for gas and heard
the sad, two-noted, wooden tune
of disparate wooden clogs
carelessly clacking over
a grease-stained filling-station floor.
(In another country[2] the clogs would all be tested.
Each pair there would have identical pitch.)
—A pity not to have heard
the other, less primitive music of the fat brown bird
who sings above the broken gasoline pump
in a bamboo church of Jesuit baroque:
three towers, five silver crosses.
—Yes, a pity not to have pondered,
blurr'dly and inconclusively,
on what connection can exist for centuries
between the crudest wooden footwear

2. Possibly the United States.

and, careful and finicky,
the whittled fantasies of wooden cages.
—Never to have studied history in
the weak calligraphy³ of songbirds' cages.
—And never to have had to listen to rain
so much like politicians' speeches:
two hours of unrelenting oratory
and then a sudden golden silence
in which the traveller takes a notebook, writes:

*"Is it lack of imagination that makes us come
to imagined places, not just stay at home?
Or could Pascal⁴ have been not entirely right
about just sitting quietly in one's room?*

*Continent, city, country, society:
the choice is never wide and never free.
And here, or there . . . No. Should we have stayed at home,
wherever that may be?"*

1956

The Armadillo

for Robert Lowell

This is the time of year
when almost every night
the frail, illegal fire balloons¹ appear.
Climbing the mountain height,

rising toward a saint²
still honored in these parts,
the paper chambers flush and fill with light
that comes and goes, like hearts.

❋   ❋   ❋

3. A decorative form of handwriting.
4. Blaise Pascal (1623–1662), a French mathematician and religious philosopher, wrote in *Pensées* that "all men's miseries derive from not being able to sit in a quiet room alone."
1. Unmanned hot-air balloons, commonly made from a large bag of paper and fueled by a container of flaming oil. When they crash, they frequently start forest fires.
2. St. John's Day (June 24) is often celebrated in Brazil by the release of fire balloons.

Once up against the sky it's hard
to tell them from the stars—
planets, that is—the tinted ones:
Venus going down, or Mars,

or the pale green one. With a wind,
they flare and falter, wobble and toss;
but if it's still they steer between
the kite sticks of the Southern Cross,[3]

receding, dwindling, solemnly
and steadily forsaking us,
or, in the downdraft from a peak,
suddenly turning dangerous.

Last night another big one fell.
It splattered like an egg of fire
against the cliff behind the house.
The flame ran down. We saw the pair

of owls who nest there flying up
and up, their whirling black-and-white
stained bright pink underneath, until
they shrieked up out of sight.

The ancient owls' nest must have burned.
Hastily, all alone,
a glistening armadillo left the scene,
rose-flecked, head down, tail down,

and then a baby rabbit jumped out,
short-eared, to our surprise.
So soft!—a handful of intangible ash
with fixed, ignited eyes.

Too pretty, dreamlike mimicry!
O falling fire and piercing cry
and panic, and a weak mailed fist
clenched ignorant against the sky!

1957

3. A constellation prominent in the Southern Hemisphere.

First Death in Nova Scotia

In the cold, cold parlor
my mother laid out Arthur[1]
beneath the chromographs:[2]
Edward, Prince of Wales,[3]
with Princess Alexandra,
and King George with Queen Mary.[4]
Below them on the table
stood a stuffed loon
shot and stuffed by Uncle
Arthur, Arthur's father.

Since Uncle Arthur fired
a bullet into him,
he hadn't said a word.
He kept his own counsel
on his white, frozen lake,
the marble-topped table.
His breast was deep and white,
cold and caressable;
his eyes were red glass,
much to be desired.

"Come," said my mother,
"Come and say good-bye
to your little cousin Arthur."
I was lifted up and given
one lily of the valley
to put in Arthur's hand.
Arthur's coffin was
a little frosted cake,
and the red-eyed loon eyed it
from his white, frozen lake.

✻   ✻   ✻

1. Bishop's young cousin Frank Boomer died in Great Village, Nova Scotia, when Bishop, a four-year-old child, was living there in 1915. The poem changes the dead child's name to Arthur, which was in fact the first name of Bishop's uncle, the deceased child's father.
2. A colored reproduction.
3. Edward, Prince of Wales, eldest son and heir to Queen Victoria, was crowned King Edward VII in 1901 upon his mother's death. He is pictured here—while still a prince—with his wife, Princess (later Queen) Alexandra. Canadians at that time often displayed images of the British royal family.
4. King George VI, the son and successor of Edward VII, is pictured with his wife, Mary.

Arthur was very small.
He was all white, like a doll
that hadn't been painted yet.
Jack Frost had started to paint him
the way he always painted
the Maple Leaf (Forever).[5]
He had just begun on his hair,
a few red strokes, and then
Jack Frost had dropped the brush
and left him white, forever.

The gracious royal couples
were warm in red and ermine;
their feet were well wrapped up
in the ladies' ermine trains.
They invited Arthur to be
the smallest page at court.
But how could Arthur go,
clutching his tiny lily,
with his eyes shut up so tight
and the roads deep in snow?

                              1962

In the Waiting Room

In Worcester, Massachusetts,
I went with Aunt Consuelo[1]
to keep her dentist's appointment
and sat and waited for her
in the dentist's waiting room.
It was winter. It got dark
early. The waiting room
was full of grown-up people,
arctics and overcoats,
lamps and magazines.
My aunt was inside

5. The maple leaf is a national symbol of Canada, and "The Maple Leaf Forever," a patriotic song, is commonly considered an unofficial Canadian national anthem.

1. This poem may be based at least partly on fact, but the poet's paternal (Bishop) aunt was named Florence.

what seemed like a long time
and while I waited and read
the *National Geographic*
(I could read) and carefully
studied the photographs:
the inside of a volcano,
black, and full of ashes;
then it was spilling over
in rivulets of fire.
Osa and Martin Johnson[2]
dressed in riding breeches,
laced boots, and pith helmets.
A dead man slung on a pole
—"Long Pig,"[3] the caption said.
Babies with pointed heads
wound round and round with string;
black, naked women with necks
wound round and round with wire
like the necks of light bulbs.[4]
Their breasts were horrifying.
I read it right straight through.
I was too shy to stop.
And then I looked at the cover:
the yellow margins, the date.
Suddenly, from inside,
came an *oh!* of pain
—Aunt Consuelo's voice—
not very loud or long.
I wasn't at all surprised;
even then I knew she was
a foolish, timid woman.
I might have been embarrassed,
but wasn't. What took me
completely by surprise
was that it was *me*:
my voice, in my mouth.

2. An American married couple well known for their explorations of Africa, the South Pacific Islands, and Borneo.
3. The name used by cannibals of the Marquesas Islands for human flesh.
4. Neck rings formed of coiled metal that are worn by women in certain African and Asian cultures.

Without thinking at all
I was my foolish aunt,
I—we—were falling, falling,
our eyes glued to the cover
of the *National Geographic,*
February, 1918.[5]

I said to myself: three days
and you'll be seven years old.
I was saying it to stop
the sensation of falling off
the round, turning world
into cold, blue-black space.
But I felt: you are an I,
you are an *Elizabeth,*
you are one of *them.*
Why should you be one, too?
I scarcely dared to look
to see what it was I was.
I gave a sidelong glance
—I couldn't look any higher—
at shadowy gray knees,
trousers and skirts and boots
and different pairs of hands
lying under the lamps.
I knew that nothing stranger
had ever happened, that nothing
stranger could ever happen.
Why should I be my aunt,
or me, or anyone?
What similarities—
boots, hands, the family voice
I felt in my throat, or even
the *National Geographic*
and those awful hanging breasts—
held us all together
or made us all just one?
How—I didn't know any

---

5. Some but not all of the images in the poem appeared in the February 1918 issue of the *National Geographic*; others appeared in previous or later issues.

word for it—how "unlikely" . . .
How had I come to be here,
like them, and overhear
a cry of pain that could have
got loud and worse but hadn't?

The waiting room was bright
and too hot. It was sliding
beneath a big black wave,
another, and another.

Then I was back in it.
The War was on.[6] Outside,
in Worcester, Massachusetts,
were night and slush and cold,
and it was still the fifth
of February, 1918.

1971

Thomas Travisano, in *Elizabeth Bishop: Her Artistic Development*, introduces "In the Waiting Room" thusly: "A young girl, surrounded by adults in a dentist's waiting room, sits alone waiting for her aunt. No one is paying attention. She has no function to serve. The girl discovers paradoxically not only her solitude but her identity with the larger world outside. She gains awareness of real alternative worlds that are strange, alluring, frightening—but just as valid as one's own. Reading the *National Geographic* (a vicarious form of travel), she discovers unsettling actualities that provoke an experience mysteriously combining knowledge of possession and identity with intimations of loss, displacement, and personal obliteration."

Poem

About the size of an old-style dollar bill,[1]
American or Canadian,
mostly the same whites, gray greens, and steel grays
—this little painting (a sketch for a larger one?)
has never earned any money in its life.
Useless and free, it has spent seventy years

6. World War I ended nine months after the events pictured here, with the Armistice of November 11, 1918.

as a minor family relic
handed along collaterally to owners
who looked at it sometimes, or didn't bother to.

It must be Nova Scotia; only there
does one see gabled wooden houses
painted that awful shade of brown.
The other houses, the bits that show, are white.
Elm trees, low hills, a thin church steeple
—that gray-blue wisp—or is it? In the foreground
a water meadow with some tiny cows,
two brushstrokes each, but confidently cows;
two minuscule white geese in the blue water,
back-to-back, feeding, and a slanting stick.
Up closer, a wild iris, white and yellow,
fresh-squiggled from the tube.
The air is fresh and cold; cold early spring
clear as gray glass; a half inch of blue sky
below the steel-gray storm clouds.
(They were the artist's specialty.)
A specklike bird is flying to the left.
Or is it a flyspeck looking like a bird?

Heavens, I recognize the place, I know it!
It's behind—I can almost remember the farmer's name.
His barn backed on that meadow. There it is,
titanium white, one dab. The hint of steeple,
filaments of brush-hairs, barely there,
must be the Presbyterian church.
Would that be Miss Gillespie's house?
Those particular geese and cows
are naturally before my time.

A sketch done in an hour, "in one breath,"
once taken from a trunk and handed over.
Would you like this? I'll probably never
have room to hang these things again.
Your Uncle George, no, mine, my Uncle George,[2]

---

1. Earlier American and Canadian dollar bills were somewhat larger than those of recent vintage.

2. George Hutchinson, Bishop's maternal great-uncle, was a Canadian artist and illustrator.

he'd be your great-uncle, left them all with Mother
when he went back to England.
You know, he was quite famous, an R.A. . . .[3]

I never knew him. We both knew this place,
apparently, this literal small backwater,
looked at it long enough to memorize it,
our years apart. How strange. And it's still loved,
or its memory is (it must have changed a lot).
Our visions coincided—"visions" is
too serious a word—our looks, two looks:
art "copying from life" and life itself,
life and the memory of it so compressed
they've turned into each other. Which is which?
Life and the memory of it cramped,
dim, on a piece of Bristol board,[4]
dim, but how live, how touching in detail
—the little that we get for free,
the little of our earthly trust. Not much.
About the size of our abidance
along with theirs: the munching cows,
the iris, crisp and shivering, the water
still standing from spring freshets,
the yet-to-be-dismantled elms,[5] the geese.

                                    1972

One Art

The art of losing isn't hard to master;
so many things seem filled with the intent
to be lost that their loss is no disaster.

Lose something every day. Accept the fluster
of lost door keys, the hour badly spent.
The art of losing isn't hard to master.

---

3. R.A.: Member of the British Royal Academy of Art. Despite the recognition Hutchinson received in England, he was not in fact a member of the Royal Academy.
4. High-quality paperboard, resembling cardboard, often used by artists.

5. Dutch elm disease, after devastating the elm tree population of the United States, arrived in northern Canada in the 1970s. Infected trees are taken down, limb by limb.

*   *   *

Then practice losing farther, losing faster:
places, and names, and where it was you meant
to travel. None of these will bring disaster.

I lost my mother's watch. And look! my last, or
next-to-last, of three loved houses went.
The art of losing isn't hard to master.

I lost two cities, lovely ones. And, vaster,
some realms I owned, two rivers, a continent.
I miss them, but it wasn't a disaster.

—Even losing you (the joking voice, a gesture
I love) I shan't have lied. It's evident
the art of losing's not too hard to master
though it may look like (*Write* it!) like disaster.

1976

"One Art" has emerged as one of the most famous and influential modern examples of the villanelle, a traditional French form in nineteen lines that follows a distinctive rhyming and stanza pattern. A villanelle has only two rhyme sounds, with the *aba* rhyme scheme of the initial three-line stanza (or tercet)—here the words "master," "intent," and "disaster"—being repeated consistently throughout the poem's following four tercets, and appearing once more in the villanelle's final four-line stanza (or quatrain) in *abaa* form. In the traditional version, which Bishop subtly varies, the first and third lines of the first stanza become rhyming refrains—repeated lines—that alternate as the last line in each successive tercet. These refrains return repeatedly to the pivotal rhyme words "master" and "disaster," and they achieve a startlingly dramatic effect when they reappear one last time in the villanelle's final couplet. "One Art" is notable for the irony, psychological intricacy, and meaningful syntactical variety that Bishop brings to this traditional form.

Pink Dog

[*Rio de Janeiro*]

The sun is blazing and the sky is blue.
Umbrellas clothe the beach in every hue.
Naked, you trot across the avenue.

Oh, never have I seen a dog so bare!
Naked and pink, without a single hair . . .
Startled, the passersby draw back and stare.

*   *   *

Of course they're mortally afraid of rabies.
You are not mad; you have a case of scabies[1]
but look intelligent. Where are your babies?

(A nursing mother, by those hanging teats.)
In what slum have you hidden them, poor bitch,
while you go begging, living by your wits?

Didn't you know? It's been in all the papers,
to solve this problem, how they deal with beggars?
They take and throw them in the tidal rivers.

Yes, idiots, paralytics, parasites
go bobbing in the ebbing sewage, nights
out in the suburbs, where there are no lights.

If they do this to anyone who begs,
drugged, drunk, or sober, with or without legs,
what would they do to sick, four-leggèd dogs?

In the cafés and on the sidewalk corners
the joke is going round that all the beggars
who can afford them now wear life preservers.

In your condition you would not be able
even to float, much less to dog-paddle.
Now look, the practical, the sensible

solution is to wear a *fantasia*.[2]
Tonight you simply can't afford to be a-
n eyesore but no one will ever see a

dog in *máscara*[3] this time of year.
Ash Wednesday'll[4] come but Carnival is here.
What sambas can you dance? What will you wear?

They say that Carnival's degenerating
—radios, Americans, or something,
have ruined it completely. They're just talking.

* * *

1. A contagious skin disease shared by both animals and humans.
2. Bishop's note: "Carnival costume."
3. Portuguese for "mask."
4. Day that marks the beginning of Lent, a time of prayer, sacrifice, and self-denial. Carnival: Rio's famous version of Mardi Gras, extravagantly celebrated with dance and dazzling costumes (*fantasias*).

Carnival is always wonderful!
A depilated[5] dog would not look well.
Dress up! Dress up and dance at Carnival!

1979

Steven Gould Axelrod has written of "Pink Dog" that "the Mardi Gras festival, with its costumed *carnavelescos* engaging in variously uncontained behaviors, provides an oppositional space of equality, disguise, heterogeneity, and pleasure. As [Mikhail] Bakhtin says, the carnivalesque crowd 'is outside of and contrary to all existing forms of the coercive socioeconomic and political organization.' Bishop's speaker advises the pink dog to take advantage of this counter-site of festival. She is also implicitly addressing all those who might be figured by the dog: the city's poor; its homosexuals (who must similarly cope with hostility and violence); herself (Bonnie Costello tells us that Bishop 'suffered from eczema and other skin ailments and as a schoolgirl was sent home for open sores'); and indeed her readers."

Sonnet

Caught—the bubble
in the spirit level,
a creature divided;
and the compass needle
wobbling and wavering,
undecided.
Freed—the broken
thermometer's mercury
running away;
and the rainbow-bird
from the narrow bevel
of the empty mirror,
flying wherever
it feels like, gay!

1979

Like many previous exercises in the genre, Bishop's "Sonnet" contemplates the paradoxical struggle between freedom and captivity embodied in this most persistently popular of traditional literary forms. In the process, she inverts the standard structure of the Petrarchan sonnet by beginning with a sestet (or six-line section; the traditional ending) and closing with an octave (or eight-line section; the traditional beginning). The mostly four-beat lines are notably shorter than the sonnet's traditional ten-beat iambic pentameter, and the rhymes are persistently irregular.

5. Hairless.

CARLOS BULOSAN
1911?–1956

Carlos bulosan, a major writer of both poetry and prose, is considered the most important founding voice in Filipino-American literature. *Look*, the popular weekly magazine of the 1940s, called his 1946 autobiographical novel, *America Is In the Heart*, "one of the fifty most important American books ever published." This book, which recounts the struggles of Filipino-American immigrants, is Bulosan's most famous novel. Along with his 1943 short-story collection, *The Laughter of My Father*, it is the first literary work by a Filipino-American writer to become well known. Bulosan also wrote poems and essays, and he belonged to the Academy of American Poets.

Bulosan enjoyed a flurry of media attention in the United States in the 1940s—especially as World War II focused attention on the Philippines and then after the war, as the country assumed its independence from the United States. Bulosan was featured in articles and on the covers of news magazines. His writing appeared in a wide range of publications—from the popular *Saturday Evening Post* to the prestigious *Poetry* magazine and the elite *New Yorker*. In 1942 Bulosan published a volume of well-received poetry called *Letter from America*. The next year he published *Voice of Bataan,* a poetic tribute to the Allied soldiers who died fighting in the Philippines during World War II. In many readers' eyes, though, his most important writing at this time may have been the essay "Freedom from Want," commissioned by President Franklin Delano Roosevelt and included in Norman Rockwell's series on the "Four Freedoms" published in *The Saturday Evening Post* in 1943.

Bulosan virtually disappeared from the literary scene in the 1950s when he was blacklisted as a labor radical and socialist writer. In 1956 he died in large part from injuries caused by racial violence, poverty, and disease. In the 1970s, his work became prominent again. His renewed visibility may have begun with the 1966 publication of *New Writing from the Philippines*, edited by Leonard Casper. Today Bulosan is viewed as a major inspiration in both Filipino-American and Filipino cultures because of his powerful writing in many genres. He has influenced such contemporary Filipino and Filipino-American writers as Benilda Santos, Nick Carbo, Jessica Hagedorn, Luisa Igloria, Fatima Lim-Wilson, David Romtvedt, and E. San Juan, Jr. In addition, he has inspired other Asian and Asian-American writers, such as Maxine Hong Kingston. Several major Filipino and Filipino-American hip-hop groups also acknowledge Bulosan as a cultural father.

Although the year of Bulosan's birth is not clear, baptismal records suggest that 1911 is the most likely year. This dating places Bulosan's birth within the early period of the U.S. colonization of the islands and about a decade after the U.S.-Filipino War. Bulosan arrived in Seattle in 1930 and was apparently sold for $5 to work in canneries. Like most Filipino immigrants, he found himself caught in the racial tensions of the Great Depression. Filipino men could be assaulted, jailed, and killed for walking in public with a woman coded as "white" by the legal authorities. Bulosan became a union organizer and a writer for union newspapers. In 1936 he became ill with tuberculosis and never fully recovered his health, though he continued working as a farmhand and a member of the cannery union in California and Washington.

Between 1900 and 1946, about 150,000 Filipinos like Bulosan emigrated to both the U.S. mainland and its territories, especially Hawaii and Alaska. Nearly a century after the first Filipinos arrived in the United States, their ethnic and class struggles continue. Bulosan's poetry still resonates. As E. San Juan, Jr. has written, "Bulosan helps us to understand the powerlessness and invisibility of being labeled a Filipino in a post–Cold War American twenty-first century." Writing in a literary journal in Hawaii, where Filipino Americans are now the third-largest demographic group, poet Jannah Manansala has stated, "we are . . . losing voice / Gaining numbers / Soon we will roar." That sense of challenge and hope carries on Bulosan's legacy as a writer and social advocate, suggesting a growing awareness of Filipino/a potential throughout the United States.

FURTHER READING

Delia D. Aguilar. "Current Challenges to Feminism: Theory and Practice." *Monthly Review*, October 18, 2006. www.mrzine.monthlyreview.org.

Carlos Bulosan. *America is in the Heart: A Personal History*. Seattle: University of Washington Press, 1973.

———. *On Becoming Filipino: Selected Writings of Carlos Bulosan*. Ed. E. San Juan, Jr. Philadelphia: Temple University Press, 1995.

Augusto Fauni Espiritu. *Five Faces of Exile: The Nation and Filipino American Intellectuals*. Palo Alto, Calif.: Stanford University Press, 2005.

Susan Evangelista. *Carlos Bulosan and His Poetry: A Biography and Anthology*. Seattle: University of Washington Press, 1985.

Jannah Manansala. "Apelyido pilni pino." *Katipunan Literary Journal*, Spring 2002: 1, 13–14.

Jane Sarmiento Schwab. *Filipino American Literature in the Shadow of Empire*. Ann Arbor: DAI, 2003.

Michael Viola. "Filipino American Hip-Hop: Renewing the Spirit of Carlos Bulosan." *Monthly Review*, April 15, 2006. www.mrzine.monthlyreview.org.

History of a Moment

Now listen. The steady fall of fine rain enriches
The land. Sunset is a red flower in the western sky.
Night breaks the moment and darkness moves eastward

Over America, and earthward, sprawling upon the continent.
It is the fluid tension of waiting in valleys and cities;
It is the last passionate longing in every heart
That beats remembering the final plunge to earth.

Listen to me then. Listen to me in the night
That ruins our illusion of violent discoveries.
Listen to my last words under the galaxies of eyes
And tongues that lash at every promise I make
For you. And now you prepare for my last will
And testament, for I leave you this heritage
Of vast patterns of land that is America . . .

Remember how I walked under the bomber that time,
Bearing a new world of longing in my eager hands;
How I approached you through the battleships,
Saying: Here is a tiny green fruit from my country.
Remember how I sat back in the small sick-bed,
After the submarines and destroyers, saying:
Here is a historic seed growing in your country.

I am the tension of waiting in valleys and cities,
The longing in every heart that beats to see
America break through the darkness moving eastward.
I warn you and prepare for the final lash
Of armies and navies and the enduring love;
Living at a time when the night must lie,
I make no promise except this historic truth.

                                                    1941

Bulosan wrote "History of a Moment" near the beginning of World War II, when the Philippines was still a colony of the United States and required its military protection. At the time the islands were in a state of tension because Japan had invaded mainland China and infiltrated the colony. Living in California, Bulosan hoped that the United States would protect the Philippines. His poem calls on the country to understand that its endangered colony required immediate preparedness and intervention. As it turned out, however, the United States was forced to retreat militarily and to rely to a great extent on the Filipinos themselves to defend the islands until the United States could regroup and retake them. But this ultimate victory did not occur until many men had died in such events as the battle of Bataan and the Bataan death march.

The poem reveals Bulosan's appropriation of his native oral tradition. Note how many times he uses such words as "listen" and refers to the listener/reader as "you." In one sense the poet is calling on all the citizens of the United States, including all Filipino

Americans, to prepare for a war that Japan's invasion of China in 1937 prophesied. This poem can be examined in relationship to other poems that reflect on World War II and its context, such as H. T. Tsiang's "Shantung," Richard Eberhart's "The Fury of Aerial Bombardment," and internment camp poetry in Volume Two as well as the poetry of Randall Jarrell and Mitsuye Yamada in this volume.

ROBERT HAYDEN
1913–1980

ROBERT HAYDEN was a master of understatement and implication, and his poetry is noted for its subtle, erudite, and nuanced exploration of the present and past of African-American culture. His work often focuses on individuals whose lives were shaped by their cultural inheritance, as in his sensitive "The Ballad of Sue Ellen Westerfield," a narrative of the life and loves of his adoptive mother. He was also a master of differing voices, as in his "Night, Death, Mississippi," which we hear through the voices of three generations of a white supremacist family who derive pleasure from the mutilation and murder of African-American men. Perhaps his most famous poem, "Those Winter Sundays," is a delicate, almost nostalgic evocation of a family environment that had made his early years deeply traumatic.

Born Asa Sheffey in Detroit in 1913, Hayden was adopted—though never formally—by Sue Ellen Westerfield and William Hayden, and thereafter he assumed his adoptive father's surname. Hayden endured a difficult childhood marked by a contentious relationship between his foster parents and by frequent beatings from his foster father. However, he listened with fascination to the African-American stories and folktales told him by his foster mother. An avid reader, Hayden attended Detroit City College (later Wayne State University), leaving without a degree in 1936 to research black history and culture for the Federal Writers' Project. In 1940, Hayden married Erma Inez Morris, a talented musician. They had one child. Between 1941 and 1945, Hayden earned a BA and MA from the University of Michigan, where he studied with the British poet W. H. Auden. Under Auden's influence, according to Arnold Rampersand, Hayden sought to write "a modernist poetry of technical and meditative complexity, in which judicious erudition and imagination, rather than pseudo-folk simplicity, or didacticism, were vital elements." Hayden championed, stated Rampersand, "an art free of crude propaganda and yet engaged with the realities of black life in America." Moreover, influenced by his wife, Hayden abandoned the Baptist religion of his childhood and embraced the Baha'i faith.

Hayden began teaching at the historically black Fisk University in 1946, returning to teach at the University of Michigan in 1969. Hayden served as Poetry Consultant to the Library of Congress (later termed the Poet Laureate) from 1976 to 1978. He died of cancer in 1980.

FURTHER READING

John Hatcher. *From the Auroral Darkness: The Life and Poetry of Robert Hayden.* Oxford, Eng.: Oxford University Press, 1984.

Robert Hayden. *Collected Poems.* Ed. Frederick Glaysher. New York: Liveright, 1985.

———. *Collected Prose.* Ed. Frederick Glaysher. Ann Arbor: University of Michigan Press, 1984.

Night, Death, Mississippi

I

A quavering cry. Screech-owl?
Or one of them?
The old man in his reek
and gauntness laughs—

one of them, I bet—
and turns out the kitchen lamp,
limping to the porch to listen
in the windowless night.

Be there with Boy and the rest
if I was well again.
Time was. Time was.
White robes like moonlight[1]

In the sweetgum dark.
Unbucked that one then
and him squealing bloody Jesus
as we cut it off.

Time was. A cry?
A cry all right.

---

1. Traditional garb of the Ku Klux Klan.

He hawks and spits,
fevered as by groinfire.

Have us a bottle,
Boy and me—
he's earned him a bottle—
when he gets home.

II
Then we beat them, he said,
beat them till our arms was tired
and the big old chains
messy and red.

O Jesus burning on the lily cross

Christ, it was better
than hunting bear
which don't know why
you want him dead.

O night, rawhead and bloodybones night

You kids fetch Paw
some water now so's he
can wash that blood
off him, she said.

O night betrayed by darkness not its own.

                                    1962

The Ballad of Sue Ellen Westerfield
(for Clyde)

She grew up in bedeviled southern wilderness,
but had not been a slave, she said,
because her father wept and set her mother free.[1]
She hardened in perilous rivertowns
and after The Surrender,[2]

---

1. Westerfield's father was a slaveholder who freed her mother after impregnating her.   2. Confederate capitulation, ending the Civil War.

went as maid upon the tarnished Floating Palaces.[3]
Rivermen reviled her for the rankling cold
sardonic pride
that gave a knife-edge to her comeliness.

When she was old, her back still straight,
her hair still glossy black,
she'd talk sometimes
of dangers lived through on the rivers.
But never told of him,
whose name she'd vowed she would not speak again
till after Jordan.[4]
Oh, he was nearer nearer now
than wearisome kith and kin.
His blue eyes followed her
as she moved about her tasks upon the *Memphis Rose*.[5]
He smiled and joshed, his voice quickening her.
She cursed the circumstance. . . .

the crazing horrors of that summer night,
the swifting flames, he fought his way to her,
the savaging panic, and helped her swim to shore.
The steamer like besieged Atlanta blazing,
the cries, the smoke and bellowing flames,
the flamelit thrashing forms in hellmouth water,
and he swimming out to them,
leaving her dazed and lost.
A woman screaming under the raddled[6] trees—

Sue Ellen felt it was herself who screamed.
The moaning of the hurt, the terrified—
she held off shuddering despair
and went to comfort whom she could.
Wagons torches bells
and whimpering dusk of morning
and blankness lostness nothingness for her
until his arms had lifted her
into wild and secret dark.

3. Gaudily furnished steamboats.
4. Death and crossing the river Jordan into heaven.
5. A steamboat destroyed by fire.
6. Worn out and broken down.

*   *   *

How long how long was it they wandered,
loving fearing loving,
fugitives whose dangerous only hidingplace
was love?[7]
How long was it before she knew
she could not forfeit what she was,
even for him—could not, ever for him,
forswear her pride?
They kissed and said farewell at last.
He wept as had her father once.
They kissed and said farewell.
Until her dying-bed,
she cursed the circumstance.

1972

Sue Ellen Westerfield, the poet's adoptive mother, was noted for her skills as a storyteller.

Those Winter Sundays

Sundays too my father got up early
And put his clothes on in the blueblack cold,
then with cracked hands that ached
from labor in the weekday weather made
banked fires blaze. No one ever thanked him.

I'd wake and hear the cold splintering, breaking.
When the rooms were warm, he'd call,
and slowly I would rise and dress,
fearing the chronic angers of that house,[1]

Speaking indifferently to him,
who had driven out the cold
and polished my good shoes as well.
What did I know, what did I know
of love's austere and lonely offices?

7. Perhaps the danger arose because of the love, in the post–Civil War South, between a white man and a black woman.

1. Presumably, the brooding conflict in Hayden's adoptive parents' home.

MURIEL RUKEYSER
1913–1980

Muriel rukeyser worked devotedly to make poetry central to everyday life and to social progress. Ideals of justice and care drive her poems, which often concern the abolition of inequality and war, the need for self-discovery, and the promise of literature and science to transform the world. Rukeyser involved herself in many of the most contentious issues of her day—from fighting fascism and corporate irresponsibility in the 1930s and 1940s to advocating civil rights and women's rights in the 1960s and 1970s. She was equally attentive to the inner world of feeling and imagination. Although she received little positive attention until her final decades, her poetry provides a model for many women writers today, and it now seems to be finding an ever-increasing audience, just as she hoped it would.

Growing up in New York City, Rukeyser was trained both in the Jewish religious tradition and at the Manhattan School of Ethical Culture, which emphasized high moral ideals and doing good in the world. She attended Vassar College and Columbia University without obtaining a degree. Instead, she was drawn to radical political action and aligned herself with the Popular Front of left-wing groups that included the Communist Party. She was arrested in Alabama at the age of twenty for protesting the conviction of the Scottsboro Boys (nine African-American youths unjustly accused of raping two white women). In 1936 she traveled to Spain to report on the People's Olympiad (an alternative to the Nazis' Berlin Olympics) and to support the Loyalist cause in the Spanish Civil War. She also investigated the deaths from silica poisoning of mine workers working for Union Carbide in West Virginia—a venture that resulted in her long documentary poem "The Book of the Dead." Such activities put her at risk during the McCarthy era of the 1940s and 1950s, and indeed the FBI kept a file on her and the American Legion tried to get her fired from her teaching job. Also during this time, Rukeyser, who was bisexual, gave birth to a son, William, whom she raised by herself.

In the 1960s and 1970s, Rukeyser focused her political energy on expanding women's rights, protecting civil liberties, and opposing the Vietnam War. She was arrested for protesting the war on the steps of the Capitol, she traveled to Vietnam on a peace mission, and she traveled to South Korea to support Kim Chi-Ha, a Catholic poet then facing execution. Having begun teaching at Sarah Lawrence College in 1954, she resigned in 1967 when she was granted tenure. She felt that being a tenured professor would make her "very nervous." Instead, she supported herself by part-time teaching and poetry readings. After decades of being neglected, she started to be honored by young feminists, who saw in her a spiritual mother. Suffering from diabetes, Rukeyser had a stroke in 1964 and a second, more serious one in 1977. She kept writing until her death in 1980 at the age of sixty-six.

The poems collected here represent the culmination of Rukeyser's journey. "To Enter That Rhythm Where the Self Is Lost" and "The Poem as Mask" portray the quest for a distinctive creative identity hidden beneath an outer shell of custom and compliance. "Poem," "The Speed of Darkness," and "Waking This Morning" reveal the poet's struggles against violence and injustice. And "Myth" and "St. Roach," written in the poet's final, parabolic style, expose the absurdity of prejudice (whether gendered, racial, religious, or national). Rukeyser's poetry evokes the inner splits, the hard-won victories, and the ceaseless imagination of a woman poet passionately connected to the people and the ideals of her time.

FURTHER READING

Burt Hatlen. "Rukeyser, Muriel." In *The Greenwood Encyclopedia of American Poets and Poetry*, vol. 4, ed. Jeffrey Gray, James McCorkle, and Mary McAleer Balkun, 1399–403 Westport, Conn.: Greenwood Press, 2006.

Anne F. Herzog and Janet E. Kaufman, eds. *"How Shall We Tell Each Other of the Poet?" The Life and Writing of Muriel Rukeyser*. New York: Palgrave, 2001.

Kathleen Carlton Johnson and Catherine Cucinella. "Muriel Rukeyser." In *Contemporary American Women Poets: An A-to-Z Guide*, ed. Catherine Cucinella, 302–8. Westport, Conn.: Greenwood Press, 2002.

Muriel Rukeyser. *Collected Poems*. Ed. Janet E. Kaufman, Anne F. Herzog, and Jan Heller Levi. Pittsburgh: University of Pittsburgh Press, 2005.

———. *The Life of Poetry*. Ashfield, Mass.: Paris Press, 1996.

———. *Out of Silence: Selected Poems*. Ed. Kate Daniels. Evanston, Ill.: TriQuarterly Books, 1992.

To Enter That Rhythm Where the Self Is Lost

To enter that rhythm where the self is lost,
where breathing : heartbeat : and the subtle music
of their relation make our dance, and hasten
us to the moment when all things become
magic, another possibility.
That blind moment, midnight, when all sight
begins, and the dance itself is all our breath,
and we ourselves the moment of life and death.
Blinded;   but given now another saving,
the self as vision, at all times perceiving,
all arts all senses being languages,

delivered of will, being transformed in truth—
for life's sake surrendering moment and images,
writing the poem;   in love making;   bringing to birth.

1962

This poem, exploring "the moment when all things become / magic," suggests the art of self-transformation, the achievement of ecstasy. In *The Life of Poetry*, Rukeyser wrote, "A poem does invite, it does require. What does it invite? A poem invites you to feel."

The Poem as Mask

Orpheus[1]

When I wrote of the women in their dances and wildness,[2] it was a mask,
on their mountain, god-hunting, singing, in orgy,
it was a mask; when I wrote of the god,
fragmented, exiled from himself, his life, the love gone down with song,
it was myself, split open, unable to speak, in exile from myself.

There is no mountain, there is no god, there is memory
of my torn life, myself split open in sleep, the rescued child
beside me among the doctors,[3] and a word
of rescue from the great eyes.

No more masks! No more mythologies!

Now, for the first time, the god lifts his hand,
the fragments join in me with their own music.

1968

This poem became a feminist anthem in the 1970s, along with Adrienne Rich's "Diving into the Wreck." Its resonant phrases "No more masks! Nor more mythologies!" became rallying cries, contributing to the title of the most significant feminist poetry anthology of the time, Florence Howe and Ellen Bass's *No More Masks!* Rukeyser's poem critiques patriarchal myth-making and specifically her own retelling of one such myth in her earlier poem "Orpheus." There, she had written about a mythic male poet as a disguise for herself. In the final lines of "The Poem as Mask," she reclaims her own story. But note

1. Figure in Greek myth who was considered the paradigmatic poet, musician, and magician. He was torn to pieces in an orgy by female followers of the god Dionysus.
2. A reference to Rukeyser's earlier, long poem "Orpheus" (1949), which depicts the death of the male poet-figure at the hands of wild women and his rebirth as a god.
3. A personal evocation of giving birth under anesthesia.

that she does not really dispense with the Orpheus myth. Instead, she adapts it to herself, producing a feminist revision of classical myth. In an interview, Rukeyser asserted that, once mythologies are dispensed with, "the myth begins again."

Poem (I lived in the first century of world wars)

I lived in the first century of world wars.
Most mornings I would be more or less insane,
The newspapers would arrive with their careless stories,
The news would pour out of various devices
Interrupted by attempts to sell products to the unseen.
I would call my friends on other devices;
They would be more or less mad for similar reasons.
Slowly I would get to pen and paper,
Make my poems for others unseen and unborn.
In the day I would be reminded of those men and women
Brave,[1] setting up signals across vast distances,
Considering a nameless way of living, of almost unimagined values.
As the lights darkened, as the lights of night brightened,
We would try to imagine them, try to find each other.
To construct peace, to make love, to reconcile
Waking with sleeping, ourselves with each other,
Ourselves with ourselves. We would try by any means
To reach the limits of ourselves, to reach beyond ourselves,
To let go the means, to wake.

I lived in the first century of these wars.

1968

Written during the Vietnam War, this poem and the next two poems all address the anguish of war. In an essay in Herzog and Kaufman's edited volume, *"How Shall We Tell Each Other of the Poet?,"* Michael True writes of "Poem": "Where else, in 20 lines, do we have such an accurate rendering of what it feels like to live at this moment in history? Who else provided such a precise, simple statement of our 'nuclear' dilemma? What other writer managed not only to identify the terror that dominates the landscape, but also to suggest a strategy for moving through its insanity toward a safer place?"

1. Historical and contemporary individuals who take a stand against the violence of war.

The Speed of Darkness

1

Whoever despises the clitoris despises the penis
Whoever despises the penis despises the cunt
Whoever despises the cunt despises the life of the child.
Resurrection music,   silence,   and surf.

2

No longer speaking
Listening with the whole body
And with every drop of blood
Overtaken by silence

But this same silence is become speech
With the speed of darkness.

3

Stillness during war, the lake.
The unmoving spruces.
Glints over the water.
Faces, voices.   You are far away.
A tree that trembles.

I am the tree that trembles and trembles.

4

After the lifting of the mist
after the lift of the heavy rains
the sky stands clear
and the cries of the city risen in day
I remember the buildings are space
walled, to let space be used for living
I mind this room is space
this drinking glass is space
whose boundary of glass
lets me give you drink and space to drink
your hand, my hand being space
containing skies and constellations
your face
carries the reaches of air

I know I am space
my words are air.

5
Between   between
the man : act   exact
woman : in curve   senses in their maze
frail orbits, green tries,   games of stars
shape of the body speaking its evidence

6
I look across at the real
vulnerable   involved   naked
devoted to the present of all I care for
the world of its history leading to this moment.

7
Life the announcer.
I assure you
there are many ways to have a child.
I bastard mother
promise you
there are many ways to be born.
They all come forth
in their own grace.

8
Ends of the earth join tonight
with blazing stars upon their meeting.

These sons,   these sons
fall burning into Asia.[1]

9
Time comes into it.
Say it.   Say it.[2]
The universe is made of stories,
not of atoms.

*   *   *

1. A reference to the Vietnam War (1965–75).
2. Perhaps an echo and revision of William
Carlos Williams's exclamation (in his poem *Paterson*), "Say it, no ideas but in things."

10
Lying
blazing beside me
you rear beautifully and up—
your thinking face—
erotic body reaching
in all its colors and light—
your erotic face
colored and lit—
not colored body-and-face
but now entire,
colors   lights   the world thinking and reaching.

11
The river flows past the city.

Water goes down to tomorrow
making its children   I hear their unborn voices
I am working out the vocabulary of my silence.

12
Big-boned man young and of my dream
Struggles to get the live bird out of his throat.
I am he am I?   Dreaming?
I am the bird am I?   I am the throat?

A bird with a curved beak.
It could slit anything, the throat-bird.

Drawn up slowly.   The curved blades, not large.
Bird emerges   wet   being born
Begins to sing.

13
My night awake
staring at the broad rough jewel
the copper roof across the way
thinking of the poet
yet unborn in this dark
who will be the throat of these hours.
No.   Of those hours.[3]

3. That is, these hours will be "those" hours from the future perspective of the "poet / yet unborn."

Who will speak these days,
if not I,
if not you?

1968

Rukeyser believed that all thirteen sections of "The Speed of Darkness" should be "treated as separate poems." The first section (or poem) condemns gendered exclusions or despisals. Subsequent sections concern the effort to make silence move into speech, the wish to relinquish domination, the compensations of eros, and the poet's need to "speak these days."

Waking This Morning

Waking this morning,
a violent woman in the violent day
Laughing.
                    Past the line of memory
along the long body of your life
in which move childhood, youth, your lifetime of touch,
eyes, lips, chest, belly, sex, legs, to the waves of the sheet.
I look past the little plant
on the city windowsill
to the tall towers bookshaped, crushed together in greed,
the river flashing flowing corroded,
the intricate harbor and the sea, the wars, the moon, the planets, all who
      people space
in the sun visible invisible.
African violets in the light
breathing, in a breathing universe.   I want strong peace, and delight,
the wild good.
I want to make my touch poems:
to find my morning, to find you entire
alive moving among the anti-touch people.

                    I say across the waves of the air to you:
today once more
I will try to be non-violent
one more day
this morning, waking the world away
in the violent day.

1973

Burt Hatlen comments: "The 'you' in the poem is the unnamed beloved, but it is also each person who opens the pages and begins to read."

Myth

Long afterward, Oedipus,[1] old and blinded, walked the
roads.   He smelled a familiar smell.   It was
the Sphinx.   Oedipus said, "I want to ask one question.
Why didn't I recognize my mother?"   "You gave the
wrong answer," said the Sphinx.   "But that was what
made everything possible," said Oedipus.   "No," she said.
"When I asked, What walks on four legs in the morning,
two at noon, and three in the evening, you answered,
Man.[2]   You didn't say anything about woman."
"When you say Man," said Oedipus, "you include women
too. Everyone knows that."   She said, "That's what
you think."

1973

St. Roach

For that I never knew you, I only learned to dread you,
for that I never touched you, they told me you are filth,
they showed me by every action to despise your kind;
for that I saw my people making war on you,
I could not tell you apart, one from another,
for that in childhood I lived in places clear of you,
for that all the people I knew met you by
crushing you, stamping you to death, they poured boiling
    water on you, they flushed you down,
for that I could not tell one from another
only that you were dark, fast on your feet, and slender.
    Not like me.
For that I did not know your poems

---

1. Oedipus, who solved the riddle of the Sphinx, is the protagonist of Sophocles's play *Oedipus Rex* (429 B.C.E.). At the play's climax, he discovers that his wife, Jocasta, is also his mother. Jocasta hangs herself, and Oedipus plunges pins from her dress into his eyes, blinding himself.
2. Oedipus's logic is that "Man" crawls on all fours as an infant, walks upright as an adult, and uses a cane in old age.

And that I do not know any of your sayings
And that I cannot speak or read your language
And that I do not sing your songs
And that I do not teach our children
       to eat your food
       or know your poems
       or sing your songs
But that we say you are filthing our food
But that we know you not at all.

Yesterday I looked at one of you for the first time.
You were lighter than the others in color, that was
  neither good nor bad.
I was really looking for the first time.
You seemed troubled and witty.

Today I touched one of you for the first time.
You were startled, you ran, you fled away
Fast as a dancer, light, strange and lovely to the touch.
I reach, I touch, I begin to know you.

                                 1978

JOHN BERRYMAN
1914–1973

JOHN BERRYMAN'S POEMS are marked by their darkly funny, linguistically inventive, and often searingly emotional explorations of the problem of selfhood in the postmodern world. His magnum opus, *The Dream Songs*, is a sequence of 385 short poems composed in a uniquely Berrymanesque language that are loosely woven together into a dreamlike, self-exploratory narrative. The first volume of this epic sequence, *77 Dream Songs*, burst on the poetic scene in 1964 with an effect of considerable surprise and shock. Early readings of *The Dream Songs* led critics to attach the label Confessional Poet to Berryman, a characterization to which he responded, in his own words, "with rage and contempt." Recently, readers have come to appreciate more fully the richness, the complexity, and the sheer artfulness of poems that are perhaps better understood as skillfully constructed surrealistic fictions than as straightforward self-revelations. For all that, both the pleasure and the pain one so often encounters in Berryman's poetry seem very real indeed.

Born John Allyn Smith, Jr., in McAlester, Oklahoma, he moved as a child with his father and mother to Florida, where his father, John Allyn Smith, Sr., lost his life savings in the Florida land boom of 1926. By June of that year, his father was distraught over his financial ruin and over the fact that his wife, Martha, the poet's mother, had filed for divorce. On the night of June 25, John, Sr., was found dead with a bullet wound in his chest and a .32-caliber revolver resting beside him. At the coroner's hearing, the poet's father's death was ruled a suicide, but neither of Berryman's biographers was able to rule out the possibility that the poet's mother had murdered his father. His mother promptly married her lover, the prosperous investor John Angus Berryman, and the poet, then eleven years old, took on his adoptive father's surname and moved north to New York with his new family. Berryman's mother proved deeply devoted to her son, supportive of his writing aspirations, yet consumingly possessive. As he grew up, Berryman himself began to suspect his mother of murder. The moral and emotional uncertainty and unsettling guilt that pervaded Berryman's emotional ties to his dead father, his usurping stepfather, and his overpowering mother haunted his personal and artistic development.

From 1932 to 1936, Berryman attended Columbia University, where he developed a close relationship with the elder poet and professor Mark Van Doren, who encouraged Berryman's own poetic aspirations. He also developed friendships with such important elder poets and critics as R. P. Blackmur and Allen Tate. In his final year at Columbia, Berryman won the Kellett Fellowship, which enabled him to do postgraduate work at Cambridge University in England, where he studied for two years and met the Welsh poet Dylan Thomas and his idol, the Irish poet W. B. Yeats. When Berryman returned to America, his relationship with his mother continued to be difficult. At the same time he befriended important poetic contemporaries such as Randall Jarrell, Robert Lowell, and Delmore Schwartz (the first two included in this anthology). Berryman would spend long hours talking with Lowell and Schwartz about the art of poetry and their artistic aspirations. After struggling to find steady work as a writer or teacher—he even briefly sold encyclopedias—Berryman located temporary teaching posts at Princeton, Harvard, and the University of Iowa before landing a long-term position, in 1954, at the University of Minnesota.

Berryman's earlier work was often laboriously conventional. His first breakthrough to a more personal style was the remarkable long poem "Homage to Mistress Bradstreet" (1953). Shortly thereafter, Berryman began to write *The Dream Songs*, the work that would define him as an artist. *The Dream Songs* give voice to a consciousness tortured by loss, anger, loneliness, and regret, and haunted by unconscious furies and desires that keep breaking into his awareness.

He is accompanied on his introspective journey by an interior companion—a split in his discursive self—who calls him "Mr. Bones" and who perhaps represents the reality principle, which the main consciousness is forever in danger of abandoning.

Berryman's alcoholism and other unhealthy living patterns ultimately caught up with him, though he had desperately tried to combat them with the help of Alcoholics Anonymous. On January 7, 1972, he jumped from the Washington Avenue Bridge in Minneapolis to the icy Mississippi River far below.

FURTHER READING

John Berryman. *Collected Poems, 1937–1971.* Ed. Charles Thornbury. New York: Farrar, Straus & Giroux, 1989.
———. *The Dream Songs.* New York: Farrar, Straus & Giroux, 2007.
———. *The Freedom of the Poet.* New York: Farrar, Straus & Giroux, 1976.
Richard J. Kelly and Alan K. Lathrop, eds. *Recovering Berryman: Essays on a Poet.* Ann Arbor: University of Michigan Press, 1993.
Paul Mariani. *Dream Song: The Life of John Berryman.* Amherst: University of Massachusetts Press, 1996.
Ernest Smith. "'Approaching Our Maturity': The Dialectic of Engagement and Withdrawal in the Political Poetry of Berryman and Lowell." In *Jarrell, Bishop, Lowell, and Co.: Middle Generation Poets in Context,* ed. Suzanne Ferguson, 287–302. Knoxville: University of Tennessee Press, 2003.
Thomas Travisano. *Midcentury Quartet: Bishop, Lowell, Jarrell, Berryman, and the Making of a Postmodern Aesthetic.* Charlottesville: University of Virginia Press, 1999.

The Ball Poem

What is the boy now, who has lost his ball,
What, what is he to do? I saw it go
Merrily bouncing, down the street, and then
Merrily over—there it is in the water!
No use to say 'O there are other balls':
An ultimate shaking grief fixes the boy
As he stands rigid, trembling, staring down
All his young days into the harbour where
His ball went. I would not intrude on him,
A dime, another ball, is worthless. Now
He senses first responsibility
In a world of possessions. People will take balls,
Balls will be lost always, little boy,
And no one buys a ball back. Money is external.
He is learning, well behind his desperate eyes,

The epistemology[1] of loss, how to stand up
Knowing what every man must one day know
And most know many days, how to stand up
And gradually light returns to the street,
A whistle blows, the ball is out of sight,
Soon part of me will explore the deep and dark
Floor of the harbour . . . I am everywhere,
I suffer and move, my mind and my heart move
With all that move me, under the water
Or whistling, I am not a little boy.

1942

Dream Song 1

Huffy Henry hid   the day,
unappeasable Henry sulked.
I see his point,—a trying to put things over.
It was the thought that they thought
they could *do* it made Henry wicked & away.
But he should have come out and talked.

All the world like a woolen lover
once did seem on Henry's side.
Then came a departure.
Thereafter nothing fell out as it might or ought.
I don't see how Henry, pried
open for all the world to see, survived.

What he has now to say is a long
wonder the world can bear & be.
Once in a sycamore I was glad
all at the top, and I sang.
Hard on the land wears the strong sea
and empty grows every bed.

1964

This poem and the nine that follow it are from *The Dream Songs*, often thought
to be Berryman's masterpiece. Henry—the leading character (who is also called

---

1. The study, in philosophy, of the nature, origins, and validity of human knowledge.

"Mr. Bones" by a perhaps imagined companion)—may be a version of Berryman himself.

Thomas Travisano warns against assuming too close a relationship between the poet and the character: "If one looks further at the issue of 'self-disclosure' or 'self-revelation' it becomes obvious that Berryman's *Dream Songs* 'confess' only to incidental and symptomatic experiences of suffering and humiliation. A core of crucial psychic material is quite deliberately withheld. Berryman's relationship with his father, who took his own life when Berryman was a boy of eleven, is merely hinted at in a few Songs. Or was his father murdered, and if so, was he murdered by the poet's mother? . . . Articulated under the weight of these fearful uncertainties, Berryman's *Dream Songs* are more remarkable for their elisions, emotional blockage, and ambiguity of reference than for specific disclosures. . . . Thus, the most compelling emotional issues of the *Dream Songs* are never *confessed* but exist only as subtext. The poem is much more effectively read for the ways it explores and represents the disturbing, symptomatic consequences of suppressed rage and repressed emotion. It is a dramatization of the desperate search for vital yet unreachable knowledge and a seemingly unattainable solace and maturity, not a catalog of factual disclosures revealing the author's shameful secrets."

Dream Song 4

Filling her compact & delicious body
with chicken páprika, she glanced at me
twice.
Fainting with interest, I hungered back
and only the fact of her husband & four other people
kept me from springing on her

or falling at her little feet and crying
'You are the hottest one for years of night
Henry's dazed eyes
have enjoyed, Brilliance.' I advanced upon
(despairing) my spumoni.—Sir Bones: is stuffed,
de world, wif feeding girls.

—Black hair, complexion Latin, jewelled eyes
downcast . . . The slob beside her   feasts . . . What wonders is
she sitting on, over there?
The restaurant buzzes. She might as well be on Mars.

Where did it all go wrong? There ought to be a law against Henry.
—Mr. Bones: there is.

1964

Dream Song 13

God bless Henry. He lived like a rat,
with a thatch of hair on his head
in the beginning.
Henry was not a coward. Much.
He never deserted anything; instead
he stuck, when things like pity were thinning.

So may be Henry was a human being.
Let's investigate that.
. . . We did; okay.
He is a human American man.
That's true. My lass is braking.
My brass is aching. Come & diminish me, & map my way.

God's Henry's enemy. We're in business . . . Why,
what business must be clear.
A cornering.
I couldn't feel more like it.—Mr. Bones,
as I look on the saffron sky,
you strikes me as ornery.

1964

Dream Song 26

The glories of the world struck me, made me aria, once.
—What happen then, Mr Bones?
if be you cares to say.
—Henry. Henry became interested in women's bodies,
his loins were & were the   scene of stupendous achievement.
Stupor. Knees, dear. Pray.

All the knobs & softnesses of, my God,
the ducking & trouble it swarm on Henry,
at one time.

—What happen   then, Mr Bones?
  you seems excited-like.
—Fell Henry back into   the original crime: art, rime

besides a sense of others, my God, my God,
and a jealousy for the honour (alive) of his country,
what can get more odd?
and discontent with the thriving gangs & pride.
—What happen then, Mr Bones?
—I had a most marvellous   piece of luck. I died.

1964

Dream Song 29

There sat down, once, a thing on Henry's heart
só heavy, if he had a hundred years
& more, & weeping, sleepless, in all them time
Henry could not make good.
Starts again always in Henry's ears
the little cough somewhere, an odour, a chime.

And there is another thing he has in mind
like a grave Sienese face[1] a thousand years
would fail to blur the still profiled reproach of. Ghastly,
with open eyes, he attends, blind.
All the bells say: too late. This is not for tears;
thinking.

But never did Henry, as he thought he did,
end anyone and hacks her body up
and hide the pieces, where they may be found.
He knows: he went over everyone, & nobody's missing.
Often he reckons, in the dawn, them up.
Nobody is ever missing.

1964

1. Alluding to the somber portraits of the Madonna painted in the Italian city of Siena by early Renaissance masters such as Duccio (ca. 1255–ca. 1319).

Dream Song 76

Henry's Confession

Nothin very bad happen to me lately.
How you explain that?—I explain that, Mr Bones,
terms o' your bafflin odd sobriety.
Sober as man can get, no girls, no telephones,
what could happen bad to Mr Bones?
—*If* life is a handkerchief sandwich,

in a modesty of death I join my father[1]
who dared so long agone leave me.
A bullet on a concrete stoop
close by a smothering southern sea
spreadeagled on an island, by my knee.
—You is from hunger, Mr Bones,

I offers you this handkerchief, now set
your left foot by my right foot,
shoulder to shoulder, all that jazz,
arm in arm, by the beautiful sea,
hum a little, Mr Bones.
—I saw nobody coming, so I went instead.

1964

Dream Song 77

Seedy Henry rose up shy in de world
& shaved & swung his barbells, duded Henry up
and p.a.'d[1] poor thousands of persons on topics of grand
moment to Henry, ah to those less & none.
Wif a book of his in either hand
he is stript down to move on.

—Come away, Mr. Bones.

        *   *   *

1. Berryman's own father, John Smith, died of a gunshot wound in 1926 on his porch in Sarasota, Florida.

1. Spoken to via a public address system.

—Henry is tired of the winter,
& haircuts, & a squeamish comfy   ruin-prone proud national
    mind,   & Spring (in the city so called).
Henry likes Fall.
Hé would be prepared to líve in a world of Fáll
for ever, impenitent Henry.
But the snows and summers grieve & dream;

thése fierce & airy occupations, and love,
raved away so many of Henry's years
it is a wonder that, with in each hand
one of his own mad books and all,
ancient fires for eyes, his head full
& his heart full, he's making ready to move on.

1964

Dream Song 90: Op. posth. no. 13

In the night-reaches dreamed he of better graces,
of liberations, and beloved faces,
such as now ere dawn he sings.
It would not be easy, accustomed to these things,
to give up the old world, but he could try;
let it all rest, have a good cry.

Let Randall[1] rest, whom your self-torturing
cannot restore one instant's good to, rest:
he's left us now.
The panic died and in the panic's dying
so did my old friend. I am headed west
also, also, somehow.

In the chambers of the end we'll meet again
I will say Randall, he'll say Pussycat[2]
and all will be as before
whenas we sought, among the beloved faces,
eminence and were dissatisfied with that
and needed more.

1969

1. Berryman's friend, the poet Randall Jarrell,   2. A nickname for Henry in *The Dream Songs*.
was struck by a car and killed in 1965.

Dream Song 101

A shallow lake, with many waterbirds,
especially egrets: I was showing Mother around,
An extraordinary vivid dream
of Betty & Douglass, and Don—his mother's estate
was on the grounds of a lunatic asylum.
He showed me around.

A policeman trundled a siren up the walk.
It was 6:05 P.M., Don was late home.
I askt if he ever saw
the inmates—'No, they never leave their cells.'
Betty was downstairs, Don called down 'A drink'
while showering.

I can't go into the meaning of the dream
except to say a sense of total Loss
afflicted me thereof:
an absolute disappearance of continuity & love
and children away at school, the weight of the cross,
and everything is what it seems.

                                          1969

Dream Song 385

My daughter's heavier. Light leaves are flying.
Everywhere in enormous numbers turkeys will be dying[1]
and other birds, all their wings.
They never greatly flew. Did they wish to?
I should know. Off away somewhere once I knew
such things.

Or good Ralph Hodgson back then did, or does.
The man is dead[2] whom Eliot praised. My praise
follows and flows too late.

1. This final poem in *The Dream Songs* sequence is set on or just before Thanksgiving Day.
2. An English poet of minor reputation, Hodgson died at the age of ninety-one on November 3, 1962. See Part IV of T. S. Eliot's "Five Finger Exercises," "Lines to Ralph Hodgson Esqre.," which begins, "How delightful to meet Mr. Hodgson! / (Everyone wants to know *him*)—."

Fall is grievy, brisk. Tears behind the eyes
almost fall. Fall comes to us as a prize
to rouse us toward our fate.

My house is made of wood and it's made well,
unlike us. My house is older than Henry;
that's fairly old.
If there were a middle   ground between things and the soul
or if the sky resembled more the sea,
I wouldn't have to scold

my heavy daughter.

1969

JULIA DE BURGOS
1914–1953

ARGUABLY PUERTO RICO'S GREATEST poet, Julia Constanza de Burgos García is enjoying a renaissance of interest in her lyrical poetry, her politics of social change, and her feminism. One major cultural indicator of her rise to the top of contemporary American poetry is her selection for a stamp issued in her honor by the U.S. Postal Service in 2010. In addition, many schools and parks have been named for her, in both Puerto Rico and the mainland United States. She is also one of the few poets to have a cultural center established in her name—the Julia de Burgos Latino Cultural Center in Harlem. Not surprisingly, such hemispheric Nobel poets as Pablo Neruda and such leading Puerto Rican modernists as Luis Llorens Torres praised and supported de Burgos as she moved through her career. Her lyrical talents have brought many musicians to her poetry, including Leonard Bernstein. Today she is considered a peer of Gabriela Mistral, Edna St. Vincent Millay, Sylvia Plath, Adrienne Rich, Audre Lorde, Joy Harjo, Marlene Nourbese Philip, and other leading women poets of the Americas.

Gifted with the ability to combine both social conscience and personal introspection with the formal subtleties of traditional lyricism, de Burgos wrote against patriarchal marriage, female subjugation, social conformity, and machismo as well as colonialism and dictatorship. Among her pioneering contributions was her absorption of African influences in her poetry and her insertion of an African dimension (or *Négritude*) into Latin American modernism (or *modernismo*). An equally important contribution was her early feminist awareness of the position of women in a society dominated by men. Also a journalist, de Burgos pursued an internationalist framework in her politics and opposed such dictators as Franco in Spain, Somoza in Nicaragua, and Trujillo in the Dominican Republic as well as U.S. and European colonialism.

Born into agrarian poverty in 1914, sixteen years after the United States had assumed control of Puerto Rico from Spain, de Burgos was the eldest of thirteen children. Six of her siblings died of malnutrition. She eventually learned that she was of African heritage, a direct descendant of slaves. After graduating from the University of Puerto Rico with a degree in teaching, she taught for several years. In 1934, she married (the marriage ended in 1937) and began working at a publicly run day care center in order to deepen her social awareness. She also began publishing articles in newspapers, and she wrote poetry, plays, and songs for radio. In 1936 she joined the Daughters of Freedom, the women's branch of the Puerto Rican Nationalist Party. Toward the end of the 1930s, she published two books of poetry, one of which included "To Julia de Burgos."

After becoming romantically involved with Dr. Juan Isidro Jiménez Grullón, a physician and public figure in the Dominican Republic, she lived in Havana, Cuba, Washington, D.C., and New York City. During World War II, she married a Puerto Rican musician named Armando Marín and worked in the Office of the Coordinator of Inter-American Affairs in Washington. After the war, she moved permanently to New York City. Divorced for a second time in 1947, she became active in New York literary circles and leftist political causes. But she gradually fell into deepening depression and alcoholism. She collapsed on a street in Spanish Harlem and died of pneumonia in a hospital at the age of thirty-nine.

FURTHER READING

Julia de Burgos. *Song of the Simple Truth: Obra Completa Poética / The Complete Poems.* Comp. and trans. Jack Agueros. Willamantic, Conn.: Curbstone Press, 1997.

Melissa Hussain. "'La masa explotada despierta': Recovering Julia de Burgos's Poetics, Politics, and Praxis." *Panini: NSU Studies in Language and Literature* 4 (2006–7): 56–106.

Vanessa Pérez Rosario, ed. *Hispanic Caribbean Literature of Migration: Narratives of Displacement.* New York: Palgrave Macmillan, 2010.

A Julia de Burgos

Ya las gentes murmuran que yo soy tu enemiga
porque dicen que en verso doy al mundo tu yo.

Mienten, Julia de Burgos. Mienten, Julia de Burgos.
La que se alza en mis versos no es tu voz: es mi voz,

porque tú eres ropaje y la esencia soy yo;
y el más profundo abismo se tiende entre las dos.

Tú eres fría muñeca de mentira social,
y yo, viril destello de la humana verdad.

Tú, miel de cortesanas hipocresías; yo no;
que en todos mis poemas desnudo el corazón.

Tú eres como tu mundo, egoísta; yo no;
que todo me lo juego a ser lo que soy yo.

Tú eres solo la grave señora señorona;
yo no; yo soy la vida, la fuerza, la mujer.

Tú eres de tu marido, de tu amo; yo no;
yo de nadie, o de todos, porque a todos, a todos,
en mi limpio sentir y en mi pensar me doy.

Tú te rizas el pelo y te pintas; yo no;
a mí me riza el viento; a mí me pinta el sol.

Tú eres dama casera, resignada, sumisa,
atada a los prejuicios de los hombres; yo no;
que yo soy Rocinante corriendo desbocado
olfateando horizontes de justicia de Dios.

Tú en ti misma no mandas; a ti todos te mandan;
en ti mandan tu esposo, tus padres, tus parientes,
el cura, la modista, el teatro, el casino,
el auto, las alhajas, el banquete, el champán,
el cielo y el infierno, y el qué dirán social.

En mí no, que en mí manda mi solo corazón,
mi solo pensamiento; quien manda en mí soy yo.

Tú, flor de aristocracia; y yo, la flor del pueblo.
Tú en ti lo tienes todo y a todos se lo debes,
mientras que yo, mi nada a nadie se la debo.

Tú, clavada al estático dividendo ancestral,
y yo, un uno en la cifra del divisor social,
somos el duelo a muerte que se acerca fatal.

*   *   *

Cuando las multitudes corran alborotadas
dejando atrás cenizas de injusticias quemadas,
y cuando con la tea de las siete virtudes,
tras los siete pecados, corran las multitudes,
contra ti, y contra todo lo injusto y lo inhumano,
yo iré en medio de ellas con la tea en la mano.

1938

[TRANS.] To Julia de Burgos

Already the people murmur that I am your enemy
because they say that in verse I give the world your "me."

They lie, Julia de Burgos. They lie, Julia de Burgos.
She who rises in my verses is not your voice: it is my voice,
because you are the clothing, and I am the essence;
and the deepest abyss spreads between the two.

You are a cold doll of social deceit,
and I, the virile spark of human truth.

You, the honey of courtesan hypocrisies; not I;
in all my poems I undress the heart.

You are like your world, selfish; not I;
I risk everything to be what I am.

You are only the ponderous lady of ladies;
not I; I am life, strength, woman.

You belong to your husband, your master; not I;
I belong to nobody, or to all, because to all, to all,
in my clear feeling and in my thought I give myself.

You curl your hair and paint yourself; not I;
the wind curls me; the sun paints me.

You are a housewife, resigned, submissive,
tied to the whims of men; not I;
I am Rocinante[1] running wildly,
sniffing out the horizons of God's justice.

✳   ✳   ✳

1. Rocinante was the name of Don Quixote's horse in Miguel de Cervantes's *Don Quixote* (1605–1615) as well as the name of the horse that belonged to Julia de Burgos's father, Francisco Burgos Hans, when she was growing up.

You do not rule yourself; everyone rules you;
your husband, your parents, your family,
the priest, the dressmaker, the theater, the dance hall,
the car, the jewels, the banquet, champagne,
heaven and hell, and the social, "What will they say?"

Not in me, I am ruled only by my heart,
my thought; I am the one who rules myself.

You, flower of aristocracy; and I, the flower of the people.
You have everything in yourself, and you owe it to everyone,
while I, my nothing is owed to no one.

You, nailed to the static ancestral dividend;
and I, a figure "one" in the social denominator,
we are the duel to death that fatally approaches.

When the multitudes run riotous
leaving ashes of burnt injustices behind,
and when with the torch of the seven virtues
the multitudes run after the seven sins,
against you, and against everything unjust and inhuman,
I will go in their midst with the torch in hand.

1938; translated 2010 by Alicia
Contreras, Lisette Ordorica Lasater,
and Steven Gould Axelrod

"To Julia de Burgos" offers a formal lyric that intertwines the anguish of the housewife, the fortitude of the rebellious poet, and, as Vanessa Pérez Rosario points out, the collective distress of Puerto Rico as a colony first of Spain and then of the United States. Images of instability, disruption, and fragmentation encourage one to consider de Burgos's own contradictory experiences as a woman, a child of poverty and racism, a fighter for social justice, a member of bourgeois society, and an artist.

RANDALL JARRELL
1914–1965

THE POEMS OF RANDALL JARRELL explore the lives of the comparatively power-less—children, holocaust victims, young soldiers whose lives are held as pawns of larger forces, or women struggling to claim a sense of identity in a man's world. Their lines combine a sharp awareness of contemporary history, and an almost encyclopedic knowledge of Western literature and thought, with a child-like wonder at the world's ambiguity and sorrow. Jarrell was a brilliant critic of the work of living poets, and as a reviewer he was widely feared for his witty and slashing style when he encountered poetry that in his judgment fell beneath the highest standards, but he also wrote with generous praise and prophetic insight about the work of such contemporaries and friends as Robert Lowell, Eliza-beth Bishop, Theodore Roethke, and John Berryman (all in this anthology), as well as such elders and mentors as Robert Frost, Marianne Moore, John Crowe Ransom, Allen Tate, and William Carlos Williams, and the British poet W. H. Auden.

Born in Nashville, Tennessee, Jarrell spent important childhood years in Hollywood, California, where he observed the dawning of America's cinematic culture, an experience that left a deep imprint on his imagination. Following his parents' divorce, Jarrell returned to Nashville and attended Vanderbilt Uni-versity, earning bachelor's and master's degrees in English while studying under poets Ransom and Tate. In 1937, Jarrell followed Ransom to Kenyon College, where he met and formed a lifelong bond with Robert Lowell. Jarrell was a gifted teacher and, following a stint at the University of Texas, served for many years on the faculty of the Women's College of North Carolina (now the Univer-sity of North Carolina–Greensboro).

Jarrell served in the Army Air Force in World War II as a celestial navigation instructor. Many of his poems of World War II, such as "Losses" and "The Death of the Ball Turret Gunner," explore the painful situations faced by young airmen trained in modern combat and sent to war before they are old enough to fully comprehend the consequences of their dedication to "the State." Others, such as "Protocols," look sharply at genocide, and at the poignant suffering and con-fusion faced by children engulfed in worldwide conflict. Jarrell's characteristic form was the dramatic monologue, and all of the poems so far named are voiced by fallen victims of World War II. In "Eighth Air Force," the poet ponders the ambiguous moral universe inhabited by young airmen who—hoping to survive a war not of their own making—must pilot their lethal war machines and in the process cause the deaths of many people they have never known.

In the 1950s Jarrell emerged as a noted author of books for children, and his postwar poetry often draws upon the dreamlike atmosphere of the fairy tales of the Brothers Grimm (some of which Jarrell translated) to plumb the curious psychological depths of the parent-child relationship, and of the child's half-bewildered confrontation with the mysteries of life, love, and death. Other poems, such as the dramatic monologues "The Woman at the Washington Zoo" and "Next Day," explore, through women's voices, the search of lonely individuals for identity as they articulate their longing for—and also their fear of—meaningful personal change.

In 1964, Jarrell experienced a deep depression, and in 1965 he was struck by a car and killed in Chapel Hill, North Carolina, while walking alongside a roadway at night. Although the coroner ruled the death accidental, many of his close friends, including Lowell and Berryman, considered it a suicide, or perhaps it was, as Bishop phrased it, "an accident of an unconscious-suicide kind . . .—because surely it was most unlike him to make some innocent motorist responsible for his death."

Jarrell left behind him a body of poetry and of criticism marked by sharp intelligence and by a willingness to take emotional risks and to explore political, moral, and psychological depths.

FURTHER READING

Stephen Burt. *Randall Jarrell and His Age*. New York: Columbia University Press, 2002.

Suzanne Ferguson, ed. *Jarrell, Bishop, Lowell, and Co.: Middle Generation Poets in Context*. Knoxville: University of Tennessee Press, 2003.

Richard Flynn. *Randall Jarrell and the Lost World of Childhood*. Athens: University of Georgia Press, 1990.

Jerome Griswold. *The Children's Books of Randall Jarrell*. Athens: University of Georgia Press, 1988.

Mary Jarrell. *Remembering Randall: A Memoir of Poet, Critic, and Teacher*. New York: Harper-Collins, 1999.

Randall Jarrell. *Complete Poems*. New York: Farrar, Straus & Giroux, 1976.

Thomas Travisano. *Midcentury Quartet: Bishop, Lowell, Jarrell, Berryman, and the Making of a Postmodern Aesthetic*. Charlottesville: University of Virginia Press, 1999.

Losses

It was not dying: everybody died.
It was not dying: we had died before
In the routine crashes—and our fields
Called up the papers, wrote home to our folks,

And the rates rose[1], all because of us.
We died on the wrong page of the almanac,[2]
Scattered on mountains fifty miles away;
Diving on haystacks, fighting with a friend,
We blazed up on the lines[3] we never saw.
We died like aunts or pets or foreigners.
(When we left high school nothing else had died
For us to figure we had died like.)

In our new planes, with our new crews, we bombed
The ranges by the desert or the shore,
Fired at towed targets, waited for our scores—
And turned into replacements and woke up
One morning, over England, operational.[4]
It wasn't different: but if we died
It was not an accident but a mistake
(But an easy one for anyone to make).
We read our mail and counted up our missions[5]—
In bombers named for girls, we burned
The cities we had learned about in school—
Till our lives wore out; our bodies lay among
The people we had killed and never seen.[6]
When we lasted long enough they gave us medals;
When we died they said, "Our casualties were low."

They said, "Here are the maps"; we burned the cities.

It was not dying—no, not ever dying;
But the night I died I dreamed that I was dead,
And the cities said to me: "Why are you dying?
We are satisfied, if you are; but why did I die?"

1944

---

1. Insurance rates.
2. Because they died earlier than peacetime sta-
tistical probability would have anticipated.
3. Both power lines and, perhaps, the headlines
of local newspapers, where their deaths were
noted.
4. On active combat duty.
5. American bomber crews in the European
Theater of Operations were required to fly a
specified number of combat missions before
rotating home.
6. Bombing missions over Europe, commonly
flown at altitudes of 25,000 feet or more, resulted
in casualties in the hundreds of thousands for
both civilian populations and bomber crews.

"Losses" is spoken in the collective voice of the young American bomber crewmen in World War II who were killed in the war, at first in training accidents at home and then on bombing raids over European cities.

The Death of the Ball Turret Gunner

From my mother's sleep I fell into the State,
And I hunched in its belly till my wet fur froze.
Six miles from earth, loosed from its dream of life,
I woke to black flak and the nightmare fighters.
When I died they washed me out of the turret with a hose.

1945

JARRELL'S NOTE: "A ball turret was a plexiglass sphere set into the belly of a B-17 or B-24 [heavy bomber], and inhabited by two .50 caliber machine-guns and one man, a short small man. When this gunner tracked with his machine-guns a fighter attacking his bomber from below, he revolved with the turret; hunched upside-down in his little sphere, he looked like the foetus in the womb. The fighters which attacked him were armed with cannon firing explosive shells. The hose was a steam hose."

Protocols

(Birkenau, Odessa; the children speak alternately.)

We went there on the train. *They had big barges that they towed,*
We stood up, there were so many I was squashed.
There was a smoke-stack, then they made me wash.
It was a factory, I think. *My mother held me up*
And I could see the ship that made the smoke.

When I was tired my mother carried me.
She said, "Don't be afraid." But I was only tired.
Where we went there is no more Odessa.
They had water in a pipe—like rain, but hot;[1]
The water there is deeper than the world

And I was tired and fell in in my sleep
And the water drank me. That is what I think.

1. Victims at Birkenau were told they were entering a shower facility rather than a lethal gas chamber, and false showerheads were affixed to the ceiling.

And I said to my mother, "Now I'm washed and dried,"
My mother hugged me, and it smelled like hay[2]
And that is how you die. And that is how you die.

1945

The title "Protocols" refers both to standard procedures used in Nazi genocide against Jews, and—with pointed irony—to *The Protocols of the Elders of Zion*, a late-nineteenth-century forged document used to justify anti-Semitism. Birkenau, a Nazi extermination camp in World War II, was part of the infamous Auschwitz complex. Jews (and others) were delivered to the Birkenau gas chambers by transport trains, and more than a million people died there, including thousands of children. The Birkenau child's speech is set in roman type. Odessa is a Russian port on the Black Sea. The poem's Odessa child speaks in *italic* type and gives voice to contemporary reports of mass drownings as the primary vehicle there of the Nazi genocide of the Jews.

Eighth Air Force

If, in an odd angle of the hutment,[1]
A puppy laps the water from a can
Of flowers, and the drunk sergeant shaving
Whistles O *Paradiso!*[2]—shall I say that man
Is not as men have said: a wolf to man?[3]

The other murderers troop in yawning;
Three of them play Pitch,[4] one sleeps, and one
Lies counting missions, lies there sweating
Till even his heart beats: One; One; One.
O *murderers!* . . . Still, this is how it's done:

This is a war . . . But since these play, before they die,
Like puppies with their puppy; since, a man,
I did as these have done, but did not die—
I will content the people as I can[5]
And give up these to them: Behold the man![6]

2. Poison gas used in the exterminations was said to "smell like hay."
1. A hut or group of huts in a military camp.
2. A tenor aria from Giacomo Meyerbeer's opera *L'Africana* (1865).
3. Roman comic playwright Plautus (ca. 254–184 B.C.E.) wrote in *Asinaria* that "man is a wolf to man."

4. A card game.
5. In the New Testament, "[Pontius] Pilate, willing to content the people, released Barabbas unto them, and delivered Jesus, when he had scourged him, to be crucified" (Mark 15:15).
6. The words of Pilate as he showed Jesus, crowned with thorns, to the Jewish people before his crucifixion (John 19:5).

* * *

I have suffered, in a dream, because of him,
Many things;[7] for this last saviour, man,
I have lied as I lie now. But what is lying?
Men wash their hands, in blood,[8] as best they can:
I find no fault in this just man.[9]

1947

JARRELL'S NOTE: "'Eighth Air Force' is a poem about the air force which bombed the
Continent from England. The man who lies counting missions has one to go before
being sent home. The phrases from the Gospels compare such criminals and scapegoats
as these with that earlier criminal and scapegoat about whom the Gospels were written."

Jarrell draws upon the King James version of the Gospels of Matthew, Mark, and John
to explore parallels between the complex patterns of innocence or guilt arising from the
Roman governor Pilate's reluctant complicity in the crucifixion of Jesus and the intricate
web of innocence or guilt involving the young soldiers who bombed German cities in
World War II.

A Quilt-Pattern

The blocked-out Tree
Of the boy's Life is gray
On the tangled quilt: the long day
Dies at last, after many tales.
Good me, bad me, the Other
Black out, and the humming stare
Of the woman—the good mother—
Drifts away; the boy falls
Through darkness, the leagues of space
Into the oldest tale of all.

All the graves of the forest
Are opened, the scaling face
Of a woman—the dead mother—

7. Pilate's wife warned her husband against crucifying Jesus: "Have thou nothing to do with that just man: for I have suffered many things this day in a dream because of him" (Matthew 27:19).
8. Pilate, reluctantly consenting that Jesus should be crucified, "washed his hands before the multitude, saying, I am innocent of the blood of this just person" (Matthew 27:24).
9. Pilate had said of Jesus to the Jewish people, "I find no fault in him" (John 19:4).

Is square in the steam of a yard
Where the cages are warmed all night for the rabbits,
All small furry things
That are hurt, but that never cry at all—
That are skinned, but that never die at all.
Good me, bad me
Dry their tears, and gather patiently
Through the loops of the chicken-wire of the cages
Blackberries, the small hairy things
They live on, here in the wood of the dream.

Here a thousand stones
Of the trail home shine from their strings
Like just-brushed, just-lost teeth.
All the birds of the forest
Sit brooding, stuffed with crumbs.
But at home, far, far away
The white moon shines from the stones of the chimney,
His white cat eats up his white pigeon.

But the house hums, "We are home." Good me, bad me
Sits wrapped in his coat of rabbit-skin
And looks for some little living thing
To be kind to, for then it will help him—
There is nothing to help; good me
Sits twitching the rabbit's-fur of his ears
And says to himself, "My mother is basting
Bad me in the bath-tub—"
                               the steam rises,
A washcloth is turned like a mop in his mouth.
He stares into the mouth
Of the whole house: there in it is waiting—
No, there is nothing.

He breaks a finger
From the wind and lifts it to his—
"Who is nibbling at me?" says the house.
The dram says, "The wind,
The heaven-born wind";
The boy says, "It is a mouse."
He sucks at the finger; and the house of bread
Calls to him in its slow singing voice:

"Feed, feed! Are you fat now?
Hold out your finger."
The boy holds out the bone of the finger.
It moves, but the house says, "No, you don't know.
Eat a littler longer."
The taste of the house
Is the taste of his—
                              "I don't know,"
Thinks the boy. "No, I don't *know*!"
His whole dream swells with the stream of the oven
Till it whispers, "You are full now, mouse—
Look, I have warmed the oven, kneaded the dough:
Creep in—ah, ah, it is warm!—
Quick, we can slip the bread in now," says the house.
He whispers, "I do not know
How I am to do it."
                              "Goose, goose," cries the house,
"It is big enough—just look!
See, if I bend a little, so—"

He has moved . . . He is still now, and holds his breath.
If something is screaming itself to death
There in the oven, it is not the mouse
Nor anything of the mouse's. Bad me, good me
Stare into each other's eyes, and timidly
Smile at each other: it was the Other.

But they are waking, waking; the last stair creaks—
Out there on the other side of the door
The house creaks, "How is my little mouse? Awake?"
It is she.
He says to himself, "I will never wake."
He says to himself, not breathing:
"Go away. Go away. Go away."

And the footsteps go away.

1950

JARRELL'S NOTE: "There is a quilt-pattern called The Tree of Life. The little boy, sick in bed, has a dream in which good me and bad me (along with the uncontrollable, unexplainable *the Other*) take the place of Hänsel and Gretel."

The poem draws pervasively for its imagery and situations on this well-known Grimm's fairy tale.

The Black Swan

When the swans turned my sister into a swan
  I would go to the lake, at night, from milking:
The sun would look out through the reeds like a swan,
  A swan's red beak; and the beak would open
And inside there was darkness, the stars and the moon.

Out on the lake a girl would laugh.
  "Sister, here is your porridge, sister,"
I would call; and the reeds would whisper,
  "Go to sleep, go to sleep, little swan."
My legs were all hard and webbed, and the silky

Hairs of my wings sank away like stars
  In the ripples that ran in and out of the reeds:
I heard through the lap and hiss of water
  Someone's "Sister . . . sister," far away on the shore,
And then as I opened my beak to answer

I heard my harsh laugh go out to the shore
  And saw—saw at last, swimming up from the green
Low mounds of the lake, the white stone swans:
  The white, named swans . . . "It is all a dream,"
I whispered, and reached from the down of the pallet

To the lap and hiss of the floor.
  And "Sleep, little sister," the swans all sang
From the moon and stars and frogs of the floor.
  But the swan my sister called, "Sleep at last, little sister,"
And stroked all night, with a black wing, my wings.

1951

JARRELL'S NOTE: "'The Black Swan' is said, long ago, by a girl whose sister is buried under the white stones of the green churchyard."

The Woman at the Washington Zoo

The saris[1] go by me from the embassies.

Cloth from the moon. Cloth from another planet.
They look back at the leopard like the leopard.[2]

And I. . . .
                        this print of mine, that has kept its color
Alive through so many cleanings; this dull null
Navy I wear to work, and wear from work, and so
To my bed, so to my grave, with no
Complaints, no comment: neither from my chief,
The Deputy Chief Assistant, nor his chief—
Only I complain. . . . this serviceable
Body that no sunlight dyes, no hand suffuses
But, dome-shadowed, withering among columns,
Wavy beneath fountains—small, far-off, shining
In the eyes of animals, these beings trapped
As I am trapped but not, themselves, the trap,
Aging, but without knowledge of their age,
Kept safe here, knowing not of death, for death—
Oh, bars of my own body, open, open!

The world goes by my cage and never sees me.
And there come not to me, as come to these,
The wild beasts, sparrows pecking the llamas' grain,
Pigeons settling on the bears' bread, buzzards
Tearing the meat the flies have clouded. . . .
                                            Vulture,
When you come for the white rat that the foxes left,
Take off the red helmet of your head, the black
Wings that have shadowed me, and step to me as man:
The wild brother at whose feet the white wolves fawn,
To whose hand of power the great lioness
Stalks, purring. . . .
                        You know what I was,
You see what I am: change me, change me!

                                            1960

---

1. Colorful cloth garments worn by women from
India and many neighboring countries.

2. One of the caged animals at the zoo in Washington, D.C.

"The Woman at the Washington Zoo" is a monologue spoken by a woman. Jarrell was a frequent visitor to the Washington, D.C., zoo when he served as Poetry Consultant to the Library of Congress (now called Poet Laureate) in 1956–58.

Next Day

Moving from Cheer to Joy, from Joy to All,[1]
I take a box
And add it to my wild rice, my Cornish game hens.
The slacked or shorted, basketed, identical
Food-gathering flocks
Are selves I overlook. Wisdom, said William James,[2]

Is learning what to overlook. And I am wise
If that is wisdom.
Yet somehow, as I buy All from these shelves
And the boy takes it to my station wagon,
What I've become
Troubles me even if I shut my eyes.

When I was young and miserable and pretty
And poor, I'd wish
What all girls wish: to have a husband,
A house and children. Now that I'm old, my wish
Is womanish:
That the boy putting groceries in my car

See me. It bewilders me he doesn't see me.
For so many years
I was good enough to eat: the world looked at me
And its mouth watered. How often they have undressed me,
The eyes of strangers!
And, holding their flesh within my flesh, their vile

Imaginings within my imagining,
I too have taken
The chance of life. Now the boy pats my dog
And we start home. Now I am good.

1. Respectively, a laundry detergent, a dish-washing liquid, and another laundry detergent heavily promoted in the 1960s.

2. American philosopher and psychologist (1842–1910).

The last mistaken,
Ecstatic, accidental bliss, the blind

Happiness that, bursting, leaves upon the palm
Some soap and water—
It was so long ago, back in some Gay
Twenties, Nineties, I don't know . . . Today I miss
My lovely daughter
Away at school, my sons away at school,

My husband away at work—I wish for them.
The dog, the maid,
And I go through the sure unvarying days
At home in them. As I look at my life,
I am afraid
Only that it will change, as I am changing:

I am afraid, this morning, of my face.
It looks at me
From the rear-view mirror, with the eyes I hate,
The smile I hate. Its plain, lined look
Of gray discovery
Repeats to me: "You're old." That's all, I'm old.

And yet I'm afraid, as I was at the funeral
I went to yesterday.
My friend's cold made-up face, granite among its flowers,
Her undressed, operated-on, dressed body
Were my face and body.
As I think of her and I hear her telling me

How young I seem; I *am* exceptional;
I think of all I have.
But really no one is exceptional,
No one has anything, I'm anybody,
I stand beside my grave
Confused with my life, that is commonplace and solitary.

                                                          1963

The House in the Woods

At the back of the houses there is the wood.
While there is a leaf of summer left, the wood

Makes sounds I can put somewhere in my song,
Has paths I can walk, when I wake, to good

Or evil: to the cage, to the oven, to the House
In the Wood. It is a part of life, or of the story

We make of life. But after the last leaf,
The last light—for each year is leafless,

Each day lightless, at the last—the wood begins
Its serious existence: it has no path,

No house, no story; it resists comparison . . .
One clear, repeated, lapping gurgle, like a spoon

Or a glass breathing, is the brook,
The wood's fouled midnight water. If I walk into the wood

As far as I can walk, I come to my own door,
The door of the House in the Wood. It opens silently:

On the bed is something covered, something humped
Asleep there, awake there—but what? I do not know.

I look, I lie there, and yet I do not know.
How far out my great echoing clumsy limbs

Stretch, surrounded only by space! For time has struck,
All the clocks are stuck now, for how many lives,

On the same second. Numbed, wooden, motionless,
We are far under the surface of the night.

Nothing comes down so deep but sound: a car, freight cars,
A high soft droning, drawn out like a wire

Forever and ever—is this the sound that Bunyan heard
So that he thought his bowels would burst within him?[1]—

1. John Bunyan (1628–1688), author of *Pilgrim's Progress,* describing the experience of religious conversion.

＊　＊　＊

Drift on, on, into nothing. Then someone screams
A scream like an old knife sharpened into nothing.

It is only a nightmare. No one wakes up, nothing happens,
Except there is gooseflesh over my whole body—

And that too, after a little while, is gone.
I lie here like a cut-off limb, the stump the limb has left . . .

Here at the bottom of the world, what was before the world
And will be after, holds me to its black

Breasts and rocks me: the oven is cold, the cage is empty,
In the House in the Wood, the witch and her child sleep.

                                              1964

GWENDOLYN BROOKS
1917–2000

GWENDOLYN BROOKS created a remarkable verbal world and social vision. Her work is a landmark of twentieth-century American poetry. She brought the urban life of working-class African Americans vividly into poetic history. Exploring her characters' particularities and circumstances with a keen eye and ready sympathy, she created a human world on the page, producing some of American poetry's most moving portraits of human beings in relation to one another. Brooks had a delight in, and reverence for, the ordinary life of city dwellers. Her poetry includes her characters' speech, and it respects their dignity, despite whatever hard times have befallen them.

Brooks provides a resonant social world through an art of implication. Her language is often spare and simple, but it is always ready to throw you for a spin. In "Boy Breaking Glass," for example, the title character "is raw: is sonic: is old-eyed première." Each of those modifiers is surprising. Each pushes the reader into thought. The modifiers tell us that this young man is different from—and more than—what we might have thought, and that the speaker's perspective on him is different, too. The poem is candid about the title character, yet it moves us to identify with him. The language depicting him does its job of accurate reporting while also going way beyond that job, placing him in unexpected contexts and stretching poetic language to do things it has never done before. Brooks's poems operate by indirection and highly wrought figuration as much as they do by clarity. Brooks's poems are at once social and verbal journeys. They take us into the heart of their depicted characters, and they perform a stunning dance that draws equally upon familiar and revolutionary word usages.

Brooks's work occupies the cultural margins, exploring the humanity of people often overlooked in her time: people of color, people who are poor, young people, women, people who are ordinary. She obliterates stereotypes. In "Sadie and Maud," two sisters live radically different lives, and the poem suggests that our conventional idea of which of them "succeeded" may be upside down. In "The Life of Lincoln West," the little boy who seems valueless to the racist eye proves to have remarkable talents and an extraordinary power to comfort himself. Brooks reconnects poetry to everyday speech and events, but she also has a social agenda: to give her neglected characters the close, approving attention they deserve. In that sense, her poetry is closely connected to the black rights and women's liberation movements of the 1950s and 1960s.

In its cultural decentering, its focus on the social margins, and its use of other people's voices (such as the young woman's in "a song in the front yard" and the young man's in "Boy Breaking Glass"), Brooks's poetry can also be seen moving toward postmodernism. It establishes a style derived from multiple discourses, from the random encounters with otherness that mark urban living, and from the unresolved perplexities of contemporary existence. Perhaps the most remarkable feature of this poetry is its magnificent goodwill—its care for, and faith in, the people it depicts with such realism and imagination.

Brooks grew up with her parents and younger brother on the south side of Chicago, in a neighborhood called Bronzeville. She began to write poetry at the age of seven, and as a teenager she read Ezra Pound and T. S. Eliot. While still a teenager, she met the great Harlem poet Langston Hughes, who read some of her poems on the spot (her mother had conveniently brought them to Hughes's lecture) and told her that she was "talented and must go on writing." Hughes became her most important mentor and inspiration. After high school, Brooks graduated from Wilson Junior College, married, and had two children. She continued to write poetry, first publishing them in *The Chicago Defender*, a black newspaper, and ultimately in volumes published by mainstream presses. Her second volume, *Annie Allen* (1949), won a Pulitzer Prize. She was the first African-American writer to win it. Additional books were published, she began a college teaching career, and she was invited by President Kennedy in 1962 to read her work at a poetry festival at the Library of Congress.

In April 1967, a significant event occurred in Brooks's intellectual life. Attending the Second Black Writers' Conference at Fisk University in Nashville, she listened as young, radical writers such as Amiri Baraka (included in this anthology) called for a new Black Arts aesthetic that derived from a politics of Black Power. The new movement would center forcefully on the pressing needs of the African-American community, forgoing Martin Luther King's ethic of nonviolence, if necessary. Some members of the militant movement viewed Brooks as part of an accommodationist past, but the poet herself responded positively to the images of cultural rebirth in the young militants' speeches. She later commented, "All I know is when young people started talking about blacks loving, respecting, and helping one another, that was enough for me." She had already been writing with a sharper political edge in the months before the conference, and the conference reinforced that trend. As she commented, "To be Black is to be political." Later she added, "To be *anything* in this world as it is 'socially' constructed, is 'political.'"

Brooks's work continued to show a fierce awareness of the value of the black community, as well as a continued feminist sensibility. Feeling a special kinship with individuals denied their equal rights, she provided support for all people, regardless of social status or identity. In the 1980s, she served as Poetry Consultant to the Library of Congress, a position now called Poet Laureate. In her autobiography, *Report from Part Two*, she quotes the African-American poet Sonia Sanchez, who told her, "You *demystified* the Library!" Brooks commented, "True! To my great delight they came—to talk about poetry. Male, female; from nine to ninety. Heterosexual, homosexual, etc. Jew. Gentile. Muslim. Aristocrat, beggar. Domestic, foreign. Senator, scientist. The sinful and the saintly. A bag lady." Brooks spent her entire career in a humanistic effort to raise up those who were oppressed and to find inventive ways for poetry to participate in that project.

FURTHER READING

B. J. Bolden. *Urban Rage in Bronzeville: Social Commentary in the Poetry of Gwendolyn Brooks, 1945–1960.* Chicago: Third World Press, 1999.

Gwendolyn Brooks. *Blacks.* Chicago: Third World Press, 1987.

———. *Maud Martha: A Novel.* Chicago: Third World Press, 1953.

———. *Report from Part Two.* Chicago: Third World Press, 1996.

Arthur P. Davis. *From the Dark Tower: Afro-American Writers, 1900–1960.* Washington, D.C.: Howard University Press, 1982.

George E. Kent. *A Life of Gwendolyn Brooks.* Lexington: University Press of Kentucky, 1990.

D. H. Melham. *Gwendolyn Brooks: Poetry and the Heroic Voice.* Lexington: University Press of Kentucky, 1987.

Maria K. Mootry and Gary Smith, eds. *A Life Distilled: Gwendolyn Brooks, Her Poetry and Fiction.* Urbana: University of Illinois Press, 1989.

a song in the front yard

I've stayed in the front yard all my life.
I want a peek at the back
Where it's rough and untended and hungry weed grows.
A girl gets sick of a rose.

I want to go in the back yard now
And maybe down the alley,
To where the charity children play.
I want a good time today.

They do some wonderful things.
They have some wonderful fun.
My mother sneers, but I say it's fine
How they don't have to go in at quarter to nine.
My mother, she tells me that Johnnie Mae
Will grow up to be a bad woman.
That George'll be taken to Jail soon or late
(On account of last winter he sold our back gate.)

But I say it's fine. Honest, I do.
And I'd like to be a bad woman, too,
And wear the brave stockings of night-black lace
And strut down the streets with paint on my face.

1945

This poem, making a symbolic contrast between the front and back yards, is a lyric spoken by a teenaged African-American girl. Although variant, it belongs to the ballad tradition, which goes back to fifteenth-century England and Scotland. Although the form was initially rural, the street ballad—set in an urban scene, as this poem is—arose in the sixteenth century. Wherever they are set, ballads tell stories of the common people, often in stanzas that alternate lines of iambic tetrameter (four beats) with iambic trimeter (three beats). This poem begins in the regulation form and then begins to modify it. Critic D. H. Melhem comments, "The girl describes her quarrel with respectable life. . . . Freudian interpretation works here—suggesting the superego front yard and the ego/id/libido backyard."

Sadie and Maud

Maud went to college.
Sadie stayed at home.
Sadie scraped life
With a fine-tooth comb.

She didn't leave a tangle in.
Her comb found every strand.
Sadie was one of the livingest chits[1]
In all the land.

Sadie bore two babies
Under her maiden name.
Maud and Ma and Papa
Nearly died of shame.
Every one but Sadie
Nearly died of shame.

When Sadie said her last so-long
Her girls struck out from home.
(Sadie had left as heritage
Her fine-tooth comb.)

Maud, who went to college,
Is a thin brown mouse.
She is living all alone
In this old house.

1945

Boy Breaking Glass

To Marc Crawford from whom the commission[1]

Whose broken window is a cry of art
(success, that winks aware
as elegance, as a treasonable faith)
is raw: is sonic: is old-eyed première.
Our beautiful flaw and terrible ornament.
Our barbarous and metal little man.

1. Wholehearted, vital young women (slang).

1. African-American writer and editor who requested the poem.

*   *   *

"I shall create! If not a note, a hole.
If not an overture, a desecration."

Full of pepper and light
and Salt and night and cargoes.

"Don't go down the plank
if you see there's no extension.
Each to his grief, each to
his loneliness and fidgety revenge.

Nobody knew where I was and now I am no longer there."

The only sanity is a cup of tea.
The music is in minors.[2]

Each one other
is having different weather.

"It was you, it was you who threw away my name!
And this is everything I have for me."

Who has not Congress, lobster, love, luau,
the Regency Room,[3] the Statue of Liberty,
runs. A sloppy amalgamation.
A mistake.
A cliff.
A hymn, a snare,[4] and an exceeding sun.

1968

The Life of Lincoln West

Ugliest little boy
that everyone ever saw.
That is what everyone said.

*   *   *

---

2. Music in a minor key is often interpreted as somber, sad, or introspective. A second meaning of "minors" may refer to the boy's young age, and a third may refer to his membership in a racial minority.

3. Common name for an elegant banquet room or ballroom in fancy hotels.

4. A trap made of wire or cord; more generally, something deceptively attractive by which one is entangled; or a snare drum.

Even to his mother it was apparent—
when the blue-aproned nurse came into the
northeast end of the maternity ward
bearing his squeals and plump bottom
looped up in a scant receiving blanket,
bending, to pass the bundle carefully
into the waiting mother-hands—that this
was no cute little ugliness, no sly baby waywardness
that was going to inch away
as would baby fat, baby curl, and
baby spot-rash. The pendulous lip, the
branching ears, the eyes so wide and wild,
the vague unvibrant brown of the skin,
and, most disturbing, the great head.
These components of That Look bespoke
the sure fibre. The deep grain.

His father could not bear the sight of him.
His mother high-piled her pretty dyed hair and
put him among her hairpins and sweethearts,
dance slippers, torn paper roses.
He was not less than these,
he was not more.

As the little Lincoln grew,
uglily upward and out, he began
to understand that something was
wrong. His little ways of trying
to please his father, the bringing
of matches, the jumping aside at
warning sound of oh-so-large and
rushing stride, the smile that gave
and gave and gave—Unsuccessful!

Even Christmases and Easters were spoiled.
He would be sitting at the
family feasting table, really
delighting in the displays of mashed potatoes
and the rich golden
fat-crust of the ham or the festive
fowl, when he would look up and find
somebody feeling indignant about him.

       ✻   ✻   ✻

What a pity what a pity. No love
for one so loving. The little Lincoln
loved Everybody. Ants. The changing
caterpillar. His much-missing mother.
His kindergarten teacher.

His kindergarten teacher—whose
concern for him was composed of one
part sympathy and two parts repulsion.
The others ran up with their little drawings.
He ran up with his.
She
tried to be as pleasant with him as
with others, but it was difficult.
For she was all pretty! all daintiness,
all tiny vanilla, with blue eyes and fluffy
sun-hair. One afternoon she
saw him in the hall looking bleak against
the wall. It was strange because the
bell had long since rung and no other
child was in sight. Pity flooded her.
She buttoned her gloves and suggested
cheerfully that she walk him home. She
started out bravely, holding him by the
hand. But she had not walked far before
she regretted it. The little monkey.
Must everyone look? And clutching her
hand like that. . . . Literally pinching
it. . . .

At seven, the little Lincoln loved
the brother and sister who
moved next door. Handsome. Well-
dressed. Charitable, often, to him. They
enjoyed him because he was resourceful, made up
games, told stories. But when
their More Acceptable friends came they turned
their handsome backs on him. He
hated himself for his feeling
of well-being when with them despite—
Everything.

*   *   *

He spent much time looking at himself
in mirrors. What could be done?
But there was no
shrinking his head. There was no
binding his ears.

"Don't touch me!" cried the little
fairy-like being in the playground.

Her name was Nerissa.
The many children were playing tag, but when
he caught her, she recoiled, jerked free
and ran. It was like all the
rainbow that ever was, going off
forever, all, all the sparklings in
the sunset west.

One day, while he was yet seven,
a thing happened. In the down-town movies
with his mother a white
man in the seat beside him whispered
loudly to a companion, and pointed at
the little Linc.
"THERE! That's the kind I've been wanting
to show you! One of the best
examples of the specie. Not like
those diluted Negroes you see so much of on
the streets these days, but the
real thing.

Black, ugly, and odd. You
can see the savagery. The blunt
blankness. That is the real
thing."

His mother—her hair had never looked so
red around the dark brown
velvet of her face—jumped up,
shrieked "Go to—" She did not finish.
She yanked to his feet the little
Lincoln, who was sitting there

staring in fascination at his assessor. At the author of his
new idea.

All the way home he was happy. Of course,
he had not liked the word
"ugly."
But, after, should he not
be used to that by now? What had
struck him, among words and meanings
he could little understand, was the phrase
"the real thing."
He didn't know quite why,
but he liked that.
He liked that very much.

When he was hurt, too much
stared at—
too much
left alone—he
thought about that. He told himself
"After all, I'm
the real thing."

It comforted him.

1970

In her autobiography, Brooks writes that "The Life of Lincoln West" presents "a small
Black boy coming to terms with outdoor and indoor opinions of his identity"—that is,
with color prejudice among both whites and blacks. Scholar Arthur P. Davis has observed
that, in her poems about color prejudice, "we get the impression that Gwendolyn Brooks
has somehow stepped into the picture and, forgetting her usual restraint, expressed intense personal feeling." Brooks herself seemed to confirm that insight when she told an
audience, "I, too, am a Lincoln West."

The Boy Died in My Alley

Without my having known.
Policeman said, next morning,
"Apparently died Alone."
"You heard a shot?" Policeman said.
Shots I hear and Shots I hear.
I never see the dead.

*   *   *

The Shot that killed him yes I heard
as I heard the Thousand shots before;
careening tinnily down the nights
across my years and arteries.

Policeman pounded on my door.
"Who is it?" "POLICE!" Policeman yelled.
"A Boy was dying in your alley.
A Boy is dead, and in your alley.
And have you known this Boy before?"

I have known this Boy before.
I have known this Boy before, who
ornaments my alley.
I never saw his face at all.
I never saw his future fall.
But I have known this Boy.

I have always heard him deal with death.
I have always heard the shout, the volley.
I have closed my heart-ears late and early.
And I have killed him ever.

I joined the Wild and killed him
with knowledgeable unknowing.
I saw where he was going.
I saw him Crossed. And seeing,
I did not take him down.

He cried not only "Father!"
but "Mother!
Sister!
Brother."
The cry climbed up the alley.
It went up to the wind.
It hung upon the heaven
for a long
stretch-strain of Moment.

The red floor of my alley
is a special speech to me.

1981

According to D. H. Melham, "The Boy Died in My Alley" was inspired by several stories, one of them involving "a tragic shooting in Brooks's neighborhood." Kenneth Alexander, an honors student in the same high school class as Brooks's daughter Nora, was killed as he ran from a policeman. Norris B. Clark, writing in A *Life Distilled*, suggests that the poem advocates "a sense of communal and individual responsibility for the spiritual and physical death of blacks."

ROBERT LOWELL
1917–1977

Robert Lowell had a poetic career notable for its range and impact. Early poems, such as "Where the Rainbow Ends," used complex formal structures to frame a quest for Christian redemption. In his middle period, he innovated a poetry of personal revelation, in such poems as "Skunk Hour," and a poetry of social witness, in such poems as "For the Union Dead." These poems are so powerful that Lowell is best remembered today as the poet who popularized "confessional poetry" and who gave poetry a political dimension. In his later work, such as "Epilogue," he reflected on the complex interrelations between life and art. By exploring difficult private and public issues, Lowell helped recover poetry's cultural centrality.

An only child, Lowell was born and raised in Boston. Among his ancestors were various Puritan patriarchs and a few notable poets, including James Russell Lowell and Amy Lowell. Despite these illustrious forebears, he grew up in a tense environment of declining income, social aspiration, and bitter conflict between his parents. Moreover, the family history itself was blemished: the patriarchs had committed brutal acts of war against Native Americans, and the family poets seemed to Lowell outdated. He grew up feeling ambivalent about history, family, and himself—the three topics that would drive his poetic career.

After two unhappy years at Harvard, Lowell came under the wing of elder poet Allen Tate, and he transferred to Kenyon College, where he studied with another elder poet, John Crowe Ransom, and befriended fellow student and poet Randall Jarrell (included in this volume). After graduating, Lowell married Jean Stafford (a fiction writer) and converted to Roman Catholicism. When inducted into the army during World War II, he protested the bombing of civilian centers by refusing to serve. Sentenced to prison, he served five and a half months, emerging (as he later said) "educated—not as they wished *re*-educated." Two years after his release in 1944, he published his first major volume, *Lord*

Weary's Castle (1946), which won the Pulitzer Prize and established him as a leading poet of his generation. Jarrell observed that the book concerns a conflict between everything that blinds or binds and everything that grows or changes. This constant struggle informs "Where the Rainbow Ends," in which Lowell's vivid language produces moments of wrenching intensity.

In the early 1950s, Lowell stopped writing poetry. He lost his faith, divorced and remarried, experienced the death of both parents, and began a series of mental breakdowns that would punctuate the rest of his life. By 1957 he was settled in Boston with his wife (literary critic Elizabeth Hardwick) and their infant daughter, and he was desperate to be writing again. Although ambivalent about Allen Ginsberg, he was impressed by the Beat poet's success in communicating his vision. He also found inspiration in the lucidity of poems by William Carlos Williams (a new mentor), Elizabeth Bishop (his close friend), and Anne Sexton (one of his students). Influenced by all of these poets, he invented a new writing style that was both personal and exploratory. Such poems as "Commander Lowell," "Waking in the Blue," and "Skunk Hour" centered on private memories rather than historical and religious themes. They had the plot, character, and humor of autobiography. They juxtaposed ironic distance with disclosure, observation with introspection, and narrative with verbal complexity. When the poems were published in *Life Studies* (1959), they created a sensation. Lowell was reborn as a poet, and American poetry was pushed along toward its appointment with postmodernism.

After the publication of these personal poems, Lowell moved with his family from Boston to New York, and he began to immerse himself again in the public sphere. "For the Union Dead" meditates on the disturbing presence of racism in American culture, while "Waking Early Sunday Morning" laments a present and future punctuated by "small war on the heels of small / war." "For Robert Kennedy 1925–68" mourns the death of a political figure who was murdered while campaigning to end the Vietnam War. Lowell himself campaigned against that war, participating, for example, in the 1967 March on the Pentagon along with such fellow poets as Allen Ginsberg and Denise Levertov.

In the 1970s, Lowell suffered from declining health and an increasingly troubled personal life. He moved to England, had a son with novelist Caroline Blackwood, divorced Hardwick, and married Blackwood. As these life-changing events occurred, he wrote books of unrhymed sonnets reflecting on his charged relations with both women, on the darker aspects of human history, and on his own poetic quest. One of these books, *The Dolphin*, brought him his second Pulitzer Prize. At the end of his life, he moved back to the United States and to Elizabeth Hardwick. He produced one final book of poems, *Day by Day*, which concludes with "Epilogue," a poem that meditates on the role memory played in his poetic project. Several days after the book's publication in 1977, Lowell died of heart failure while en route from a visit with Blackwood back to his home with Hardwick.

From his early prophetic words to his last meditative ones, Lowell made himself a central creator in American poetry. His early work brought modernist poetry to one sort of blazing conclusion, his middle period encapsulated the characteristics of Cold War poetry, and his later work moved toward the indeterminacy and self-reflexivity of postmodernism. From the beginning of his career to the end, he wrote poems that became American landmarks.

FURTHER READING

Steven Gould Axelrod. *Robert Lowell: Life and Art*. Princeton: Princeton University Press, 1978.

———, ed. *The Critical Response to Robert Lowell*. Westport, Conn.: Greenwood Press, 1999.

Steven Gould Axelrod and Helen Deese, eds. *Robert Lowell: New Essays on the Poetry*. New York: Cambridge University Press, 1986.

Suzanne Ferguson, ed. *Jarrell, Bishop, Lowell, and Co.: Middle Generation Poets in Context*. Knoxville: University of Tennessee Press, 2003.

Robert Lowell. *Collected Poems*. Ed. Frank Bidart and David Gewanter. New York: Farrar, Straus & Giroux, 2003.

———. *Letters*. Ed. Saskia Hamilton. New York: Farrar, Straus & Giroux, 2005.

——— and Elizabeth Bishop. *Words in Air: The Complete Correspondence Between Elizabeth Bishop and Robert Lowell*. Ed. Thomas Travisano with Saskia Hamilton. New York: Farrar, Straus & Giroux, 2008.

Paul Mariani. *Lost Puritan: A Life of Robert Lowell*. New York: W. W. Norton, 1994.

Marjorie Perloff. *The Poetic Art of Robert Lowell*. Ithaca, N.Y.: Cornell University Press, 1973.

Richard Tillinghast. *Robert Lowell's Life and Work: Damaged Grandeur*. Ann Arbor: University of Michigan Press, 1995.

Thomas Travisano. *Midcentury Quartet: Bishop, Lowell, Jarrell, Berryman, and the Making of a Postmodern Aesthetic*. Charlottesville: University of Virginia Press, 1999.

Where the Rainbow Ends

I saw the sky descending, black and white,
Not blue,[1] on Boston where the winters wore
The skulls to jack-o'-lanterns on the slates,[2]
And Hunger's skin-and-bone retrievers tore
The chickadee and shrike.[3] The thorn tree waits
Its victim and tonight
The worms will eat the deadwood to the foot
Of Ararat:[4] the scythers, Time and Death,

1. Perhaps an echo of the New Testament book of Revelation 6:12–13: "And the sun became black as sackcloth of hair, and the moon became as blood; and the stars of heaven fell unto the earth."
2. Slate gravestones.
3. The chickadee is a small, gregarious bird, whereas the shrike is a bird of prey. The thorn tree may be an evocation of Christ's crucifixion.
4. Mountains where Noah's ark came to rest (Genesis 8:4).

Helmed locusts,[5] move upon the tree of breath;
The wild ingrafted olive[6] and the root

Are withered, and a winter drifts to where
The Pepperpot,[7] ironic rainbow, spans
Charles River and its scales of scorched-earth miles.[8]
I saw my city in the Scales,[9] the pans
Of judgment rising and descending. Piles
Of dead leaves char the air[10]—
And I am a red arrow on this graph
Of Revelations. Every dove is sold.
The Chapel's sharp-shinned eagle[11] shifts its hold
On serpent-Time, the rainbow's epitaph.

In Boston serpents whistle at the cold.
The victim climbs the altar steps and sings:
"Hosannah to the lion, lamb, and beast[12]
Who fans the furnace-face of IS[13] with wings:
I breathe the ether of my marriage feast."[14]
At the high altar, gold
And a fair cloth. I kneel and the wings beat
My cheek. What can the dove of Jesus give
You now but wisdom, exile? Stand and live,[15]
The dove has brought an olive branch to eat.[16]

1946

5. In Revelation 9:3, "there came out of the smoke locusts upon the earth." Tree of breath: reminiscent of the "tree of life" of Jewish and Christian tradition (Genesis 2:9; Revelation 22:2).
6. The grafted olive branch is a metaphor for a Christian in Romans 11:17–24.
7. The picturesque Longfellow Bridge, also known as the "Pepperpot" or "Salt and Pepper" Bridge because of the appearance of its towers, spans the Charles River between Boston and Cambridge.
8. In Revelation 16:8, one of seven angels is instructed by an angry God "to scorch men with fire."
9. Either scales for weighing or measuring (as in Isaiah 40:12) or a covering, like fish scales, over the eyes (as in Acts 9:18).
10. In Revelation 8:7, "the third part of trees burnt up, and all green grass was burnt up."
11. In Revelation 12:14–16, a great "eagle" pro-

tects a woman from Satan in the shape of a "serpent."
12. In Revelation 4, 5, and 13, the lamb is Christ the redeemer, whereas the lion and beast are demonic figures. Here they seem part of a single entity (taking a singular verb in the next line).
13. Perhaps a reference to Exodus 3:14 in the Jewish and Christian scriptures, in which God says to Moses, "I AM THAT I AM."
14. Perhaps a reference to the marriage supper of the Lamb, or Jesus Christ, in Revelation 19:9–10.
15. Speaking of the Lamb, or Christ, Revelation asks, "the great day of his wrath is come; and who shall be able to stand?" (6:17).
16. In Genesis 8:11, the dove and the olive signaled to Noah the end of the flood: "And the dove came in to him in the evening, and, lo, in her mouth was an olive leaf plucked off: so Noah knew that the waters were abated from off the earth."

The title of "Where the Rainbow Ends" refers to the story of Noah and the flood, which concludes with God setting a rainbow in a cloud to signify his promise that there will be no further destructive floods (Genesis 9:13–15). Lowell wrote this poem in his twenties, during his period of fervent Roman Catholic faith. He placed it as the final poem in *Lord Weary's Castle* (1946), the volume that made him famous. When Lowell's best friend, poet Randall Jarrell, read the poem in manuscript, he wrote to Lowell that it was "one of the best religious poems in hundreds of years."

Commander Lowell

(1887–1950)

There were no undesirables or girls in my set,
when I was a boy at Mattapoisett—
only Mother, still her Father's daughter.
Her voice was still electric
with a hysterical, unmarried panic,
when she read to me from the Napoleon book.
Long-nosed Marie Louise
Hapsburg[1] in the frontispiece
had a downright Boston bashfulness,
where she grovelled to Bonaparte, who scratched his navel,
and bolted his food—just my seven years tall!
And I, bristling and manic,
skulked in the attic,
and got two hundred French generals by name,
from A to V—from Augereau to Vandamme.
I used to dope myself asleep,
naming those unpronounceables like sheep.

Having a naval officer
for my Father was nothing to shout
about to the summer colony at "Matt."
He wasn't at all "serious,"
when he showed up on the golf course,
wearing a blue serge jacket and numbly cut
white ducks he'd bought
at a Pearl Harbor commissariat . . .
and took four shots with his putter to sink his putt.

1. The archduchess Marie-Louise Hapsburg married Napoleon Bonaparte in 1810.

"Bob," they said, "golf's a game you really ought to know how to play,
if you play at all."
They wrote him off as "naval,"
naturally supposed his sport was sailing.
Poor Father, his training was engineering!
Cheerful and cowed
among the seadogs at the Sunday yacht club,
he was never one of the crowd.

"Anchors aweigh," Daddy boomed in his bathtub,
"Anchors aweigh,"
when Lever Brothers offered to pay
him double what the Navy paid.
I nagged for his dress sword with gold braid,
and cringed because Mother, new
caps on all her teeth, was born anew
at forty. With seamanlike celerity,
Father left the Navy,
and deeded Mother his property.

He was soon fired. Year after year,
he still hummed "Anchors aweigh" in the tub—
whenever he left a job,
he bought a smarter car.
Father's last employer
was Scudder, Stevens and Clark, Investment Advisors,
himself his only client.
While Mother dragged to bed alone,
read Menninger,[2]
and grew more and more suspicious,
he grew defiant.
Night after night,
à la clarté déserte de sa lampe,[3]
he slid his ivory Annapolis slide rule
across a pad of graphs—
piker speculations! In three years
he squandered sixty thousand dollars.

*   *   *

2. Karl Menninger (1893–1990), American psychiatrist and author.
3. "In the deserted light of his lamp" (French); taken from Stéphane Mallarmé's poem "Brise Marine."

Smiling on all,
Father was once successful enough to be lost
in the mob of ruling-class Bostonians.
As early as 1928,
he owned a house converted to oil,
and redecorated by the architect
of St. Mark's School. . . . Its main effect
was a drawing room, "longitudinal as Versailles,"
its ceiling, roughened with oatmeal, was blue as the sea.
And once
nineteen, the youngest ensign in his class,
he was "the old man" of a gunboat on the Yangtze.[4]

1959

One of the *Life Studies* poems, "Commander Lowell" portrays Robert Lowell's father, a former naval officer who died some years before Lowell composed the poem. According to biographer Paul Mariani, Lowell's father had graduated Annapolis in 1907 at the age of twenty: "He was an engineer, a slide rule man, a wizard in math and the nascent science of radio."

Waking in the Blue

The night attendant, a B.U.[1] sophomore,
rouses from the mare's-nest of his drowsy head
propped on *The Meaning of Meaning.*[2]
He catwalks down our corridor.
Azure day
makes my agonized blue window bleaker.
Crows maunder[3] on the petrified fairway.
Absence! My heart grows tense[4]
as though a harpoon were sparring for the kill.
(This is the house for the "mentally ill.")

What use is my sense of humor?
I grin at Stanley, now sunk in his sixties,
once a Harvard all-American fullback,

4. River in China; Lowell's father served there during his naval duty.
1. Boston University. Ironically, Lowell taught at Boston University during this period.
2. A well-known study of language and meaning by linguist C. K. Ogden and literary scholar I. A. Richards, originally published in 1923.
3. To move without aim or to speak indistinctly.
4. Compare the common saying, "Absence makes the heart grow fonder."

(if such were possible!)
still hoarding the build of a boy in his twenties,
as he soaks, a ramrod
with the muscle of a seal
in his long tub,
vaguely urinous from the Victorian plumbing.
A kingly granite profile in a crimson golf-cap,[5]
worn all day, all night,
he thinks only of his figure,
of slimming on sherbet and ginger ale—
more cut off from words than a seal.

This is the way day breaks in Bowditch Hall at McLean's;[6]
the hooded night lights bring out "Bobbie,"
Porcellian '29,[7]
a replica of Louis XVI[8]
without the wig—
redolent and roly-poly as a sperm whale,
as he swashbuckles about in his birthday suit
and horses at chairs.

These victorious figures of bravado ossified young.

In between the limits of day,
hours and hours go by under the crew haircuts
and slightly too little nonsensical bachelor twinkle
of the Roman Catholic attendants.
(There are no Mayflower
screwballs in the Catholic Church.)

After a hearty New England breakfast,
I weigh two hundred pounds
this morning. Cock of the walk,
I strut in my turtle-necked French sailor's jersey
before the metal shaving mirrors,
and see the shaky future grow familiar
in the pinched, indigenous faces

---

5. Crimson was designated Harvard's official color in 1910.
6. A private psychiatric hospital near Boston.

7. "Bobbie" belonged to an exclusive student club at Harvard and graduated in 1929.
8. French king (1754–1793) who ruled from 1774 to 1792 and was executed by revolutionaries.

of these thoroughbred mental cases,
twice my age and half my weight.
We are all old-timers,
each of us holds a locked razor.

1959

"Waking in the Blue," like the poem that precedes it and the one that follows it, originally appeared in *Life Studies* (1959), the volume in which Lowell turned away from his earlier dense rhetoric and religious aspiration and toward autobiography or even "confession" (a term he disliked but which has frequently been used). This poem is based on his treatment for a bipolar mood disorder. Lowell commented that the *Life Studies* poems were "not always factually true. There's a good deal of tinkering with fact. You leave out a lot, and emphasize this and not that. Your actual experience is a complete flux. I've invented facts and changed things, and the whole balance of the poem was something invented. So there's a lot of artistry, I hope, in the poems. Yet there is this thing: if a poem is autobiographical . . . you want the reader to say, this is true." Many other poets participated in this new, personal style of poetry, including Allen Ginsberg, Anne Sexton, John Berryman, Sylvia Plath, and ultimately Elizabeth Bishop.

Skunk Hour

(FOR ELIZABETH BISHOP)[1]

Nautilus Island's hermit
heiress still lives through winter in her Spartan cottage;
her sheep still graze above the sea.
Her son's a bishop. Her farmer
is first selectman in our village;
she's in her dotage.

Thirsting for
the hierarchic privacy
of Queen Victoria's century,
she buys up all
the eyesores facing her shore,
and lets them fall.

The season's ill—
we've lost our summer millionaire,

---

1. Included in this anthology, Bishop was one of Lowell's closest friends. Lowell explained that he dedicated the poem to her "because rereading her suggested a way of breaking through the shell of my old manner." He added that he modeled "Skunk Hour" on Bishop's "The Armadillo."

who seemed to leap from an L. L. Bean[2]
catalogue. His nine-knot yawl
was auctioned off to lobstermen.
A red fox stain[3] covers Blue Hill.

And now our fairy
decorator brightens his shop for fall;
his fishnet's filled with orange cork,
orange, his cobbler's bench and awl;
there is no money in his work,
he'd rather marry.

One dark night,
my Tudor Ford[4] climbed the hill's skull;
I watched for love-cars. Lights turned down,
they lay together, hull to hull,
where the graveyard shelves on the town. . . .
My mind's not right.

A car radio bleats,
"Love, O careless Love. . . ."[5] I hear
my ill-spirit sob in each blood cell,
as if my hand were at its throat. . . .
I myself am hell;[6]
nobody's here—

only skunks,[7] that search
in the moonlight for a bite to eat.
They march on their soles up Main Street:
white stripes, moonstruck eyes' red fire
under the chalk-dry and spar spire
of the Trinitarian Church.

   ✳ ✳ ✳

2. Mail-order company based in Maine that specializes in outdoor clothing.
3. Lowell wrote that the red stain is "meant to describe the rusty reddish color of autumn on Blue Hill, a Maine mountain near where we were living."
4. Two-door Ford sedan. Hill's skull: resonant of Golgotha, the "place of a skull," where Jesus Christ was crucified.
5. A traditional song that has been sung in folk, blues, jazz, country, and pop styles. A radio in the 1950s might have been playing a version recorded by Bessie Smith, Pete Seeger, Elvis Presley, or Fats Domino.
6. An echo of Satan in John Milton's *Paradise Lost* (IV:75): "Which way I fly is hell; my self am hell."
7. Lowell wrote, "Most people take the skunks as cheerful [but] they are horrible blind energy, at the same time . . . a wish and a fear of annihilation, i.e., dropping to a simpler form of life, and a hopeful wish for that simpler energy."

I stand on top
of our back steps and breathe the rich air—
a mother skunk with her column of kittens swills the garbage pail.
She jabs her wedge-head in a cup
of sour cream, drops her ostrich tail,
and will not scare.

1959

"Skunk Hour" climaxes the *Life Studies* sequence, even though in real life the events it depicts preceded those depicted in "Waking in the Blue." "Skunk Hour" takes place in Castine, Maine, where Lowell and his wife had a summer cottage. The poet commented: "The first four stanzas are meant to give a dawdling more or less amiable picture of a declining Maine sea town. I move from the ocean inland. Sterility howls through the scenery. . . . Then all comes alive in stanzas V and VI. This is the dark night. I hoped my readers would remember John of the Cross's poem. My night is not gracious, but secular, puritan, and agnostic. An existentialist night. Somewhere in my mind was a passage from Sartre or Camus about reaching some point of final darkness where the one free act is suicide. Out of this comes the march and affirmation, an ambiguous one, of my skunks in the last two stanzas. The skunks are both quixotic and barbarously absurd, hence the tone of amusement and defiance."

For the Union Dead

"Relinquunt Omnia Servare Rem Publicam."[1]

The old South Boston Aquarium stands
in a Sahara of snow now. Its broken windows are boarded.
The bronze weathervane cod has lost half its scales.
The airy tanks are dry.

Once my nose crawled like a snail on the glass;
my hand tingled
to burst the bubbles
drifting from the noses of the cowed, compliant fish.

My hand draws back. I often sigh still
for the dark downward and vegetating kingdom
of the fish and reptile. One morning last March,
I pressed against the new barbed and galvanized

---

1. "They give up all to serve the state" (Latin). This epigraph is the same as the one on the Civil War memorial in Boston Common except that Lowell has changed "he" to "they."

* * *

fence on the Boston Common. Behind their cage,
yellow dinosaur steamshovels were grunting
as they cropped up tons of mush and grass
to gouge their underworld garage.[2]

Parking spaces luxuriate like civic
sandpiles in the heart of Boston.
A girdle of orange, Puritan-pumpkin colored girders
braces the tingling Statehouse,

shaking over the excavations, as it faces Colonel Shaw
and his bell-cheeked Negro infantry
on St. Gaudens'[3] shaking Civil War relief,
propped by a plank splint against the garage's earthquake.

Two months after marching through Boston,
half the regiment was dead;
at the dedication,
William James could almost hear the bronze Negroes breathe.[4]

Their monument sticks like a fishbone
in the city's throat.
Its Colonel is as lean
as a compass-needle.

He has an angry wrenlike vigilance,
a greyhound's gentle tautness;
he seems to wince at pleasure,
and suffocate for privacy.

He is out of bounds now. He rejoices in man's lovely,
peculiar power to choose life and die—
when he leads his black soldiers to death,
he cannot bend his back.

* * *

2. An underground public parking garage, with hellish connotations supplied by the "underworld."

3. Augustus Saint-Gaudens (1848–1907), sculptor of the bronze bas-relief that depicts Robert Gould Shaw (1837–1863) and the Massachusetts Fifty-fourth, situated at the northwest corner of Boston Common, facing the Massachusetts statehouse.

4. At the dedication of the monument, philosopher William James (1842–1910) said that they are "so true to nature that one can almost hear them breathing."

On a thousand small town New England greens,
the old white churches hold their air
of sparse, sincere rebellion; frayed flags
quilt the graveyards of the Grand Army of the Republic.

The stone statues of the abstract Union Soldier[5]
grow slimmer and younger each year—
wasp-waisted, they doze over muskets
and muse through their sideburns . . .

Shaw's father wanted no monument
except the ditch,
where his son's body was thrown
and lost with his "niggers."[6]

The ditch is nearer.
There are no statues for the last war here;[7]
on Boylston Street, a commercial photograph
shows Hiroshima boiling

over a Mosler Safe,[8] the "Rock of Ages"
that survived the blast. Space is nearer.[9]
When I crouch to my television set,
the drained faces of Negro school-children rise like balloons.[10]

Colonel Shaw
is riding on his bubble,
he waits
for the blessèd break.

    ✻   ✻   ✻

5. In his dedication speech, William James said that "abstract soldiers'-monuments have been reared on every village green."

6. After the battle, the Confederate commanding officer was purported to have ordered that Shaw be buried "with his niggers," a phrase that became a rallying cry for black and white Union soldiers in the months after the event. When the war was over, Shaw's father refused to allow his son to be dug up and reburied in a private grave, feeling that it was more fitting that he remain buried with the other soldiers.

7. World War II. The poem overlooks the Korean War.

8. The Mosler Safe Company placed a photograph of the Hiroshima mushroom cloud in its window on Boylston Street in Boston, with the caption "The Hiroshima Story Comes to Life with a Bang."

9. The Soviet Union launched *Sputnik 1*, the world's first artificial satellite, into space in 1957. "Space," here, may suggest a moral void as well as the region beyond the earth's atmosphere.

10. In September 1957, nine African-American teenagers, escorted by federal troops, braved a screaming, threatening crowd to integrate a formerly all-white high school in Little Rock, Arkansas.

The Aquarium is gone. Everywhere,
giant finned cars nose forward like fish;
a savage servility
slides by on grease.

                                        1964

"For the Union Dead," a Civil War poem, concerns the first Union Army regiment composed of free African-American soldiers. About two months into battle, the regiment was
ambushed, and half the men were killed, including the white commanding officer, Colonel Robert Gould Shaw. All of the dead were unceremoniously dumped into a common
grave or "ditch." Thirty-four years later, a monument to Shaw and his men was unveiled
in Boston Common, where it may still be seen today.

When Lowell first read the poem in public, he commented that it "is about childhood memories, the evisceration of our modern cities, civil rights, nuclear warfare, and
more particularly, Colonel Robert Shaw and his Negro regiment, the Massachusetts
Fifty-fourth. I brought in early personal memories because I wanted to avoid the fixed,
brazen tone of the set-piece and official ode." The poem weaves together personal and
public subject matter through the use of linking images, such as fish, noses, bubbles, and
ditches.

Steven Gould Axelrod observes that "the poem is literally born of time, focusing on
various historical moments. . . . Even within the poem itself, the process of time can be
seen: in the first stanza the aquarium still 'stands,' but by the last it 'is gone.' By his act
of historical memory, Lowell seeks to counter the prevailing mood of his age which is
fiercely antagonistic to traces of the past—aquarium, memorial, and all else. By obliterat-
ing its past, modern society has become a stranger to itself. As a result we ignorantly repeat
the sins of our ancestors; the brutal regimental deaths and burial are replicated in the
bombing of Hiroshima. Lowell hopes to redeem time by identifying Colonel Shaw and
the Massachusetts Fifty-fourth, William James, and the black school-children as models
of humane and courageous public acts and discourse."

Waking Early Sunday Morning

O to break loose, like the chinook
salmon jumping and falling back,
nosing up to the impossible
stone and bone-crushing waterfall—
raw-jawed, weak-fleshed there, stopped by ten
steps of the roaring ladder, and then
to clear the top on the last try,
alive enough to spawn and die.

                ✳   ✳   ✳

Stop, back off. The salmon breaks
water, and now my body wakes
to feel the unpolluted joy
and criminal leisure of a boy—
no rainbow smashing a dry fly[1]
in the white run is free as I,
here squatting like a dragon on
time's hoard before the day's begun!

Vermin run for their unstopped holes;
in some dark nook a fieldmouse rolls
a marble, hours on end, then stops;
the termite in the woodwork sleeps—
listen, the creatures of the night
obsessive, casual, sure of foot,
go on grinding, while the sun's
daily remorseful blackout dawns.

Fierce, fireless mind, running downhill.
Look up and see the harbor fill:
business as usual in eclipse
goes down to the sea in ships[2]—
wake of refuse, dacron rope,
bound for Bermuda or Good Hope,
all bright before the morning watch
the wine-dark[3] hulls of yawl and ketch.

I watch a glass of water wet
with a fine fuzz of icy sweat,
silvery colors touched with sky,
serene in their neutrality—
yet if I shift, or change my mood,
I see some object made of wood,
background behind it of brown grain,
to darken it, but not to stain.

O that the spirit could remain
tinged but untarnished by its strain!

---

1. A fishing lure that rides on the water's surface, as opposed to a "wet" fly, which is submerged.
2. Ironic echo of Psalm 107: "They that go down to the sea in ships, that do business in great wa- ters; / these see the works of the LORD, and his wonders of the deep" (23–24).
3. Epithet for the sea in Homer's *Odyssey*. Yawl and ketch: kinds of small boats.

Better dressed and stacking birch,
or lost with the Faithful at Church—
anywhere, but somewhere else!
And now the new electric bells,
clearly chiming, "Faith of our fathers,"[4]
and now the congregation gathers.

O Bible chopped and crucified
in hymns we hear but do not read,
none of the milder subtleties
of grace or art will sweeten these
stiff quatrains shoveled out four-square—
they sing of peace, and preach despair;
yet they gave darkness some control,
and left a loophole for the soul.

No, put old clothes on, and explore
the corners of the woodshed for
its dregs and dreck:[5] tools with no handle,
ten candle-ends not worth a candle,
old lumber banished from the Temple,
damned by Paul's precept and example,
cast from the kingdom, banned in Israel,
the wordless sign, the tinkling cymbal.[6]

When will we see Him face to face?
Each day, He shines through darker glass.[7]
In this small town where everything
is known, I see His vanishing
emblems, His white spire and flag-
pole sticking out above the fog,
like old white china doorknobs, sad,
slight, useless things to calm the mad.

Hammering military splendor,
top-heavy Goliath[8] in full armor—

4. Protestant hymn composed in the nineteenth century.
5. Trash (German and Yiddish).
6. Allusion to St. Paul's warning in the New Testament: "Though I speak with the tongues of men and of angels, and have not charity, I am become as sounding brass or a tinkling cymbal" (I Corinthians 13:1).

7: Another echo of Paul: "For now we see through a glass, darkly, but then face to face" (I Corinthians 13:12).
8. Philistine giant, encased in a helmet of brass and a coat of mail, whom David nonetheless slays in the Hebrew Scriptures (I Samuel 17:4–54).

little redemption in the mass
liquidations of their brass,
elephant and phalanx moving
with the times and still improving,
when that kingdom hit the crash:
a million foreskins stacked like trash . . .[9]

Sing softer! But what if a new
diminuendo[10] brings no true
tenderness, only restlessness,
excess, the hunger for success,
sanity of self-deception
fixed and kicked by reckless caution,
while we listen to the bells—
anywhere, but somewhere else!

O to break loose. All life's grandeur
is something with a girl in summer . . .
elated as the President[11]
girdled by his establishment
this Sunday morning, free to chaff
his own thoughts with his bear-cuffed[12] staff,
swimming nude, unbuttoned, sick
of his ghost-written rhetoric!

No weekends for the gods now. Wars
flicker, earth licks its open sores,
fresh breakage, fresh promotions, chance
assassinations,[13] no advance.
Only man thinning out his kind
sounds through the Sabbath noon, the blind
swipe of the pruner and his knife
busy about the tree of life . . .[14]

Pity the planet, all joy gone
from this sweet volcanic cone;

9. In lieu of a dowry, King Saul asks David to bring him "a hundred foreskins of the Philistines, to be avenged of the king's enemies," and David brings him two hundred instead (I Samuel 18:25–27).
10. Gradually diminishing volume in music (Italian).
11. Lyndon B. Johnson (1908–1973), president of the United States between 1963 and 1969.
12. Struck or slapped, perhaps playfully.
13. President John F. Kennedy was assassinated on November 22, 1963, the event that elevated Johnson to the presidency.
14. Phrase that appears in Genesis 2:9 and elsewhere in the Bible.

peace to our children when they fall
in small war on the heels of small
war—until the end of time
to police the earth,[15] a ghost
orbiting forever lost
in our monotonous sublime.

1967

In 1965, President Lyndon Johnson invited Lowell to attend a White House Festival of the Arts. Lowell declined, based on his growing apprehensions about the escalation of the Vietnam War. He wrote to Johnson: "We are in danger of imperceptibly becoming an explosive and suddenly chauvinistic nation. . . . At this anguished, delicate and perhaps determining moment, I feel I am serving you and our country best by not taking part in the White House Festival of the Arts." This single public act, Lowell later observed, "brought more publicity than all my poems, and I felt miscast, felt burdened to write on the great theme, private, and almost 'global.'" The result was "Waking Early Sunday Morning."

For Robert Kennedy 1925–68

Here in my workroom, in its listlessness
of Vacancy, like the old townhouse we shut for summer,
airtight and sheeted from the sun and smog,
far from the hornet yatter[1] of his gang—
is loneliness, a thin smoke thread of vital
air. But what will anyone teach you now?
Doom was woven in your nerves, your shirt,
woven in the great clan;[2] they too were loyal,
and you too were loyal to them, to death.
For them like a prince, you daily left your tower
to walk through dirt in your best cloth. Untouched,
alone in my Plutarchan bubble, I miss
you, you out of Plutarch,[3] made by hand—
forever approaching our maturity.

1973

15. Political columnist Walter Lippmann had written skeptically about American foreign policy that "our official doctrine is that we must be prepared to police the world" (*Newsweek*, May 24, 1965, 23).
1. Chatter.
2. The Kennedy family, which included Robert

F. Kennedy and his eight siblings, among them Joseph Kennedy, Jr. (killed in World War II), President John F. Kennedy, Special Olympics founder Eunice Kennedy Shriver, and Senator Edward (Ted) Kennedy.
3. Biographer (46–120 C.E.) of Greek and Roman notables, and author of *Parallel Lives*.

Senator Robert F. Kennedy was running for the Democratic nomination for president on an antiwar platform when he was assassinated on June 6, 1968. When someone suggested to Lowell that the poem's final words be changed to "your maturity," he replied that "our" was the proper pronoun, since it meant "man's or mankind's, or the future of our country." Nevertheless, he allowed the poem to be printed with the phrase "your maturity" in one edition. This poem and the three that follow are from Lowell's sonnet sequences published between 1969–1973.

Reading Myself

Like thousands, I took just pride and more than just,
struck matches that brought my blood to a boil;
I memorized the tricks to set the river on fire—
somehow never wrote something to go back to.
Can I suppose I am finished with wax flowers
and have earned my grass on the minor slopes of Parnassus. . . .[1]
No honeycomb is built without a bee
adding circle to circle, cell to cell,
the wax and honey of a mausoleum—
this round dome proves its maker is alive;
the corpse of the insect lives embalmed in honey,
prays that its perishable work live long
enough for the sweet-tooth bear to desecrate—
this open book . . . my open coffin.

1973

End of a Year

These conquered kings pass furiously away;
gods die in flesh and spirit and live in print,
each library a misquoted tyrant's home.
A year runs out in the movies, must be written
in bad, straightforward, unscanning sentences—
stamped, trampled, branded on backs of carbons,
lines, words, letters nailed to letters, words, lines—
the typescript looks like a Rosetta Stone. . . .[1]

1. Mountain in central Greece that in Greek myth was sacred to Apollo and home to the seven muses.
1. Egyptian text carved in 196 B.C.E. that includes three translations of a single passage, thus helping scholars learn how to decipher hieroglyphic Egyptian writing.

One more annus mirabilis,[2] its hero *hero demens*
ill-starred of men and crossed by his fixed stars,
running his ship past sound-spar on the rocks. . . .
The slush-ice on the east bank of the Hudson
is rose-heather in the New Year sunset;
bright sky, bright sky, carbon[3] scarred with ciphers.

1973

According to Frank Bidart and David Gewanter, in this poem's final line, "re-used carbon paper becomes the bright night sky: where a [typewriter] key struck, a gap shows light."

Dolphin

My Dolphin, you only guide me by surprise,
captive as Racine,[1] the man of craft,
drawn through his maze of iron composition
by the incomparable wandering voice of Phèdre.
When I was troubled in mind, you made for my body
caught in its hangman's-knot of sinking lines,
the glassy bowing and scraping of my will. . . .
I have sat and listened to too many
words of the collaborating muse,
and plotted perhaps too freely with my life,
not avoiding injury to others,
not avoiding injury to myself—
to ask compassion . . . this book, half fiction,
an eelnet made by man for the eel fighting—

my eyes have seen what my hand did.

1973

This poem—a non-metered, non-rhyming sonnet with one extra line—evokes the presence of Lowell's third wife, Caroline Blackwood, as a "Dolphin." Just as legendary dolphins saved drowning sailors, so this "Dolphin" saves the poet's life. The poem also

---

2. Wonderful year. *Hero demens*: "demented hero."
3. Constituent of coal and petroleum, but here probably carbon paper, a lightweight paper with one side coated black, used for making copies of typewritten pages.
1. French dramatist Jean Racine (1639–1699), author of the play *Phèdre* (1677), which was named after its tragic heroine.

meditates on the complex interactions between Lowell's life and his poetry. The final line may suggest that the poet's eyes saw first what his hand later wrote down, but also that his eyes saw (and took responsibility for) the writing that the hand performed.

Epilogue

Those blessèd structures, plot and rhyme—
why are they no help to me now
I want to make
something imagined, not recalled?
I hear the noise of my own voice:
The painter's vision is not a lens,
it trembles to caress the light.
But sometimes everything I write
with the threadbare art of my eye
seems a snapshot,
lurid, rapid, garish, grouped,
heightened from life,
yet paralyzed by fact.
All's misalliance.
Yet why not say what happened?
Pray for the grace of accuracy
Vermeer[1] gave to the sun's illumination
stealing like the tide across a map
to his girl solid with yearning.
We are poor passing facts,
warned by that to give
each figure in the photograph
his living name.

1977

In this poem Lowell reflects on his poetic quest. Critic Helen Deese (in *Robert Lowell: Essays on The Poetry*) noted that Vermeer, like Lowell himself, excelled "in recording compositionally what the eye has seen."

1. Jan Vermeer (1632–1675), Dutch painter noted for his subtle domestic scenes and his masterly treatment of light.

ROBERT DUNCAN
1919–1988

ROBERT DUNCAN was both a visionary poet, in the tradition of Dante and William Blake, and a poet of collage, fragmentation, and allusion, helping initiate a tradition that flowered among such contemporary poets as Susan Howe, Lyn Hejinian, and Rae Armantrout (all included in this anthology). His learned and at times ecstatic poetry has classical, medieval, and Romantic roots. Yet in its style of disconnection and contingency, and in its poignant implications and silences, it gave rise to a kind of process poetry we associate with post-1970 postmodernism. Receptive to visionaries of the past, Duncan proved to be a kind of visionary poet himself—a culture hero, someone ahead of his time who inaugurates a new age.

Duncan's mother died in childbirth, and his father, a day laborer, put him up for adoption. At the age of six months, he was adopted by Edwin and Minnehaha Symmes, an architect and his wife. The poet was raised in Oakland and Bakersfield, California, in a "theosophist" home filled with séances, mysticism, and magic. Although as an adult he changed his name back from Symmes to Duncan and rejected his family culture for an identity as an innovative poet, the family discourse about supersensible realities left a permanent impact on him and his writing. In his teens and twenties, he sporadically attended the University of California, Berkeley, where he studied in a wide variety of fields but particularly in medieval and Renaissance literature. He was drafted into the army and soon discharged for homosexuality. After numerous affairs and a brief marriage to a woman, he formed a lifelong domestic partnership with the visual artist Jess Collins.

Duncan associated himself with various Bay Area poets, including Kenneth Rexroth and Allen Ginsberg, and with the Black Mountain school of poets, which included Charles Olson, Denise Levertov, and Robert Creeley (all included in this anthology). He established himself as a major poet in the 1960s, with such poems as "Often I Am Permitted to Return to a Meadow." In 1968, he vowed not to publish again for fifteen years in order to replenish his gift and not repeat himself. True to his word, he did not publish again until 1984. He died at the age of sixty-nine from a heart attack probably brought on by years of kidney disease.

Robert Duncan tried to write each of his poems in one sitting, feeling that if he allowed himself to revise he wouldn't try hard enough to get it right the first time. When he recited his work, he paid close attention to his breathing, as if to insist that poems were a bodily function, made to be read aloud and closely associated with music. Like his hero Walt Whitman, he was a poet whose work reflected "the immediate impulse of psychic life." He sought to produce "open forms" to match an "open universe." "Our demand for truth," he asserted, "is not to reach a conclusion but to keep our exposure to what we do not know." Interested in the imagination, in the border between sleeping and waking, in human love with all of its complexities, in social equality, in material objects, and in what is deeper and more real than material objects, Duncan fostered a notion of aesthetic and cosmic immediacy. He believed "that the Kingdom is here, that we have only now in which to live—that the universe has only now in which to live."

FURTHER READING

Robert J. Bertholf. "Duncan, Robert." In *The Greenwood Encyclopedia of American Poets and Poetry*, vol. 2, ed. Jeffrey Gray, James McCorkle, and Mary McAleer Balkun, 431–35. Westport, Conn.: Greenwood Press, 2006.

Michael Davidson. *The San Francisco Renaissance: Poetics and Community at Mid-Century*. New York: Cambridge University Press, 1989.

Robert Duncan. *Selected Poems*. Revised and Enlarged. Ed. Robert J. Bertholf. New York: New Directions, 1997.

———. *A Selected Prose*. Ed. Robert J. Bertholf. New York: New Directions, 1995.

——— and Denise Levertov. *The Letters of Robert Duncan and Denise Levertov*. Ed. Robert J. Bertholf and Albert Gelpi. Stanford: Stanford University Press, 2003.

Often I Am Permitted to Return to a Meadow

as if it were a scene made-up by the mind,
that is not mine, but is a made place,

that is mine, it is so near to the heart,
an eternal pasture folded in all thought
so that there is a hall therein

that is a made place, created by light
wherefrom the shadows that are forms fall.[1]

Wherefrom fall all architectures I am
I say are likenesses of the First Beloved
whose flowers are flames lit to the Lady.[2]

1. Allusion to Plato's allegory of the cave. In *The Republic*, Plato portrays a group of people chained in a cave whose only reality is watching shadows flickering on the wall. Plato analogizes those shadows to material objects and the light to a more fundamental, ideal reality, of which material objects are but a shadowy reflection.

2. Perhaps an allusion to "the Lady," the female principle imagined as a deity, who is evoked in H.D.'s *Trilogy*.

*　*　*

She it is Queen Under The Hill[3]
whose hosts are a disturbance of words within words
that is a field folded.

It is only a dream of the grass blowing
east against the source of the sun
in an hour before the sun's going down

whose secret we see in a children's game
of ring a round of roses told.[4]

Often I am permitted to return to a meadow
as if it were a given property of the mind
that certain bounds hold against chaos,

that is a place of first permission,
everlasting omen of what is.

1960

The meadow in "Often I Am Permitted to Return to a Meadow" is at once a natural place, a mystical reality, and a space of intimacy and imagination. Robert J. Bertholf writes: "Duncan combines a dream of children dancing, an Atlantean dream, references to the 'first beloved' as in medieval and courtly hymns to the 'lady,' Platonic thought, Charles Olson's idea of field composition, and the romantic idea of visionary wonder. . . . The mythopoetic process creates a field of action, a meadow of thought and feeling that in turn provides a place of habitation for the poet."

Poetry, A Natural Thing

Neither our vices nor our virtues
further the poem. "They came up
and died
just like they do every year
on the rocks."

*　*　*

3. Persephone, queen of the underworld in Greek mythology. The daughter of Demeter (the goddess of earth), she was abducted by Hades (god of the underworld). Although ultimately returned to Demeter, Persephone was forced thereafter to spend a season underground every year, a pattern that corresponds to the death and rebirth cycle of the seasons.

4. Reference to the nineteenth-century nursery rhyme "Ring Around the Rosie." A playground game involves children singing this song as they stand in a circle, hold hands, skip, and then fall down. Popular beliefs linking the game to the Great Plague of London in 1665 appear to be historically invalid.

The poem
feeds upon thought, feeling, impulse,
      to breed itself,
a spiritual urgency at the dark ladders leaping.

This beauty is an inner persistence
      toward the source
striving against (within) down-rushet[1] of the river,
      a call we heard and answer
in the lateness of the world
      primordial bellowings
from which the youngest world might spring,

salmon not in the well where the
      hazelnut falls
but at the falls battling, inarticulate,
      blindly making it.

This is one picture apt for the mind.

A second: a moose painted by Stubbs,[2]
where last year's extravagant antlers
      lie on the ground.
The forlorn moosey-faced poem wears
      new antler-buds,
      the same,

"a little heavy, a little contrived",

his only beauty to be
      all moose.

1960

Roots and Branches

Sail, Monarchs,[1] rising and falling
orange merchants in spring's flowery markets!
messengers of March in warm currents of news floating,

---

1. An invented word perhaps based on "freshet," which is a freshwater stream or a sudden rise in the level of a stream.
2. George Stubbs (1724–1806), an English painter of horses and other animals.

1. The monarch butterfly, the best known of all North American butterflies, has an orange and black pattern on its wings.

flitting into areas of aroma,
tracing out of air unseen roots and branches of sense
I share in thought,
filaments woven and broken where the world might light
casual certainties of me. There are

echoes of what I am in what you perform
this morning. How you perfect my spirit!
almost restore
an imaginary tree of the living in all its doctrines
by fluttering about,
intent and easy as you are, the profusion of you!
awakening transports of an inner view of things.

1964

My Mother Would Be a Falconress

My mother would be a falconress,[1]
And I, her gay falcon treading her wrist,
would fly to bring back
from the blue of the sky to her, bleeding, a prize,
where I dream in my little hood[2] with many bells
jangling when I'd turn my head.

My mother would be a falconress,
and she sends me as far as her will goes.
She lets me ride to the end of her curb[3]
where I fall back in anguish.
I dread that she will cast me away,
for I fall, I mis-take, I fail in her mission.

She would bring down the little birds.
And I would bring down the little birds.
When will she let me bring down the little birds,
pierced from their flight with their necks broken,
their heads like flowers limp from the stem?

*　*　*

1. A coined term for a female falconer; that is, a woman who trains falcons—a kind of hawk—for bringing back small birds.
2. Essential in training a falcon, the hood covers the falcon's head to ensure that the bird remains calm in the presence of human beings.
3. Control; curve.

I tread my mother's wrist and would draw blood.
Behind the little hood my eyes are hooded.
I have gone back into my hooded silence,
talking to myself and dropping off to sleep.

For she has muffled my dreams in the hood she has made me,
sewn round with bells, jangling when I move.
She rides with her little falcon upon her wrist.
She uses a barb[4] that brings me to cower.
She sends me abroad to try my wings
and I come back to her. I would bring down
the little birds to her
I may not tear into, I must bring back perfectly.

I tear at her wrist with my beak to draw blood,
and her eye holds me, anguisht, terrifying.
She draws a limit to my flight.
Never beyond my sight, she says.
She trains me to fetch and to limit myself in fetching.
She rewards me with meat for my dinner.
But I must never eat what she sends me to bring her.

Yet it would have been beautiful, if she would have carried me,
always, in a little hood with the bells ringing,
at her wrist, and her riding
to the great falcon hunt, and me
flying up to the curb of my heart from her heart
to bring down the skylark from the blue to her feet,
straining, and then released for the flight.

My mother would be a falconress,
and I her gerfalcon,[5] raised at her will,
from her wrist sent flying, as if I were her own
pride, as if her pride
knew no limits, as if her mind
sought in me flight beyond the horizon.

Ah, but high, high in the air I flew.
And far, far beyond the curb of her will,

---

4. A sharp projection extending backward to prevent easy extraction; metaphorically, a pointedly critical remark.

5. Variant of *gyrfalcon*, a large falcon of the arctic regions, about two feet long and more powerful than the peregrine falcon.

were the blue hills where the falcons nest.
And then I saw west to the dying sun—
it seemd my human soul went down in flames.

I tore at her wrist, at the hold she had for me,
until the blood ran hot and I heard her cry out,
far, far beyond the curb of her will •

to horizons of stars beyond the ringing hills of the world where the falcons nest
I saw, and I tore at her wrist with my savage beak.
I flew, as if sight flew from the anguish in her eye beyond her sight,
sent from my striking loose, from the cruel strike at her wrist,
striking out from the blood to be free of her.

My mother would be a falconress,
and even now, years after this,
when the wounds I left her had surely heald,
and the woman is dead,
her fierce eyes closed, and if her heart
were broken, it is stilld •

I would be a falcon and go free.
I tread her wrist and wear the hood,
talking to myself, and would draw blood.

1968

In a prefatory note, Duncan explained how this poem arose: "I wakend in the night with the lines '*My mother would be a falconress—And I a falcon at her wrist*' being repeated in my mind. Was the word *falconress* or *falconess*?—the troubled insistence of the lines would not let go of me, and I got up and took my notebook." Whether the poem alludes to Duncan's biological mother, who died in childbirth, or his adoptive mother, who died before the poem was written, or neither, it nonetheless resonates the attachments and alienations of the family relationship.

Childhood's Retreat

It's in the perilous boughs of the tree
out of blue sky   the wind
sings loudest surrounding me.

And solitude,   a wild solitude
's reveald,   fearfully,   high   I'd climb
into the shaking uncertainties,

＊　＊　＊

part out of longing, part   daring my self,
part to see that
widening of the world,   part

to find my own, my secret
hiding sense and place, where from afar
all voices and scenes come back

—the barking of a dog,   autumnal burnings,
far calls,   close calls—   the boy I was
calls out to me
here the man where I am   "Look!

I've been where you
most fear to be."

1984

JAMES DICKEY
1923–1997

JAMES DICKEY drew inspiration from the white, Southern social world of his upbringing and from the natural environment that he loved. Unlike poets who emphasized formal innovation, Dickey found excitement in the lives and minds of ordinary people. "A Birth," for example, explores the complex interrelations between memory and fantasy, and between consciousness and perception. "Falling" imagines a more sensational story: the fatal fall from an airplane of a young female flight attendant. "The Sheep Child," derived from oral legend, is equally disturbing. It evokes a doomed being who speaks from the transgressive border between the human and non-human orders. Whereas other poets of his era, such as Theodore Roethke and Robert Lowell, sometimes examined extreme emotional states that appeared to be their own, Dickey was more apt to imagine the extreme experiences of others. Belonging to no poetic movement, his poems engage with the traditions of Southern fiction, exemplified by such writers as William Faulkner and Flannery O'Connor.

Dickey was born in Buckhead, Georgia, a suburb of Atlanta. He served in a Night Fighter Squadron in World War II, flying dangerous missions over Japan.

After marrying and receiving his B.A. and M.A. degrees in English from Vanderbilt University, he was recalled to military service for the Korean War. He subsequently worked in an advertising agency and taught English at various colleges, ending up as an honored poet-in-residence at the University of South Carolina. His volumes of poetry received wide acclaim, and his shocking novel, *Deliverance* (1972), became a best-seller and the basis for a motion picture. He was a major figure in American culture for thirty years before his death from lung disease at the age of seventy-four.

On the one hand, Dickey was a gifted, charismatic, and award-winning poet who mesmerized audiences and who was chosen to read at President Jimmy Carter's inaugural celebration. But on the other hand, he was an alcoholic who lived a chaotic life and engaged in outrageous behavior. He recognized his inner contradictions and convinced himself that they were necessary—that in order to create poetry, you must "make a monster out of your own mind." As quoted by Henry Hart, he claimed that writers consume alcohol first to aid the monster and then to get rid of him. "But by that time," he said, "the monster is so highly developed he cannot be got rid of." Yet despite his destructive descent, he produced poems about ecstasy and redemption, and they shine brightly today, long after the turmoil of his life ceased.

FURTHER READING

Ronald Baughman. *Understanding James Dickey*. Columbia: University of South Carolina Press, 1985.

Christopher Dickey. *Summer of Deliverance: A Memoir of Father and Son*. New York: Touchstone/Simon and Schuster, 1999.

James Dickey. *Deliverance*. Boston: Houghton Mifflin, 1970.

———. *The James Dickey Reader*. Ed. Henry Hart. New York: Touchstone/Simon and Schuster, 1999.

———. *Self-Interviews*. Baton Rouge: Louisiana State University Press, 1984.

Henry Hart. *James Dickey: The World as a Lie*. New York: Picador/St. Martin's, 2000.

Robert Kirschten. *James Dickey and the Gentle Ecstasy of Earth*. Baton Rouge: Louisiana State University Press, 1988.

A Birth

Inventing a story with grass,
I find a young horse deep inside it.
I cannot nail wires around him;
My fence posts fail to be solid,

And he is free, strangely, without me.
With his head still browsing the greenness,

He walks slowly out of the pasture
To enter the sun of his story.

My mind freed of its own creature,
I find myself deep in my life
In a room with my child and my mother,
When I feel the sun climbing my shoulder

Change, to include a new horse.

1962

Falling

A 29-year-old stewardess fell . . . to her death tonight
when she was swept through an emergency door
that suddenly sprang open. . . . The body . . . was
found . . . three hours after the accident.
  —*New York Times*

The states when they black out and lie there rolling   when they turn
To something transcontinental   move by   drawing moonlight out of the great
One-sided stone hung off the starboard wingtip   some sleeper next to
An engine is groaning for coffee   and there is faintly coming in
Somewhere the vast beast-whistle of space. In the galley with its racks
Of trays   she rummages for a blanket   and moves in her slim tailored
Uniform to pin it over the cry at the top of the door. As though she blew

The door down with a silent blast from her lungs   frozen   she is black
Out finding herself   with the plane nowhere and her body taking by the throat
The undying cry of the void   falling   living   beginning to be something
That no one has ever been and lived through   screaming without enough air
Still neat   lipsticked   stockinged   girdled by regulation   her hat
Still on   her arms and legs in no world   and yet spaced also strangely
With utter placid rightness on thin air   taking her time   she holds it
In many places   and now, still thousands of feet from her death she seems
To slow   she develops interest   she turns in her maneuverable body

To watch it. She is hung high up in the overwhelming middle of things in her
Self   in low body-whistling wrapped intensely   in all her dark dance-weight
Coming down from a marvellous leap   with the delaying, dumfounding ease
Of a dream of being drawn   like endless moonlight to the harvest soil
Of a central state of one's country   with a great gradual warmth coming

Over her　　floating　　finding more and more breath in what she has been using
For breath　　as the levels become more human　　seeing clouds placed honestly
Below her left and right　　riding slowly toward them　　she clasps it all
To her and can hang her hands and feet in it in peculiar ways　　and
Her eyes opened wide by wind, can open her mouth as wide　　wider and suck
All the heat from the cornfields　　can go down on her back with a feeling
Of stupendous pillows stacked under her　　and can turn　　turn as to someone
In bed　　smile, understood in darkness　　can go away　　slant　　slide
Off tumbling　　into the emblem of a bird with its wings half-spread
Or whirl madly on herself　　in endless gymnastics in the growing warmth
Of wheatfields rising toward the harvest moon.　　There is time to live
In superhuman health　　seeing mortal unreachable lights far down seeing
An ultimate highway with one late priceless car probing it　　arriving
In a square town　　and off her starboard arm the glitter of water catches
The moon by its one shaken side　　scaled, roaming silver　　My God it is good
And evil　　lying in one after another of all the positions for love
Making　　dancing　　sleeping　　and now cloud wisps at her no
Raincoat　　no matter　　all small towns brokenly brighter from inside
Cloud　　she walks over them like rain　　bursts out to behold a Greyhound
Bus shooting light through its sides　　it is the signal to go straight
Down like a glorious diver　　then feet first　　her skirt stripped beautifully
Up　　her face in fear-scented cloths　　her legs deliriously bare　　then
Arms out　　she slow-rolls over　　steadies out　　waits for something great
To take control of her　　trembles near feathers　　planes head-down
The quick movements of bird-necks turning her head　　gold eyes　　the insight-
eyesight of owls blazing into the hencoops　　a taste for chicken overwhelming
Her　　the long-range vision of hawks enlarging all human lights of cars
Freight trains　　looped bridges　　enlarging the moon racing slowly
Through all the curves of a river　　all the darks of the midwest blazing
From above. A rabbit in a bush turns white　　the smothering chickens
Huddle　　for over them there is still time for something to live
With the streaming half-idea of a long stoop　　a hurtling　　a fall
That is controlled　　that plummets as it wills　　turns gravity
Into a new condition, showing its other side like a moon　　shining
New Powers　　there is still time to live on a breath made of nothing
But the whole night　　time for her to remember to arrange her skirt
Like a diagram of a bat　　tightly it guides her　　she has this flying-skin
Made of garments　　and there are also those sky-divers on TV　　sailing
In sunlight　　smiling under their goggles　　swapping batons back and forth
And He who jumped without a chute and was handed one by a diving
Buddy. She looks for her grinning companion　　white teeth　　nowhere

She is screaming   singing hymns   her thin human wings spread out
From her neat shoulders   the air beast-crooning to her   warbling
And she can no longer behold the huge partial form of the world   now
She is watching her country lose its evoked master shape   watching it lose
And gain   get back its houses and peoples   watching it bring up
Its local lights   single homes   lamps on barn roofs   if she fell
Into water she might live   like a diver   cleaving   perfect   plunge

Into another   heavy silver   unbreathable   slowing   saving
Element: there is water   there is time to perfect all the fine
Points of diving   feet together   toes pointed   hands shaped right
To insert her into water like a needle   to come out healthily dripping
And be handed a Coca-Cola   there they are   there are the waters
Of life   the moon packed and coiled in a reservoir   so let me begin
To plane across the night air of Kansas   opening my eyes superhumanly
Bright   to the damned moon   opening the natural wings of my jacket
By Don Loper[1]   *moving like a hunting owl toward the glitter of water*
One cannot just fall   *just tumble screaming all that time   one must use*
It   she is now through with all   through all   clouds   damp   hair
Straightened   the last wisp of fog pulled apart on her face like wool revealing
New darks   new progressions of headlights along dirt roads   from chaos

And night   a gradual warming   a new-made, inevitable world of one's own
Country   a great stone of light in its waiting waters   hold   hold out
For water: who knows when what correct young woman must take up her body
And fly   and head for the moon-crazed inner eye of midwest imprisoned
Water   stored up for her for years   the arms of her jacket slipping
Air up her sleeves to go   all over her? What final things can be said
Of one who starts out sheerly in her body in the high middle of night
Air   to track down water like a rabbit where it lies like life itself
Off to the right in Kansas? She goes toward   the blazing-bare lake
Her skirts neat   her hands and face warmed more and more by the air
Rising from pastures of beans   and under her   under chenille[2]   bedspreads
The farm girls are feeling the goddess in them struggle and rise brooding
On the scratch-shining posts of the bed   dreaming of female signs
Of the moon   male blood like iron   of what is really said by the moan
Of airliners passing over them at dead of midwest midnight   passing
Over brush fires   burning out in silence on little hills   and will wake

1. Loper (1906–1972) was a well-known costume   2. Soft, puffy fabric.
designer of the 1940s through the 1960s. He
modernized the outfit worn by flight attendants.

To see the woman they should be   struggling on the rooftree to become
Stars: for her the ground is closer   water is nearer   she passes
It   then banks   turns   her sleeves fluttering differently as she rolls
Out to face the east, where the sun shall come up from wheatfields she must
Do something with water   fly to it   fall in it   drink it   rise
From it   but there is none left upon earth   the clouds have drunk it back
The plants have sucked it down   there are standing toward her only
The common fields of death   she comes back from flying to falling
Returns to a powerful cry   the silent scream with which she blew down
The coupled door of the airliner   nearly   nearly losing hold
Of what she has done   remembers   remembers the shape at the heart
Of cloud   fashionably swirling   remembers she still has time to die
Beyond explanation. Let her now take off her hat in summer air the contour
Of cornfields   and have enough time to kick off her one remaining
Shoe with the toes   of the other foot   to unhook her stockings
With calm fingers, noting how fatally easy it is to undress in midair
Near death   when the body will assume without effort any position
Except the one that will sustain it   enable it to rise   live
Not die   nine farms hover close   widen   eight of them separate, leaving
One in the middle   then the fields of that farm do the same   there is no
Way to back off   from her chosen ground   but she sheds the jacket
With its silver sad impotent wings   sheds the bat's guiding tailpiece
Of her skirt   the lightning-charged clinging of her blouse   the intimate
Inner flying-garment of her slip in which she rides like the holy ghost
Of a virgin   sheds the long windsocks of her stockings   absurd
Brassiere   then feels the girdle required by regulations squirming
Off her: no longer monobuttocked   she feels the girdle flutter   shake
In her hand   and float   upward   her clothes rising off her ascending
Into cloud   and fights away from her head the last sharp dangerous shoe
Like a dumb bird   and now will drop in   SOON   now will drop

In like this   the greatest thing that ever came to Kansas   down from all
Heights   all levels of American breath   layered in the lungs from the frail
Chill of space to the loam where extinction slumbers in corn tassels thickly
And breathes like rich farmers counting: will come along them after
Her last superhuman act   the last slow careful passing of her hands
All over her unharmed body   desired by every sleeper in his dream:
Boys finding for the first time their loins filled with heart's blood
Widowed farmers whose hands float under light covers to find themselves
Arisen at sunrise   the splendid position of blood unearthly drawn
Toward clouds   all feel something   pass over them as she passes
Her palms over *her* long legs   *her* small breasts   and deeply between

Her thighs   her hair shot loose from all pins   streaming in the wind
Of her body   let her come openly   trying at the last second to land
On her back   This is it   THIS
                              All those who find her impressed
In the soft loam   gone down   driven well into the image of her body
The furrows for miles flowing in upon her where she lies very deep
In her mortal outline   in the earth as it is in cloud   can tell nothing
But that she is there   inexplicable   unquestionable   and remember
That something broke in them as well   and began to live and die more
When they walked for no reason into their fields to where the whole earth
Caught her   interrupted her maiden flight   told her how to lie she cannot
Turn   go away   cannot move   cannot slide off it and assume another
Position   no sky-diver with any grin could save her   hold her in his arms
Plummet with her   unfold above her his wedding silks   she can no longer
Mark the rain with whirling women that take the place of a dead wife
Or the goddess in Norwegian farm girls   or all the back-breaking whores
Of Wichita. All the known air above her is not giving up quite one
Breath it is all gone   and yet not dead   not anywhere else
Quite   lying still in the field on her back   sensing the smells
Of incessant growth try to lift her   a little sight left in the corner
Of one eye   fading   seeing something wave   lies believing
That she could have made it   at the best part of her brief goddess
State   to water   gone in headfirst   come out smiling   invulnerable
Girl in a bathing-suit ad   but she is lying like a sunbather at the last
Of moonlight   half-buried in her impact on the earth   not far
From a railroad trestle   a water tank   she could see if she could
Raise her head from her modest hole   with her clothes beginning
To come down all over Kansas   into bushes   on the dewy sixth green
Of a golf course   one shoe   her girdle coming down fantastically
On a clothesline, where it belongs   her blouse on a lightning rod:

Lies in the fields   in *this* field   on her broken back as though on
A cloud she cannot drop through   while farmers sleepwalk without
Their women from houses   a walk like falling toward the far waters
Of life   in moonlight   toward the dreamed eternal meaning of their farms
Toward the flowering of the harvest in their hands   that tragic cost
Feels herself go   go toward   go outward   breathes at last fully
Not   and tries   less   once   tries   tries   AH, GOD—

                                                    1967

In *Self-Interviews*, Dickey explained that "Falling" is "a record of the way [the stewardess] feels as she falls: panic at first and then a kind of goddess-like invulnerability." Scholar

Robert Kirschten adds: "To see how the stewardess' 'brief goddess / State' is linked to those Midwesterners above whom she falls, we may best read 'Falling' not simply as an accidental spectacular fall from a plane but as a ritual reenactment of the primitive practice of killing a god of vegetation to ensure both the perpetuation of crops and the continuation of the human species itself."

The Sheep Child

Farm boys wild to couple[1]
With anything   with soft-wooded trees
With mounds of earth   mounds
Of pinestraw   will keep themselves off
Animals by legends of their own:
In the hay-tunnel dark
And dung of barns, they will
Say   I have heard tell

That in a museum in Atlanta
Way back in a corner somewhere
There's this thing that's only half
Sheep   like a woolly baby
Pickled in alcohol   because
Those things can't live   his eyes
Are open   but you can't stand to look
I heard from somebody who . . .

But this is now almost all
Gone. The boys have taken
Their own true wives in the city,
The sheep are safe in the west hill
Pasture   but we who were born there
Still are not sure. Are we,
Because we remember, remembered
In the terrible dust of museums?

Merely with his eyes, the sheep-child may

Be saying   saying

I am here, in my father's house.
I who am half of your world, came deeply

1. To join in sexual union.

To my mother in the long grass
Of the west pasture, where she stood like moonlight
Listening for foxes. It was something like love
From another world that seized her
From behind, and she gave, not lifting her head
Out of dew, without ever looking, her best
Self to that great need. Turned loose, she dipped her face
Farther into the chill of the earth, and in a sound
Of sobbing   of something stumbling
Away, began, as she must do,
To carry me. I woke, dying,

In the summer sun of the hillside, with my eyes
Far more than human. I saw for a blazing moment
The great grassy world from both sides,
Man and beast in the round of their need,
And the hill wind stirred in my wool,
My hoof and my hand clasped each other,
I ate my one meal
Of milk, and died
Staring. From dark grass I came straight

To my father's house, whose dust
Whirls up in the halls for no reason
When no one comes   piling deep in a hellish mild corner,
And, through my immortal waters,
I meet the sun's grains eye
To eye, and they fail at my closet of glass.
Dead, I am most surely living
In the minds of farm boys: I am he who drives
Them like wolves from the hound bitch and calf
And from the chaste ewe[2] in the wind.
They go into woods   into bean fields   they go
Deep into their known right hands. Dreaming of me,
They groan   they wait   they suffer
Themselves, they marry, they raise their kind.

1967

Dickey's biographer, Henry Hart, suggests that "The Sheep Child" uses "a legend about sex with animals to dramatize the origin of sexual taboos and to show how a fear of breaking taboos drove men toward civilized institutions like marriage."

2. A female sheep.

DENISE LEVERTOV
1923–1997

Denise Levertov dedicated her career to exploring connections among nations, cultures, and spiritual traditions. Levertov was born in Ilford, England, to a Welsh mother with roots in Christian mysticism and a father, Paul Levertoff, who was a Russian Hasidic Jew who migrated from Germany to the United Kingdom and became an Anglican priest. Her father's published writings in the field of theology study the common ground between Judaism and Christianity. Levertov investigates these Christian and Jewish spiritual connections in her early poem "Illustrious Ancestors." She was educated by her family at home and, aside from ballet lessons, never attended formal schooling. Levertov served as a civilian nurse during the German bombing of London in World War II. In 1948 she moved to the United States, having married the American writer Mitchell Goodman the previous year. She eventually divorced Goodman in 1974.

Although Levertov had announced her intention to become a writer at age five, she did not find her own voice until, after publishing two volumes of verse in a traditional vein, she began to identify closely with modern and contemporary movements in American poetry (she had become a naturalized American citizen in 1955). Of central importance were her discovery of the work of the New Jersey poet William Carlos Williams and her artistic alliance with the poets of the Black Mountain school, including, most notably, Robert Duncan. Levertov and Duncan, who saw one another as "companions in art," carried on an extensive and distinguished correspondence, ultimately published in 2004 as *The Letters of Robert Duncan and Denise Levertov.*

In the 1960s, Levertov—as evident in poems such as "What Were They Like?"—became deeply involved with resistance to the Vietnam War, a stance that caused eventual strain in her artistic relationship with Duncan, who also opposed the war but disapproved of poetry that was overtly political. Other poems, such as "A Solitude" and the later "A Woman Alone," sensitively explore the exquisite balance an individual in search of self-realization must strike between self-sufficiency and human connection. At its best, Levertov's work is marked by acute observation and a flowing, conversational style that imparts feeling with great naturalness, poise, spontaneity, and simplicity. Her poems glide gracefully between the sensual and the spiritual.

In her later years, Levertov became a successful college and university teacher, working first in the Boston area at Brandeis University, MIT, and Tufts. She then moved to the West Coast, where she taught at the University of Washington before concluding her teaching career with a professorship at Stanford University from 1982 to 1993. When Levertov died in 1997 of complications from lymphoma, she left behind more than thirty volumes of poetry.

FURTHER READING

Denise Levertov. *Collected Earlier Poems, 1940–1960*. New York: New Directions, 1979.
——— and Robert Duncan. *The Letters of Robert Duncan and Denise Levertov*. Ed. Robert J. Bertholf and Albert Gelpi. Palo Alto: Stanford University Press, 2003.
———. *Selected Poems*. New York: New Directions, 1986.

Illustrious Ancestors

The Rav[1]
of Northern White Russia declined,
in his youth, to learn the
language of birds, because
the extraneous did not interest him; nevertheless
when he grew old it was found
he understood them anyway, having
listened well, and as it is said, 'prayed
      with the bench and the floor.' He used
what was at hand—as did
Angel Jones of Mold,[2] whose meditations
were sewn into coats and britches.
      Well, I would like to make,
thinking some line still taut between me and them,
poems direct as what the birds said,
hard as a floor, sound as a bench,
mysterious as the silence when the tailor
would pause with his needle in the air.

         1958

"Illustrious Ancestors" meditates on Levertov's connections, as a poet, to the well-known Russian Jewish mystic and the noted Welsh Christian mystic from whom she was descended on her father's and mother's sides.

1. Shneur Zalman (1745–1813), who founded the Habad branch of Hasidic Judaism, was, as Levertov noted, "my father's great-grandfather."

2. A Welsh mystic, by trade a tailor, and an ancestor of Levertov's mother.

To the Reader

As you read, a white bear leisurely
pees, dyeing the snow
saffron,

and as you read, many gods
lie among lianas:[1] eyes of obsidian
are watching the generations of leaves,

and as you read
the sea is turning its dark pages,
turning
its dark pages.

1961

A Solitude

A blind man. I can stare at him
ashamed, shameless. Or does he know it?
No, he is in a great solitude.

O, strange joy,
to gaze my fill at a stranger's face.
No, my thirst is greater than before.

In his world he is speaking
almost aloud. His lips move.
Anxiety plays about them. And now joy

of some sort trembles into a smile.
A breeze I can't feel
crosses that face as if it crossed water.

The train moves uptown, pulls in and
pulls out of the local stops. Within its loud
jarring movement a quiet,

*   *   *

---

1. Climbing vines found in the canopy of tropical forests. Obsidian: a shiny volcanic glass, usually black.

the quiet of people not speaking,
some of them eyeing the blind man,
only a moment though, not thirsty like me,

and within that quiet his
different quiet, not quiet at all, a tumult
of images, but what are his images,

he is blind? He doesn't care
that he looks strange, showing
his thoughts on his face like designs of light

flickering on water, for he doesn't know
what **look** is.
I see he has never seen.

And now he rises, he stands at the door ready,
knowing his station is next. Was he counting?
No, that was not his need.

When he gets out I get out.
'Can I help you towards the exit?'
'Oh, alright.' An indifference.

But instantly, even as he speaks,
even as I hear indifference, his hand
goes out, waiting for me to take it,

and now we hold hands like children.
His hand is warm and not sweaty,
the grip firm, it feels good.

And when we have passed through the turnstile,
he going first, his hand at once
waits for mine again.

'Here are the steps. And here we turn
to the right. More stairs now.' We go
up into sunlight. He feels that,

      *   *   *

the soft air. 'A nice day,
isn't it?' says the blind man. Solitude
walks with me, walks

beside me, he is not with me, he continues
his thoughts alone. But his hand and mine
know one another,

it's as if my hand were gone forth
on its own journey. I see him
across the street, the blind man,

and now he says he can find his way. He knows
where he is going, it is nowhere, it is filled
with presences. He says, **I am**.

1961

What Were They Like?

1) Did the people of Viet Nam
   use lanterns of stone?
2) Did they hold ceremonies
   to reverence the opening of buds?
3) Were they inclined to quiet laughter?
4) Did they use bone and ivory,
   jade and silver, for ornament?
5) Had they an epic poem?
6) Did they distinguish between speech and singing?

1) Sir, their light hearts turned to stone.
   It is not remembered whether in gardens
   stone gardens illumined pleasant ways.
2) Perhaps they gathered once to delight in blossom,
   but after their children were killed
   there were no more buds.
3) Sir, laughter is bitter to the burned mouth.
4) A dream ago, perhaps. Ornament is for joy.
   All the bones were charred.

5) It is not remembered. Remember,
   most were peasants; their life
   was in rice and bamboo.
   When peaceful clouds were reflected in the paddies
   and the water buffalo stepped surely along terraces,
   maybe fathers told their sons old tales.
   When bombs smashed those mirrors
   there was time only to scream.
6) There is an echo yet
   of their speech which was like a song.
   It was reported their singing resembled
   the flight of moths in moonlight.
   Who can say? It is silent now.

1967

In 1965, the United States Air Force began a sustained bombing campaign aimed at targets in North Vietnam. By the time this campaign—which fostered widespread protest in the United States and elsewhere—ended three years later, North Vietnam had suffered 72,000 civilian casualties, according to Pentagon estimates.

A Woman Alone

When she cannot be sure
which of two lovers it was with whom she felt
this or that moment of pleasure, of something fiery
streaking from head to heels, the way the white
flame of a cascade streaks a mountainside
seen from a car across a valley, the car
changing gear, skirting a precipice,
climbing . . .
When she can sit or walk for hours after a movie
talking earnestly and with bursts of laughter
with friends, without worrying
that it's late, dinner at midnight, her time
spent without counting the change . . .
When half her bed is covered with books
and no one is kept awake by the reading light
and she disconnects the phone, to sleep till noon . . .

Then
self-pity dries up, a joy
untainted by guilt lifts her.
She has fears, but not about loneliness;
fears about how to deal with the aging
of her body—how to deal
with photographs and the mirror. She feels
so much younger and more beautiful
than she looks. At her happiest
—or even in the midst of
some less than joyful hour, sweating
patiently through a heatwave in the city
or hearing the sparrows at daybreak, dully gray,
toneless, the sound of fatigue—
a kind of sober euphoria makes her believe
in her future as an old woman, a wanderer
seamed and brown,
little luxuries of the middle of life all gone,
watching cities and rivers, people and mountains,
without being watched; not grim nor sad,
an old winedrinking woman, who knows
the old roads, grass-grown, and laughs to herself . . .
She knows it can't be:
that's Mrs. Doasyouwouldbedoneby[1] from
                                        The Water Babies,
no one can walk the world any more,
a world of fumes and decibels.
But she thinks maybe
she could get to be tough and wise, some way,
anyway. Now at least
she is past the time of mourning,
now she can say without shame or deceit,
O blessed Solitude.

                                                    1978

---

1. In Charles Kingsley's fairy tale *The Water Babies* (1863), a gentle caretaker of children and "the loveliest fairy in the world."

The May Mornings

May mornings wear
light cashmere shawls of quietness,
brush back waterfalls of
burnished silk from
clear and round brows.
When we see them approaching
over lawns, trailing
dewdark shadows and footprints,
we remember, ah
yes, the May mornings,
how could we have forgotten,
what solace
it would be in the bitter violence
of fire then ice again we
apprehend—but
it seems the May mornings
are a presence known
only as they pass
light stepped, seriously smiling, bearing
each a leaflined basket
of wakening flowers.

1982

MITSUYE YAMADA
b. 1923

Poet, short story writer, feminist, activist, and teacher, Mitsuye Yamada explores themes of human rights and self-development in a conflict-ridden world. Her work combines the personal revelation associated with the confessional poets with the insistence on gender and ethnic equality central to many multicultural poets. As Traise Yamamoto has written, Yamada's project is one of "reclaiming denied subjectivity," and this project involves "collective recovery through personal experience." Yamada moves the Asian-American female subject into a space where she may speak for herself. Highlighting her social identity as an Asian American and a woman, she uses her poetry to instantiate an ethic of interpersonal justice and care.

Yamada was born in Kyushu, Japan, while her mother, a Japanese American, was visiting Japan. She immigrated to the United States with her mother at the age of two, growing up with her parents and three brothers in Seattle. During World War II, her father (an interpreter for the U.S. Immigration Service) was falsely charged with espionage, and she (then nineteen) and the rest of her family were interned for two years at Camp Minidoka, Idaho. After internment, Yamada attended the University of Cincinnati, New York University (from which she received a B.A. in English and art), and the University of Chicago (from which she received an M.A. in English). She married a research chemist, had four children, and worked as a professor of English at Cypress College in California and as a visiting associate professor of Asian American studies at the University of California, Irvine. She has served on the board of directors of Amnesty International and the Interfaith Prisoner of Conscience Project, and she founded the Multicultural Women Writers group of Orange County, California.

In her internment poetry Yamada mourns the trauma of racism. In her post-internment poetry she reflects on the persistent effects of racism and patriarchy on those who have suffered from them. Her mourning does not turn into paralyzing melancholy but rather yields activism and wisdom. Her poetry ties remembrance to insight, recovery, and social change.

FURTHER READING

Helen Jasoski. "A MELUS Interview: Mitsuye Yamada." *MELUS* 15:1 (Spring 1988): 97–107.

Allie Light and Irving Saraf, producers. *Mitsuye and Nellie: Asian American Poets*. PBS documentary. San Francisco: Light-Saraf Films, 1981.

Karen L. Polster. "Mitsuye Yamada." In *Contemporary American Women Poets: An A-to-Z Guide*, ed. Catherine Cucinella. Westport, Conn.: Greenwood Press, 2002.

Mitsuye Yamada. *Camp Notes and Other Writings*. New Brunswick, N.J.: Rutgers University Press, 1998.

———, Merle Woo, and Nellie Wong. *Three Asian American Writers Speak Out on Feminism*. Columbia, S.C.: Red Letter Press, 2003.

Traise Yamamoto. *Masking Selves, Making Subjects: Japanese American Women, Identity, and the Body*. Berkeley: University of California Press, 1999.

What Your Mother Tells You

haha ga ima yu-koto
sono uchi ni
wakatte kuru

*   *   *

What your mother tells you now
in time
you will come to know.

1976

The first three lines of this poem represent the mother's words in Japanese, and the second three lines are the daughter's English translation. This poem begins the first section of Yamada's *Camp Notes*, a section titled "My Issei Parents, Twice Pioneers, Now I Hear Them."

Evacuation

As we boarded the bus
bags on both sides
(I had never packed
two bags before
on a vacation
lasting forever)
the *Seattle Times*
photographer said
Smile!
so obediently I smiled
and the caption the next day
read:

Note smiling faces
a lesson to Tokyo.

1976

In this poem, the speaker and her family are being forcibly removed from their home in Seattle and transported to a concentration camp at Minidoka, Idaho, during World War II. The following two poems evoke their life in the camp.

Harmony at the Fair Grounds

Why is the soldier boy in a cage
like that?
In the freedom of the child's
universe
the uniformed guard

stood trapped in his outside cage.
We walked away from the gate and
grated guard
on sawdusted grounds
where millions trod once
to view prize cows
at the Puyallup Fair.

They gave us straws to sleep on
encased in muslin ticks.
Some of us were stalled under grandstand
seats
the egg with
parallel lines.[1]

Lines formed for food
lines for showers
lines for the john
lines for shots.

1976

Block 4 Barrack 4 Apt C

The barbed fence
protected us
from wildly twisted
sagebrush.
Some were taken
by old men with gnarled
hands.
These sinewed branches
were rubbed and polished
shiny with sweat and body oil.

They creeped on
under and around our coffee table
with apple crate stands.

✳   ✳   ✳

---

1. That is, the grandstand was egg shaped.

Lives spilled over us
through plaster walls
came mixed voices.
Bared too
a pregnant wife
while her man played *go*
all day
she sobbed alone
and a barracksful
of ears shed tears.

1976

Thirty Years Under

I had packed up
my wounds in a cast
iron box
sealed it
labeled it
do not open . . .
ever . . .

and traveled blind
for thirty years

until one day I heard
a black man with huge bulbous eyes
say
there is nothing more
humiliating
more than beatings
more than curses
than being spat on

like a dog.

1976

Many years after internment and release, the speaker of this poem hears a chance comment by an African-American stranger that enables her to uncover a long-repressed memory. The painful memory itself is evoked in the following poem, which takes place just
after Yamada left the internment camp to attend the University of Cincinnati. The year
is 1944.

Cincinnati

Freedom at last
in this town aimless
I walked against the rush
hour traffic
My first day
in a real city
where

no one knew me.

No one except one
hissing voice that said
dirty jap
warm spittle on my right cheek.
I turned and faced
the shop window
and my spittled face
spilled onto a hill
of books.
Words on display.

In Government Square
people criss-crossed
the street
like the spokes of
a giant wheel.

I lifted my right hand
but it would not obey me.
My other hand fumbled
for a hankie.

My tears would not
wash it. They stopped
and parted.
My hankie brushed
the forked
tears and spittle
together.
I edged toward the curb

loosened my fisthold
and the bleached laced
mother-ironed hankie blossomed in
the gutter atop teeth marked
gum wads and heeled candy wrappers.

Everyone knew me.

1976

Mirror Mirror

People keep asking where I come from
says my son.
Trouble is   I'm american on the inside
         and oriental on the outside

         No Kai
         Turn that outside in
         THIS is what American looks like

1976

Drowning in My Own Language

         My world is a brain
         shaped island encrusted
         from decades of crevices
         rumblings seethe
         without cracking

         the open half
         of me is
         sinking on a small
         land mass into the sea

         as I watch rows
         of animated people in
         white suits
         converse on dry
         land inches away with
         out seeing

me single-handed
clawing
my way up grasping
exposed root ends
crying
out
slow
ly
still
sinking

tas-keh-tehhh[1]
wrong language
the line of white heels
in half
moons over my head
fade away
waves scoop
more land
I look
round-eyed fish
in the mouth

helllllllllllp

still
wrong language

I will come up for air
in another language
all my own.

                    1988

Compare this poem to Adrienne Rich's "Diving into the Wreck" (included in this anthology).

---

1. A cry for help (Japanese).

ROBERT CREELEY
1926–2005

Robert creeley was deeply involved in exploring the unfolding texture of individual emotion as conveyed through the possibilities of language. His poems, which have been characterized as "short, terse and poignant," reflect an affinity for and extension of contemporary verse experimentalism and of the potentialities for verse created by such masters of jazz as Charlie Parker, who Creeley acknowledged helped shape his work "in his uses of silence, in his rhythmic structure." For Creeley, poetry was a mode of perception as much as—or more than—it was a mode of expression. It recorded the nuances of experience and self-knowledge in intricate rhythms and pregnant pauses. He compressed this view into his dictum, "Form is never more than an extension of content," which strongly influenced Charles Olson and other innovative poets of his time. As poet Charles Bernstein has observed, Creeley also adduced the trenchant corollary, "Content is never more than the extension of form."

Creeley lost his father, a medical doctor, when he was very young, and he was raised by his mother in rural Afton, Massachusetts. He later confessed a lingering affinity for small-town America. After two earlier stints at Harvard University and a term in the American Field Service in Burma during World War II, Creeley in 1955 earned a bachelor's degree from Black Mountain College, where he would later teach, and where he developed important lifelong connections with poets such as Charles Olson and Robert Duncan, and shortly thereafter with Allen Ginsberg. Creeley also corresponded frequently with such elder poets as William Carlos Williams, Louis Zukofsky, and Ezra Pound, whose work he published in various little magazines. In 1967, Creeley joined the English faculty at the University at Buffalo (sometimes referred to as Black Mountain II), where he served as an influential teacher until 2003. When he died in 2005, Creeley left behind an important legacy as an avant-garde poet, poetic theorist, editor, and mentor to many younger poets.

FURTHER READING

Robert Creeley. *Collected Essays*. Berkeley: University of California Press, 1989.
———. *Collected Prose*. Cmampaign, IL: Dalkey Archive Press, 2001.
———. *Selected Poems, 1945–2005*. Ed. Benjamin Friedlander. Berkeley: University of California Press, 2008.
———. *Tales Out of School: Selected Interviews*. Ann Arbor: University of Michigan Press, 1993.
Stephen Fredman and Steve McCaffery, eds. *Form, Power and Person in Robert Creeley's Life and Work*. Iowa City: University of Iowa Press, 2010.

The Rain

All night the sound had
come back again,
and again falls
this quiet, persistent rain.

What am I to myself
that must be remembered,
insisted upon
so often? Is it

that never the ease,
even the hardness,
of rain falling
will have for me

something other than this,
something not so insistent—
am I to be locked in this
final uneasiness.

Love, if you love me,
lie next to me.
Be for me, like rain,
the getting out

of the tiredness, the fatuousness, the semi-
lust of intentional indifference.
Be wet
with a decent happiness.

                                        1962

For No Clear Reason

I dreamt last night
the fright was over, that
the dust came, and then water,
and women and men, together
again, and all was quiet
in the dim moon's light.

        *   *   *

A paean of such patience—
laughing, laughing at me,
and the days extend over
the earth's great cover,
grass, trees, and flower-
ing season, for no clear reason.

1962

The Flower

I think I grow tensions
like flowers
in a wood where
nobody goes.

Each wound is perfect,
encloses itself in a tiny
imperceptible blossom,
making pain.

Pain is a flower like that one,
like this one,
like that one,
like this one.

1962

The Language

Locate *I*
love you some-
where in

teeth and
eyes, bite
it but

take care not
to hurt, you
want so

⁂

much so
little. Words
say everything

I
love you
again,

then what
is emptiness
for. To

fill, fill.
I heard words
and words full

of holes
aching. Speech
is a mouth.
1967

ALLEN GINSBERG
1926–1997

ALLEN GINSBERG, perhaps the best-known American poet after World War II, changed the face of poetry and culture. Bob Dylan has written that Ginsberg's "Howl" signaled "a new type of human existence." Declaiming his poems in coffeehouses and auditoriums, Ginsberg made himself a celebrity. He aligned poetic innovation with popular culture. He brought political dissidence into the poetic mainstream, and—along with such poets as Robert Lowell and Anne Sexton—he refashioned poetry to make it a medium for intimate self-disclosure. He was also the first public figure to bring an explicit self-representation as a homosexual into the center of American culture. A pioneer, a rebel, and an original, Ginsberg expanded the scope of poetry in both its public and its personal dimensions. He challenged and rocked American culture, and at the same time he used his charm and humor to achieve the popular approval he craved.

Born in Newark, New Jersey, to a family of Jewish-Russian immigrants, Ginsberg grew up in working-class Paterson. Already a rebel in elementary school, he adopted the slogan "Do what you want to when you want to." Reading Walt Whitman in high school only strengthened his iconoclastic character. Ginsberg's later position as both a community member and an outsider reflected his difficult early years. His father was a dutiful high school teacher and poet, whereas his mother, who suffered from schizophrenia, paranoia, and epilepsy, belonged to an idealistic wing of the American Communist Party and was obsessed with helping suffering workers. Ginsberg attended Columbia University on a scholarship, and after graduation he worked as a dishwasher, spot welder, member of the merchant marine, and book reviewer for *Newsweek* magazine. But, with the encouragement of his mentor William Carlos Williams, he devoted his life to poetry. After experiencing a hallucination in which the English poet William Blake spoke to him, he concentrated on establishing a new poetic movement, which he called "New Vision." In the 1950s, this movement transformed itself into what Jack Kerovac called "the Beat Generation," the era's noisiest and most creative opponents of Cold War conformity.

After a series of heterosexual and homosexual affairs, and time spent in a mental hospital, Ginsberg moved to San Francisco, where he worked as a market researcher and lived an openly gay life with his lover, the poet Peter Orlovsky. By the mid-1950s, the San Francisco Bay Area had become a vital center of Beat culture, and Ginsberg—along with novelists Jack Kerouac and William S. Burroughs and poet Diane DiPrima—was one of its leading lights. In 1955 he wrote and performed his Beat epic, "Howl," which had an immediate effect as a shocking and mesmerizing text. The next year, "Howl" was published, seized by authorities as obscene, and found by a court to have "redeeming social significance." The poem, published together with some shorter poems (including "A Supermarket in California," "Sunflower Sutra," and "America") in an inexpensive City Lights edition, was hugely successful. Ginsberg became a national celebrity, a position he was never to lose. Funny, provocative, thoughtful, personable, and fiercely independent, he transfixed the nation for the next thirty years.

In 1956, Ginsberg's mother, Naomi, died, after years of being in and out of mental hospitals. Ginsberg mourned the loss in his long poem, "Kaddish." He then continued to write and to travel, publishing his poems in inexpensive editions (and later in more conventional volumes); becoming a political spokesman for justice, equality, and peace; exploring Buddhist and other spiritual traditions; and, in the 1960s, making the transition from Beat to hippy culture. In the 1960s, he befriended such popular culture icons as the Beatles, the Rolling Stones, and especially Bob Dylan. John Lennon made a reference to Ginsberg in "Give

Peace a Chance." Ginsberg sang a duet with the Rolling Stones. He appeared with Dylan in videos, films, and concert tours. He was instrumental in the cross-fertilization of poetry with rock and roll in the 1960s and 1970s. Ginsberg also became a major figure in opposition to the Vietnam War, writing poems against the war (such as "Anti-Vietnam War Peace Mobilization"), appearing on television and in newspapers, and participating in protests and sit-ins.

The 1980s and 1990s were a quieter period for Ginsberg. In the 1980s, he traveled widely, taught at the Naropa Institute (a facility for education and spiritual awareness located in Boulder, Colorado), and continued to write poetry. His revolutionary zeal appeared to wane, though he never abandoned his devotion to peace and freedom causes. He continued to explore the intersections of poetry and popular culture, performing and recording many of his poems as songs (for example, on the album *New York Blues*)—featured in recordings by such rock groups as Rage Against the Machine, the Clash, Sonic Youth, and They Might Be Giants—and appearing in videos and films. In a Thansgiving episode of *The Simpsons*, Lisa Simpson paid homage to Ginsberg in her poem "Howl of the Unappreciated." By the 1990s, Ginsberg was living in New York and adopting an introspective mood in such late poems as "It's All So Brief" and "Yiddishe Kopf."

Ginsberg died at home of liver cancer at the age of seventy-one. The illness was the endgame of a case of hepatitis he had picked up during a visit to the Amazon while in his mid-twenties. Buddhist monks chanted in one corner of his room. Friends recited a Jewish prayer in another. Asked if he wanted to sleep, he answered, "Oh yes." They were his last words—a fitting conclusion to a life spent in the affirmative.

FURTHER READING

Graham Caveney. *Screaming with Joy: The Life of Allen Ginsberg*. New York: Broadway Books, 1999.
Ann Charters, ed. *The Portable Beat Reader*. New York: Penguin, 1992.
Allen Ginsberg. *Collected Poems, 1947–1997*. New York: HarperCollins, 2006.
———. *Deliberate Prose: Selected Essays, 1952–1995*. Ed. Bill Morgan. New York: HarperCollins, 2000.
———. *Howl: Original Draft Facsimile, Transcript & Variant Versions, Fully Annotated by Author*. Ed. Barry Miles. New York: Harper and Row, 1986.
———. *Letters*. Ed. Bill Morgan. New York: Da Capo Press, 2008.
———. *Spontaneous Mind: Selected Interviews, 1958–1996*. Ed. David Carter. New York: HarperCollins, 2001.
Bill Morgan. *I Celebrate Myself: The Somewhat Private Life of Allen Ginsberg*. New York: Viking, 2006.
Paul Portugés. *The Visionary Poetics of Allen Ginsberg*. Santa Barbara: Ross-Erikson, 1978.
Jonah Raskin. *American Scream: Allen Ginsberg's Howl and the Making of the Beat Generation*. Berkeley: University of California Press, 2004.
Michael Schumacher. *Dharma Lion: A Biography of Allen Ginsberg*. New York: St. Martin's Press, 1992.

Howl

For Carl Solomon[1]

I

I saw the best minds of my generation destroyed by madness, starving hysterical
>   naked,

dragging themselves through the negro streets at dawn looking for an angry fix,[2]

angelheaded hipsters burning for the ancient heavenly connection[3] to the
>   starry dynamo in the machinery of night,

who poverty and tatters and hollow-eyed and high sat up smoking in the
>   supernatural darkness of cold-water flats floating across the tops of cities
>   contemplating jazz,[4]

who bared their brains to Heaven under the El[5] and saw Mohammedan angels
>   staggering on tenement roofs illuminated,

who passed through universities with radiant cool eyes hallucinating Arkansas
>   and Blake-light tragedy among the scholars of war,[6]

who were expelled from the academies for crazy & publishing obscene odes on
>   the windows of the skull,[7]

who cowered in unshaven rooms in underwear, burning their money in
>   wastebaskets[8] and listening to the Terror through the wall,

who got busted in their pubic beards returning through Laredo[9] with a belt of
>   marijuana for New York,

who ate fire in paint hotels or drank turpentine in Paradise Alley,[10] death, or
>   purgatoried their torsos night after night

with dreams, with drugs, with waking nightmares, alcohol and cock and
>   endless balls,

1. Carl Solomon (1928–1993) was a fellow writer whom Ginsberg had met in 1949 in a mental institution. When Ginsberg began to write "Howl," he had just learned that Solomon was back in another mental hospital. Ginsberg intended the dedication as "a gesture of wild solidarity, a message into the asylum, a sort of heart's trumpet call."

2. Ginsberg's friend Herbert Huncke (1915–1997) "cruised Harlem and Times Square areas at irregular hours" seeking heroin (Ginsberg's note).

3. Ambiguously implying either a spiritual connection or a drug connection. Starry dynamo: an image "derived from Dylan Thomas's mixture of Nature and Machinery" (Ginsberg's note).

4. "The jazz was late bop Charlie Parker played in Bowery loft jam sessions in those years" (Ginsberg's note).

5. "Part of Manhattan's subway system, the Third Avenue elevated railway, one of those familiarly called the 'El,' was demolished in the mid-'50s" (Ginsberg's note).

6. "Refers to author's adventures at Columbia College" (Ginsberg's note). Ginsberg had a mystical vision while reading the poetry of William Blake (1757–1827) in 1948. In the 1940s, Columbia scientists worked on constructing the atom bomb.

7. Ginsberg was suspended twice from Columbia, once for writing obscenities in the grime on his dorm room window and once when he was confined to a psychiatric institution.

8. Solomon burned money "while upset about the evils of materialism" (Solomon's note).

9. City in Texas on the Mexican border.

10. A cold-water-flat courtyard in New York's Lower East Side, an area where Ginsberg and his friends lived and socialized in the late 1940s and early 1950s.

incomparable blind streets of shuddering cloud and lightning in the mind
   leaping toward poles of Canada & Paterson,[11] illuminating all the
   motionless world of Time between,

Peyote[12] solidities of halls, backyard green tree cemetery dawns, wine
   drunkenness over the rooftops, storefront boroughs of teahead joyride neon
   blinking traffic light, sun and moon and tree vibrations in the roaring winter
   dusks of Brooklyn, ashcan rantings and kind king light of mind,

who chained themselves to subways for the endless ride from Battery[13] to holy
   Bronx on benzedrine until the noise of wheels and children brought them
   down shuddering mouth-wracked and battered bleak of brain all drained of
   brilliance in the drear light of Zoo,

who sank all night in submarine light of Bickford's[14] floated out and sat through
   the stale beer afternoon in desolate Fugazzi's, listening to the crack of doom
   on the hydrogen jukebox,

who talked continuously seventy hours from park to pad to bar to Bellevue[15] to
   museum to the Brooklyn Bridge,

a lost battalion of platonic conversationalists jumping down the stoops[16] off fire
   escapes off windowsills off Empire State out of the moon,

yacketayakking screaming vomiting whispering facts and memories and
   anecdotes and eyeball kicks and shocks of hospitals and jails and wars,

whole intellects disgorged in total recall for seven days and nights with brilliant
   eyes, meat for the Synagogue cast on the pavement,

who vanished into nowhere Zen New Jersey leaving a trail of ambiguous
   picture postcards of Atlantic City Hall,

suffering Eastern sweats and Tangerian bone-grindings[17] and migraines of
   China under junk-withdrawal in Newark's bleak furnished room,

who wandered around and around at midnight in the railroad yard wondering
   where to go, and went, leaving no broken hearts,

11. New Jersey city where Ginsberg was born and which William Carlos Williams immortalized in his epic poem *Paterson*.

12. Cactus native to northern Mexico and southwestern United States that produces a stimulant drug used in religious ceremonials by some Indian peoples. Tree vibrations: "ref. author's first peyote experience" (Ginsberg's note).

13. The southern tip of Manhattan. The Battery and the Bronx were the southern and northern ends of a subway line. Zoo: the Bronx Zoo. This line was "a conscious attempt to go all the way from A to Z (Zoo)" (Ginsberg's note)—or perhaps, more precisely, from B to Z.

14. New York cafeteria where Ginsberg mopped floors. Fugazzi's: a bar in New York's bohemian Greenwich Village. Hydrogen jukebox: the phrase juxtaposes two very different contexts that were both central to the 1950s: nuclear bombs and popular music.

15. New York public hospital and psychiatric clinic. Ginsberg's friend Ruth "one day began a flight of talk in Washington Square that continued through the day and night for 72 hours until she was finally committed to Bellevue" (Ginsberg's note).

16. Front porches.

17. Reference to beat writer William S. Burroughs's heroin withdrawals in Tangiers, Morocco. Newark's bleak furnished room: Ginsberg's brother, Eugene Brooks, "lived in one such studying law, late forties" (Ginsberg's note).

who lit cigarettes in boxcars boxcars boxcars racketing through snow toward
lonesome farms in grandfather night,

who studied Plotinus[18] Poe St. John of the Cross telepathy and bop kabbalah
because the cosmos instinctively vibrated at their feet in Kansas,

who loned it through the streets of Idaho seeking visionary indian angels who
were visionary indian angels,

who thought they were only mad when Baltimore gleamed in supernatural
ecstasy,

who jumped in limousines with the Chinaman of Oklahoma on the impulse
of winter midnight streetlight smalltown rain,

who lounged hungry and lonesome through Houston seeking jazz or sex or
soup, and followed the brilliant Spaniard to converse about America and
Eternity, a hopeless task, and so took ship to Africa,

who disappeared into the volcanoes of Mexico leaving behind nothing but the
shadow of dungarees and the lava and ash of poetry scattered in fireplace
Chicago,

who reappeared on the West Coast investigating the FBI in beards and shorts
with big pacifist eyes sexy in their dark skin passing out incomprehensible
leaflets,

who burned cigarette holes in their arms protesting the narcotic tobacco haze
of Capitalism,

who distributed Supercommunist pamphlets in Union Square[19] weeping and
undressing while the sirens of Los Alamos wailed them down, and wailed
down Wall, and the Staten Island ferry also wailed,

who broke down crying in white gymnasiums naked and trembling before the
machinery of other skeletons,

who bit detectives in the neck and shrieked with delight in policecars
for committing no crime but their own wild cooking pederasty[20] and
intoxication,

who howled on their knees in the subway and were dragged off the roof waving
genitals and manuscripts,

who let themselves be fucked in the ass by saintly motorcyclists, and screamed
with joy,

who blew and were blown by those human seraphim, the sailors, caresses of
Atlantic and Caribbean love,

18. Ginsberg studied this mystical writer, and the others named, in college. Bop: a style of jazz developed in the late 1940s and early 1950s. Kabbalah: a Jewish mystical system of interpreting the Hebrew scriptures.

19. Public square in Manhattan, site of radical speeches and protests, especially in the 1930s. Los Alamos: laboratory in New Mexico where the atomic bomb was developed. Wall: Wall Street in New York, the nation's financial center, but at the same time the Wailing Wall (or Western Wall) in Jerusalem, a sacred spot where religious Jews gather in prayer.

20. Anal intercourse. Here the poem begins a frank evocation of sexuality, especially homosexuality.

who balled in the morning in the evenings in rosegardens and the grass of
    public parks and cemeteries scattering their semen freely to whomever
    come who may,

who hiccuped endlessly trying to giggle but wound up with a sob behind a
    partition in a Turkish Bath when the blond & naked angel came to pierce
    them with a sword,

who lost their loveboys to the three old shrews of fate[21] the one eyed shrew
    of the heterosexual dollar the one eyed shrew that winks out of the womb
    and the one eyed shrew that does nothing but sit on her ass and snip the
    intellectual golden threads of the craftsman's loom,

who copulated ecstatic and insatiate with a bottle of beer a sweetheart a
    package of cigarettes a candle and fell off the bed, and continued along
    the floor and down the hall and ended fainting on the wall with a vision of
    ultimate cunt and come eluding the last gyzym of consciousness,

who sweetened the snatches of a million girls trembling in the sunset, and
    were red eyed in the morning but prepared to sweeten the snatch of the
    sunrise, flashing buttocks under barns and naked in the lake,

who went out whoring through Colorado in myriad stolen night-cars, N.C.,[22]
    secret hero of these poems, cocksman and Adonis of Denver—joy to the
    memory of his innumerable lays of girls in empty lots & diner backyards,
    moviehouses' rickety rows, on mountaintops in caves or with gaunt
    waitresses in familiar roadside lonely petticoat upliftings & especially secret
    gas-station solipsisms of johns, & hometown alleys too,

who faded out in vast sordid movies, were shifted in dreams, woke on a sudden
    Manhattan, and picked themselves up out of basements hung-over with
    heartless Tokay[23] and horrors of Third Avenue iron dreams & stumbled to
    unemployment offices,

who walked all night with their shoes full of blood on the snowbank docks
    waiting for a door in the East River to open to a room full of steam-heat and
    opium,

who created great suicidal dramas on the apartment cliff-banks of the Hudson
    under the wartime blue floodlight of the moon & their heads shall be
    crowned with laurel in oblivion,

21. The three Fates, in Greek and Roman myth, were goddesses who determined the course of human lives by spinning threads and then cutting them.
22. Neal Cassady (1926–1968), Ginsberg's friend and lover, was also a friend of novelists Jack Kerouac and Ken Kesey. Kerouac portrayed him as Dean Moriarty in *On the Road* (1957) and Kesey as Superman in "The Day after Superman Died" in *Demon Box* (1986). Adonis of Denver: in Greek myth, Adonis was a beautiful young man beloved of Aphrodite, the goddess of love; Cassady grew up in Denver.
23. Sweet Hungarian white wine with a high alcohol content.

who ate the lamb stew of the imagination or digested the crab at the muddy
 bottom of the rivers of Bowery,[24]
who wept at the romance of the streets with their pushcarts full of onions and
 bad music,
who sat in boxes breathing in the darkness under the bridge, and rose up to
 build harpsichords in their lofts,[25]
who coughed on the sixth floor of Harlem crowned with flame under the
 tubercular sky surrounded by orange crates of theology,
who scribbled all night rocking and rolling over lofty incantations which in the
 yellow morning were stanzas of gibberish,
who cooked rotten animals lung heart feet tail borsht[26] & tortillas dreaming of
 the pure vegetable kingdom,
who plunged themselves under meat trucks looking for an egg,
who threw their watches off the roof to cast their ballot for Eternity outside of
 Time, & alarm clocks fell on their heads every day for the next decade,
who cut their wrists three times successively unsuccessfully, gave up and were
 forced to open antique stores where they thought they were growing old and
 cried,
who were burned alive in their innocent flannel suits[27] on Madison Avenue
 amid blasts of leaden verse & the tanked-up clatter of the iron regiments
 of fashion & the nitroglycerine shrieks of the fairies of advertising & the
 mustard gas of sinister intelligent editors, or were run down by the drunken
 taxicabs of Absolute Reality,
who jumped off the Brooklyn Bridge this actually happened and walked away
 unknown and forgotten into the ghostly daze of Chinatown soup alleyways
 & firetrucks, not even one free beer,
who sang out of their windows in despair, fell out of the subway window,
 jumped in the filthy Passaic,[28] leaped on negroes, cried all over the street,
 danced on broken wineglasses barefoot smashed phonograph records of
 nostalgic European 1930s German jazz finished the whiskey and threw up

---

24. The lower part of Third Avenue in Manhattan, frequented by alcoholics and homeless people.

25. Possible reference to the first and last sections of Hart Crane's epic poem *The Bridge* (1930).

26. Russian beet soup, a dish cooked by Ginsberg's mother.

27. Sloane Wilson's best-selling novel, *The Man in the Gray Flannel Suit* (1955), identified businessmen as typically wearing flannel suits. Madison Avenue: location of many New York advertising agencies.

28. The Passaic River flows through Paterson, New Jersey, where both Ginsberg and his mentor, William Carlos Williams, grew up. The phrase "filthy Passaic" comes from Williams's 1915 poem "The Wanderer," in which the river provides the poet with inspiration. German jazz: refers to the songs "O Show Me the Way to the Next Whiskey Bar" and "Benares Song" in Kurt Weill and Bertolt Brecht's opera *Rise and Fall of the City of Mahagonny* (Ginsberg's note).

groaning into the bloody toilet, moans in their ears and the blast of colossal
steamwhistles,

who barreled down the highways of the past journeying to each other's hotrod-
Golgotha[29] jail-solitude watch or Birmingham jazz incarnation,

who drove crosscountry seventytwo hours to find out if I had a vision or you
had a vision or he had a vision to find out Eternity,

who journeyed to Denver, who died in Denver,[30] who came back to Denver
& waited in vain, who watched over Denver & brooded & loned in Denver
and finally went away to find out the Time, & now Denver is lonesome for
her heroes,

who fell on their knees in hopeless cathedrals praying for each other's salvation
and light and breasts, until the soul illuminated its hair for a second,

who crashed through their minds in jail waiting for impossible criminals with
golden heads and the charm of reality in their hearts who sang sweet blues
to Alcatraz,

who retired to Mexico to cultivate a habit,[31] or Rocky Mount to tender Buddha
or Tangiers to boys or Southern Pacific to the black locomotive or Harvard
to Narcissus to Woodlawn to the daisychain or grave,

who demanded sanity trials accusing the radio of hypnotism[32] & were left with
their insanity & their hands & a hung jury,

who threw potato salad at CCNY[33] lecturers on Dadaism and subsequently
presented themselves on the granite steps of the madhouse with shaven
heads and harlequin speech of suicide, demanding instantaneous lobotomy,

and who were given instead the concrete void of insulin[34] Metrazol electricity
hydrotherapy psychotherapy occupational therapy pingpong & amnesia,

29. In the New Testament, Golgotha, "a place of a skull," is the site of Christ's crucifixion (Matthew 27:33).

30. "Lyric lines by Kerouac: 'Down in Denver, / Down in Denver, / All I did was die'" (Ginsberg's note).

31. The Beat writer and drug addict William S. Burroughs lived in Mexico for a time. Rocky Mount: a town in North Carolina where Kerouac briefly lived. Tangiers: Moroccan city where both Burroughs and Ginsberg lived for a time. Southern Pacific: Neal Cassady worked as a brakeman for the Southern Pacific Railroad. Narcissus: in Greek myth, a youth who fell in love with his own reflection in a pool. Woodlawn: a large cemetery in the Bronx, which Ginsberg's mother could see from her window.

32. Naomi Ginsberg, the poet's mother, suffered from a paranoid delusion that the radio was communicating to her personally.

33. City College of New York. Dadaism: avant-garde literary and artistic movement of the 1910s and 1920s that emphasized absurdity and chance. Carl Solomon threw potato salad at a lecturer at Brooklyn College, an act that he said "was supposed to be Dadaism" but that led to his incarceration in a psychiatric hospital.

34. Used for shock therapy in the 1940s and 1950s. Metrazol: a drug used in convulsive shock therapy in the 1950s. Electricity: another form of shock therapy. Naomi Ginsberg was given both insulin shock and electroshock treatments. Allen Ginsberg himself only "received hydrotherapy, psychotherapy, occupational therapy (oil painting) and played Ping-Pong with Carl Solomon at N. Y. State Psychiatric Institute" (Ginsberg's note).

who in humorless protest overturned only one symbolic pingpong table,[35]
     resting briefly in catatonia,
returning years later truly bald except for a wig of blood, and tears and fingers,
     to the visible madman doom of the wards of the madtowns of the East,
Pilgrim State's Rockland's and Greystone's foetid halls,[36] bickering with the
     echoes of the soul, rocking and rolling in the midnight solitude-bench
     dolmen-realms of love, dream of life a nightmare, bodies turned to stone as
     heavy as the moon,
with mother finally ******,[37] and the last fantastic book flung out of the
     tenement window, and the last door closed at 4 A.M. and the last telephone
     slammed at the wall in reply and the last furnished room emptied down
     to the last piece of mental furniture, a yellow paper rose twisted on a wire
     hanger in the closet, and even that imaginary, nothing but a hopeful little
     bit of hallucination—
ah, Carl, while you are not safe I am not safe,[38] and now you're really in the
     total animal soup of time—
and who therefore ran through the icy streets obsessed with a sudden flash
     of the alchemy of the use of the ellipsis catalogue a variable meter & the
     vibrating plane,
who dreamt and made incarnate gaps in Time & Space through images
     juxtaposed, and trapped the archangel of the soul between 2 visual images
     and joined the elemental verbs and set the noun and dash of consciousness
     together jumping with sensation of Pater Omnipotens Aeterna Deus[39]
to recreate the syntax and measure of poor human prose and stand before you
     speechless and intelligent and shaking with shame, rejected yet confessing

35. Carl Solomon overturned a ping-pong table at New York State Psychiatric Institute in a "big burst of anti-authoritarian rage on arrival" (Solomon's note).

36. Three mental hospitals in the New York area. Carl Solomon was incarcerated at Pilgrim State; Naomi Ginsberg, the poet's mother, was a patient at Pilgrim State and Greystone. Dolmen-realms: a dolmen is a prehistoric monument found in Britain and France and thought to be a tomb. "Dolmens mark a vanished civilization" (Ginsberg's note). At the time "Howl" was composed, the poet's mother was living her last months at Pilgrim State Hospital and Carl Solomon had recently been admitted there.

37. Ginsberg's initial draft reads, "mother finally fucked," an expression of long-repressed incestuous desire. "Author replaced letters with asterisks in final draft of poem to introduce appropriate element of uncertainty" (Ginsberg's note).

38. In response to this line addressed to him, Carl Solomon responded ironically, "It's safer in hospital than outside."

39. "All-powerful Father, Eternal God" (Latin). The phrase is from a letter written by the French Post impressionist painter Paul Cézanne (1839–1906), in which he describes the overpowering sensations he feels in observing nature. Ginsberg commented in *Spontaneous Mind*: "The last part of 'Howl' was really an homage to art but also in specific terms an homage to Cézanne's method. . . . Just as Cézanne doesn't use perspective lines to create space, but it's a juxtaposition of one color against another color . . . , so, I had the idea, perhaps over-refined, that by the unexplainable, unexplained nonperspective line, that is, juxtaposition of one *word* against another, . . . there'd be a *gap* between the two words, which the mind would fill in with the sensation of existence."

out the soul to conform to the rhythm of thought in his naked and endless head,

the madman bum and angel beat in Time, unknown, yet putting down here what might be left to say in time come after death,

and rose reincarnate in the ghostly clothes of jazz in the goldhorn shadow of the band and blew the suffering of America's naked mind for love into an eli eli lamma lamma sabacthani[40] saxophone cry that shivered the cities down to the last radio

with the absolute heart of the poem of life butchered out of their own bodies good to eat a thousand years.

II

What sphinx[41] of cement and aluminum bashed open their skulls and ate up their brains and imagination?

Moloch![42] Solitude! Filth! Ugliness! Ashcans and unobtainable dollars! Children screaming under the stairways! Boys sobbing in armies! Old men weeping in the parks!

Moloch! Moloch! Nightmare of Moloch! Moloch the loveless! Mental Moloch! Moloch the heavy judger of men![43]

Moloch the incomprehensible prison! Moloch the crossbone soulless jailhouse and Congress of sorrows! Moloch whose buildings are judgment! Moloch the vast stone of war! Moloch the stunned governments!

Moloch whose mind is pure machinery! Moloch whose blood is running money! Moloch whose fingers are ten armies! Moloch whose breast is a cannibal dynamo! Moloch whose ear is a smoking tomb!

Moloch whose eyes are a thousand blind windows![44] Moloch whose skyscrapers stand in the long streets like endless Jehovahs! Moloch whose factories dream and croak in the fog! Moloch whose smoke-stacks and antennae crown the cities!

Moloch whose love is endless oil and stone! Moloch whose soul is electricity and banks! Moloch whose poverty is the specter of genius! Moloch whose fate is a cloud of sexless hydrogen! Moloch whose name is the Mind!

40. "My God, my God, why hast thou forsaken me" (Aramaic). These are Christ's words on the cross in the New Testament (Matthew 27:46).
41. Fearsome mythic creature that speaks in riddles.
42. "'Moloch': or Molech, the Canaanite fire god, whose worship was marked by parents' burning their children as propitiatory sacrifice. 'And thou shalt not let any of thy seed pass through the fire to Molech' (Leviticus 18:21)"

(Ginsberg's note). Boys sobbing in armies: the Cold War draft was instituted in 1948.
43. "Ref. also world-shock 1953 N. Y. electric chair executions Julius & Ethel Rosenberg spy convicts" (Ginsberg's note).
44. According to Ginsberg, the appearance of the upper stories of the Sir Francis Drake Hotel in San Francisco inspired this section of the poem. Skyscrapers: "Ref. cinema images for robot megalopolis centrum, Fritz Lang's *Metropolis*, Berlin, 1932" (Ginsberg's note).

Moloch in whom I sit lonely! Moloch in whom I dream Angels! Crazy in
 Moloch! Cocksucker in Moloch! Lacklove and manless in Moloch!
Moloch who entered my soul early! Moloch in whom I am a consciousness
 without a body! Moloch who frightened me out of my natural ecstasy!
 Moloch whom I abandon![45] Wake up in Moloch! Light streaming out of
 the sky!
Moloch! Moloch! Robot apartments! invisible suburbs! skeleton treasuries!
 blind capitals! demonic industries! spectral nations! invincible madhouses!
 granite cocks! monstrous bombs!
They broke their backs lifting Moloch to Heaven! Pavements, trees, radios,
 tons! lifting the city to Heaven which exists and is everywhere about us!
Visions! omens! hallucinations! miracles! ecstasies! gone down the American
 river!
Dreams! adorations! illuminations! religions! the whole boatload of sensitive
 bullshit!
Breakthroughs! over the river! flips and crucifixions! gone down the flood!
 Highs! Epiphanies! Despairs! Ten years' animal screams and suicides!
 Minds! New loves! Mad generation! down on the rocks of Time!
Real holy laughter in the river! They saw it all! the wild eyes! the holy yells!
 They bade farewell! They jumped off the roof! to solitude! waving! carrying
 flowers! Down to the river! into the street!

III

Carl Solomon! I'm with you in Rockland[46]
 where you're madder than I am[47]
I'm with you in Rockland
 where you must feel very strange
I'm with you in Rockland
 where you imitate the shade of my mother[48]
I'm with you in Rockland
 where you've murdered your twelve secretaries
I'm with you in Rockland
 where you laugh at this invisible humor
I'm with you in Rockland
 where we are great writers on the same dreadful typewriter

45. "This verse seems to objectify a recognition uncovered in the act of composition, a crux of the poem" (Ginsberg's note).
46. Mental hospital near New York City. Carl Solomon commented: "I was never in Rockland . . . Neither of us has ever been in Rockland." Solomon was actually in Pilgrim State Hospital at the time.
47. Ginsberg later recanted this assertion, saying he was thankful for Solomon's "sanity and generosity."
48. Naomi Ginsberg was then in Pilgrim State Hospital, as was Carl Solomon.

I'm with you in Rockland
> where your condition has become serious and is reported on the radio

I'm with you in Rockland
> where the faculties of the skull no longer admit the worms of the senses

I'm with you in Rockland
> where you drink the tea of the breasts of the spinsters of Utica[49]

I'm with you in Rockland
> where you pun on the bodies of your nurses the harpies of the Bronx[50]

I'm with you in Rockland
> where you scream in a straightjacket[51] that you're losing the game of the actual pingpong of the abyss

I'm with you in Rockland
> where you bang on the catatonic piano the soul is innocent and immortal it should never die ungodly in an armed madhouse

I'm with you in Rockland
> where fifty more shocks will never return your soul to its body again from its pilgrimage to a cross in the void

I'm with you in Rockland
> where you accuse your doctors of insanity and plot the Hebrew socialist revolution against the fascist national Golgotha[52]

I'm with you in Rockland
> where you will split the heavens of Long Island and resurrect your living human Jesus from the superhuman tomb

I'm with you in Rockland
> where there are twentyfive thousand mad comrades all together singing the final stanzas of the Internationale[53]

I'm with you in Rockland
> where we hug and kiss the United States under our bedsheets the United States that coughs all night and won't let us sleep

I'm with you in Rockland
> where we wake up electrified out of the coma by our own souls' airplanes roaring over the roof they've come to drop angelic bombs the hospital illuminates itself   imaginary walls collapse   O skinny legions run outside   O starry-spangled shock of mercy the eternal war is here   O victory forget your underwear we're free

49. City in upstate New York.
50. Solomon's mother and aunts had lived in the Bronx, as had Ginsberg's mother and aunts.
51. Solomon commented that he was straight-jacketed at Pilgrim State Hospital "rather often."
52. Site of Christ's crucifixion, according to the New Testament. Solomon was not a socialist but a liberal Democrat.
53. Composed by Eugène Pottier in 1871 to celebrate the Paris Commune, this song has served as the anthem of workers, socialists, and communists.

I'm with you in Rockland
    in my dreams you walk dripping from a sea-journey on the highway across
    America in tears to the door of my cottage in the Western night

                                                                        1956

"Howl" is a landmark of American poetry. By turns melancholy, shocking, and celebratory, it diagnoses American culture after World War II, and at the same time it reflects on the poet's personal experience. It reveals aspects of both civilization and the author that would traditionally have remained hidden. One way to view "Howl" is as the signature poem of the Beat movement—an act of opposition to the culture of conformity that predominated in Cold War America. If that era could be termed by social scientists as a time of "the lonely crowd" and "the organization man," Ginsberg compellingly portrayed a self that was at odds with both crowds and organizations. Ginsberg himself characterized the poem in a variety of different ways: as an effort to show readers that they could be "angels"; as "an homage to art"; as a "coming out of the closet"; and as an "emotional time bomb that would continue exploding in U. S. consciousness."

A small epic based on free association, "Howl" recounts the deeds of its hero and his companions. It is also a tissue of paradoxes, depicting the contemporary world as a hell but also as a potential paradise. The speaker's tone of voice is simultaneously prophetic and injured (perhaps prophetic *because* injured). He dwells on social margins but with an abiding good humor. He looks at gritty realities while engaging in quests for spiritual transcendence and aesthetic achievement. Love it or hate it, "Howl" expanded the boundaries of what a poem could say and be.

Ginsberg wrote and revised the poem—not sure at first that it *was* a poem—in the North Beach district of San Francisco. Soon after finishing Part I, he read it publicly at the Six Gallery in San Francisco on October 7, 1955. A little-known, virtually unpublished poet when he began to speak, he was a sensation by the end of the evening. Scholar Jonah Raskin describes the event: "After several hours of drinking cheap red wine, Ginsberg was drunk, but as he read he became increasingly sober, and as he gathered momentum he was surprised by his own 'strange ecstatic intensity.' He developed a deeper sense of his own identity than he had ever had before. He thought of himself, he said, as a rabbi reading rhythmically to a congregation. Indeed, there was something of the Old Testament prophet about him. In the process of reading the poem, he found himself forging a new identity as a public poet sharing his private thoughts and feelings with eager, admiring listeners. . . . 'Everyone was yelling Go! Go! Go!' Kerouac wrote. No one had ever been at a poetry reading that was so emotional and so cathartic."

Upon the poem's publication, its publisher, Lawrence Ferlinghetti, was charged with obscenity, though he was found innocent. As a result of the trial's notoriety, "Howl" immediately became a best-seller. It has remained hugely popular ever since, inspiring several generations of rock and roll artists, including Bob Dylan, the Beatles, the Rolling Stones, and Patti Smith. The footnotes ascribed to Ginsberg and Carl Solomon in our text derive from Ginsberg's *Howl: Original Draft Facsmile, Transcript & Variant Versions* (included in "Further Reading" above).

A Supermarket in California

What thoughts I have of you tonight, Walt Whitman, for I walked down the sidestreets under the trees with a headache self-conscious looking at the full moon.

In my hungry fatigue, and shopping for images, I went into the neon fruit supermarket, dreaming of your enumerations!

What peaches and what penumbras![1] Whole families shopping at night! Aisles full of husbands! Wives in the avocados, babies in the tomatoes!—and you, García Lorca,[2] what were you doing down by the watermelons?

I saw you, Walt Whitman, childless, lonely old grubber, poking among the meats in the refrigerator and eyeing the grocery boys.

I heard you asking questions of each: Who killed the pork chops? What price bananas? Are you my Angel?

I wandered in and out of the brilliant stacks of cans following you, and followed in my imagination by the store detective.

We strode down the open corridors together in our solitary fancy tasting artichokes, possessing every frozen delicacy, and never passing the cashier.

Where are we going, Walt Whitman? The doors close in an hour. Which way does your beard point tonight?

(I touch your book and dream of our odyssey in the supermarket and feel absurd.)

Will we walk all night through solitary streets? The trees add shade to shade, lights out in the houses, we'll both be lonely.

Will we stroll dreaming of the lost America of love past blue automobiles in driveways, home to our silent cottage?

Ah, dear father, graybeard, lonely old courage-teacher, what America did you have when Charon[3] quit poling his ferry and you got out on a smoking bank and stood watching the boat disappear on the black waters of Lethe?

1956

While lamenting "the lost America of love," the speaker of "A Supermarket in California" reveals his personal struggle with loneliness and his need for others. More questioning than prophetic, this poem uses paragraphs to acquire some of the informality of prose,

---

1. Partial shadows with a fringe of light.
2. Federico García Lorca (1898–1936), a Spanish dramatist and poet. He was killed at the beginning of the Spanish Civil War, perhaps because of his liberal views or his homosexual identity.
3. In Greek myth, Charon (pronounced *Keren*) is the ferryman of Hades who carries souls of the newly dead across the rivers dividing the world of the living from the world of the dead. Lethe: the river of forgetfulness, one of five rivers in Hades.

and it employs surreal humor ("Who killed the pork chops?") to complicate the tone of suffering. "A Supermarket in California" pays tribute to Walt Whitman (1819–1892), who wrote an analogous poem called "Hours continuing long, sore and heavy hearted." The speaker here begins to restore himself by reconnecting with Whitman and with his own imagination.

Sunflower Sutra

I walked on the banks of the tincan banana dock and sat down under the huge
    shade of a Southern Pacific locomotive to look at the sunset over the box
    house hills and cry.
Jack Kerouac[1] sat beside me on a busted rusty iron pole, companion, we
    thought the same thoughts of the soul, bleak and blue and sad-eyed,
    surrounded by the gnarled steel roots of trees of machinery.
The oily water on the river mirrored the red sky, sun sank on top of final Frisco
    peaks,[2] no fish in that stream, no hermit in those mounts, just ourselves
    rheumy-eyed and hung-over like old bums on the riverbank, tired and wily.
Look at the Sunflower, he said, there was a dead gray shadow against the sky,
    big as a man, sitting dry on top of a pile of ancient sawdust—
—I rushed up enchanted—it was my first sunflower, memories of Blake[3]—my
    visions—Harlem
and Hells of the Eastern rivers, bridges clanking Joes Greasy Sandwiches, dead
    baby carriages, black treadless tires forgotten and unretreaded, the poem of
    the riverbank, condoms & pots, steel knives, nothing stainless, only the dank
    muck and the razor-sharp artifacts passing into the past—
and the gray Sunflower poised against the sunset, crackly bleak and dusty with
    the smut and smog and smoke of olden locomotives in its eye—
corolla[4] of bleary spikes pushed down and broken like a battered crown, seeds
    fallen out of its face, soon-to-be-toothless mouth of sunny air, sunrays
    obliterated on its hairy head like a dried wire spiderweb,
leaves stuck out like arms out of the stem, gestures from the sawdust root, broke
    pieces of plaster fallen out of the black twigs, a dead fly in its ear,
Unholy battered old thing you were, my sunflower O my soul, I loved you
    then!
The grime was no man's grime but death and human locomotives,

1. Ginsberg's friend and sometime lover Kerouac (1922–1969) wrote such classic Beat novels as *On the Road, The Subterraneans,* and *The Dharma Bums.*
2. The highest peaks in San Francisco are Mount Davidson and Twin Peaks.
3. In 1948 Ginsberg had a mystical vision of the English poet William Blake (1757–1827) reciting "Ah! Sun-flower" and several other poems.
4. Petals of a flower.

all that dress of dust, that veil of darkened railroad skin, that smog of cheek,
    that eyelid of black mis'ry, that sooty hand or phallus or protuberance of
    artificial worse-than-dirt—industrial—modern—that civilization spotting
    your crazy golden crown—
and those blear[5] thoughts of death and dusty loveless eyes and ends and
    withered roots below, in the home-pile of sand and sawdust, rubber dollar
    bills, skin of machinery, the guts and innards of the weeping coughing car,
    the empty lonely tincans with their rusty tongues alack, what more could
    I name, the smoked ashes of some cock cigar, the cunts of wheelbarrows
    and the milky breasts of cars, wornout asses out of chairs & sphincters of
    dynamos—all these
entangled in your mummied roots—and you there standing before me in the
    sunset, all your glory in your form!
A perfect beauty of a sunflower! a perfect excellent lovely sunflower existence!
    a sweet natural eye to the new hip moon, woke up alive and excited
    grasping in the sunset shadow sunrise golden monthly breeze!
How many flies buzzed round you innocent of your grime, while you cursed
    the heavens of the railroad and your flower soul?
Poor dead flower? when did you forget you were a flower? when did you look at
    your skin and decide you were an impotent dirty old locomotive? the ghost
    of a locomotive? the specter and shade of a once powerful mad American
    locomotive?
You were never no locomotive, Sunflower, you were a sunflower!
And you Locomotive, you are a locomotive, forget me not!
So I grabbed up the skeleton thick sunflower and stuck it at my side like a
    scepter,[6]
and deliver my sermon to my soul, and Jack's soul too, and anyone who'll
    listen,
—We're not our skin of grime, we're not our dread bleak dusty imageless
    locomotive, we're all golden sunflowers inside, blessed by our own seed
    & hairy naked accomplishment-bodies growing into mad black formal
    sunflowers in the sunset, spied on by our eyes under the shadow of the mad
    locomotive riverbank sunset Frisco hilly tincan evening sitdown vision.

1956

In Hindu tradition a sutra is an aphorism or a series of aphorisms, whereas in Buddhism a sutra is a canonical narrative, especially the dialogues of the Buddha. The sunflower of Ginsberg's title alludes to William Blake's "Ah! Sun-flower." Paul Portugés writes: "The best example of Ginsberg's visionary quest, ending in a vision of Eternity, is 'Sunflower

5. Dim, blurry.　　　　　　　　6. Royal staff or baton.

Sutra.' The poem specifically refers to his Blake experience and also describes his perceptions of a dying sunflower, dying because the soot and grime of a thoughtless, mechanical
society have weighed so heavily upon it. . . . Ginsberg transcends the forces of our society
by coming forth with a vision of Eternity that claims we are all spirits, all angels."

America

America I've given you all and now I'm nothing.
America two dollars and twentyseven cents January 17, 1956.
I can't stand my own mind.
America when will we end the human war?
Go fuck yourself with your atom bomb.
I don't feel good don't bother me.
I won't write my poem till I'm in my right mind.
America when will you be angelic?
When will you take off your clothes?
When will you look at yourself through the grave?
When will you be worthy of your million Trotskyites?[1]
America why are your libraries full of tears?
America when will you send your eggs to India?
I'm sick of your insane demands.
When can I go into the supermarket and buy what I need with my good looks?
America after all it is you and I who are perfect not the next world.
Your machinery is too much for me.
You made me want to be a saint.
There must be some other way to settle this argument.
Burroughs[2] is in Tangiers I don't think he'll come back it's sinister.
Are you being sinister or is this some form of practical joke?
I'm trying to come to the point.
I refuse to give up my obsession.
America stop pushing I know what I'm doing.
America the plum blossoms are falling.[3]
I haven't read the newspapers for months, everyday somebody goes on trial for
    murder.

---

1. Leon Trotsky (1879–1940) was a leader and
theorist of the Communist revolution in Russia.
Eventually deported by Stalin, he was assassinated in Mexico by one of Stalin's agents.
2. William S. Burroughs (1914–1997), Ginsberg's
friend and the author of such novels as *Junky*
and *Naked Lunch*.
3. Compare Ezra Pound's *Cantos*: "The blossoms of the apricot / blow from the east to the
west, / And I have tried to keep them from falling" (Canto 13).

America I feel sentimental about the Wobblies.[4]
America I used to be a communist when I was a kid I'm not sorry.
I smoke marijuana every chance I get.
I sit in my house for days on end and stare at the roses in the closet.
When I go to Chinatown I get drunk and never get laid.
My mind is made up there's going to be trouble.
You should have seen me reading Marx.[5]
My psychoanalyst thinks I'm perfectly right.
I won't say the Lord's Prayer.
I have mystical visions and cosmic vibrations.
America I still haven't told you what you did to Uncle Max after he came over
    from Russia.
I'm addressing you.
Are you going to let your emotional life be run by Time Magazine?
I'm obsessed by Time Magazine.
I read it every week.
Its cover stares at me every time I slink past the corner candystore.
I read it in the basement of the Berkeley Public Library.
It's always telling me about responsibility. Businessmen are serious. Movie
    producers are serious. Everybody's serious but me.
It occurs to me that I am America.
I am talking to myself again.

Asia is rising against me.
I haven't got a chinaman's chance.
I'd better consider my national resources.
My national resources consist of two joints of marijuana millions of genitals
    an unpublishable private literature that jetplanes 1400 miles an hour and
    twentyfive-thousand mental institutions.
I say nothing about my prisons nor the millions of underprivileged who live in
    my flowerpots under the light of five hundred suns.
I have abolished the whorehouses of France, Tangiers is the next to go.
My ambition is to be President despite the fact that I'm a Catholic.

America how can I write a holy litany in your silly mood?
I will continue like Henry Ford[6] my strophes are as individual as his
    automobiles more so they're all different sexes.

4. Members of the Industrial Workers of the World, an activist American labor organization of the 1910s and 1920s. Ginsberg thought they had an "Anarchist-Buddhist-Populist tinge."
5. Karl Marx (1818–1883), German social philosopher and revolutionary.
6. Industrialist (1863–1947) who founded Ford Motor Company and established the assembly line as a means of mass production. Strophes: stanzas.

America I will sell you strophes $2500 apiece $500 down on your old strophe
America free Tom Mooney[7]
America save the Spanish Loyalists[8]
America Sacco & Vanzetti[9] must not die
America I am the Scottsboro boys.[10]
America when I was seven momma took me to Communist Cell meetings
   they sold us garbanzos a handful per ticket a ticket costs a nickel and
   the speeches were free everybody was angelic and sentimental about the
   workers it was all so sincere you have no idea what a good thing the party
   was in 1835 Scott Nearing[11] was a grand old man a real mensch Mother
   Bloor the Silk-strikers' Ewig-Weibliche made me cry I once saw the Yiddish
   orator Israel Amter plain. Everybody must have been a spy.
America you don't really want to go to war.
America it's them bad Russians.
Them Russians them Russians and them Chinamen. And them Russians.
The Russia wants to eat us alive. The Russia's power mad. She wants to take
   our cars from out our garages.
Her wants to grab Chicago. Her needs a Red *Reader's Digest*. Her wants our
   auto plants in Siberia. Him big bureaucracy running our fillingstations.
That no good. Ugh. Him make Indians learn read. Him need big black niggers.
   Hah. Her make us all work sixteen hours a day. Help.
America this is quite serious.
America this is the impression I get from looking in the television set.
America is this correct?
I'd better get right down to the job.
It's true I don't want to join the Army or turn lathes in precision parts factories,
   I'm nearsighted and psychopathic anyway.
America I'm putting my queer shoulder to the wheel.

1956

7. Labor organizer (1882–1942) who spent twenty-three years in jail on a probably false charge of bomb-throwing.
8. Opponents of the Nationalists in the Spanish Civil War of 1936–39, ultimately defeated.
9. Nicola Sacco and Bartolomeo Vanzetti, Italian-American immigrants executed for armed robbery and murder in 1927 after a controversial trial.
10. Nine African-American teenagers convicted in 1931 in Alabama for an alleged gang rape of two young white women that probably never occurred. They spent as many as seventeen years in jail for a crime they did not commit.
11. Radical economist, opponent of World War I, and advocate of simple living (1883–1983). Mensch: an adult, a good person (Yiddish). Mother Bloor: Ella Reeve Bloor (1862–1951) was a Communist Party organizer and writer in New York. Ewig-Weibliche: the eternal feminine, the power of women to inspire (German). Israel Amter: Communist Party leader in Ohio and New York. Compare Robert Browning's line, "Ah, did you once see Shelley plain?" in his poem "Memorabilia" (1855).

Michael Schumacher, one of Ginsberg's biographers, has written of this poem: "'America' was a poem that demanded discipline and restraint on the part of the poet. If the poem went on too long, it could lose its impact; if it overextended its use of hyperbole, it would lose the seriousness of its intent. . . . Allen worked carefully on the poem, working with its rhythms until he had built a poem with a series of emotional peaks and valleys. A section would build momentum, reach a climax, and then Ginsberg would repeat the process. The poem's parting shot—'America I'm putting my queer shoulder to the wheel'—became one of Ginsberg's most famous lines, one that managed to encompass both the humor and sense of determination present throughout the work."

Anti-Vietnam War Peace Mobilization

White sunshine on sweating skulls
Washington's Monument pyramided high granite clouds
over a soul mass, children screaming in their brains on quiet grass
(black man strapped hanging in blue denims from an earth cross)—
Soul brightness under blue sky
Assembled before White House filled with mustached Germans
& police buttons, army telephones, CIA Buzzers, FBI bugs
Secret Service walkie-talkies, Intercom squawkers to Narco
Fuzz[1] & Florida Mafia Real Estate Speculators.
One hundred thousand bodies naked before an Iron Robot
Nixon's brain Presidential cranium case spying thru binoculars
from the Paranoia Smog Factory's East Wing.

                                                                1972

"Anti-Vietnam War Peace Mobilization" evokes one of many protest rallies Ginsberg attended during the Vietnam War. A pacifist, Ginsberg remained (in the words of biographer Michael Schumacher) "one of the war's most visible and outspoken critics." This poem was written five days after the Kent State shooting of May 4, 1970, in which four unarmed college students were killed, and a fifth was permanently paralyzed, by shots fired by the Ohio National Guard. The event precipitated national protests.

---

1. Police. Florida Mafia Real Estate Speculators: probably a reference to Charles "Bebe" Rebozo (1912–1998), a Florida banker and real estate investor and a close friend of President Richard Nixon.

"Don't Grow Old"

I

Twenty-eight years before on the living room couch he'd stared at me, I said
"I want to see a psychiatrist—I have sexual difficulties—homosexuality"
I'd come home from troubled years as a student. This was the weekend I would
　　talk with him.
A look startled his face, "You mean you like to take men's penises in your
　　mouth?"
Equally startled, "No, no," I lied, "that isn't what it means."

Now he lay naked in the bath, hot water draining beneath his shanks.
Strong shouldered Peter,[1] once ambulance attendant, raised him up
in the tiled room. We toweled him dry, arms under his, bathrobe over his
　　shoulder—
he tottered thru the door to his carpeted bedroom
sat on the soft mattress edge, exhausted, and coughed up watery phlegm.
We lifted his swollen feet talcum'd white, put them thru pajama legs,
tied the cord round his waist, and held the nightshirt sleeve open for his hand,
　　slow.
Mouth drawn in, his false teeth in a dish, he turned his head round
looking up at Peter to smile ruefully, "Don't ever grow old."

II

At my urging, my eldest nephew came
to keep his grandfather company, maybe sleep overnight in the apartment.
He had no job, and was homeless anyway.
All afternoon he read the papers and looked at old movies.
Later dusk, television silent, we sat on a soft-pillowed couch,
Louis sat in his easy-chair that swiveled and could lean back—
"So what kind of job are you looking for?"
"Dishwashing but someone told me it makes your hands' skin scaly red."
"And what about officeboy?" His grandson finished highschool with marks too
　　poor for college.
"It's unhealthy inside airconditioned buildings under fluorescent light."
The dying man looked at him, nodding at the specimen.
He began his advice. "You might be a taxidriver, but what if a car crashed into
　　you? They say you can get mugged too.
Or you could get a job as a sailor, but the ship could sink, you could get
　　drowned.

1. Peter Orlovsky (1933–2010), American poet and longtime companion of Allen Ginsberg.

Maybe you should try a career in the grocery business, but a box of bananas
    could slip from the shelf,
you could hurt your head. Or if you were a waiter, you could slip and fall down
    with a loaded tray, & have to pay for the broken glasses.
Maybe you should be a carpenter, but your thumb might get hit by a hammer.
Or a lifeguard—but the undertow at Belmar beach[2] is dangerous, and you
    could catch a cold.
Or a doctor, but sometimes you could cut your hand with a scalpel that had
    germs, you could get sick & die"

Later, in bed after twilight, glasses off, he said to his wife
"Why doesn't he comb his hair? It falls all over his eyes, how can he see?
Tell him to go home soon, I'm too tired."

    III.

    Resigned

A year before visiting a handsome poet and my Tibetan guru,[3]
    Guests after supper on the mountainside
we admired the lights of Boulder spread glittering below
        through a giant glass window—
After coffee, my father bantered wearily
"Is life worth living? Depends on the liver—"
The Lama smiled to his secretary—
It was an old pun I'd heard in childhood.
Then he fell silent, looking at the floor
    and sighed, head bent heavy
        talking to no one—
            "What can you do . . . ?"

                1982

"'Don't Grow Old'" recalls the final months of Ginsberg's father, Louis Ginsberg (1896–1976), a high school teacher and poet. Ginsberg wrote the poem in 1978, two years after his father's death from cancer. Part I includes description similar to that found in a letter Allen Ginsberg wrote to a friend in 1976: "Louis is dying in Paterson. Wasted thin arms and wrinkled breasts, big belly, skull nose, speckled feet, thin legs, can't stand up out of a bathtub."

2. In northern New Jersey.

3. Chogyam Trungpa (1939–1987), Allen Ginsberg's spiritual advisor, a Buddhist scholar and meditation master, and the founder of Naropa Institute in Boulder, Colorado, where Ginsberg sometimes taught.

It's All So Brief

I've got to give up
Books, checks, letters
File cabinets, apartment
pillows, bodies and skin
even the ache in my teeth.

1986

Yiddishe Kopf

I'm Jewish because love my family matzoh ball soup.[1]
I'm Jewish because my fathers mothers uncles grandmothers said "Jewish," all
    the way back to Vitebsk[2] & Kaminetz-Podolska via Lvov.
Jewish because reading Dostoyevsky at 13 I write poems at restaurant tables
    Lower East Side, perfect delicatessen intellectual.
Jewish because violent Zionists make my blood boil, Progressive indignation.
Jewish because Buddhist,[3] my anger's transparent hot air, I shrug my shoulders.
Jewish because monotheist Jews Catholics Moslems're intolerable intolerant—
Blake[4] sd. "6000 years of sleep" since antique Nobodaddy Adonai's mind trap—
    Oy! such Meshuggeneh absolutes—
Senior Citizen Jewish paid my dues got half-fare card buses subways, discount
    movies—
Can't imagine how these young people make a life, make a living.
How can they stand it, going out in the world with only $10 and a hydrogen
    bomb?

1994

The title, "Yiddishe Kopf," means "Jewish head" (Yiddish). The poem critiques the ab-
solutism of the Abrahamic religions (Judaism, Christianity, and Islam) while employing
Jewish terms and cultural attitudes in a positive way.

1. Chicken soup and a dumpling made of matzoh meal, a traditional Eastern European Jewish
dish.
2. A town in Belarus. Kaminetz-Podolska: a town
in Ukraine. Lvov: a city in Ukraine.
3. Ginsberg was a Jewish Buddhist, a common
phenomenon in which an ethnically Jewish person follows both Buddhist and Jewish traditions.

4. English poet and mystic William Blake (1757–
1827). Nobodaddy: title character of Blake's
poem "To Nobodaddy," a pejorative image of
the Judeo-Christian God as a "silent & invisible / Father." Adonai: Lord or God (Hebrew).
Oy!: oh, used to express dismay or exasperation
(Yiddish). Meshuggeneh: crazy, impractical
(Yiddish).

JAMES MERRILL
1926–1995

DEFTLY WITTY, AND BRIMMING with gracious allusion and subtle wordplay, James Merrill's poems often create a tone of rarified amusement that seems to glide above the fray of ordinary existence. Yet his poems nonetheless remain deeply immersed in the everyday details of contemporary experience, and they can turn from playful lightness or whimsical nostalgia to stark seriousness—and back again—with a dazzling swiftness and exactitude. Love and loss are persistent Merrill themes, and in his work the world offers a confounding paradox: it is full of attractions and tantalizing possibilities, yet one faces this world weighted down by the burdens of one's past and by the limitations imposed by one's individual character and one's participation in the imperfections inherent in humanity.

Merrill was born in New York City, where his father, Charles E. Merrill, enjoyed considerable power and prestige as a founding partner in the Merrill Lynch investment firm. He was raised in an environment of wealth and privilege, but when his parents separated when he was eleven, and later divorced, he suffered keenly, and a melancholic sense of distance or separation haunts much of his later work. Merrill attended Amherst College and, before graduation, published *The Black Swan*, the first of his many volumes of poetry. His early verse was predominantly lyric, but in 1976 he published *Divine Comedies*, the first volume in a personal epic, focusing on himself and his partner of four decades, the writer and artist David Jackson, and involving—rather surprisingly—a dialogue with a lively colloquy of departed spirits via the Ouija board. The second volume, *Mirabell: Books of Number* (1978), was followed by a final, comprehensive volume, *The Changing Light of Sandover*, in 1982. In his later years, Merrill's poetry returned again to the lyric mode. He died of a heart attack due to complications from AIDS in 1995, having recently finished his last, valedictory volume of poems, *A Scattering of Salts*.

Although he inherited great wealth from his financier father and from his mother, Hellen Ingram Merrill, he lived simply and devoted much of his income to the support of literature and the arts, particularly through the creation of the influential Ingram Merrill Foundation. Friendship with fellow artists is a frequent theme of his poetry, as can be seen in "The Victor Dog," dedicated to his close friend, the poet Elizabeth Bishop (also included in this anthology). That poem also reveals Merrill's fascination with the smorgasbord of ancient, modern, and contemporary culture—a feast that sometimes threatens to overwhelm the feaster—as does his "Self-Portrait in Tyvek™ Windbreaker," a late poem that explores the irony of staking out a pro-ecology position by wearing a jacket so synthetic as to bear the trademark of a corporate chemical giant. The ironies of human circumstance—and the paradoxes of individual and collective fate—remain Merrill's persistent preoccupations, and few poets have handled these with such lightness of touch or such gentle, yet penetrating, irony.

FURTHER READING

Rachel Hadas. *Merrill, Cavafy, Poems, and Dreams.* Ann Arbor: University of Michigan Press, 2000.
Timothy Materer. *James Merrill's Apocalypse.* Ithaca, N.Y.: Cornell University Press, 2000.
James Merrill. *Selected Poems.* Ed. J. D. McClatchy and Stephen Yenser. New York: Knopf, 2008.

The Victor Dog

for Elizabeth Bishop

Bix to Buxtehude to Boulez,[1]
The little white dog on the Victor label
Listens long and hard as he is able.
It's all in a day's work, whatever plays.

From judgment, it would seem, he has refrained.
He even listens earnestly to Bloch,[2]
Then builds a church upon our acid rock.[3]
He's man's—no—he's the Leiermann's[4] best friend,

Or would be if hearing and listening were the same.
Does he hear? I fancy he rather smells
Those lemon-gold arpeggios in Ravel's
"Les jets d'eau du palais de ceux qui s'aiment."[5]

     ✳   ✳   ✳

1. Merrill's updating of the traditional "Three B's" (Bach, Beethoven, and Brahms) features jazz cornetist Bix Beiderbecke (1903–1931), baroque composer Dietrich Buxtehude (1637–1707), and avant-garde composer and conductor Pierre Boulez (1925–).
2. Ernst Bloch (1880–1859), classical composer known for his somber, even earnest style.
3. A multilayered pun: Jesus said to his leading disciple, "Thou art Peter, and upon this rock I will build my church" (Matthew 16:18)—the word *Peter* (Petros) resembles *rock* (petra) in ancient Greek. Acid rock: a late-1960s rock music style featuring lyrics and musical effects suggestive of psychedelic experience.
4. Literally, "The Organ-Grinder." A reference to "Der Leiermann," the final song in Franz Schubert's cycle *Winterreise* (1827).
5. Merrill playfully extends the title of Maurice Ravel's shimmeringly impressionistic "Les Jeux d'Eau" (1901); Merrill's version might be translated, "The Fountains of the Palace of Those Who Love Each Other."

He ponders the Schumann Concerto's[6] tall willow hit
By lightning, and stays put. When he surmises
Through one of Bach's eternal boxwood mazes[7]
The oboe pungent as a bitch in heat,

Or when the calypso[8] decants its raw bay rum
Or the moon in *Wozzeck*[9] reddens ripe for murder,
He doesn't sneeze or howl; just listens harder.
Adamant needles[10] bear down on him from

Whirling of outer space, too black, too near—
But he was taught as a puppy not to flinch,
Much less to imitate his bête noire Blanche
Who barked, fat foolish creature, at King Lear.[11]

Still others fought in the road's filth over Jezebel,[12]
Slavered on hearths of horned and pelted barons.
His forebears lacked, to say the least, forebearance.
Can nature change in him? Nothing's impossible.

The last chord fades. The night is cold and fine.
His master's voice rasps through the grooves' bare groves.
Obediently, in silence like the grave's
He sleeps there on the still-warm gramophone

Only to dream he is at the première of a Handel
Opera long thought lost—*Il Cane Minore.*[13]
Its allegorical subject is his story!
A little dog revolving round a spindle

Gives rise to harmonies beyond belief,
A cast of stars. . . . Is there in Victor's heart

---

6. Robert Schumann's popular piano concerto (1845) is romantically evocative of nature.

7. That is, the intricately interwoven patterns found in the fugues and other contrapuntal writings of J. S. Bach (1685–1750). Bach had a special gift for writing for the oboe.

8. A Caribbean musical style of African origin featuring rhythmic syncopation and ironic commentary on local events and politics.

9. 1925 opera by Alban Berg that culminates in homicide.

10. Literally, the gemstone (frequently diamond) needles that press into the grooves of phonograph records to extract the sound.

11. Shakespeare's *King Lear*, "The little dogs and all, / Tray, Blanch, and Sweetheart, see, they bark at me" (3.6).

12. Jezebel, the pagan wife of King Ahab of Israel, was thrown from a window and her body was devoured by dogs (2 Kings 9:30–37).

13. George Frideric Handel (1685–1759) composed many operas in Italian, but *Il Cane Minore* ("The Smaller Dog") is Merrill's invention.

No honey for the vanquished? Art is art.
The life it asks of us is a dog's life.

1972

The title of "The Victor Dog" does not quite mean what it may appear at first glance to mean. The logo for the Victor Talking Machine Company—later RCA Victor—showed a white dog listening to a gramophone, straining to hear (or so the trademarked slogan went) "His Master's Voice." The poem meditates on the extraordinary range of music that this virtual Victor Dog might have experienced as his image spun round the spindles of millions of 33-rpm and 78-rpm record players—perhaps including the poet's own. The dedicatee, the poet Elizabeth Bishop, was a close friend of Merrill's and, like him, a devotee of a wide range of musical styles.

Self-Portrait in Tyvek™ Windbreaker

The windbreaker is white with a world map.
DuPont contributed the seeming-frail,
Unrippable stuff[1] first used for Priority Mail.
Weightless as shores reflected in deep water,
The countries are violet, orange, yellow, green;
Names of the principal towns and rivers, black.
A zipper's hiss, and the Atlantic Ocean closes
Over my blood-red T-shirt from the Gap.

I found it in one of those vaguely imbecile
Emporia catering to the collective unconscious
Of our time and place. This one featured crystals,
Cassettes of whalesong and rain-forest whistles,
Barometers, herbal cosmetics, pillows like puffins,
Recycled notebooks, mechanized lucite coffins
For sapphire waves that crest, break, and recede,
As they presumably do in nature still.

Sweat-panted and Reeboked,[2] I wear it to the gym.
My terry-cloth headband is green as laurel.[3]
A yellow plastic Walkman[4] at my hip
Sends shiny yellow tendrils to either ear.

---

1. Tyvek™ is a light, unrippable, nonporous, trademarked synthetic fabric developed by the DuPont Chemical Corporation.
2. Wearing Reebok brand sneakers.

3. An ironic metamorphosis of the poet's laurel crown.
4. Portable cassette or CD player, branded by Sony.

All us street people got our types on tape,
Turn ourselves on with a sly fingertip.
Today I felt like Songs of Yesteryear
Sung by Roberto Murolo.[5] Heard of him?

Well, back before animal species began to become
Extinct, a dictator named Mussolini banned
The street-singers of Naples. One smart kid
Learned their repertoire by heart, and hid.
Emerging after the war with his guitar,
He alone bearing the old songs of the land
Into the nuclear age sang with a charm,
A perfect naturalness that thawed the numb

Survivors and reinspired the Underground.
From love to grief to gaiety his art
Modulates effortlessly, like a young man's heart,
Tonic to dominant—the frets so few
And change so strummed into the life of things
That Nature's lamps burn brighter when he sings
Nanetta's fickleness, or chocolate,
Snow on a flower, the moon, the seasons' round.

I picked his tape in lieu of something grosser
Or loftier, say the Dead[6] or Arvo Pärt,
On the hazy premise that what fills the mind
Shows on the face. My face, as a small part
Of nature, hopes this musical sunscreen
Will keep the wilderness within it green,
Yet looks uneasy, drawn. I detect behind
My neighbor's grin the oncoming bulldozer

And cannot stop it. Ecosaints[7]—their karma
To be Earth's latest, maybe terminal, fruits—
Are slow to ripen. Even this dumb jacket
Probably still believes in Human Rights,

5. Neapolitan singer, guitarist, and actor (1912–2003). The poem's subsequent two stanzas tell Murolo's story. In 1963, Murolo published a twelve-LP set covering the entire history of Neapolitan popular song, annotated and sung by himself.

6. The rock band The Grateful Dead. Arvo Pärt: Estonian classical composer (1935–).
7. Presumably, saints devoted to ecology or to the preservation of the earth.

Thinks in terms of "nations," urban centers,
Cares less (can Tyvek breathe?) for oxygen
Than for the innocents evicted when
Ford bites the dust and Big Mac buys the farm.

Hah. As if greed and savagery weren't the tongues
We've spoken since the beginning. My point is, those
Prior people, fresh from scarifying
Their young and feasting in triumph on their foes,
Honored the gods of Air and Land and Sea.
We, though . . . Cut to dead forests, filthy beaches,
The can of hairspray, oil-benighted creatures,
A star-scarred x-ray of the North Wind's lungs.

Still, not to paint a picture wholly black,
Some social highlights: Dead white males in malls.
Prayer breakfasts. Pay-phone sex. "Ring up as meat."
Oprah. The GNP. The contour sheet.
The painless death of History. The stick
Figures on Capitol Hill. Their rhetoric,
Gladly—no, rapturously (on Prozac) suffered!
Gay studies. Right to Lifers. The laugh track.

And clothes. Americans, blithe as the last straw,
Shrug off accountability by dressing
Younger than their kids—jeans, ski-pants, sneakers,
A baseball cap, a happy-face T-shirt . . .
Like first-graders we "love" our mother Earth,
Know she's been sick, and mean to care for her
When we grow up. Seeing my windbreaker,
People hail me with nostalgic awe.

"Great jacket!" strangers on streetcorners impart.
The Albanian doorman pats it: "Where you buy?"
Over his ear-splitting drill a hunky guy
Yells, "Hey, you'll always know where you are, right?"
"Ever the fashionable cosmopolite,"
Beams Ray. And "Voilà mon pays"[8]—the carrot-haired
Girl in the bakery, touching with her finger
The little orange France above my heart.

---

8. "There is my country."

*   *   *

Everyman, c'est moi,[9] the whole world's pal!
The pity is how soon such feelings sour.
As I leave the gym a smiling-as-if-I-should-know-her
Teenager—oh but I *mean* she's wearing "our"
Windbreaker, and assumes . . . Yet I return her wave
Like an accomplice. For while all humans aren't
Countable as equals, we must behave
As if they were, or the spirit dies (Pascal).[10]

"We"? A few hundred decades of relative
Lucidity glinted-through by minnow schools
Between us and the red genetic muck—
Everyman's underpainting. We look up, shy
Creatures, from our trembling pool of sky.
Caught wet-lipped in light's brushwork, fleet but sure,
Flash on shudder, folk of the first fuck,
Likeness breathes likeness, fights for breath—*I live*—

Where the crush thickens. And by season's end,
The swells of fashion cresting to collapse
In breaker upon breaker on the beach,
Who wants to be caught dead in this cliché
Of mere "involvement"? Time to put under wraps
Its corporate synthetic global pitch;
Not throwing out motley once reveled in,
Just learning to live down the wrinkled friend.

Face it, reproduction of any kind leaves us colder
Though airtight-warmer (greenhouse effect) each year.
Remember the figleaf's lesson. Styles betray
Some guilty knowledge. What to dress ours in—
A seer's blind gaze, an infant's tender skin?
All that's been seen through. The eloquence to come
Will be precisely what we cannot say
Until it parts the lips. But as one grows older

*   *   *

9. "I am Everyman." An echo of Louis XIV's pronouncement "*L'etat, c'est moi*" or "I am the State."

10. Blaise Pascal (1623–1662), French philosopher and mathematician.

—I should confess before that last coat dries—
The wry recall of thunder does for rage.
Erotic torrents flash on screen instead
Of drenching us. Exclusively in dream,
These nights, does a grandsire rear his saurian head,
And childhood's inexhaustible brain-forest teem
With jewel-bright lives. No way now to restage
Their sacred pageant under our new skies'

Irradiated lucite. What then to wear
When—hush, it's no dream! It's my windbreaker
In black, with starry longitudes, Archer, Goat,[11]
Clothing an earphoned archangel of Space,
Who hasn't read Pascal, and doesn't wave . . .
What far-out twitterings he learns by rote,
What looks they'd wake upon a human face,
Don't ask, Roberto.[12] Sing our final air:

Love, grief, etc. **** for good reason.
Now only ******* STOP signs
Meanwhile ***** if you or I've ex-
ceeded our [?] *** ~~more than time~~ was needed
To fit a text airless and ** as Tyvek
With breathing spaces and between the lines
Days brilliantly recurring, as once *we* did,
To keep the blue wave dancing in its prison.

1995

Merrill's title, "Self-Portrait in Tyvek™ Windbreaker," alludes to his contemporary John Ashbery's long poem "Self-Portrait in a Convex Mirror" (1976), which itself refers to the painting also titled "Self-Portrait in a Convex Mirror" (1524) by the Italian Renaissance painter Parmigianino. The gaps and cancellations in the final stanza perhaps indicate the poet's recognition of the difficulty of reconciling and completing the conflicting thoughts in the poem.

11. A black version of the Tyvek windbreaker, covered with constellations.

12. The Neapolitan singer Roberto Murolo, mentioned above.

FRANK O'HARA
1926–1966

F RANK O'HARA — often campy and witty, frequently provocative, and sometimes
  tense and introverted — celebrated everyday life in New York City. Writing in
the 1950s and 1960s, he chronicled dailiness in a city that was emerging as the
cultural capital of the Cold War West. Like his fellow member of the New York
school of poetry, John Ashbery, O'Hara was deeply involved in both the city's art
scene and its poetry scene. Art curator and critic as well as poet, O'Hara negotiated those roles simultaneously in his Manhattan-based world, serving as curator
of the Museum of Modern Art and as art reviewer for *ArtNews*, while innovating
a poetry notable for its spontaneity, sophistication, and humor. While writing
some of the finest lyrics in American poetry, O'Hara also "proved that friendship is an art form," as art critic Deborah Solomon has written. At his funeral,
artist Larry Rivers said, "There are at least sixty people in New York who thought
Frank O'Hara was their best friend." Not surprisingly, dozens of homages to him
were written by friends and other people whose lives he touched.

O'Hara lived within an urban community composed of loosely knit, sometimes conflicting friendships and alliances. He frequently served as a bridge and
mediator as well as an advocate competing for position; a powerbroker himself,
he both won and lost cultural wars. In addition, O'Hara's life was complicated
by his position as a self-identified gay man coping with the rigid constraints that
Cold War culture imposed on homosexuals. Historic confrontations between
the diverse gay communities in New York and the police took place during the
1950s and 1960s, and these simmering tensions and restrictions were part of the
social fabric that O'Hara negotiated.

All of the cultural arts in Manhattan competed heatedly in midcentury America for patronage, media attention, public support, and governmental and foundation funding. As the center of the arts in the Cold War, New York attracted
thousands of young artists with all kinds of talents from around the world. This
era saw a large-scale renaissance in the arts. O'Hara proved an inspiration to
many developing artists and poets because he would both guide them and step
aside to allow them their individuality. O'Hara worked across competing cultural lines within the American scene as well as across national boundaries. Associating with such New York School poets as Ashbery and with such Beat poets
as Allen Ginsberg and Amiri Baraka, he also followed literary developments in
Africa and translated European writers such as Jean Genet. O'Hara mediated the
long-lasting competition in the visual arts between the Jackson Pollock faction

(allied with critic Clement Greenberg) and the Wilhem de Kooning camp (with its advocate Harold Rosenberg). In addition, he sought support for new artists from Spain and elsewhere. His interests in music and dance included Aaron Copland's work with Agnes de Mille in postwar New York and Vaslav Nijinsky's collaboration with Igor Stravinsky in modernist Paris.

O'Hara enjoyed the benefits of a wide variety of artistic perspectives, ranging from the classical to the postmodern. At times he was a Romantic lyricist (as in "Autobiographia Literaria"). He half-facetiously founded a movement he called "Personism," in which the poem must "address itself to one person" (as in "Avenue A" and "Having a Coke with You"), though O'Hara sardonically added that "if I wanted to I could use the telephone instead." He also developed such modernist and postmodernist methods as bricolage, or collage-building, which layered popular and elite cultural references (as in "The Day Lady Died"). Even as O'Hara's poetic practice places him firmly within the modernist-postmodernist spectrum, it also reveals a poetic inheritance from earlier eras. His diary-like rhetoric in the so-called "I do this/I do that" poems such as "The Day Lady Died" indicate his affinity with fellow New England poet Emily Dickinson. His embrace of global culture, especially its urbanity, is reminiscent of fellow New Yorker Walt Whitman's vision of cultural links stretching around the world.

Beyond his interest in the arts and in the social world of artists and bohemians, O'Hara also foregrounded the cultures of childhood and adolescence, and their relationship to the adult self (as in "Autobiographia Literaria"). Until the early postwar years, adolescence was not a well-defined period in psychological development; and childhood—aside from infancy—remained vaguely developed. While biographers such as Brad Gooch have documented O'Hara's active social life, several critics, especially Mutlu Blasing, have indicated that he was deeply aware of his isolation and that his writing regularly contains a sense of impending doom—as though he is one step away from disaster. One can also say, however, that O'Hara often seems ahead of others as well—in the vanguard of aesthetics and ideas.

Born in Baltimore, Frank (Francis Russell) O'Hara grew up in Grafton, Massachusetts, near Worcester, in an Irish-American Catholic family. He studied piano for three years at the New England Conservatory of Music from 1941 to 1944. During World War II, he served in the navy and was stationed in the South Pacific and Japan. When he returned from the war, O'Hara attended Harvard University, studying music while also majoring in English and working on the campus newspaper. He fit in easily with the postwar generation of poets there, which included Ashbery, Kenneth Koch, and Robert Creeley. He then studied at the University of Michigan, receiving a master's degree in English in 1951. During this period, he continued to write poetry and to experiment with both music and plays.

When O'Hara reached New York after graduate school, he was immediately attracted to the visual arts and began working at the Museum of Modern Art. He rose to the position of associate curator and organized exhibits for the major art stars Franz Kline and Robert Motherwell while producing a book on Jackson Pollock. He collaborated frequently with such artists as Larry Rivers and immersed himself in the worlds of first- and second-generation Abstract Expressionists. At the same time, as Marjorie Perloff has written, he continued to highlight older experimental movements such as French Dadaism and Surrealism. O'Hara also collaborated with composers, frequently with Ned Rorem. In addition, he documented the world of sound (musical, mechanical, industrial, and domestic) in his poetry and films, setting, for example, a musical theme by composer Leonard Bernstein against the buzz of electricity found in street lamps, telephone wires, and mass transit.

O'Hara enjoyed the artistic ferment of his time from the day he arrived in New York City in 1951 to the day of his accidental death on a beach in Fire Island in 1966. He wrote at the center of a swirling concatenation of poetry, painting, music, performance, film, and the hum of urban life. His work is saturated with signs of cutting-edge and popular culture, ranging from the painters named in "Avenue A" to the jazz singer Billie Holiday, who is lamented so passionately in "The Day Lady Died." His poetry transmitted a sense of how exciting, pleasurable, and painful postmodern life could be.

FURTHER READING

Mutlu Konuk Blasing. *Politics and Form in Postmodern Poetry: O'Hara, Bishop, Ashbery & Merrill*. Cambridge, Eng.: Cambridge University Press, 1995.

Russell Ferguson. *In Memory of My Feelings: Frank O'Hara and American Art*. Berkeley: University of California Press, 1999.

Brad Gooch. *City Poet: The Life and Times of Frank O'Hara*. New York: Harper, 1994.

Robert Hampson and Will Montgomery, eds. *Frank O'Hara Now: New Essays on the American Poet*. Liverpool, Eng.: Liverpool University Press, 2010.

David Lehman. *The Last Avant-Garde: The Making of the New York School of Poets*. New York: Doubleday, 1998.

Frank O'Hara. *The Collected Poems of Frank O'Hara*. Ed. Donald Allen. Berkeley: University of California Press, 1995.

Marjorie Perloff. *Frank O'Hara: Poet Among Painters*. Chicago: University of Chicago Press, 1977.

Camille Roman. "Frank O'Hara and Music as Ethnography: The Example of 'The Day Lady Died.'" In *Yearbook of Interdisciplinary Studies in the Fine Arts*, eds., William E. Grim and Michael B. Harper. Lewiston, N.Y.: Edwin Mellen Press, 1992. 15–33.

Deborah Solomon. "When Artists and Writers Shared the Scene." *New York Times*. 4 July 1999: AR 25.

Autobiographia Literaria

When I was child
I played by myself in a
corner of the schoolyard
all alone.

I hated dolls and I
hated games, animals were
not friendly and birds
flew away.

If anyone was looking
for me I hid behind a
tree and cried out "I am
an orphan."

And here I am, the
center of all beauty!
writing these poems!
Imagine!

1971

Composed in 1949–50 but published posthumously, "Autobiographia Literaria" offers a crucial glimpse into O'Hara's aesthetics. It acknowledges his debt to British Romanticism beginning with the title, which alludes to Samuel Taylor Coleridge's *Biographia Literaria*. The poem also reveals O'Hara's sense of modernist alienation and his refusal to employ the "wise" and "saintly" child trope configured in so much Romantic painting and poetry.

The Day Lady Died

It is 12:20 in New York a Friday
three days after Bastille day,[1] yes
it is 1959 and I go get a shoeshine
because I will get off the 4:19 in Easthampton[2]
at 7:15 and then go straight to dinner
and I don't know the people who will feed me

*   *   *

1. July 14, France's major national holiday.   2. A beach town on Long Island.

I walk up the muggy street beginning to sun
and have a hamburger and a malted and buy
an ugly NEW WORLD WRITING[3] to see what the poets
in Ghana are doing these days
                                    I go on to the bank
and Miss Stillwagon (first name Linda I once heard)
doesn't even look up my balance for once in her life
and in the GOLDEN GRIFFIN[4] I get a little Verlaine
for Patsy[5] with drawings by Bonnard although I do
think of Hesiod,[6] trans. Richmond Lattimore or
Brendan Behan's[7] new play or *Le Balcon* or *Les Nègres*
of Genet, but I don't, I stick with Verlaine
after practically going to sleep with quandariness

and for Mike[8] I just stroll into the PARK LANE
Liquor Store and ask for a bottle of Strega[9] and
then I go back where I came from to 6th Avenue
and the tobacconist in the Ziegfeld Theatre[10] and
casually ask for a carton of Gauloises[11] and a carton
of Picayunes,[12] and a NEW YORK POST with her face on it

and I am sweating a lot by now and thinking of
leaning on the john door in the 5 SPOT[13]
while she whispered a song along the keyboard
to Mal Waldron[14] and everyone and I stopped breathing

                                                    1964

"The Day Lady Died" is an elegy for Billie Holiday (1915–1959). Her nickname from the saxophonist Lester Young was "Lady Day," which, as Camille Roman has written, is evoked in O'Hara's title for the poem. Perhaps the greatest jazz and blues singer in U.S.

3. A paperback magazine that featured significant new writing, in print from 1951 until 1964.
4. New York City bookstore. Verlaine: The speaker buys a small edition of the French poet Paul Verlaine (1844–1896), with illustrations by the French artist Pierre Bonnard (1867–1947).
5. Patsy Southgate, his hostess for the evening, a writer and translator.
6. Greek poet (eighth century B.C.E.), whose work Richmond Lattimore translated into English.
7. Irish playwright (1923–1964), author of *The Hostage* (1958). *Le Balcon* (1956) and *Les Nègres* (1958) are plays by the French playwright Jean Genet (1910–1986).

8. Michael Goldberg, his host for the evening, an avant-garde visual artist and husband of Patsy Southgate.
9. Yellow-colored Italian liqueur made with fennel, mint, and saffron.
10. Broadway theater, named for the famed Broadway impresario Florenz Ziegfeld.
11. French brand of cigarette.
12. American brand of cigarette, originally manufactured in New Orleans.
13. New York jazz club.
14. Malcolm Waldron (1925–2002), American jazz pianist and composer, was a regular accompanist for Billie Holiday from 1957 until her death in 1959.

history, Holiday is memorialized by O'Hara through the textual representation of sound. Her name is emphasized in the opening of the poem through the repetition of "Day" in the title and the first two lines.

Although "The Day Lady Died" belongs to the elegiac tradition, Marjorie Perloff observes that "O'Hara dispenses with all the traditional props of elegy—the statement of lament, the consolation motif, the procession of mourners, the pathetic fallacy, and so on—and still manages to pay an intensely moving tribute to the great jazz singer. . . . [A] disconnection characterizes the network of proper names and place references in the poem. On the one hand, the poet's consciousness is drawn to the foreign or exotic. . . . On the other, the poem contains a set of native American references. . . . As a person, Billie Holiday was, of course, quintessentially American: a southern Black who had experienced typical hardships on the road to success, a woman of great passions who finally succumbed to her terrible drug addiction, a victim of FBI agents and police raids. In this sense, hers is the world of muggy streets, hamburgers and malteds, the john door, the '5 Spot.' But her great voice transcends what she is in life, linking her to the poets, dramatists, and artists cited in the first part."

It should be noted that Holiday was ill in the later years of her life and lacked a stable work routine and regular paycheck. She exhausted herself because society treated her as a second-class citizen. She was not given the same pay as the instrumentalists working with her and could not stay in all-white hotels with some of the other musicians. Considering how hard and long she worked under adverse conditions, it is astonishing that she achieved so much.

Avenue A

We hardly ever see the moon any more
                                   so no wonder
        it's so beautiful when we look up suddenly
and there it is gliding broken-faced over the bridges
brilliantly coursing, soft, and a cool wind fans
        your hair over your forehead and your memories
                of Red Grooms' locomotive landscape[1]
I want some bourbon/you want some oranges[2]/I love the leather
                jacket Norman[3] gave me
                                   and the corduroy coat David[4]
        gave you, it is more mysterious than spring, the El Greco

1. Red Grooms (b. 1937) is an American multimedia artist known for his frantic scenes of urban life.
2. The reference to oranges may suggest artist Grace Hartigan's painting entitled *Oranges*.
3. Visual artist Norman Bluhm (1921–1999), O'Hara's friend and collaborator.
4. Writer and artist David Jackson (1922–2001), who was known for wearing corduroy jackets. Jackson collaborated with his life partner, poet James Merrill, on many of his major works.

heavens breaking and open then reassembling like lions
    in a vast tragic veldt[5]
   that is far from our small selves and our temporally united
passions in the cathedral of Januaries

   everything is too comprehensible
   these are my delicate and caressing poems
I suppose there will be more of those others to come, as in the past
                  so many!
but for now the moon is revealing itself like a pearl
                  to my equally naked heart
                      1965

"Avenue A" is a love poem addressed to the dancer Vincent Warren (b. 1938), who was O'Hara's lover, 1959–61. O'Hara wrote forty-four love poems to Warren. Beyond being a "delicate and caressing" erotic lyric, "Avenue A" is concerned with O'Hara's Manhattan neighborhood. O'Hara's home on East 49th Street near Avenue A, which runs along East Greenwich Village and Tompkins Square Park, attracted a great deal of attention from admirers. Biographer Brad Gooch quotes poet Ted Berrigan, who treated it as a shrine: "[I] used to stand on Avenue A staring up patiently at O'Hara's apartment before we even met." Other artists and poets, such as Fairfield Porter and Bill Berkson, also lived nearby.

Having a Coke with You

is even more fun than going to San Sebastian, Irún, Hendaye, Biarritz,
   Bayonne[1]
or being sick to my stomach on the Travesera de Gracia[2] in Barcelona
partly because in your orange shirt you look like a better happier St. Sebastian[3]
partly because of my love for you, partly because of your love for yoghurt
partly because of the fluorescent orange tulips around the birches
partly because of the secrecy our smiles take on before people and statuary
it is hard to believe when I'm with you that there can be anything as still
as solemn as unpleasantly definitive as statuary when right in front of it
in the warm New York 4 o'clock light we are drifting back and forth
between each other like a tree breathing through its spectacles

      *   *   *

5. African grassland that is usually fairly level, intermixed with scattered shrubs or trees, and chiefly located in southern and eastern Africa (Afrikaans).

1. Cities and towns in the Basque region of northeastern Spain and southwestern France.
2. Street in Barcelona, in the autonomous region of Catalonia in Spain.
3. Christian martyr and saint (d. ca. 288).

and the portrait show seems to have no faces in it at all, just paint
you suddenly wonder why in the world anyone ever did them
                                                              I look
at you and I would rather look at you than all the portraits in the world
except possibly for the *Polish Rider*[4] occasionally and anyway it's in the Frick
which thank heavens you haven't gone to yet so we can go together the
    first time
and the fact that you move so beautifully more or less takes care of Futurism[5]
just as at home I never think of the *Nude Descending a Staircase*[6] or
at a rehearsal a single drawing of Leonardo or Michelangelo[7] that used to
    wow me
and what good does all the research of the Impressionists[8] do them
when they never got the right person to stand near the tree when the sun sank
or for that matter Marino Marini[9] when he didn't pick the rider as carefully
as the horse

            it seems they were all cheated of some marvellous experience
which is not going to go wasted on me which is why I'm telling you about it
                                                              1965

"Having a Coke with You," like "Avenue A" above, is a love poem to the dancer Vincent Warren. It wittily addresses the relative value of life and art. Marjorie Perloff observes that "the object of the poet's love (Warren) is comically compared and found superior to Rembrandt's *Polish Rider*, Duchamp's *Nude Descending a Staircase*, and the equestrian figures of Marino Marini." Weighing out whether the love object is superior to Rembrandt's painting, the speaker tries to resolve his feelings by looking at Warren and the art work simultaneously.

4. Portrait of a handsome man on a horse by the Dutch painter Rembrandt van Rijn (1606–1669). The Frick: The Frick Collection, a museum in Manhattan with a noted collection of paintings, sculptures, and items of material culture.
5. A movement in art, music, and literature begun in Italy around 1910 and marked by an effort to give formal expression to the dynamic energy and movement of processes.
6. A 1912 painting by the French artist Marcel Duchamp (1887–1968), widely regarded as one of the landmarks of modernism.
7. Leonardo da Vinci (1452–1519) and Michelangelo (1475–1564), masterly Italian visual artists.
8. French artists of about 1870 who painted objects by dabbing primary unmixed colors in order to imitate reflected light, their subject matter generally being outdoor scenes painted from observation.
9. Italian sculptor (1901–1980) noted for equestrian statues.

JOHN ASHBERY
b. 1927

JOHN ASHBERY, a great poet of interior states, also explores the interiors of language. He troubles the relation of word to meaning, exploring poetry's capacity for indirection, implication, and condensation. He emphasizes the importance of both subjective and material reality by positing that language can depict them only partially and peripherally. Thus, his poems have a dual focus: on the objects, events, and feelings that are always just out of reach and on the poetic rhetorics that both promise and compromise the communication of information. Foregrounding their own language use, Ashbery's poems suggest that verbal creativity is less a divine power than an assembly plant, in which diverse parts are combined to form something new. The poems disperse our preexistent certainties as they invent verbal combinations that are at once indeterminate, seductive, and surprising.

Ashbery's dreamlike poems tend to subvert any frame of reference the instant one becomes visible. In his *Selected Prose*, he self-mockingly writes that he is "sometimes considered a harebrained, homegrown surrealist whose poetry defies even the rules and logic of Surrealism." His poems never allow language to recede into the background or to become transparent. They use words like pieces of stained glass, arranging them into a design of their own. In the process, the illusion of a masterly author or of a single correct perspective vanishes. Instead, we are left with the play of language across a set of momentous issues, such as time, memory, consciousness, regret, loss, death, affection, and love.

Empty of literal meaning, Ashbery's poems are filled with verbal energy. They channel the ebb and flow of the poet's intellectual and emotional environment and the far horizon of what can be said in language. "The Instruction Manual," for example, describes precisely what is not to be seen—the never-visited city of Guadalajara—in a rhetoric that flaunts its artificiality. "The Tennis Court Oath" suggests bewilderment in a discourse so fragmented that no transcendence can shine through. "Daffy Duck in Hollywood" travels through a carnivalesque wordscape of hyperbolic cultural phenomena. "The Big Cloud" envelops itself in a cloud of ideas, feelings, and dreams. Ashbery's language is always inventive and in motion, and the things in his poems never stay tied down for long.

Born in Rochester, New York, Ashbery grew up on a farm near Sodus, also in upstate New York. He lived with his father (a farmer), his mother (a former biology teacher), his two brothers, and for a time with his maternal grandparents. Entering Harvard with the intention of becoming a painter, he was already writing poetry, and he soon made that his full-time occupation. He received his B.A. in English from Harvard and an M.A. in English from Columbia. He then worked as an art critic and editor for many years, in an attempt to support his "poetry habit" (as he puts it in *Selected Prose*). Living in Paris between 1955 and 1965 and then in New York, he served as the editor of *ArtNews* and as an art reviewer for *Newsweek*. Along with his friend Frank O'Hara and his student John Yau, Ashbery was associated with the New York school of poetry, writing poems that reflected his experience of New York's rich artistic and cultural scene.

Ashbery's books of poetry have received admiring reviews, and he has garnered many major awards, including the Pulitzer Prize and the National Book Award. Now retired from teaching at Brooklyn College and Bard College, he lives with his partner, David Kermani, in New York City and rural Hudson, New York. He is one of the most respected, influential, and beloved poets of his era.

FURTHER READING

John Ashbery. *Can You Hear, Bird*. New York: Farrar, Straus & Giroux, 1995.
———. *Collected Poems, 1956–1987*. Ed. Mark Ford. New York: Library of America, 2008.
———. *Selected Prose*. Ed. Eugene Richie. Ann Arbor: University of Michigan Press, 2005.
———. *A Worldly Country*. New York: Ecco Press, 2007.
Sue Gangel. "John Ashbery." In *American Poetry Observed: Poets on Their Work*, ed. Joe David Bellamy, 9–20. Urbana: University of Illinois Press, 1988.
Jeffrey Gray. *Mastery's End: Travel and Postwar American Poetry*. Athens: University of Georgia Press, 2005.
David Herd. *John Ashbery and American Poetry*. Manchester, Eng.: University of Manchester Press, 2003.
John Shoptaw. *On the Outside Looking Out: John Ashbery's Poetry*. Cambridge, Mass.: Harvard University Press, 1994.

The Instruction Manual

As I sit looking out of a window of the building
I wish I did not have to write the instruction manual on the uses of a new metal.
I look down into the street and see people, each walking with an inner peace,
And envy them—they are so far away from me!
Not one of them has to worry about getting out this manual on schedule.
And, as my way is, I begin to dream, resting my elbows on the desk and leaning out of the window a little,
Of dim Guadalajara! City of rose-colored flowers!
City I wanted most to see, and most did not see, in Mexico!
But I fancy I see, under the press of having to write the instruction manual,

Your public square, city, with its elaborate little bandstand!
The band is playing *Scheherazade* by Rimsky-Korsakov.[1]
Around stand the flower girls, handing out rose- and lemon-colored flowers,
Each attractive in her rose-and-blue striped dress (Oh! such shades of rose and
    blue),
And nearby is the little white booth where women in green serve you green
    and yellow fruit.
The couples are parading; everyone is in a holiday mood.
First, leading the parade, is a dapper fellow
Clothed in deep blue. On his head sits a white hat
And he wears a mustache, which has been trimmed for the occasion.
His dear one, his wife, is young and pretty; her shawl is rose, pink, and white.
Her slippers are patent leather, in the American fashion,
And she carries a fan, for she is modest, and does not want the crowd to see her
    face too often.
But everybody is so busy with his wife or loved one
I doubt they would notice the mustachioed man's wife.
Here come the boys! They are skipping and throwing little things on the
    sidewalk
Which is made of gray tile. One of them, a little older, has a toothpick in his
    teeth.
He is silenter than the rest, and affects not to notice the pretty young girls in
    white.
But his friends notice them, and shout their jeers at the laughing girls.
Yet soon all this will cease, with the deepening of their years,
And love bring each to the parade grounds for another reason.
But I have lost sight of the young fellow with the toothpick.
Wait—there he is—on the other side of the bandstand,
Secluded from his friends, in earnest talk with a young girl
Of fourteen or fifteen. I try to hear what they are saying
But it seems they are just mumbling something—shy words of love, probably.
She is slightly taller than he, and looks quietly down into his sincere eyes.
She is wearing white. The breeze ruffles her long fine black hair against her
    olive cheek.
Obviously she is in love. The boy, the young boy with the toothpick, he is in
    love too;
His eyes show it. Turning from this couple,
I see there is an intermission in the concert.

1. Nikolai Rimsky-Korsakov (1844–1908) was a Russian composer of classical music, one of whose
best-known works was the symphonic suite *Scheherazade*, inspired by the legendary Persian storyteller of *One Thousand and One Nights*.

The paraders are resting and sipping drinks through straws
(The drinks are dispensed from a large glass crock by a lady in dark blue),
And the musicians mingle among them, in their creamy white uniforms, and
    talk
About the weather, perhaps, or how their kids are doing at school.

Let us take this opportunity to tiptoe into one of the side streets.
Here you may see one of those white houses with green trim
That are so popular here. Look—I told you!
It is cool and dim inside, but the patio is sunny.
An old woman in gray sits there, fanning herself with a palm leaf fan.
She welcomes us to her patio, and offers us a cooling drink.
"My son is in Mexico City," she says. "He would welcome you too
If he were here. But his job is with a bank there.
Look, here is a photograph of him."
And a dark-skinned lad with pearly teeth grins out at us from the worn leather
    frame.
We thank her for her hospitality, for it is getting late
And we must catch a view of the city, before we leave, from a good high place.
That church tower will do—the faded pink one, there against the fierce blue of
    the sky. Slowly we enter.
The caretaker, an old man dressed in brown and gray, asks us how long we
    have been in the city, and how we like it here.
His daughter is scrubbing the steps—she nods to us as we pass into the tower.
Soon we have reached the top, and the whole network of the city extends
    before us.
There is the rich quarter, with its houses of pink and white, and its crumbling,
    leafy terraces.
There is the poorer quarter, its homes a deep blue.
There is the market, where men are selling hats and swatting flies
And there is the public library, painted several shades of pale green and beige.
Look! There is the square we just came from, with the promenaders.
There are fewer of them, now that the heat of the day has increased,
But the young boy and girl still lurk in the shadows of the bandstand.
And there is the home of the little old lady—
She is still sitting in the patio, fanning herself.
How limited, but how complete withal, has been our experience of
    Guadalajara!
We have seen young love, married love, and the love of an aged mother for her
    son.
We have heard the music, tasted the drinks, and looked at colored houses.

What more is there to do, except stay? And that we cannot do.
And as a last breeze freshens the top of the weathered old tower, I turn my gaze
Back to the instruction manual which has made me dream of Guadalajara.

1956

Guadalajara, which dates from the sixteenth century, is the capital of the Mexican state of Jalisco. With a population of more than a million and a half people, it is Mexico's second-largest city. Jeffrey Gray writes that "in 'The Instruction Manual,' the earliest instance in which Ashbery introduces the idea of an unrecoverable presence (the 'real' Guadalajara), we see, through a hackneyed touristic narrative, that the staged and the unstaged are indistinguishable."

Sue Gangel quotes Ashbery on the autobiographical matrix of this poem: "I was working for a publisher, writing and editing college textbooks. I never actually wrote an instruction manual, but I wrote the poem in an office of McGraw-Hill in New York. There wasn't any window in the room so that was an invention. To me, it is more 'confessional' than it appears to be on the surface. The poem really ends with me returning to the boring task I have to do, where the poem began." Critic John Shoptaw observes that, "if anything, Ashbery's noncommittal poem is 'counter-confessional' in that it tells what didn't happen. Ashbery had vacationed in Mexico . . . in the summer of 1955, but didn't visit the promising city."

The Picture of Little J. A. in a Prospect of Flowers

He was spoilt from childhood by the
future, which he mastered rather early
and apparently without great difficulty

—Boris Pasternak

I

Darkness falls like a wet sponge
And Dick gives Genevieve a swift punch
In the pajamas. "Aroint thee, witch."[1]
Her tongue from previous ecstasy
Releases thoughts like little hats.

"He clap'd me first during the eclipse.
Afterwards I noted his manner
Much altered. But he sending

1. William Shakespeare, *Macbeth* 1.3.6. *Aroint* means "begone."

At that time certain handsome jewels
I durst not seem to take offence."[2]

In a far recess of summer
Monks are playing soccer.

II
So far is goodness a mere memory
Or naming of recent scenes of badness
That even these lives, children,
You may pass through to be blessed,
So fair does each invent his virtue.

And coming from a white world, music
Will sparkle at the lips of many who are
Beloved. Then these, as dirty handmaidens
To some transparent witch, will dream
Of a white hero's subtle wooing,
And time shall force a gift on each.

That beggar to whom you gave no cent
Striped the night with his strange descant.[3]

III
Yet I cannot escape the picture
Of my small self in that bank of flowers:
My head among the blazing phlox[4]
Seemed a pale and gigantic fungus.
I had a hard stare, accepting

Everything, taking nothing,
As though the rolled-up future might stink
As loud as stood the sick moment
The shutter clicked.[5] Though I was wrong,
Still, as the loveliest feelings

Must soon find words, and these, yes,
Displace them, so I am not wrong

2. Invented quotation, perhaps in the style of the eighteenth-century English novelist Daniel Defoe.
3. Highly ornamental melody.
4. American plant with red, purple, or variegated flowers.
5. Sound of a camera taking a photograph.

In calling this comic version of myself
The true one. For as change is horror,
Virtue is really stubbornness

And only in the light of lost words
Can we imagine our rewards.

1956

The title of this poem parodies "The Picture of Little T. C. in a Prospect of Flowers" by
the English poet Andrew Marvell (1621–1678). The epigraph is from the Russian novelist Boris Pasternak's memoir *Safe Conduct* (1931). The poem provides a "comic version"
of the poet as a young boy ("little J. A."), and it meditates on the changes that occur as
experiences are displaced by words and memories.

The Tennis Court Oath

What had you been thinking about
the face studiously bloodied
heaven blotted region
I go on loving you like water but
there is a terrible breath in the way all of this
You were not elected president, yet won the race
All the way through fog and drizzle
When you read it was sincere the coasts
stammered with unintentional villages the
horse strains fatigued I guess . . . the calls . . .
I worry

the water beetle head
why of course reflecting all
then you redid you were breathing
I thought going down to mail this
of the kettle you jabbered as easily in the yard
you come through but
are incomparable the lovely tent
mystery you don't want surrounded the real
you dance
in the spring there was clouds

*   *   *

The mulatress[1] approached in the hall—the
lettering easily visible along the edge of the *Times*
in a moment the bell would ring but there was time
for the carnation laughed here are a couple of "other"

to one in yon[2] house

The doctor and Philip had come over the road
Turning in toward the corner of the wall his hat on
reading it carelessly as if to tell you your fears were justified
the blood shifted you know those walls
wind off the earth had made him shrink
undeniably an oboe now the young
were there there was candy
to decide the sharp edge of the garment
like a particular cry not intervening called the dog "he's coming! he's coming"
    with an emotion felt it sink into peace

there was no turning back but the end was in sight
he chose this moment to ask her in detail about her family and the others
The person. pleaded—"have more of these
not stripes on the tunic[3]—or the porch chairs
will teach you about men—what it means"
to be one in a million pink stripe
and now could go away the three approached the doghouse
the reef. Your daughter's
dream of my son understand prejudice
darkness in the hole
the patient finished
They could all go home now the hole was dark
lilacs blowing across his face glad he brought you

                                                    1962

The title of "The Tennis Court Oath" refers to a meeting held on June 20, 1789, in the
early days of the French Revolution when the commoners, barred from a regular meeting of the Estates General in Versailles, met at an indoor tennis court and vowed to draft
a national constitution. Jacques-Louis David painted a famously unfinished depiction of
this historical event two years later, with its figures undressed and posing heroically. Like

1. Obsolete term for a woman of mixed African
and European ancestry.
2. Something that lies distant; yonder (a dialect
term).

3. An outer garment worn in public by citizens
of ancient Rome.

"The Instruction Manual," this poem has a misleading title that points to what the poem is not about. Assuming that master narratives are no longer plausible, the poem presents a collage of fragments, abruptly interrupted at the ends of lines or in the middle of them, where they collide with other fragments, with no punctuation mark to note the transition. The serial juxtaposition of discursive segments produces an effect of incoherence, and yet the fragments also possess a novelistic suggestiveness. The fragments of discourse and the curtailed "I" that occasionally appears in those fragments hint at uncompleted narratives of love, loss, illness, and death. But they produce no consistent, authoritative story. To borrow one of Ashbery's own descriptions of his poetry, the poem is "opacity illustrated."

Daffy Duck in Hollywood

Something strange is creeping across me.
La Celestina[1] has only to warble the first few bars
Of "I Thought about You"[2] or something mellow from
Amadigi di Gaula[3] for everything—a mint-condition can
Of Rumford's Baking Powder,[4] a celluloid earring, Speedy
Gonzales,[5] the latest from Helen Topping Miller's fertile
Escritoire,[6] a sheaf of suggestive pix on greige, deckle-edged
Stock—to come clattering through the rainbow trellis
Where Pistachio Avenue rams the 2300 block of Highland
Fling Terrace. He promised he'd get me out of this one,
That mean old cartoonist, but just look what he's
Done to me now! I scarce dare approach me mug's attenuated
Reflection in yon[7] hubcap, so jaundiced, so *déconfit*
Are its lineaments—fun, no doubt, for some quack phrenologist's[8]
Fern-clogged waiting room, but hardly what you'd call
Companionable. But everything is getting choked to the point of
Silence. Just now a magnetic storm hung in the swatch of sky

1. The name of a lead character—a matchmaker or procuress—in *Tragicomedy of Calisto and Melibea*, a Spanish novel in dialogue by Fernando de Rojas (1499). Celestina was also the popular name of an eighteenth-century opera singer, Celeste Resse.
2. Popular song written by Johnny Mercer and Jimmy Van Heusen (1939), recorded by the Mills Brothers and by Billie Holiday.
3. Opera by George Frideric Handel first performed in 1715, based on the sixteenth-century Spanish chivalric romance, *Amadis de Gaula*.
4. A venerable brand of baking powder, now owned by Clabber Girl Baking Products.
5. An animated cartoon character termed "The Fastest Mouse in All Mexico." He appeared with Daffy Duck in a series of Warner Brothers cartoons in the 1960s. Helen Topping Miller: American romance writer (1884–1960).
6. Writing desk or bureau. Greige: beige or gray. Deckle-edged: with a jagged edge.
7. Yonder. *Déconfit*: discomfited (French).
8. Nineteenth-century practitioner of a pseudo-science that regarded skull shape as an indicator of mental faculties and character traits.

Over the Fudds'[9] garage, reducing it—drastically—
To the aura of a plumbago-blue log cabin on
A Gadsden Purchase[10] commemorative cover. Suddenly all is
Loathing. I don't want to go back inside any more. You meet
Enough vague people on this emerald traffic-island—no,
Not people, comings and goings, more: mutterings, splatterings,
The bizarrely but effectively equipped infantries of happy-go-nutty
Vegetal jacqueries,[11] plumed, pointed at the little
White cardboard castle over the mill run. "Up
The lazy river, how happy we could be?"[12]
How will it end? That geranium glow
Over Anaheim's had the riot act read to it by the
Etna-size firecracker that exploded last minute into
A *carte du Tendre*[13] in whose lower right-hand corner
(Hard by the jock-itch sand-trap that skirts
The asparagus patch of algolagnic[14] *nuits blanches*) Amadis
Is cozening the Princesse de Cleves[15] into a midnight micturition spree
On the Tamigi[16] with the Wallets (Walt, Blossom, and little
Sleezix) on a lamé barge "borrowed" from Ollie
Of the Movies'[17] dread mistress of the robes. Wait!
I have an announcement! This wide, tepidly meandering,
Civilized Lethe[18] (one can barely make out the maypoles
And *châlets de nécessité*[19] on its sedgy shore) leads to Tophet, that
Landfill-haunted, not-so-residential resort from which
Some travellers return! This whole moment is the groin
Of a borborygmic[20] giant who even now
Is rolling over on us in his sleep. Farewell bocages,[21]

---

9. Elmer J. Fudd, like Daffy Duck, was a cartoon character created by Tex Avery in the 1930s. He was famous as Bugs Bunny's arch enemy, but he also appeared in several Daffy Duck cartoons.
10. Territory purchased by the United States from Mexico in 1853, comprising southern parts of what are now Arizona and New Mexico.
11. Peasant revolts (French).
12. Lyric adapted from the popular song "(Up a) Lazy River," composed by Hoagy Carmichael and Sidney Arolin in 1931.
13. French allegorical map of love, popular in the seventeenth century.
14. Sadomasochistic. *Nuits blanches*: sleepless nights (French). Amadis: adventure-seeking hero of the Spanish romance *Amadis de Gaula* (1508).

15. Heroine of the French psychological novel *La Princesse de Clèves* (1678) by Madame de Lafayette. Micturition: urination.
16. The Thames River (Italian). The Wallets: characters in the long-running comic strip *Gasoline Alley*, created by Frank King in 1918.
17. Early comic strip.
18. River of forgetfulness, one of the rivers of Hades in Greek myth.
19. "Public conveniences" (French). Tophet: Hell.
20. Making a rumbling sound in his intestine because of the movement of gas.
21. Landscapes of western France marked by patches of woodlands, heath, fields, hedgerows, and orchards.

Tanneries, water-meadows. The allegory comes unsnarled
Too soon; a shower of pecky[22] acajou harpoons is
About all there is to be noted between tornadoes. I have
Only my intermittent life in your thoughts to live
Which is like thinking in another language. Everything
Depends on whether somebody reminds you of me.
That this is a fabulation,[23] and that those "other times"
Are in fact the silences of the soul, picked out in
Diamonds on stygian[24] velvet, matters less than it should.
Prodigies of timing may be arranged to convince them
We live in one dimension, they in ours. While I
Abroad through all the coasts of dark destruction seek
Deliverance for us all,[25] think in that language: its
Grammar, though tortured, offers pavilions
At each new parting of the ways. Pastel
Ambulances scoop up the quick and hie[26] them to hospitals.
"It's all bits and pieces, spangles, patches, really; nothing
Stands alone. What happened to creative evolution?"
Sighed Aglavaine.[27] Then to her Sélysette: "If his
Achievement is only to end up less boring than the others,
What's keeping us here? Why not leave at once?
I have to stay here while they sit in there,
Laugh, drink, have fine time. In my day
One lay under the tough green leaves,
Pretending not to notice how they bled into
The sky's aqua, the wafted-away no-color of regions supposed
Not to concern us. And so we too
Came where the others came: nights of physical endurance,
Or if, by day, our behavior was anarchically
Correct, at least by New Brutalism[28] standards, all then
Grew taciturn by previous agreement. We were spirited
Away *en bateau*,[29] under cover of fudge dark.
It's not the incomplete importunes,[30] but the spookiness

---

22. Discolored. Acajou: wood of cashew, laurel oak, or mahogany.
23. A fantastic or false tale.
24. Associated with the River Styx in Greek myth—hence hellish, gloomy, or deathly.
25. Spoken by Satan in John Milton's *Paradise Lost*, book 2, lines 463–65.
26. Hasten.

27. Character in Maurice Maeterlinck's play *Aglavaine et Sélysette* (1897).
28. Post–World War II architectural style associated with Le Corbusier that was notable for its use of poured concrete.
29. "In a boat" (French).
30. Verb meaning to trouble with demands, to annoyingly urge.

Of the finished product. True, to ask less were folly, yet
If he is the result of himself, how much the better
For him we ought to be! And how little, finally,
We take this into account! Is the puckered garance[31] satin
Of a case that once held a brace of dueling pistols our
Only acknowledging of that color? I like not this,
Methinks, yet this disappointing sequel to ourselves
Has been applauded in London and St. Petersburg. Somewhere
Ravens pray for us."
                         The storm finished brewing. And thus
She questioned all who came in at the great gate, but none
She found who ever heard of Amadis,[32]
Nor of stern Aureng-Zebe,[33] his first love. Some
They were to whom this mattered not a jot: since all
By definition is completeness (so
In utter darkness they reasoned), why not
Accept it as it pleases to reveal itself? As when
Low skyscrapers from lower-hanging clouds reveal
A turret there, an art-deco escarpment[34] here, and last perhaps
The pattern that may carry the sense, but
Stays hidden in the mysteries of pagination.
Not what we see but how we see it matters; all's
Alike, the same, and we greet him who announces
The change as we would greet the change itself.
All life is but a figment; conversely, the tiny
Tome that slips from your hand is not perhaps the
Missing link in this invisible picnic whose leverage
Shrouds our sense of it. Therefore bivouac we
On this great, blond highway, unimpeded by
Veiled scruples, worn conundrums. Morning is
Impermanent. Grab sex things, swing up
Over the horizon like a boy
On a fishing expedition. No one really knows
Or cares whether this is the whole of which parts
Were vouchsafed—once—but to be ambling on's
The tradition more than the safekeeping of it. This mulch for
Play keeps them interested and busy while the big,

---

31. Red dye made from the madder flower.
32. Hero of the Spanish romance *Amadis de Gaula* (see note 14).

33. Emperor of India who is the protagonist of John Dryden's play *Aureng-Zebe* (1675).
34. Steep slope in front of a fortification.

Vaguer stuff can decide what it wants—what maps, what
Model cities, how much waste space. Life, our
Life anyway, is between. We don't mind
Or notice any more that the sky is green, a parrot
One, but have our earnest where it chances on us,
Disingenuous, intrigued, inviting more,
Always invoking the echo, a summer's day.

1977

The title, "Daffy Duck in Hollywood," is also the title of an animated cartoon produced by Tex Avery in 1938 for Warner Brothers. Daffy Duck arose in the late 1930s as a "daffy" character, often appearing as a friend or rival of the trickster Bugs Bunny. He starred in about 130 cartoons from the late 1930s to the late 1960s. David Herd suggests that Daffy is the speaker of the poem and an avatar of the poet. His allusive style and "the cartoonic speed" of his transitions affirm the rich productivity of culture, including popular culture, as against demands for a conservative, static conception of culture. Daffy seems to endorse cultural change toward the end of the poem when he says that "to be ambling on's / The tradition more than the safekeeping of it."

The Big Cloud

For ages man has labored to put his dreams in order. Look at the result.
Once an idea like the correct time is elucidated
It must fade or spread. Decay, under the old tree, is noted.
That's why we frame them, try to keep them on a wall,
Though it is decreed that the companionable
Trooping down to be with us, to partly become us
Must continue for them[1] and us to flourish:
The obliging feathers once parted,
The object of our sight, grass, just sits there
Like an empty flowerpot on a windowsill.

And a new dream gets us involved further
In that closeness. Yes, I knew there
Were sheets of tulips and pointed leaves
To screen us from each other, what we were all about,
And an announcement made against the lukewarm atmosphere of the room
To all that did or did not belong in it.

*   *   *

1. That is, ideas.

Finally, it seems, they have scattered.
Not one specimen was actually available.
And they call this peace, living our lives, and so on.
To point the finger of blame—ah, surely, at no one?
Each system trickles out into its set numbers of instances.
Poles strike bottom,
Finding the river sludge good to them, a companionable feeling.
Meetings occur under grotesquely overscaled arcades,
Last words are uttered, and first love
Ascends to its truly majestic position unimpaired.

Letters were strewn across the floor,
Singing the joyful song of how no one was ever going to read them.
Trees and wisteria rose and sank in the breeze,
And laughter danced in the dim fields beyond the schoolhouse:
It was existence again in all its tautness,
Playing its adolescent joke, its pictures
Teasing our notion of fragility with their monumental permanence.
But life was never the same again. Something faltered,
Something went away.

1987

Twilight Park

Surely the lodger hadn't returned yet.
He had, but she hadn't heard him.
He was waiting five steps below the landing:
a black cloth in one black-gloved hand,
a band of light from the streetlamp like masking tape
across his eyes. He wanted to write something that would *sell*,
and this seemed the only way.
                    Desperate are the remedies
when one is broke, and no longer all that young or handsome.

Attention, secondary characters, and that means you,
Edith Fernandez:[1] The snow is no longer pallid enough
to sum up your footfalls. One is ever so impatient;
now the tape falls, now carnival music

---

1. Invented character, perhaps in homage to Wallace Stevens's "Ramon Fernandez" in "The Idea of Order at Key West."

bashes in the front door. One can never be wholly
right, or wrong, catsup or ketchup? We must reread this.
The ending is considered particularly fine.

1995

Anticipated Stranger,

the bruise will stop by later.
For now, the pain pauses in its round,
notes the time of day, the patient's temperature,
leaves a memo for the surrogate: What the *hell*
did you think you were doing? I mean . . .
Oh well, less said the better, they all say.
I'll post this at the desk.

God will find the pattern and break it.

2007

The comma in the title suggests that the title is to be read as the beginning of the poem's
first sentence. The poem seems to be contemplating illness, injury, and death in relation
to a series of linked characters called "stranger," "patient," "surrogate," and "God."

ANNE SEXTON
1928–1974

ANNE SEXTON was a leader in the "confessional" school of poetry, though she
disavowed that term. As an offshoot of her Freudian analysis, she began exploring hidden, raw, and unassuaged feelings in poetry. Other poets such as Robert
Lowell and Sylvia Plath (both included in this anthology) may have learned the
technique from her. She conceived of writing as an "axe for the frozen sea within
us" (a line she quoted from Franz Kafka). She thus propelled the introspective
method and the interest in psychological extremes that characterize American
poetry of the Cold War era, especially the poetry published between about 1959
and 1966.

Beyond focusing on personal traumas, Sexton pinpointed the presence of love, anger, conflict, and devotion in family relations, thereby opening up that heretofore private realm as an arena for poetic exploration. Moreover, her poems are always inflected with a woman's perspective. They frankly tell women's stories, which often run counter to the patriarchal subject matter and vocabulary that previously had dominated poetic discourse. In all of these ways, Sexton proved an innovator and what critic Delmore Schwartz would have called a "culture hero." She opened up new vistas of thought and feeling in poetry.

Sexton was born into an upper-middle-class white family in Newton, Massachusetts. After attending junior college for a year, she married at the age of nineteen, worked as a fashion model and salesperson, and then gave birth to two daughters. By the time she was in her mid-twenties, her growing despair led to a series of mental breakdowns, suicide attempts, and hospitalizations. On her psychiatrist's advice, she undertook poetry as therapy and soon began to distinguish herself, especially after taking writing seminars taught by poets John Clellan Holmes and Robert Lowell. Sexton's example probably influenced Lowell's decision to expose details from his own personal life in *Life Studies*, and it influenced Sylvia Plath, her fellow student, to do the same in *Ariel*. Sexton's first volume, *To Bedlam and Part Way Back*, recounting her time in mental hospitals, appeared in 1960 to great acclaim and controversy. The work broke through the refined surface of poetic tradition to reveal socially unsanctioned emotions and experiences. The poems displayed a human richness that traditionally had seemed the terrain of fiction.

In subsequent years, Sexton published additional volumes (eleven in all), which were increasingly feminist in orientation, and she began to receive multiple forms of recognition, including a Pulitzer Prize, a Shelley Award, a Guggenheim Fellowship, and a Professorship of Creative Writing at Boston University. She achieved popular success as well. A riveting reader of her own poems, she was much in demand on the college poetry circuit. Yet her personal life continued to be troubled, and her psyche was burdened by pain. After divorcing her husband, she published a volume called *The Death Notebooks* (in 1974) but could not follow it up with a promised volume to be called *The Life Notebooks*; as she told an acquaintance, she had not yet begun to live again. On October 4, 1974, at the age of forty-six, she sealed herself in her garage, turned her car on, and killed herself by monoxide poisoning. Her close friend, the poet Maxine Kumin, said afterward that only Sexton's writing had kept her from performing this act years before.

FURTHER READING

Rise B. Axelrod. "'I Dare to Live': The Transforming Art of Anne Sexton." In *Critical Essays on Anne Sexton*, ed. Linda Wagner-Martin. 177–85, Boston: G. K. Hall, 1989.

Stephen E. Colburn, ed. *Anne Sexton: Telling the Tale*. Ann Arbor: University of Michigan Press, 1988.

Diana Hume George. *Oedipus Anne: The Poetry of Anne Sexton*. Urbana: University of Illinois Press, 1987.

Diane Wood Middlebrook. *Anne Sexton: A Biography*. Boston: Houghton Mifflin, 1991.

Anne Sexton. *Anne Sexton: A Self-Portrait in Letters*. Ed. Linda Gray Sexton and Lois Ames. Boston: Houghton Mifflin, 1977.

———. *Complete Poems*. Ed. Linda Gray Sexton. Boston: Houghton Mifflin, 1981.

———. *No Evil Star: Selected Essays, Interviews, and Prose*. Ed. Stephen E. Colburn. Ann Arbor: University of Michigan Press, 1985.

You, Doctor Martin

You, Doctor Martin, walk
from breakfast to madness. Late August,
I speed through the antiseptic tunnel
where the moving dead still talk
of pushing their bones against the thrust
of cure. And I am queen of this summer hotel
or the laughing bee on a stalk

of death. We stand in broken
lines and wait while they unlock
the door and count us at the frozen gates
of dinner. The shibboleth[1] is spoken
and we move to gravy in our smock
of smiles. We chew in rows, our plates
scratch and whine like chalk

in school. There are no knives
for cutting your throat. I make
moccasins all morning. At first my hands
kept empty, unraveled for the lives
they used to work. Now I learn to take
them back, each angry finger that demands
I mend what another will break

* * *

1. Catchword or slogan. Traditionally, a "shibboleth" is a word or phrase regarded as a criterion for distinguishing members of one social class, sect, or party from those who are not of that group; in this case, it signals that the inmates are permitted to be fed.

tomorrow. Of course, I love you;
you lean above the plastic sky,
god of our block, prince of all the foxes.
The breaking crowns are new
that Jack wore.[2] Your third eye
moves among us and lights the separate boxes
where we sleep or cry.

What large children we are
here. All over I grow most tall
in the best ward. Your business is people,
you call at the madhouse, an oracular
eye in our nest. Out in the hall
the intercom pages you. You twist in the pull
of the foxy children who fall

like floods of life in frost.
And we are magic talking to itself,
noisy and alone. I am queen of all my sins
forgotten. Am I still lost?
Once I was beautiful. Now I am myself,
counting this row and that row of moccasins
waiting on the silent shelf.

1960

This poem is the first in Sexton's premier volume, *To Bedlam and Part Way Back*. The following three poems derive from this volume as well. Evoking the poet's hospitalization for clinical depression, the poem introduces her key themes of madness and despair along with her distinctively witty and observant style. The psychiatrist in the poem, "Doctor Martin," walks like a god among his death-haunted, broken patients. The poem's speaker feels "love" for him, in a classical example of Freud's concept of transference, in which the patient unconsciously redirects feelings about someone loved in childhood (usually a parent) to the psychiatrist. As Rise B. Axelrod has pointed out, the speaker's task of making "moccasins" may punningly indicate her wish to mock her own "sins" as well.

2. A puzzling reference to the Mother Goose nursery rhyme "Jack and Jill" (and perhaps "This Is the House That Jack Built" as well). In "Jack and Jill," "Jack fell down and broke his crown" (or head) and must therefore go "to bed to mend his head." Perhaps the speaker of Sexton's poem analogizes Jack's broken and mended head to the injured psyches of the patients in the mental hospital. Third eye: perhaps a reference to a light or mirror attached to the psychiatrist's forehead and/or a reference to the ancient mystical concept of a space in the brow or forehead that leads to higher consciousness and visionary power.

Music Swims Back to Me

Wait Mister. Which way is home?
They turned the light out
and the dark is moving in the corner.
There are no sign posts in this room,
four ladies, over eighty,
in diapers every one of them.
La la la, Oh music swims back to me
and I can feel the tune they played
the night they left me
in this private institution on a hill.[1]

Imagine it. A radio playing
and everyone here was crazy.
I liked it and danced in a circle.
Music pours over the sense
and in a funny way
music sees more than I.
I mean it remembers better;
remembers the first night here.
It was the strangled cold of November;
even the stars were strapped in the sky
and that moon too bright
forking through the bars to stick me
with a singing in the head.
I have forgotten all the rest.

They lock me in this chair at eight a.m.
and there are no signs to tell the way,
just the radio beating to itself
and the song that remembers
more than I. Oh, la la la,
this music swims back to me.
The night I came I danced a circle
and was not afraid.
Mister?

1960

---

1. Perhaps a reference to Westwood Lodge or Glenside, two mental institutions where Sexton was hospitalized during her breakdown of 1955.

Sexton's biographer, Diane Wood Middlebrook, writes of this poem: "What made this a milestone in Sexton's development was the daring representation of the perspective of a madwoman. Some kind of breakdown has exiled her to an asylum. Which way is home? Further into madness. . . . In Sexton's metaphor, the music is a former identity that overtakes her: not a memory, but a consciousness that unfolds."

Her Kind

I have gone out, a possessed witch,
haunting the black air, braver at night;
dreaming evil, I have done my hitch
over the plain houses, light by light:
lonely thing, twelve-fingered,[1] out of mind.
A woman like that is not a woman, quite.
I have been her kind.

I have found the warm caves in the woods,
filled them with skillets, carvings, shelves,
closets, silks, innumerable goods;
fixed the suppers for the worms and the elves:
whining, rearranging the disaligned.
A woman like that is misunderstood.
I have been her kind.

I have ridden in your cart, driver,[2]
waved my nude arms at villages going by,
learning the last bright routes, survivor
where your flames still bite my thigh
and my ribs crack where your wheels wind.
A woman like that is not ashamed to die.
I have been her kind.

1960

Sexton here expresses at the same time her personal experience and women's collective identity by referring to the legendary figure of the witch, a character associated with both social persecution and female power.

1. In the medieval and early modern periods, physical differences were often seen as signs of wickedness, and six fingers on one hand could be taken as a sign that the person was a witch.

2. Perhaps a member of the hostile majority. The flames, below, may indicate a witch-burning.

For John, Who Begs Me Not to Enquire Further

Not that it was beautiful,
but that, in the end, there was
a certain sense of order there;
something worth learning
in that narrow diary of my mind,
in the commonplaces of the asylum
where the cracked mirror
or my own selfish death
outstared me.
And if I tried
to give you something else,
something outside of myself,
you would not know
that the worst of anyone
can be, finally,
an accident of hope.
I tapped my own head;
it was glass, an inverted bowl.
It is a small thing
to rage in your own bowl.
At first it was private.
Then it was more than myself;
it was you, or your house
or your kitchen.
And if you turn away
because there is no lesson here
I will hold my awkward bowl,
with all its cracked stars shining
like a complicated lie,
and fasten a new skin around it
as if I were dressing an orange
or a strange sun.
Not that it was beautiful,
but that I found some order there.
There ought to be something special
for someone
in this kind of hope.
This is something I would never find
in a lovelier place, my dear,
although your fear is anyone's fear,

like an invisible veil between us all . . .
and sometimes in private,
my kitchen, your kitchen,
my face, your face.

1960

The poet John Clellan Holmes, who taught a writing class that Sexton attended, advised her not to publish her mental hospital poems in a book. Sexton sent him this poem in response. The title alludes to a passage by the philosopher Arthur Schopenhauer: "It is the courage to make a clean breast of it in face of every question that makes the philosopher. He must be like Sophocles's Oedipus, who, seeking enlightenment concerning his terrible fate, pursues his indefatigable enquiry, even when he divines that appalling horror awaits him in the answer. But most of us carry in our heart the Jocasta who begs Oedipus for God's sake not to enquire further."

The Truth the Dead Know

For my mother, born March 1902, died March 1959
and my father, born February 1900, died June 1959

Gone, I say and walk from church,
refusing the stiff procession to the grave,
letting the dead ride alone in the hearse.
It is June. I am tired of being brave.

We drive to the Cape. I cultivate
myself where the sun gutters[1] from the sky,
where the sea swings in like an iron gate
and we touch. In another country people die.

My darling, the wind falls in like stones
from the whitehearted water and when we touch
we enter touch entirely. No one's alone.
Men kill for this, or for as much.

And what of the dead? They lie without shoes
in their stone boats. They are more like stone
than the sea would be if it stopped. They refuse
to be blessed, throat, eye and knucklebone.

1962

---

1. To cut channels in, to flow in rivulets, or to incline downward in a draft of wind (used of a candle or lamp flame).

Old Dwarf Heart

True. All too true. I have never been at home in life.
All my decay has taken place upon a child.

—*Henderson the Rain King,* by Saul Bellow

When I lie down to love,
old dwarf heart shakes her head.
Like an imbecile she was born old.
Her eyes wobble as thirty-one thick folds
of skin open to glare at me on my flickering bed.
She knows the decay we're made of.

When hurt she is abrupt.
Now she is solid, like fat,
breathing in loops like a green hen
in the dust. But if I dream of loving, then
my dreams are of snarling strangers. *She* dreams that . . .
strange, strange, and corrupt.

Good God, the things she knows!
And worse, the sores she holds
in her hands, gathered in like a nest
from an abandoned field. At her best
she is all red muscle, humming in and out, cajoled
by time. Where I go, she goes.

Oh now I lay me down to love,
how awkwardly her arms undo,
how patiently I untangle her wrists
like knots. Old ornament, old naked fist,
even if I put on seventy coats I could not cover you . . .
mother, father, I'm made of.

1962

Lessons in Hunger

"Do you like me?"
I asked the blue blazer.
No answer.
Silence bounced out of his books.

Silence fell off his tongue
and sat between us
and clogged my throat.
It slaughtered my trust.
It tore cigarettes out of my mouth.
We exchanged blind words,
and I did not cry,
and I did not beg,
but blackness filled my ears,
blackness lunged in my heart,
and something that had been good,
a sort of kindly oxygen,
turned into a gas oven.

Do you like me?
How absurd!
What's a question like that?
What's a silence like that?
And what am I hanging around for,
riddled with what his silence said?

1974

This poem, one of the last Sexton completed, was dated August 7, 1974. She ended her life less than two months later.

JOSEPH AWAD
1929–2009

JOSEPH AWAD, like his modernist precursors Wallace Stevens and William Carlos Williams, maintained two professional identities. During the day he was "a man in a suit" who worked as a public relations executive, and at night he wrote poetry on legal pads and notebooks at the kitchen table of his family home in Virginia. Relatively unknown nationally until recently, he is emerging as a major pioneer for the current generation of Arab-American poets. His poetry radiates a mood of modesty and honesty as it explores the poet's intimate thoughts and feelings. The author of four books of poetry, Awad has been anthologized in collections of Arab-American, Irish-American, multicultural, and Roman Catholic poetry. Among his awards and honors were the poet laureateship of Virginia from 1998 to 2000 and an Edgar Allan Poe Prize. He served as president of the Poetry Society of Virginia and as vice president of the Virginia Writers Club.

A second-generation Lebanese- and Irish-American, Awad was born in the coal-mining town of Shenandoah, Pennsylvania. His mother died when he was eight years old, and when his father moved to Washington, D.C., and opened a barber shop at the Mayflower Hotel, he lived with his grandparents. In fifth grade, he joined his father in Washington. After graduating with a degree in English from Georgetown University, he worked in the Washington bureau of *The New York Daily News* and at the Dave Herman public relations firm. He also took graduate classes at George Washington University and studied art at the Corcoran School of Art. He spent his career in the corporate world and retired in 1993 as an executive vice president for public relations at Reynolds Metals. He served as the national president of the Public Relations Society of America in 1982, published *The Power of Public Relations* with Praeger Publishing in 1985, and was inducted into the Virginia Communications Hall of Fame in 1992. Awad and his wife, Doris, had ten children and lived in Richmond, Virginia.

FURTHER READING

Joseph Awad. Poems. In *Grape Leaves: A Century of Arab-American Poetry*, ed. Gregory Orfalea and Sharif Elmusa, 133–46, New York: Interlink Publishing, 1999.
Ellen Robertson. "Reynolds PR Executive, poet Joseph Awad dies." *Richmond Times-Dispatch.* July 19, 2009. www.timesdispatch.com.

Stopping at the Mayflower

Father, your hallowed ghost
Will always haunt me here. The old hotel
Is being renovated. In the ballrooms
Moldings and golden bas reliefs[1]
Have been restored to their original splendor.
(If only they could restore that golden grin.)
And so this morning, early,
I descended the dim staircase off the lobby
To see the barber shop before it's shorn[2]
Of my particular memories, redone
Beyond our time together. Your poet son

1. Sculptures in which figures emerge from a surrounding flat surface.   2. Cut off.

Climbed the shoe shine stand, unrecognized
By the aging man who worked there in his prime
When you were manager. He could not know
His busy presence brought me close to you.

I could see, inside the shop, the barber chair
You worked from eight to six, six days a week.
I thought of my Georgetown years, lost afternoons
When I dropped by near quitting time. I'd peruse
The old *Times-Herald* or *The Daily News*
Until you finished your last customer,
Who, introduced, would say, as if on cue,
"Your dad is very proud of you."

You would clip and cut my hair, shave my neck,
Give me a shampoo and a steaming towel,
Order me a shine. "The works," you'd quip,
Treating me better than your biggest tipper.
I'd wait while you checked out the register
As I did long years before in Shenandoah.[3]
(We lived behind your shop then. I'd rush in
On Saturday, your busiest day, demanding
In front of all your grinning customers,
A quarter for the movies . . . and some candy.)

As the old man brushed and buffed my shoes
I stared hard at your empty chair.
For an instant you were standing there
In your white tunic, shaking out the hair
From a barber cloth, and calling, "Next."
Spying me, you smiled, father-wise,
Lighting the Lebanese midnight of your eyes.

The shine was finished now. The man was waiting.
(I remembered Shenandoah long ago.
The morning of mother's funeral we walked uptown
Dressed in our Sunday suits and new black ties.
You bought us both shine.) With hurting eyes
And heart, I went up to the lobby, found the doors.

✻   ✻   ✻

3. Coal-mining town in Pennsylvania where Awad was born.

You would hardly know Connecticut Avenue.
New buildings have crowded out the old.
Your favorite restaurant's gone. The wind was cold,
I walked the block or so to the cathedral
Where you went to Mass before or after work
Or during lunch on holy days. Before
The altar of our God (my faith in him
Your precious gift to me) I prayed,
Remembering a dream I had one night
Shortly after you died. You were in the shop
In Shenandoah, busy at your chair,
Honing your razor on the leather strop,[4]
Preparing to shave a customer tilted back.
Reclining corpse-like under the white cloth.
The customer lifted his head.
It was Jesus and, accusing me
With eyes that pierced me through, he said,
"Your dad is very proud of you."

1999

The Mayflower Hotel, which opened in 1925, is an historic hotel on Connecticut Avenue in Washington, D.C. The largest luxury hotel in the capital, it hosts an Inaugural Ball that has often been considered nearly equal to the White House balls in prestige. Awad remembers in this poem, with great devotion and love, his father's barbershop inside this famous hotel. He focuses especially on his father's care for him, while also memorializing the deaths of both of his parents.

You might wish to consider this poem in the context of other works by Arab-American poets, such as Naomi Shihab Nye and Elmaz Abinader. Or compare it to other poems about the speaker's father, such as Robert Lowell's "Commander Lowell," Sylvia Plath's "Daddy," or Li-Young Lee's "The Gift."

4. Piece of leather used to straighten and polish a straight razor blade.

ADRIENNE RICH
b. 1929

THROUGHOUT HER LONG and distinguished career, Adrienne Rich's poetry has been continuously engaged with a series of interrelated preoccupations. These include the issues of sexual equality and cultural identity; the challenge of finding a persuasive and compelling poetic voice—and of giving voice to the silenced—while employing, of necessity, "the oppressor's language"; and the difficulty of reconciling the needs of the private self with the need for public and political expression. Ultimately, for Rich, the private, the public, and the political can never be truly separate. Like that of the African-American author W. E. B. DuBois (1868–1963), Rich's work remains persistently engaged with the problem of perceiving the world through the prism of a double conscious-ness—in her case, a consciousness that grows particularly out of the experiences of outsiderhood associated with being half-Jewish in a Christian-dominated cul-ture, a woman in a male-dominated culture, and a lesbian in a straight culture. That double consciousness extends to being a poet committed to the ambiva-lence, ambiguity, emotional honesty, and original and expressive use of form and language that characterize the best lyric poetry while engaging in a political arena where simple binaries of good and evil, and the slipperiest deployment of language, hold continual sway. Rich is also a formidable prose writer, and her essays and interviews chart an evolution of thought and feeling that moves in parallel with her verse, revealing a tale of personal and artistic development that spans the second half of the twentieth century and into the early years of the new millennium.

Rich was born in Baltimore, Maryland, in 1929. Her father, Arnold Rich, was a medical researcher and non-practicing Jew, and her mother was a Christian. Rich was raised in the Episcopalian church and, according to her prose piece "Split at the Root: An Essay in Jewish Identity" (1982), began to explore and un-derstand the Jewish half of ancestry only when she attended Radcliffe College and started contemplating "the daily, mundane anti-Semitisms of my entire life." Her intellectual and artistic development commenced early, while "reading my way through" her father's extensive (and "very Victorian, very Pre-Raphaelite") library, and she won the Yale Younger Poets Award (judged by W. H. Auden) at the unusually early age of twenty-two. Her first poems demonstrate a fluid mas-tery of traditional forms, yet they tend to deal only obliquely with what would later become her major personal and political preoccupations. Rich married the Harvard economist Alfred Conrad in 1953 and by 1959 had given birth to three sons. In the mid-1960s, Rich became increasingly engaged politically, at first with protesting the Vietnam War and later with the problems of urban poverty and inequality of education (brought home to her while working in the SEEK program at City College of New York). This move toward political engagement is reflected with great complexity in such poems as "The Burning of Paper Instead of Children." In the tragic aftermath of her husband's suicide in 1970, and in the light of her experiences as a woman and a mother, Rich increased her already deep engagement with women's liberation. She explores these concerns—along with such themes as the need to come to grips with one's cultural inheritance, however imperfect it might be, as well as the rewards and dangers of fame and recognition—in such poems as "Diving into the Wreck" and "Power." By the mid-1970s, in writings that include the essay "Women and Honor: Some Notes on Lying" (1975), Rich disclosed her lesbian identity, declaring that "the institutions of heterosexuality have forced lesbians to dissemble" and that "in lying to others we also lie to ourselves." It is this need for emotional honesty, in both the private and the public spheres, that Rich explores in the landmark sequence, "Twenty-One Love Poems."

Rich's work never assumes the superiority of the poet over the reader—reader and poet, her writings suggest, are engaged in parallel struggles for identity, dignity, and self-expression. In such later work as the final section of her long poem "The Atlas of the Difficult World," Rich posits a reader whose life is far from easy: "I know you are reading this poem for something, torn between bitterness and hope." In "Tattered Kaddish," Rich returns to the theme of Jewish identity, and the need to praise in a world where loss, disappointment, and despair are endemic.

Along with writing, Rich maintained a career as an influential teacher, serving as professor at such colleges and universities as Swarthmore, Columbia, CCNY, Brandeis, Rutgers, Cornell, Scripps, San Jose State, and finally Stanford. Despite the chronic pain of rheumatoid arthritis, Rich has had a remarkably active and honor-filled career, publishing numerous books of poetry as well as important collections of intellectual prose. Considered as a whole, Rich's poetic career is among the most individual and representative of the past six decades, a career marked by political courage, emotional honesty, and a dedication to the challenges and adventures of artistic craft.

FURTHER READING

Cheri Colby Langdell. *Adrienne Rich: The Moment of Change*. Westport, Conn.: Praeger, 2004.

Adrienne Rich. *Adrienne Rich's Poetry and Prose*. Norton Critical Edition. Ed. Barbara Charlesworth Gelpi and Albert Gelpi. New York: Norton, 1993.

———. *Arts of the Possible: Essays and Conversations*. New York: Norton, 2001.

———. *Blood, Bread, and Poetry: Selected Prose, 1979–1985*. New York: Norton, 1986.

———. *The Fact of a Doorframe: Poems, 1950–2001*. New Edition. New York: Norton, 2002.

———. *A Human Eye: Essays on Art in Society, 1997–2008*. New York: Norton, 2010.
———. *Of Woman Born: Motherhood as Experience and Institution*. New York: Norton, 1976.
———. *On Lies, Secrets, and Silences: Selected Prose, 1966–1978*. New York: Norton, 1979.
———. *The School Among the Ruins: Poems, 2000–2004*. New York: Norton, 2011.
———. *Telephone Ringing in the Labyrinth: Poems, 2004–2006*. New York: Norton, 2009.
———. *What Is Found There: Notebooks on Poetry and Politics*. Expanded Edition. New York: Norton, 2003.

The Burning of Paper Instead of Children

I was in danger of verbalizing my moral impulses out of existence.

—*Daniel Berrigan,*[1] *on trial in Baltimore*

1. My neighbor, a scientist and art-collector, telephones me in a state of violent emotion. He tells me that my son and his, aged eleven and twelve, have on the last day of school burned a mathematics textbook in the backyard. He has forbidden my son to come to his house for a week, and has forbidden his own son to leave the house during that time. "The burning of a book," he says, "arouses terrible sensations in me, memories of Hitler; there are few things that upset me so much as the idea of burning a book."

Back there: the library, walled
with green Britannicas
Looking again
in Dürer's *Complete Works*
for MELANCOLIA,[2] the baffled woman

the crocodiles in Herodotus[3]
the Book of the Dead[4]
the *Trial of Jeanne d'Arc,*[5] so blue
I think, It is her color

and they take the book away
because I dream of her too often

1. Jesuit priest who was convicted in 1968 of willfully injuring government property after burning Selective Service draft records in Baltimore in protest against the Vietnam War.
2. Engraving (1514) by the German artist Albrecht Dürer (1471–1528) that features a brooding female figure surrounded by symbolic objects.
3. The ancient Greek historian Herodotus (ca. 484–ca. 425 B.C.) colorfully describes the habits of crocodiles in his *Histories*.

4. Ancient Egyptian funerary text.
5. Transcription of the trial of the French peasant girl Joan of Arc (ca. 1412–1431) who, in response to divine promptings, led the French army to a series of victories during the Hundred Years' War. Captured by her English enemies, she was tried and condemned by a British ecclesiastical court and burned at the stake. She was later canonized.

*   *   *

love and fear in a house
knowledge of the oppressor
I know it hurts to burn

2. To imagine a time of silence
or few words
a time of chemistry and music

the hollows above your buttocks
traced by my hand
or, *hair is like flesh,* you said

an age of long silence

relief

from this tongue   this slab of limestone
or reinforced concrete
fanatics and traders
dumped on this coast wildgreen clayred
that breathed once
in signals of smoke
sweep of the wind

knowledge of the oppressor
this is the oppressor's language

yet I need it to talk to you

3. *People suffer highly in poverty and it takes dignity and intelligence to
overcome this suffering. Some of the suffering are: a child did not had dinner
last night: a child steal because he did not have money to buy it: to hear a
mother say she do not have money to buy food for her children and to see
a child without cloth it will make tears in your eyes.*[6]

(the fracture of order
the repair of speech
to overcome this suffering)

*   *   *

6. Rich quotes one of her students in the Open Admissions Program at City College of New York.

4. We lie under the sheet
after making love, speaking
of loneliness
relieved in a book
relived in a book
so on that page
the clot and fissure
of it appears
words of a man
in pain
a naked word
entering the clot
a hand grasping
through bars:

deliverance

What happens between us
has happened for centuries
we know it from literature

still it happens

sexual jealousy
outflung hand
beating bed

dryness of mouth
after panting

there are books that describe all this
and they are useless

You walk into the woods behind a house
there in that country
you find a temple
built eighteen hundred years ago
you enter without knowing
what it is you enter

so it is with us

*   *   *

no one knows what may happen
though the books tell everything

burn the texts said Artaud[7]

5. I am composing on the typewriter late at night, thinking of today. How
well we all spoke. A language is a map of our failures. Frederick Douglass[8]
wrote an English purer than Milton's. People suffer highly in poverty. There
are methods but we do not use them. Joan, who could not read, spoke some
peasant form of French. Some of the suffering are: it is hard to tell the truth;
this is America; I cannot touch you now. In America we have only the present
tense. I am in danger. You are in danger. The burning of a book arouses
no sensation in me. I know it hurts to burn. There are flames of napalm in
Catonsville, Maryland.[9] I know it hurts to burn. The typewriter is overheated,
my mouth is burning, I cannot touch you and this is the oppressor's language.

1968

Diving into the Wreck

First having read the book of myths,
and loaded the camera,
and checked the edge of the knife-blade,
I put on
the body-armor of black rubber
the absurd flippers
the grave and awkward mask.
I am having to do this
not like Cousteau[1] with his
assiduous team
aboard the sun-flooded schooner
but here alone.

There is a ladder.
The ladder is always there

7. Antonin Artaud (1896–1948), the French surrealist poet, asserted that "written poetry is worth
reading once, and then should be destroyed. Let
the dead poets make way for others."
8. The black abolitionist (1817?–1895), who
was born into slavery, self-liberated, and self-
educated, is noted for the directness and elegant
simplicity of his prose style.

9. In 1968, Daniel Berrigan and eight others,
using homemade napalm, destroyed draft records in Catonsville, Maryland.
1. Jacques Cousteau (1910–1997), French undersea explorer, famous for his books and a television series featuring the schooner *Calypso*, on
which he undertook his voyages.

hanging innocently
close to the side of the schooner.
We know what it is for,
we who have used it.
Otherwise
it is a piece of maritime floss
some sundry equipment.

I go down.
Rung after rung and still
the oxygen immerses me
the blue light
the clear atoms
of our human air.
I go down.
My flippers cripple me,
I crawl like an insect down the ladder
and there is no one
to tell me when the ocean
will begin.

First the air is blue and then
it is bluer and then green and then
black I am blacking out and yet
my mask is powerful
it pumps my blood with power
the sea is another story
the sea is not a question of power
I have to learn alone
to turn my body without force
in the deep element.

And now: it is easy to forget
what I came for
among so many who have always
lived here
swaying their crenellated fans
between the reefs
and besides
you breathe differently down here.

      ✳   ✳   ✳

I came to explore the wreck.
The words are purposes.
The words are maps.
I came to see the damage that was done
and the treasures that prevail.
I stroke the beam of my lamp
slowly along the flank
of something more permanent
than fish or weed

the thing I came for:
the wreck and not the story of the wreck
the thing itself and not the myth
the drowned face always staring
toward the sun
the evidence of damage
worn by salt and away into this threadbare beauty
the ribs of the disaster
curving their assertion
among the tentative haunters.

This is the place.
And I am here, the mermaid whose dark hair
streams black, the merman in his armored body.
We circle silently
about the wreck
we dive into the hold.
I am she: I am he

whose drowned face sleeps with open eyes
whose breasts still bear the stress
whose silver, copper, vermeil[2] cargo lies
obscurely inside barrels
half-wedged and left to rot
we are the half-destroyed instruments
that once held to a course
the water-eaten log
the fouled compass

    * * *

2. Silver-gilt.

We are, I am, you are
by cowardice or courage
the one who find our way
back to this scene
carrying a knife, a camera
a book of myths
in which
our names do not appear.

1972

In "Diving into the Wreck," the speaker's form of preparation for her dive (that is, reading "the book of myths"), along with the fact that she undertakes the effort alone, suggests that the poem's undersea exploration might be a journey into mythical and psychological—as well as literal—depths. Nonetheless, the physical preparations for the dive, and the gear involved, are rendered in meticulous detail. Note that her "body-armor of black rubber" and her "mask" make her prescribed gender designation unreadable as she takes her journey.

Power

Living   in the earth-deposits   of our history

Today a backhoe divulged   out of a crumbling flank of earth
one bottle   amber   perfect   a hundred-year-old
cure for fever   or melancholy   a tonic[1]
for living on this earth   in the winters of this climate.

Today I was reading about Marie Curie:[2]
she must have known she suffered   from radiation sickness
her body bombarded for years   by the element
she had purified
It seems she denied to the end
the source of the cataracts on her eyes
the cracked and suppurating skin   of her finger-ends
till she could no longer hold   a test-tube or a pencil

⁂   ⁂   ⁂

---

1. That is, a patent medicine.
2. Marie Skłodowska Curie (1867–1934), Polish chemist and physicist. She shared a Nobel Prize in physics with her French husband, Pierre Curie, for her pioneering work on radioactivity, and she was the sole winner, in 1911, of a Nobel Prize in chemistry for isolating radium in its pure form.

She died   a famous woman   denying
her wounds
denying
her wounds   came   from the same source as her power.

1974

FROM *Twenty-One Love Poems*

I

Whenever in this city, screens flicker
with pornography, with science-fiction vampires,
victimized hirelings bending to the lash,
we also have to walk . . . if simply as we walk
through the rainsoaked garbage, the tabloid cruelties
of our own neighborhoods.
We need to grasp our lives inseparable
from those rancid dreams, that blurt of metal, those disgraces,
and the red begonia perilously flashing
from a tenement sill six stories high,
or the long-legged young girls playing ball
in the junior highschool playground.
No one has imagined us. We want to live like trees,
sycamores blazing through the sulfuric air,
dappled with scars, still exuberantly budding,
our animal passion rooted in the city.

II

I wake up in your bed. I know I have been dreaming.
Much earlier, the alarm broke us from each other,
You've been at your desk for hours. I know what I dreamed:
our friend the poet comes into my room
where I've been writing for days,
drafts, carbons, poems are scattered everywhere,
and I want to show her one poem
which is the poem of my life. But I hesitate,
and wake. You've kissed my hair
to wake me. *I dreamed you were a poem,*
I say, *a poem I wanted to show someone . . .*
and I laugh and fall dreaming again
of the desire to show you to everyone I love,

to move openly together
in the pull of gravity, which is not simple,
which carries the feathered grass a long way down the upbreathing air.

III
Since we're not young, weeks have to do time
for years of missing each other. Yet only this odd warp
in time tells me we're not young.
Did I ever walk the morning streets at twenty,
my limbs streaming with a purer joy?
did I lean from my window over the city
listening for the future
as I listen with nerves tuned for your ring?
And you, you move towards me with the same tempo.
Your eyes are everlasting, the green spark
of the blue-eyed grass of early summer,
the green-blue wild cress washed by the spring.
At twenty, yes: we thought we'd live forever.
At forty-five, I want to know even our limits.
I touch you knowing we weren't born tomorrow,
and somehow, each of us will help the other live,
and somehow, each of us must help the other die.

IX
Your silence today is a pond where drowned things live
I want to see raised dripping and brought into the sun.
It's not my own face I see there, but other faces,
even your face at another age.
Whatever's lost there is needed by both of us—
a watch of old gold, a water-blurred fever chart,
a key. . . . Even the silt and pebbles of the bottom
deserve their glint of recognition. I fear this silence,
this inarticulate life. I'm waiting
for a wind that will gently open this sheeted water
for once, and show me what I can do
for you, who have often made the unnameable
nameable for others, even for me.

XIII
The rules break like a thermometer,
quicksilver spills across the charted systems,

we're out in a country that has no language
no laws, we're chasing the raven and the wren
through gorges unexplored since dawn
whatever we do together is pure invention
the maps they gave us were out of date
by years . . . we're driving through the desert
wondering if the water will hold out
the hallucinations turn to simple villages
the music on the radio comes clear—
neither *Rosenkavalier* nor *Götterdämmerung*[1]
but a woman's voice singing old songs
with new words, with a quiet bass, a flute
plucked and fingered by women outside the law.

XX

That conversation we were always on the edge
of having, runs on in my head,
at night the Hudson trembles in New Jersey light
polluted water yet reflecting even
sometimes the moon
and I discern a woman
I loved, drowning in secrets, fear wound round her throat
and choking her like hair.[2] And this is she
with whom I tried to speak, whose hurt, expressive head
turning aside from pain, is dragging down deeper
where it cannot hear me,
and soon I shall know I was talking to my own soul.

XXI

The dark lintels, the blue and foreign stones
of the great round rippled by stone implements
the midsummer night light rising from beneath
the horizon—when I said "a cleft of light"
I meant this. And this is not Stonehenge
simply nor any place but the mind
casting back to where her solitude,
shared, could be chosen without loneliness,

---

1. Operas by German composers Richard Strauss
and Richard Wagner whose female protagonists,
the Marschallin and Brünnhilde, face the pain
of lost love and renunciation.

2. See Robert Browning's poem "Porphyria's
Lover" (1836).

not easily nor without pains to stake out
the circle, the heavy shadows, the great light.
I choose to be the figure in that light,
half-blotted by darkness, something moving
across that space, the color of stone
greeting the moon, yet more than stone:
a woman. I choose to walk here. And to draw this circle.

1974–76

The "Twenty-One Love Poems" sequence, in its surrealistic technique and its blending of love and politics, recalls Chilean poet Pablo Neruda's *Twenty Love Songs and a Poem of Despair* (1924). Moreover, although none of its unrhymed free verse lyrics are in traditional sonnet form—fourteen lines of iambic pentameter following a specific rhyming pattern—such elements as the length of the songs (ranging in this selection from twelve to seventeen lines), along with the songs' preoccupation with the problems of love and language, and their intimate address to a poet's real or imagined lover, recall notable sonnet sequences such as those by Petrarch, Shakespeare, Sir Philip Sidney, Elizabeth Barrett Browning, and Edna St. Vincent Millay.

Tattered Kaddish

Taurean[1] reaper of the wild apple field
messenger from earthmire gleaning
transcripts of fog
in the nineteenth year and the eleventh month
speak your tattered Kaddish for all suicides:

Praise to life though it crumbled in like a tunnel
on ones we knew and loved

> Praise to life though its windows blew shut
> on the breathing-room of ones we knew and loved

Praise to life though ones we knew and loved
loved it badly, too well, and not enough

> Praise to life though it tightened like a knot
> on the hearts of ones we thought we knew loved us

*   *   *

---

1. Taurus: constellation (also known as "The Bull") near Orion and Aries; also Rich's astrological sign.

Praise to life giving room and reason
to ones we knew and loved who felt unpraisable

Praise to them, how they loved it, when they could.
1989

The Mourner's Kaddish is the traditional Jewish prayer for the dead. The word *Kaddish* means "holy" or "sanctified." The prayer does not refer directly to the dead person but instead exalts God's name and presence. It is recited toward the end of Jewish services, at funerals and memorials, and when mourning the death of a loved one.

Rich has provided this commentary for the poem's first line: "The Reapers of the Field are the Comrades, masters of this wisdom, because *Mahlkut* is called the Apple Field, and She grows sprouts of secrets and new meanings of Torah. Those who constantly create new interpretations of Torah are the ones who reap Her."

FROM *An Atlas of the Difficult World*

XIII (Dedications)
I know you are reading this poem
late, before leaving your office
of the one intense yellow lamp-spot and the darkening window
in the lassitude of a building faded to quiet
long after rush-hour.   I know you are reading this poem
standing up in a bookstore far from the ocean
on a grey day of early spring, faint flakes driven
across the plains' enormous spaces around you.
I know you are reading this poem
in a room where too much has happened for you to bear
where the bedclothes lie in stagnant coils on the bed
and the open valise speaks of flight
but you cannot leave yet.   I know you are reading this poem
as the underground train loses momentum and before running
        up the stairs
toward a new kind of love
your life has never allowed.
I know you are reading this poem by the light
of the television screen where soundless images jerk and slide
while you wait for the newscast from the *intifada*.[1]

---

1. Arabic word that means "shaking off," "rebellion," or "resistance to oppression"; often used in reference to Palestinian uprisings against Israeli rule.

I know you are reading this poem in a waiting-room
of eyes met and unmeeting, of identity with strangers.
I know you are reading this poem by fluorescent light
in the boredom and fatigue of the young who are counted out,
count themselves out, at too early an age.   I know
you are reading this poem through your failing sight, the thick
lens enlarging these letters beyond all meaning yet you read on
because even the alphabet is precious.
I know you are reading this poem as you pace beside the stove
warming milk, a crying child on your shoulder, a book in your
     hand
because life is short and you too are thirsty.
I know you are reading this poem which is not in your language
guessing at some words while others keep you reading
and I want to know which words they are.
I know you are reading this poem listening for something, torn
     between bitterness and hope
turning back once again to the task you cannot refuse.
I know you are reading this poem because there is nothing else
     left to read
there where you have landed, stripped as you are.

1990–91

Section 13 of "An Atlas of the Difficult World" is the final section of the sequence.

GARY SNYDER
b. 1930

Gary snyder has been leading a countercultural movement founded on
heightened ecological and spiritual awareness since the 1950s. He is a leading
"eco" poet of the United States and the Pacific Rim, having published more than
twenty-five books to date. His poetry, as Patrick Murphy has written, is transcultural. It combines an elliptical, spare, avant-garde style with a consciousness suffused in the circumambient natural world. The work celebrates archaic values
and visionary states of being, far apart from conventional motives or actions.

Snyder's writings place him in several major poetic traditions. He belongs to the Beat Generation, along with Allen Ginsberg, Diane di Prima, and the early Amiri Baraka. Novelist Jack Kerouac modeled his protagonist Japhy Ryder in *The Dharma Bums* after him. Yet Snyder's focus on the Western wilderness also places him in the longer American literary tradition of nature writing associated with such nineteenth-century poets as William Cullen Bryant, Ralph Waldo Emerson, and Emily Dickinson; such twentieth-century poets as Robert Frost and Robinson Jeffers; and such present-day poets as Joy Harjo. Snyder's work on Japan and on Buddhism links him to such poets as Ernest Fenollosa and Sadakichi Hartmann at the end of the nineteenth century and Yone Noguchi, Kenneth Rexroth, and (again) Allen Ginsberg in the twentieth. His verbal experimentalism reveals the influence of the modernist masters Ezra Pound and William Carlos Williams. Finally, Snyder's eco poetry is often discussed in relationship to Native American writing, which ranges from the communal voices of earlier centuries to the work of Joy Harjo, Linda Hogan, and Sherman Alexie today.

Snyder was born in San Francisco in 1930 and grew up in Oregon and Washington. Having studied Buddhism, literature, and mythology, he graduated from Reed College in 1951 with a bachelor's degree in anthropology. Then he attended the University of California, Berkeley, to study Oriental languages. From 1953 to 1956, he worked with the Beat poets in the San Francisco area. In 1956 he moved to Japan, where he resided for about twelve years, translating Zen texts and studying Rinzai Zen Buddhism. In 1962 he met the Dalai Lama in India. After his return from Japan, he chose to reside mostly in California's Sierra Nevada mountains. He taught for many years at the University of California, Davis. Among his many awards are the Pulitzer Prize, the Ruth Lilly Poetry Prize, the Shelley Memorial Poetry Award, the Bollingen Prize for Poetry, and the John Hay Award for Nature Writing.

FURTHER READING

Timothy Gray. *Gary Snyder and the Pacific Rim: Creating Countercultural Community*. Iowa City: University of Iowa Press, 2006.

Patrick Murphy. *A Place for Wayfaring: The Poetry and Prose of Gary Snyder*. Corvallis: Oregon State University Press, 2000.

Gary Snyder. *The Gary Snyder Reader: Prose, Poetry, and Translations, 1952–1998*. Berkeley, Calif.: Counterpoint, 2000.

———. *Riprap and Cold Mountain Poems*. Berkeley, Calif.: Counterpoint, 2010.

———. *Turtle Island*. New York: New Directions, 1974.

John Whalen-Bridge and Gary Storhoff, eds. *The Emergence of Buddhist American Literature*. New York: SUNY Press, 2009.

O Waters

O waters,
wash us, me,
under the wrinkled granite
straight-up slab,

and sitting by camp in the pine shade
Nanao[1] sleeping,
mountains humming and crumbling
snowfields melting
soil
building on tiny ledges

for wild onions and the flowers
Blue
Polemonium[2]

great
earth
sangha[3]

1974

"O Waters" melds Snyder's experience in the Sierra Nevada with his recollections of
Nanao, Japan, a medium-sized city founded in 1939. *Nanao* means "seven tails." Seven
mountain ridges surround Nanao; they can be viewed from the castle ruins in the city.

Walking Through Myoshin-ji

Straight stone walks
up lanes between mud walls

. . . the sailors who handled the ships
from Korea and China,
the carpenters, chisels like razors,

✻   ✻   ✻

1. City in Japan on the coast of the Sea of Japan.
2. A North American plant that produces laven-
der-blue flowers in spring and summer.

3. Refers either to a group of ordained Buddhist
monks and nuns or to Buddhists who have at-
tained a level of "spiritual awakening."

young monks working on *mu*,[1]

and the pine trees
that surrounded this city.
the Ancient Ones, each one
anonymous.
green needles.
lumber,
ash.

VII, 81, Kyoto

1983

Myoshin-ji is a Buddhist temple complex in Kyoto, Japan, founded in 1342. Snyder visited the temple complex in 1981.

DEREK WALCOTT
b. 1930

DEREK WALCOTT IS ONE OF THE FEW poets from the Americas to receive a Nobel Prize in literature. In addition to his success as a poet, Walcott enjoys a worldwide reputation as a playwright in both drama and musical theater. His writing places him at the intersections of U.S., British, African, Dutch, Caribbean, and postcolonial cultures and literatures. In addition to many poetry collections, plays, and prose works, Walcott has published the book-length poem *Omeros*—a late-twentieth-century version of the *Iliad* and the *Odyssey* set in his native Caribbean. In addition to the Nobel Prize, he has received a MacArthur Foundation "genius" award, a Royal Society of Literature Award, and the Queen's Medal for Poetry. He is an honorary member of the American Academy and Institute of Arts and Letters. Jeffrey Gray has called Walcott "the most celebrated poet of the Caribbean and one of the most important postcolonial writers of the world."

Walcott was born in Castries on the island of Saint Lucia, one of the Lesser Antilles. He is of mixed African, English, and Dutch ancestry. His mother was

1. Literally "not," "nothing," or "non being" (Japanese). Central to the Rinzai school of Zen Buddhism, the word is used to interrupt and question everyday logic.

connected to the town's Methodist school; his father, who died early in his life, was a watercolorist. Both grandmothers were descendants of slaves. Walcott studied at Saint Mary's College on Saint Lucia and at the University of the West Indies in Jamaica. He then moved to Trinidad, where he worked as a theater and art critic. Later he began teaching at Boston University, where he founded the university's Boston Playwrights' Theater. Since the 1960s he has divided his time between the United States and the Caribbean.

FURTHER READING

Paula Burnett. *Derek Walcott: Politics and Poetics.* Gainesville: University Press of Florida, 2001.
Jeffrey Gray. "Walcott, Derek." In *The Greenwood Encyclopedia of American Poets and Poetry,* vol. 5, ed. Jeffrey Gray, James McCorkle, and Mary McAleer Balkun, 1644–50. Westport, Conn.: Greenwood Press, 2006.
Jahan Ramazani. *A Transnational Poetics.* Chicago: University of Chicago Press, 2009.
Guy L. Rotella. *Castings: Monuments and Monumentality in Poems by Elizabeth Bishop, Robert Lowell, James Merrill, Derek Walcott, and Seamus Heaney.* Nashville, Tenn.: Vanderbilt University Press, 2004.
Derek Walcott. *Collected Poems, 1948–1984.* New York: Farrar Straus & Giroux, 1986.
———. *Omeros.* New York: Farrar Straus & Giroux, 1992.
———. *White Egrets.* New York: Farrar Straus & Giroux, 2010.

Love After Love

The time will come
when, with elation
you will greet yourself arriving
at your own door, in your own mirror
and each will smile at the other's welcome.

And say, sit here. Eat.
You will love again the stranger who was your self.
Give wine. Give bread. Give back your heart
to itself, to the stranger who has loved you

all your life, whom you ignored
for another, who knows you by heart.
Take down the love letters from the bookshelf,

the photographs, the desperate notes,
peel your own image from the mirror.
Sit. Feast on your life.

1986

"Love After Love" provides a series of metaphors ("door," "feast") for self-healing and self-acceptance, perhaps in the aftermath of depression or a failed relationship.

Dark August

So much rain, so much life like the swollen sky
of this black August. My sister, the sun,
broods in her yellow room and won't come out.

Everything goes to hell; the mountains fume
like a kettle, rivers overrun; still,
she will not rise and turn off the rain.

She is in her room, fondling old things,
my poems, turning her album. Even if thunder falls
like a crash of plates from the sky,

she does not come out.
Don't you know I love you but am hopeless
at fixing the rain? But I am learning slowly

to love the dark days, the steaming hills,
the air with gossiping mosquitoes,
and to sip the medicine of bitterness,

so that when you emerge, my sister,
parting the beads of the rain,
with your forehead of flowers and eyes of forgiveness,

all will not be as it was, but it will be true
(you see they will not let me love
as I want), because, my sister, then

I would have learnt to love black days like bright ones,
the black rain, the white hills, when once
I loved only my happiness and you.

1986

"Dark August" was influenced by the hurricane season in the Caribbean as well as the volcanic origins of Walcott's home island, Saint Lucia.

SYLVIA PLATH
1932–1963

SYLVIA PLATH wrote poems with meticulous care and blazing intensity. She channeled into her poetry all of her personal anguish and fierceness as well as the political opposition to war, injustice, and iniquitous gender roles that was circulating through segments of Anglo-American culture in the late 1950s and early 1960s. She pioneered a new, more assertive and explicit voice for women poets. Her brief career as a poet, foreshortened by her suicide at the age of thirty, showed just how close to the bone poetry could get. Plath's poetry laid bare private wounds and desires, brought public traumas up close and personal, and subtly explored the powers and limits of language. By revealing the Shakespearean complexities and intensities of contemporary life, Plath exposed raw nerves in many readers and in society. Poetry has never been quite the same.

Plath was born in Boston in 1932, the first child of Otto Plath (a professor of zoology) and Aurelia Plath (a well-educated homemaker). Plath's father, a German immigrant, was consumed with his work, giving his wife and children little time and attention. Plath's mother, the daughter of Austrian immigrants, provided an enriched, if highly controlled, intellectual environment for Sylvia and her younger brother, Warren. Otto Plath died from the effects of untreated diabetes when Sylvia was eight. This loss of an already somewhat absent father was devastating to his daughter. She was later to compose some of her most famous poems about him, such as "Daddy" and "Lady Lazarus." After his death, Aurelia Plath went to work as an instructor of secretarial skills, ultimately teaching at Boston University, where her husband had taught. Sylvia Plath's mixed feelings toward her mother resonate in such poems as "The Disquieting Muses" and "Medusa." Plath's poetry registers the impact of her interrupted childhood at every stage of her career.

Encouraged by her mother, Plath became a stellar student. After graduating from Wellesley High School, she attended Smith College on full scholarship. Graduating from Smith summa cum laude, she won a scholarship to study at Cambridge University in England, where she received a master's in English literature. Yet despite her academic success, Plath's personal life was troubled. At the age of twenty, she tried to commit suicide by taking an overdose of sleeping pills—an event reflected in her autobiographical novel, *The Bell Jar*. Institutionalized at McLean Hospital, she received excellent psychiatric care from Dr. Ruth Beuscher and made a quick recovery. But her problems with bipolar mood disorder had only begun, and they would not end until her death ten years later.

At Cambridge, Plath met the young English poet Ted Hughes, whom she married after a whirlwind courtship in 1956. The couple moved to the United States, where Plath took a creative writing class from Robert Lowell, who was just then making his "breakthrough" into a more personal style of poetry. Among the other students in the class was the autobiographical poet Anne Sexton, who was to become a close friend. (Both Lowell and Sexton are included in this anthology.) Plath and Hughes returned to England in 1959. The next year saw the birth of their first child, a daughter named Frieda (now a poet herself), and the publication of Plath's first book of poetry. In 1961 Plath and Hughes moved to a country home in Devon. Cold (the house was unheated) and exhausted, Plath spent the year writing poems and *The Bell Jar*.

Early in 1962 Plath's son, Nicholas, was born. Soon thereafter, Plath discovered that her husband was having an affair. After a heated confrontation, he left her, and she moved back to London with her children. She sought to support herself through writing, supplemented by gifts from her mother. Emotionally devastated and physically ill, she composed the poems that ultimately brought her great fame. In October 1962, the month of her thirtieth birthday, she experienced a creative frenzy, writing "Daddy," "Medusa," "The Jailer," and "Lady Lazarus." Sophisticated yet primitive, "Daddy" instantly became the apex of the "confessional" movement that Robert Lowell had spawned. It is one of the most powerful and oft-cited poems of the century. Four days later Plath composed a companion piece about a mother-figure, "Medusa," and one day after that she completed her family trilogy by composing a poem about a husband called "The Jailer." "Lady Lazarus," written a few days later, returns to the scene of "Daddy," entwining domestic relations with the imagery of Nazi Germany.

By early 1963 Plath was writing eerily detached short poems with one-word titles such as "Kindness," "Words," and "Edge." "Edge," perhaps the last poem she wrote, calmly states, "We have come so far, it is over." Six days later, on February 11, Plath put her head in the kitchen oven and turned on the gas. By the time she was discovered, she had suffocated.

Plath's poems do not transparently reproduce her lived experience. She thought of "Daddy," for example, as a story about an invented character. Nevertheless, her poems do bear the emotional weight of her private life. In her texts we witness a young woman's struggle for voice, creativity, and social standing in a patriarchal culture. We encounter feelings of abandonment, anger, loneliness, self-doubt, desire, love, and despair. We enter a verbal world in which personal and public discourses rub off on each other, creating a contingent kinship between the suffering private self and the wretched of the earth. And, always, we observe the struggle for an expressive, artistic language that was at the core of Plath's enterprise. In her best poems she was able to merge personal disclosure with social implication, revelation with spectacle, vulnerability with irony, and language with emotion. She composed some of the most vital poems of her era, by breaking through the limits of what lyric poetry could and should do.

FURTHER READING

Steven Gould Axelrod. *Sylvia Plath: The Wound and the Cure of Words*. Baltimore: Johns
 Hopkins University Press, 1990.
Sally Bayley and Tracy Brain, eds. *Representing Sylvia Plath*. Cambridge, Eng.: Cambridge
 University Press, 2011.
Christina Britzolakis, *Sylvia Plath and the Theatre of Mourning*. Oxford: Clarendon Press,
 1999.
Kathleen Connors and Sally Bayley, eds. *Eye Rhymes: Sylvia Plath's Art of the Visual*. Oxford,
 Eng.: Oxford University Press, 2007.
Jo Gill, ed. *The Cambridge Companion to Sylvia Plath*. Cambridge, Eng.: Cambridge Uni-
 versity Press, 2006.
Anita Helle, ed. *The Unraveling Archive: Essays on Sylvia Plath*. Ann Arbor: University of
 Michigan Press, 2007.
Sylvia Plath. *The Bell Jar*. New York: Harper, 2009.
———. *Collected Poems*. Ed. Ted Hughes. New York: Harper, 2008.
———. *Johnny Panic and the Bible of Dreams: Short Stories, Prose, and Diary Excerpts*. New
 York: Harper, 2008.
———. *Letters Home: Correspondence, 1950–1963*, ed. Aurelia S. Plath. New York: Harper,
 1992.
———. *Unabridged Journals*. Ed. Karen V. Kukil. New York: Random House–Anchor, 2000.
Jacqueline Rose. *The Haunting of Sylvia Plath*. Cambridge, Mass.: Harvard University Press,
 1991.
Linda Wagner-Martin. *Sylvia Plath: A Biography*. New York: Simon & Schuster, 1987.

The Moon and the Yew Tree

This is the light of the mind, cold and planetary.
The trees of the mind are black. The light is blue.
The grasses unload their griefs on my feet as if I were God,
Prickling my ankles and murmuring of their humility.
Fumy, spiritous mists inhabit this place
Separated from my house by a row of headstones.
I simply cannot see where there is to get to.

The moon is no door. It is a face in its own right,
White as a knuckle and terribly upset.
It drags the sea after it like a dark crime; it is quiet
With the O-gape of complete despair. I live here.
Twice on Sunday, the bells startle the sky—
Eight great tongues affirming the Resurrection.
At the end, they soberly bong out their names.

✳   ✳   ✳

The yew tree points up. It has a Gothic shape.
The eyes lift after it and find the moon.
The moon is my mother. She is not sweet like Mary.
Her blue garments unloose small bats and owls.
How I would like to believe in tenderness—
The face of the effigy, gentled by candles,
Bending, on me in particular, its mild eyes.

I have fallen a long way. Clouds are flowering
Blue and mystical over the face of the stars.
Inside the church, the saints will be all blue,
Floating on their delicate feet over the cold pews,
Their hands and faces stiff with holiness.
The moon sees nothing of this. She is bald and wild.
And the message of the yew tree is blackness—blackness and silence.

1961

"The Moon and the Yew Tree" evokes a nighttime scene visible from Plath's house in rural Devon, England. The yew—a large evergreen tree—was situated to the west of the house in a churchyard.

Elm

For Ruth Fainlight[1]

I know the bottom, she says. I know it with my great tap root:[2]
It is what you fear.
I do not fear it: I have been there.

Is it the sea you hear in me,
Its dissatisfactions?
Or the voice of nothing, that was your madness?

Love is a shadow.
How you lie and cry after it.
Listen: these are its hooves: it has gone off, like a horse.

All night I shall gallop thus, impetuously,
Till your head is a stone, your pillow a little turf,
Echoing, echoing.

1. English poet and short-story writer, born in the United States (in 1931), a friend of Plath.   2. Primary root.

＊　＊　＊

Or shall I bring you the sound of poisons?
This is rain now, this big hush.
And this is the fruit of it: tin-white, like arsenic.[3]

I have suffered the atrocity of sunsets.
Scorched to the root
My red filaments burn and stand, a hand of wires.

Now I break up in pieces that fly about like clubs.
A wind of such violence
Will tolerate no bystanding: I must shriek.

The moon, also, is merciless: she would drag me
Cruelly, being barren.
Her radiance scathes me. Or perhaps I have caught her.

I let her go. I let her go
Diminished and flat, as after radical surgery.
How your bad dreams possess and endow me.

I am inhabited by a cry.
Nightly it flaps out
Looking, with its hooks, for something to love.

I am terrified by this dark thing
That sleeps in me;
All day I feel its soft, feathery turnings, its malignity.

Clouds pass and disperse.
Are those the faces of love, those pale irretrievables?
Is it for such I agitate my heart?

I am incapable of more knowledge.
What is this, this face
So murderous in its strangle of branches?——

Its snaky acids kiss.
It petrifies[4] the will. These are the isolate, slow faults
That kill, that kill, that kill.

1962

---

3. Metalloid element used commercially as a poison.

4. Literally: turns to stone. Metaphorically: deadens, paralyzes, frightens, amazes.

A very large elm tree overshadowed Plath's home in Devon. In this poem, the elm speaks to a human listener.

Daddy

You do not do, you do not do
Any more, black shoe
In which I have lived like a foot[1]
For thirty years, poor and white,
Barely daring to breathe or Achoo.

Daddy, I have had to kill you.
You died before I had time—
Marble-heavy, a bag full of God,
Ghastly statue with one gray toe
Big as a Frisco seal

And a head in the freakish Atlantic
Where it pours bean green over blue
In the waters off beautiful Nauset.[2]
I used to pray to recover you.
Ach, du.[3]

In the German tongue, in the Polish town[4]
Scraped flat by the roller
Of wars, wars, wars.
But the name of the town is common.
My Polack friend

Says there are a dozen or two.
So I never could tell where you
Put your foot, your root,
I never could talk to you.
The tongue stuck in my jaw.

It stuck in a barb wire snare.
Ich, ich, ich, ich,[5]
I could hardly speak.

1. Possibly an echo of the nursery rhyme "There Was an Old Woman Who Lived in a Shoe."
2. A beach on Cape Cod, Massachusetts, named after the original Native American inhabitants.
3. Ah, you (German).
4. Otto Plath, Sylvia Plath's father, was born in Grabów, which historically has been part of both Poland and Germany.
5. I, I, I, I (German).

I thought every German was you.
And the language obscene

An engine, an engine
Chuffing me off like a Jew.
A Jew to Dachau, Auschwitz, Belsen.[6]
I began to talk like a Jew.
I think I may well be a Jew.

The snows of the Tyrol,[7] the clear beer of Vienna
Are not very pure or true.
With my gipsy ancestress and my weird luck
And my Taroc pack and my Taroc pack[8]
I may be a bit of a Jew.

I have always been scared of you,
With your Luftwaffe,[9] your gobbledygoo.
And your neat mustache
And your Aryan[10] eye, bright blue.
Panzer-man,[11] panzer-man, O You——

Not God but a swastika
So black no sky could squeak through.
Every woman adores a Fascist,
The boot in the face, the brute
Brute heart of a brute like you.

You stand at the blackboard, daddy,
In the picture I have of you,
A cleft in your chin instead of your foot
But no less a devil for that, no not
Any less the black man[12] who

Bit my pretty red heart in two.
I was ten when they buried you.
At twenty I tried to die

6. Death camps.
7. A region of the Alps, mostly in Austria.
8. A taroc or tarot pack of divining cards is used for fortune-telling.
9. German air force before and during World War II (German). Gobbledygoo: gobbledygook, an American colloquial term of World War II vintage meaning nonsensical language.
10. In Nazi racism, people or traits corresponding to the Nordic "master race"; in U.S. white supremacism, people or traits deriving from northern Europe.
11. A German soldier belonging to a panzer (armored tank) unit.
12. In American colonial times, the devil was sometimes called "the black man" because he was understood to live in the forest shadows.

And get back, back, back to you.
I thought even the bones would do.

But they pulled me out of the sack,
And they stuck me together with glue.
And then I knew what to do.
I made a model of you,
A man in black[13] with a Meinkampf look

And a love of the rack and the screw.[14]
And I said I do, I do.
So daddy, I'm finally through.
The black telephone's off at the root,
The voices just can't worm through.

If I've killed one man, I've killed two—
The vampire who said he was you
And drank my blood for a year,
Seven years, if you want to know.
Daddy, you can lie back now.

There's a stake in your fat black heart
And the villagers never liked you.
They are dancing and stamping on you.
They always knew it was you.
Daddy, daddy, you bastard, I'm through.

1962

Although "Daddy" has often been read as confessional, its details depart significantly from the facts of Plath's life. Her father, Otto Plath, had no Nazi sympathies, and Plath herself had no known Jewish or Gypsy ancestry. In a BBC radio program, Plath presented the poem as simply a fiction: "Here is a poem spoken by a girl with an Electra complex. Her father died while she thought he was God. Her case is complicated by the fact that her father was also a Nazi and her mother very possibly part Jewish. In the daughter the two strains marry and paralyze each other—she has to act out the awful little allegory once over before she is free of it." Nevertheless, the poem does have autobiographical resonances. Plath's father died when she was young (eight, not ten), and Plath had separated from her husband before composing this poem—a loss that could have revived feelings

13. Popular conception of a demon. Plath's husband, Ted Hughes, often dressed in black. Meinkampf: *Mein Kampf* (German for "My Struggle") was the title of an anti-Semitic, mili- taristic autobiography by Adolf Hitler (1889– 1945).
14. Medieval torture devices.

about the earlier loss. Steven Gould Axelrod suggests that the poem does indeed figure Plath's "unresolved conflicts with paternal authority" and her "paralyzing self-division" but that it does so in the context of a woman poet's struggle to speak, as indicated by the poem's emphasis on "talk" and "tongue." Alternatively, one could consider this poem as an act of the historical imagination, portraying the horror of the Holocaust through a fantasy of dysfunctional domestic life.

Medusa

Off that landspit of stony mouth-plugs,
Eyes rolled by white sticks,
Ears cupping the sea's incoherences,
You house your unnerving head—God-ball,
Lens of mercies,

Your stooges
Plying their wild cells in my keel's shadow,
Pushing by like hearts,
Red stigmata[1] at the very center,
Riding the rip tide to the nearest point of departure,

Dragging their Jesus hair.
Did I escape, I wonder?
My mind winds to you
Old barnacled umbilicus, Atlantic cable,
Keeping itself, it seems, in a state of miraculous repair.

In any case, you are always there,
Tremulous breath at the end of my line,
Curve of water upleaping
To my water rod, dazzling and grateful,
Touching and sucking.

I didn't call you.
I didn't call you at all.
Nevertheless, nevertheless
You steamed to me over the sea,
Fat and red, a placenta[2]

*   *   *

1. Scars, stains, marks; sometimes the wounds on the crucified body of Christ.

2. Organ that unites a fetus to the maternal uterus.

Paralysing the kicking lovers.
Cobra light
Squeezing the breath from the blood bells
Of the fuchsia. I could draw no breath,
Dead and moneyless,

Overexposed, like an X-ray.
Who do you think you are?
A Communion wafer? Blubbery Mary?
I shall take no bite of your body,
Bottle in which I live,

Ghastly Vatican.
I am sick to death of hot salt.
Green as eunuchs,[3] your wishes
Hiss at my sins.
Off, off, eely tentacle!

There is nothing between us.

1962

In Greek myth, Medusa was one of the Gorgon monsters. Her head covered with serpents rather than hair, she had wings, claws, and enormous teeth, and she turned anyone who looked at her to stone. The hero Perseus approached her by viewing her through a mirror, cut her head off, and presented it to the goddess Athena, who put it on her shield. Medusa is also another name for jellyfish, one genus of which is called the Aurelia. Sylvia Plath's mother was named Aurelia. Like the poems preceding and following it, this poem was written as Plath's thirtieth birthday approached, after she had separated from her husband and after her mother had visited from the United States offering help and advice. Steven Gould Axelrod comments that the speaker's last sentence "implies not only that she and her mother have nothing in common but also that there is nothing dividing them."

The Jailer

My night sweats grease his breakfast plate.
The same placard of blue fog is wheeled into position
With the same trees and headstones.
Is that all he can come up with,
The rattler of keys?

3. Castrated men.

*   *   *

I have been drugged and raped.
Seven hours knocked out of my right mind
Into a black sack
Where I relax, foetus or cat,
Lever of his wet dreams.

Something is gone.
My sleeping capsule,[1] my red and blue zeppelin
Drops me from a terrible altitude.
Carapace[2] smashed,
I spread to the beaks of birds.

O little gimlets[3]—
What holes this papery day is already full of!
He has been burning me with cigarettes,
Pretending I am a negress with pink paws.
I am myself. That is not enough.

The fever trickles and stiffens in my hair.
My ribs show. What have I eaten?
Lies and smiles.
Surely the sky is not that color,
Surely the grass should be rippling.

All day, gluing my church of burnt matchsticks,
I dream of someone else entirely.
And he, for this subversion,
Hurts me, he
With his armor of fakery,

His high cold masks of amnesia.
How did I get here?
Indeterminate criminal,
I die with variety—
Hung, starved, burned, hooked.

I imagine him
Impotent as distant thunder,

1. Perhaps Phenobarbital, a powerful barbiturate widely prescribed in the 1950s and 1960s.
2. Shell.
3. Woodworking tools with screw points, used for boring holes.

In whose shadow I have eaten my ghost ration.
I wish him dead or away.
That, it seems, is the impossibility.

That being free. What would the dark
Do without fevers to eat?
What would the light
Do without eyes to knife, what would he
Do, do, do without me?

1962

Linda Wagner-Martin describes "The Jailer" as Plath's response to Ted Hughes's final abandonment of her: "Sylvia continued to write out her vengeance. On October 17, she wrote 'The Jailer,' the most vindictive of her late poems. In it, the male protagonist treats the speaker like a slave. She is worn to exhaustion. His rejection of her turns her to a skeleton."

Lady Lazarus

I have done it again.
One year in every ten
I manage it——

A sort of walking miracle, my skin
Bright as a Nazi lampshade,[1]
My right foot

A paperweight,
My face a featureless, fine
Jew linen.

Peel off the napkin
O my enemy.
Do I terrify?——

The nose, the eye pits, the full set of teeth?
The sour breath
Will vanish in a day.

*   *   *

1. At several Nazi death camps, administrators experimented with using the skin of dead victims as wallpaper and lamp shades.

Soon, soon the flesh
The grave cave ate will be
At home on me

And I a smiling woman.
I am only thirty.
And like the cat I have nine times to die.

This is Number Three.
What a trash
To annihilate each decade.

What a million filaments.
The peanut-crunching crowd
Shoves in to see

Them unwrap me hand and foot——
The big strip tease.
Gentlemen, ladies

These are my hands
My knees.
I may be skin and bone,[2]

Nevertheless, I am the same, identical woman.
The first time it happened I was ten.
It was an accident.

The second time I meant
To last it out and not come back at all.
I rocked shut

As a seashell.
They had to call and call
And pick the worms off me like sticky pearls.

Dying
Is an art, like everything else.
I do it exceptionally well.

    ✻   ✻   ✻

2. In the manuscript, the first two lines of this stanza were combined as one, and a different third line appeared: "I may be Japanese." It was probably a reference to the dead at Hiroshima and Nagasaki. On the advice of a critic, Plath omitted this line.

I do it so it feels like hell.
I do it so it feels real.
I guess you could say I've a call.

It's easy enough to do it in a cell.
It's easy enough to do it and stay put.
It's the theatrical

Comeback in broad day
To the same place, the same face, the same brute
Amused shout:

'A miracle!'
That knocks me out.
There is a charge

For the eyeing of my scars, there is a charge
For the hearing of my heart——
It really goes.

And there is a charge, a very large charge
For a word or a touch
Or a bit of blood

Or a piece of my hair or my clothes.
So, so, Herr[3] Doktor.
So, Herr Enemy.

I am your opus,
I am your valuable,
The pure gold baby

That melts to a shriek.
I turn and burn.
Do not think I underestimate your great concern.

Ash, ash——
You poke and stir.
Flesh, bone, there is nothing there——

*   *   *

3. Mister, lord (German). Doktor: doctor (German). A reference to Nazi doctors who performed gruesome experiments on Jews, the disabled, and others.

A cake of soap,[4]
A wedding ring,
A gold filling.[5]

Herr God, Herr Lucifer
Beware
Beware.

Out of the ash
I rise with my red hair
And I eat men like air.

1962

Introducing "Lady Lazarus" on a BBC radio program, Plath said, "The speaker is a woman who has the great and terrible gift of being reborn. The only trouble is, she has to die first. She is the Phoenix, the libertarian spirit, what you will. She is also just a good, plain, very resourceful woman." Deborah Nelson (in Jo Gill's *Cambridge Companion to Sylvia Plath*) interprets "Herr Doktor" as the figure of an Anglo-American psychoanalyst, waiting for his patient to proffer intimate details: "When the speaker tells 'Herr Doktor' that 'I am your opus, / I am your valuable,' we can now understand the subsequent sneering line, 'Do not think I underestimate your great concern.' The doctor has his own prestige and authority tied up in the patient, who has been turned into his opus, that is, his work of art. The shriek at the end of the poem resists confession by frustrating his appropriation of her words." Conversely, Ann Keniston (in Anita Helle's *The Unraveling Archive*) interprets "Herr Doktor" as a Nazi torturer. She argues that in the poem's description of the speaker as body parts and in its antagonistic attitude toward auditors, "Lady Lazarus" reveals the uncertainties central to trauma and "the difficulty of representing the Holocaust itself."

Poppies in October

Even the sun-clouds this morning cannot manage such skirts.
Nor the woman in the ambulance
Whose red heart blooms through her coat so astoundingly—

A gift, a love gift
Utterly unasked for
By a sky

*   *   *

4. At one Nazi death camp, the fat from dead bodies was allegedly used to produce soap.

5. Nazis systematically pried gold fillings and wedding rings from the remains of the dead.

Palely and flamily
Igniting its carbon monoxides, by eyes
Dulled to a halt under bowlers.[1]

O my God, what am I
That these late mouths should cry open
In a forest of frost, in a dawn of cornflowers.

1962

Kindness

Kindness glides about my house.
Dame Kindness, she is so nice!
The blue and red jewels of her rings smoke
In the windows, the mirrors
Are filling with smiles.

What is so real as the cry of a child?
A rabbit's cry may be wilder
But it has no soul.
Sugar can cure everything, so Kindness says.
Sugar is a necessary fluid,

Its crystals a little poultice.[1]
O kindness, kindness
Sweetly picking up pieces!
My Japanese silks, desperate butterflies,
May be pinned any minute, anesthetized.

And here you come, with a cup of tea
Wreathed in steam.
The blood jet is poetry,
There is no stopping it.
You hand me two children, two roses.

1963

"Kindness" and the next two poems were written in the final weeks of Plath's life.

---

1. Derby hats.

1. Healing substance spread on cloth for application to sores or inflamed areas to relieve pain.

Words

Axes
After whose stroke the wood rings,
And the echoes!
Echoes traveling
Off from the center like horses.

The sap
Wells like tears, like the
Water striving
To re-establish its mirror
Over the rock

That drops and turns,
A white skull,
Eaten by weedy greens.
Years later I
Encounter them on the road——

Words dry and riderless,
The indefatigable hoof-taps.
While
From the bottom of the pool, fixed stars
Govern a life.[1]

1963

Edge

The woman is perfected.
Her dead

Body wears the smile of accomplishment,
The illusion of a Greek necessity

Flows in the scrolls of her toga,
Her bare

✳   ✳   ✳

---

1. In Shakespeare's *King Lear*, Kent says, "It is the stars, / the stars above us, govern our conditions" (4.4.34–35).

Feet seem to be saying:
We have come so far, it is over.

Each dead child coiled, a white serpent,
One at each little

Pitcher of milk, now empty.
She has folded

Them back into her body as petals
Of a rose close when the garden

Stiffens and odors bleed
From the sweet, deep throats of the night flower.

The moon[1] has nothing to be sad about,
Staring from her hood of bone.

She is used to this sort of thing.
Her blacks crackle and drag.

1963

"Edge" appears to be the last poem that Plath composed. Christina Britzolakis (in *Sylvia Plath and The Theatre of Mourning*) argues that, despite its air of finality, the poem is fluid in meaning: "The aesthetic and ideological closure represented by the image of the 'perfected' woman is more apparent than real. It is, after all, 'the *illusion* of a Greek necessity' which 'flows in the scrolls of her toga,' while 'her bare / Feet *seem* to be saying: / We have come so far, it is over.' . . . Although 'Edge' has so often served as the telos of a completed psychobiographical narrative, it can equally be read as insisting on the deceptiveness of such totalizations."

"Context"

The issues of our time which preoccupy me at the moment are the incalculable genetic effects of fallout and a documentary article on the terrifying, mad, omnipotent marriage of big business and the military in America— "Juggernaut, The Warfare State," by Fred J. Cook in a recent *Nation*. Does this influence the kind of poetry I write? Yes, but in a sidelong fashion. I am not gifted with the tongue of Jeremiah, though I may be sleepless enough before my vision of the apocalypse. My poems do not turn out to be about Hiroshima,

---

1. Traditionally conceived in different cultures as a female deity: for example, Selene and Artemis (Greek), Luna and Diana (Roman), and Chang'e or Chang-O (Chinese).

but about a child forming itself finger by finger in the dark. They are not about the terrors of mass extinction, but about the bleakness of the moon over a yew tree in a neighboring graveyard. Not about the testaments of tortured Algerians, but about the night thoughts of a tired surgeon.

In a sense, these poems are deflections. I do not think they are an escape. For me, the real issues of our time are the issues of every time—the hurt and wonder of loving; making in all its forms—children, loaves of bread, paintings, buildings; and the conservation of life of all people in all places, the jeopardizing of which no abstract doubletalk of "peace" or "implacable foes" can excuse.

I do not think a "headline poetry" would interest more people any more profoundly than the headlines. And unless the up-to-the-minute poem grows out of something closer to the bone than a general, shifting philanthropy and is, indeed, that unicorn-thing—a real poem—it is in danger of being screwed up[1] as rapidly as the news sheet itself.

The poets I delight in are possessed by their poems as by the rhythms of their own breathing. Their finest poems seem born all-of-a-piece, not put together by hand; certain poems in Robert Lowell's *Life Studies*, for instance; Theodore Roethke's greenhouse poems; some of Elizabeth Bishop and a very great deal of Stevie Smith ("Art is wild as a cat and quite separate from civilization").

Surely the great use of poetry is its pleasure—not its influence as religious or political propaganda. Certain poems and lines of poetry seem as solid and miraculous to me as church altars or the coronation of queens must seem to people who revere quite different images. I am not worried that poems reach relatively few people. As it is, they go surprisingly far—among strangers, around the world, even. Farther than the words of a classroom teacher or the prescriptions of a doctor; if they are very lucky, farther than a lifetime.

1962

---

1. Twisted into a roll (and, implicitly, tossed away).

AMIRI BARAKA (LEROI JONES)
b. 1934

A PROLIFIC AND CONTROVERSIAL AUTHOR who is equally at home in many genres — including drama, music criticism, fiction, essays, and autobiography — Amiri Baraka has written poetry marked by an inimitably jazzy, profane, free-wheeling, ironically charged, and transgressive style that mixes jagged rhythms with edgy wit in support of serious cultural and political aims. His career as a writer can be defined, at least partially, by a series of major shifts in aesthetics, ideology, and personal, racial, and political identity, developments that Baraka himself describes as "my own changing and diverse motion, of where I have been and why, and how I got to where I was when I next appeared or was heard from." Radical as these changes have been, Baraka has never disowned his past, seeing each stage as an essential step in a process of individual and cultural becoming. In his comprehensive *LeRoi Jones / Amiri Baraka Reader*, Baraka and co-editor William J. Harris divide Baraka's career into four phases: "The Beat Period (1957–1962)," "The Transitional Period (1963–1965)," "The Black Nationalist Period (1965–1974)," and "The Third World Marxist Period (1974–)." Baraka acknowledges, however, that "the typology that lists my ideological changes and so forth as 'Beat-Black Nationalist-Communist' has brevity going for it, and there's something to be said for that, but, like notations of [the jazz pianist Thelonious] Monk, it doesn't show the complexity of real life."

Even as the poet's work has gone through a series of meaningful mutations, so too has the poet's name. Baraka was born in Newark, New Jersey, in 1934 as Everett LeRoy Jones, the son of a postal employee and a social worker. Jones started college with a scholarship to Rutgers University in 1951, and he began using LeRoi as his first name in 1952. That same year, he transferred to historically black Howard University in Washington, D.C., where he worked with noted black scholars and with the venerable black poet Sterling Brown. But he failed to complete a degree because, as he later said, "the Howard thing let me understand the Negro sickness. They teach you how to pretend to be white." He served in the Air Force from 1954 to 1957, then settled in Greenwich Village, where he absorbed the influences of such avant-garde poets as Charles Olson, Allen Ginsberg, and Frank O'Hara. There he began to publish his own work, founded the Totem Press, and edited the literary magazine *Yugen* with his first wife, Hettie Cohen. National recognition came in 1964 when his controversial play *Dutchman* received an Obie award.

Baraka's early Beat phase is reflected in such examples as "Political Poem" and "A Poem for Speculative Hipsters." Following the assassination of Malcolm

X in 1965, he moved from Greenwich Village to Harlem, where he declared himself a Black Nationalist, divorced Cohen, and founded the Black Arts Repertory Theatre. He would soon change his name from LeRoi Jones to Imamu Amiri Baraka ("blessed spiritual leader"), though he ultimately dropped the Islamic prefix Imamu. He married his second wife, Sylvia Robinson, in 1966. Baraka helped to found the Black Arts movement and energetically promoted it through his writing and organizing efforts. Poems from his Black Nationalist period include "leroy" and "Return of the Native." However, by 1974, Baraka announced his rejection of Black Nationalism, because he had come to feel that the movement's often anti-white and sometimes anti-Semitic rhetoric—which he too had practiced—was in itself racist and was not addressing the core problems of poverty and discrimination. Baraka would later say that "Nationalism, so-called, when it says 'all non-blacks are our enemies,' is sickness or criminality, in fact a form of fascism."

Identifying Black Nationalism as "bourgeois" and concluding, in a radio interview with David Barsamian, that "skin color is not a determinant of political content," Baraka began to advocate socialism as the way forward for the poor and culturally disenfranchised worldwide, and he became a supporter of the global economic perspectives of Third World Marxism, a viewpoint that led to the sardonic cultural critique in such poems as "A New Reality Is Better than a New Movie!"

Along with his writing, Baraka has had an extensive teaching career, serving as a professor at the New School of Social Research, San Francisco State University, Yale University, George Washington University, and finally (from 1980 on) at the State University of New York, Stony Brook. He remains a highly individualistic, inventive poet and a provocative and controversial advocate for political and social change.

FURTHER READING

Amiri Baraka. *The Autobiography of LeRoi Jones*. Revised edition. Chicago: Lawrence Hill & Co., 1995.
———. *The LeRoi Jones / Amiri Baraka Reader*. Ed. William J. Harris with Baraka. New York: Basic Books, 1999.
———. *Transbluesency: Selected Poems*. Ed. Paul Vengelisti. New York: Marsilio Publishers, 1995.
W. J. Harris. *The Poetry and Politics of Amiri Baraka: The Jazz Aesthetic*. Columbia, MO.: University of Missouri Press, 1985.
Charlie Reilly et al., eds. *Conversations With Amiri Baraka*. 1994.
Jerry Watts. *Amiri Baraka: The Politics and Art of a Black Intellectual*. New York: New York University Press, 2001.
Komozi Woodard. *A Nation Within a Nation: Amiri Baraka (LeRoi Jones) and Black Power Politics*. Chapel Hill: University of North Carolina Press, 1999.

Political Poem

(for Basil)

Luxury, then, is a way of
being ignorant, comfortably
An approach to the open market
of least information. Where theories
can thrive, under heavy tarpaulins
without being cracked by ideas.

(I have not seen the earth for years
and think now possibly "dirt" is
negative, positive, but clearly
social. I cannot plant a seed, cannot
recognize the root with clearer dent
than indifference. Though I eat
and shit as a natural man. (Getting up
from the desk to secure a turkey sandwich
and answer the phone: the poem undone
undone by my station, by my station,
and the bad words of Newark.) Raised up
to the breech, we seek to fill for this
crumbling century. The darkness of love,
in whose sweating memory all error is forced.

Undone by the logic of any specific death. (Old gentlemen
who still follow fires, tho are quieter
and less punctual. It is a polite truth
we are left with. Who are you? What are you
saying? Something to be dealt with, as easily.
The noxious game of reason, saying, "No, No,
you cannot feel," like my dead lecturer
lamenting thru gipsies his fast suicide.

1964

A Poem for Speculative Hipsters

He had got, finally,
to the forest
of motives. There were no
owls, or hunters. No Connie Chatterleys[1]
resting beautifully
on their backs, having casually
brought socialism
to England.
   Only ideas,
and their opposites.
     Like,
   he was *really*
   nowhere.

       1964

leroy

I wanted to know my mother when she sat
looking sad across the campus in the late 20's
into the future of the soul, there were black angels
straining above her head, carrying life from our ancestors,
and knowledge, and the strong nigger feeling. She sat
(in that photo in the yearbook I showed Vashti) getting into
new blues, from the old ones, the trips and passions
showered on her by her own. Hypnotizing me, from so far
ago, from that vantage of knowledge passed on to her passed on
to me and all the other black people of our time.
When I die, the consciousness I carry I will to
black people. May they pick me apart and take
the useful parts, the sweet meat of my feelings. And leave
the bitter bullshit rotten white parts
alone.

       1969

1. Protagonist of D. H. Lawrence's novel *Lady Chatterley's Lover* (1928).

Return of the Native

Harlem is vicious
modernism. BangClash.
Vicious the way its made.
Can you stand such beauty?
So violent and transforming.
The trees blink naked, being
so few. The women stare
and are in love with them
selves. The sky sits awake
over us. Screaming
at us. No rain.
Sun, hot cleaning sun
drives us under it.

The place, and place
meant of
black people. Their heavy Egypt.
(Weird word!) Their minds, mine,
the black hope mine. In Time.
We slide along in pain or too
happy. So much love
for us. All over, so much of
what we need. Can you sing
yourself, your life, your place
on the warm planet earth.
And look at the stones

the hearts, the gentle hum
of meaning. Each thing, life
we have, or love, is meant
for us in a world like this.
Where we may see ourselves
all the time. And suffer
in joy, that our lives
are so familiar.

1969

A New Reality Is Better Than a New Movie!

How will it go, crumbling earthquake, towering inferno,[1] jugger-
    naut, volcano, smashup,
in reality, other than the feverish nearreal fantasy of the capitalist
    flunky film hacks
tho they sense its reality breathing a quake inferno scar on their
    throat even snorts of
100% pure cocaine cant cancel the cold cut of impending death
    to this society. On all the
screens of america, the joint blows up every hour and a half for
    two dollars an fifty cents.
They have taken the niggers out to lunch, for a minute, made us
    partners nigger Charlie) or
surrogates (boss nigger) for their horror. But just as superafrikan
    mobutu[2] cannot leop
    ardskinhat his
way out of responsibility for lumumba's[3] death, nor even with his
    incredible billions
    rockefeller[4]
cannot even save his pale ho's titties in the crushing weight of
things as they really are.
How will it go, does it reach you, getting up, sitting on the side
of the bed, getting ready to go to work. Hypnotized by the machine, and the cement floor, the jungle treachery of
    trying
to survive with no money in a money world, of making the boss
100,000 for every 200
    dollars
you get, and then having his brother get you for the rent, and if
you want to buy the car
    you

1. *The Towering Inferno*, a big-budget Hollywood disaster film (1974).
2. Mobutu Sese Seko, authoritarian ruler of the Republic of the Congo from 1965 to 1997. His trademark was a leopardskin hat.
3. Patrice Lumumba, the first legally elected prime minister of the Republic of the Congo. He was deposed by a coup organized by Mobutu in 1961 and later executed by a firing squad.
4. Nelson Rockefeller, former governor of New York and grandson of John D. Rockefeller, the billionaire founder of Standard Oil. In 1974, following President Nixon's resignation, Rockefeller had been chosen under the Twenty-fifth Amendment to serve as vice president by Nixon's successor, Gerald Ford, a nomination later confirmed by Congress.

helped build, your downpayment paid for it, the rest goes to buy
his old lady a foam
    rubber
rhinestone set of boobies for special occasions when kissinger[5]
drunkenly fumbles with her blouse, forgetting himself.
If you don't like it, what you gonna do about it. That was the
question we asked each
    other, &
still right regularly need to ask. You don't like it? Whatcha
gonna do, about it??
The real terror of nature is humanity enraged, the true
technicolor spectacle that
    hollywood
cant record. They cant even show you how you look when you
go to work, or when you
    come back.
They cant even show you thinking or demanding the new socialist reality, its the ultimate
    tidal
wave. When all over the planet, men and women, with heat in
their hands, demand that
    society
be planned to include the lives and self determination of all the
people ever to live. That is the scalding scenario with a cast of
just under two billion that they dare not even whisper. Its called,
"We Want It All . . . The Whole World!"

                                                                    1975

---

5. Henry Kissinger, Secretary of State under Presidents Nixon and Ford from 1973 to 1977.

DIANE DI PRIMA
b. 1934

IN THE LATE 1950S AND EARLY 1960S, DIANE DI PRIMA was the most prominent woman poet of the Beat Generation. She wrote in the Beat style of social non-conformity and conversational free association, though more succinctly than did many of her peers. After 1968, her poetry became more focused on Buddhist self-awareness and social, ecological, ethnological, mythological, and feminist concerns. In this later phase, she has exposed the cross-hatching of political and imaginative concerns (as in "Rant) and has constructed a feminine and feminist aesthetic (as in the *Loba* poems). Her friend Allen Ginsberg once wrote of her: "Diane di Prima, revolutionary activist of the 1960s Beat literary renaissance, heroic in life and poetics: a learned humorous bohemian, classically educated and twentieth-century radical, her writing informed by Buddhist equanimity, is exemplary in imagist, political and mystical modes."

Di Prima was born in Brooklyn into an Italian-American family. After drop-ping out of Swarthmore College, she moved to Greenwich Village in Man-hattan and joined the Beat movement. She lived a bohemian existence that included editing, theater, music, performance, art, sex, drugs, and, above all, poetry. She and Amiri Baraka became lovers, and she became friends with Allen Ginsberg, Denise Levertov, Frank O'Hara, and John Ashbery (all included in this anthology). She also knew such performers as Bob Dylan, Joan Baez, Fred Herko, and Janice Joplin. Refusing to accept the choice—then almost compul-sory—between career and motherhood, she had five children with four different men, even as she continued to produce poems and do other creative work.

In 1968 di Prima moved to San Francisco, where she received Buddhist in-struction and participated in the hippie counterculture. Her poems grew in spiritual, environmental, and feminist awareness, influenced now by H.D. as well as Walt Whitman. Di Prima continued to involve herself in poetry per-formance, art, music, and editing, and she became active in a variety of edu-cational endeavors, leading classes for such institutions as the New College of California, the San Francisco Institute of Magical and Healing Arts, the Naropa Institute, and the California Poets in the Schools program. From the early 1970s to 1998, she wrote an epic sequence called *Loba*, in which a wolf goddess encap-sulates the varied images, experiences, and myths of womanhood. Still active, di Prima has published forty-three books thus far, and her work has been translated into twenty languages. In his foreword to di Prima's *Pieces of Song*, poet Robert Creeley wrote, "Her search for human center is among the most moving I have witnessed."

FURTHER READING

Diane di Prima. *Loba.* New York: Penguin, 1998.
————. *Memoirs of a Beatnik.* New York: Penguin, 1998.
————. *Pieces of a Song: Selected Poems.* San Francisco: City Lights, 2001.
————. *Recollections of My Life as a Woman: The New York Years.* New York: Viking, 2001.
————. *Revolutionary Letters.* San Francisco: Last Gasp, 2007.
Brenda Knight. *Women of the Beat Generation: The Writers, Artists and Muses at the Heart of a Revolution* (Berkeley: Conari Press, 1998).

Three Laments

1
Alas
I believe
I might have become
a great writer
but
the chairs
in the library
were too hard

2
I have
the upper hand
but if I keep it
I'll lose the circulation
in one arm

3
So here I am the coolest in New York
what dont swing I dont push.

In some Elysian field[1]
by a big tree
I chew my pride
like cud.

1958

1. In Greek and Roman myth, the Elysian Fields were the final resting place of the happy souls of virtuous persons.

Song for Baby-O, Unborn

Sweetheart
when you break thru
you'll find
a poet here
not quite what one would choose.

I won't promise
you'll never go hungry
or that you won't be sad
on this gutted
breaking
globe

but I can show you
baby
enough to love
to break your heart
forever

1958

"Song for Baby-O, Unborn" expresses love for the pregnant poet's unborn first daughter. As in other early poems, di Prima uses spare, conversational language.

Poetics

I have deserted my post, I cdnt hold it
rearguard/to preserve the language/lucidity:
let the language fend for itself.
it turned over god knows enough carts in the city streets
its barricades are my nightmares

preserve the language—there are
         enough fascists &
         enough socialists
on both sides
so that no one will lose this war

    ✳   ✳   ✳

the language shall be my element, I plunge in
I suspect that I cannot drown
like a fat brat catfish, smug
       a hoodlum fish
I move more & more gracefully
       breathe it in,
success written on my mug till the fishpolice
corner me in the coral & I die

                      1975

On Sitting Down to Write, I Decide Instead to Go to Fred Herko's Concert

As water, silk
the quiver of fish
or the long cry of goose
      or some such bird
      I never heard
your orange tie
a sock in the eye
      as Duncan[1]
        might forcibly note
are you sitting under the irregular drums
of Brooklyn Joe Jones[2]
(in a loft which I know to be dirty
& probably cold)
or have you scurried already
         hurried already
uptown
on a Third Avenue Bus
toward smelly movies & crabs I'll never get
and you all perfumed too
as if they'd notice

        ✻   ✻   ✻

1. San Francisco poet Robert Duncan (1919–1988; also included in this anthology) was a friend of di Prima.
2. Joe Jones (1934–1993), born in Brooklyn, was an avant-garde musician who gained fame through his experiments with mechanical musical instruments.

O the dark caves of obligation
into which I must creep
    (alack)
like downstairs & into a coat
    O all that wind
Even Lord & Taylor[3] don't quite keep out
that wind

1975

Fred Herko (1936–1964) was a close friend of di Prima. A dancer, choreographer, and musician, he also acted in several of Andy Warhol's early films. Plagued by poverty, drug use, and chronic depression, he leapt to his death from a fifth-story apartment window while dancing to Mozart's Coronation Mass at the age of twenty-eight. Jill Johnston, dance critic for the *Village Voice*, described one of his performances: "The five sections of Mr. Herko's *Binghamton Birdie* cohere with that strange logic of parts that have no business being together, but which go together anyway because anything in life can go with anything else if you know what you're doing. The only moment that missed for me was the overextended display of Brooklyn Joe Jones' marvelous mechanical musical construction (suspended from the balcony). Mr. Herko danced around after that on one roller skate, but I don't think he did it soon enough. The pure choreography of the second and last section . . . is lovely. So is the first event: Herko squat walking in a black cape with a black umbrella for canopy, making a few sweet notes on a flute."

Rant

You cannot write a single line w/out a cosmology
a cosmogony[1]
laid out, before all eyes

there is no part of yourself you can separate out
saying, this is memory, this is sensation
this is the work I care about, this is how I
make a living

it is whole, it is a whole, it always was whole
you do not "make" it so
there is nothing to integrate, you are a presence
you are an appendage of the work, the work stems from
hangs from the heaven you create

---

3. Fashionable women's clothing store in New York.

1. Theory of the origin and development of the universe.

*   *   *

every man / every woman carries a firmament inside
& the stars in it are not the stars in the sky

w/out imagination there is no memory
w/out imagination there is no sensation
w/out imagination there is no will, desire

history is a living weapon in yr hand
& you have imagined it, it is thus that you
"find out for yourself"
history is the dream of what can be, it is
the relation between things in a continuum

of imagination
what you find out for yourself is what you select
out of an infinite sea of possibility
no one can inhabit yr world

yet it is not lonely,
the ground of imagination is fearlessness
discourse is video tape of a movie of a shadow play
but the puppets are in yr hand
your counters in a multidimensional chess
which is divination[2]
      & strategy

the war that matters is the war against the imagination
all other wars are subsumed in it.

the ultimate famine is the starvation
of the imagination

it is death to be sure, but the undead
seek to inhabit someone else's world

the ultimate claustrophobia is the syllogism
the ultimate claustrophobia is "it all adds up"
nothing adds up & nothing stands in for
anything else

*   *   *

2. The art of foreseeing future events or discovering hidden knowledge, usually by reading omens
or signs.

THE ONLY WAR THAT MATTERS IS THE WAR AGAINST
                                    THE IMAGINATION
THE ONLY WAR THAT MATTERS IS THE WAR AGAINST
                                    THE IMAGINATION
THE ONLY WAR THAT MATTERS IS THE WAR AGAINST
                                    THE IMAGINATION

ALL OTHER WARS ARE SUBSUMED IN IT

There is no way out of the spiritual battle
There is no way you can avoid taking sides
There is no way you can *not* have a poetics
no matter what you do: plumber, baker, teacher

you do it in the consciousness of making
or not making yr world
you have a poetics: you step into the world
like a suit of readymade clothes

or you etch in light
your firmament spills into the shape of your room
the shape of the poem, of yr body, of yr loves

A woman's life / a man's life is an allegory

Dig[3] it

There is no way out of the spiritual battle
the war is the war against the imagination
you can't sign up as a conscientious objector

the war of the worlds[4] hangs here, right now, in the balance
it is a war for this world, to keep it
a vale of soul-making[5]

the taste in all our mouths is the taste of our power
and it is bitter as death

        *   *   *

3. Understand (African-American and Beat slang).
4. Allusion to the title of a science fiction novel written by H. G. Wells (1898), a radio broadcast devised by Orson Welles (1938), and a science fiction film produced by George Pal (1953).
5. In a letter of 1819, poet John Keats denied that the world is "a vale of tears," insisting instead that it is "a vale of Soul-Making."

bring yr self home to yrself, enter the garden
the guy at the gate w/the flaming sword is yrself

the war is the war for the human imagination
and no one can fight it but you/ & no one can fight it for you

The imagination is not only holy, it is precise
it is not only fierce, it is practical
men die every day for the lack of it[6]
it is vast & elegant

intellectus[7] means "light of the mind"
it is not discourse it is not even language
the inner man

the *polis*[8] is constellated around the sun
the fire is central

1990

Written in opposition to the Vietnam War (1965–75), "Rant" follows the mystical English poet William Blake (1757–1827) in conceiving of war as a violation of the imagination. The tone and typographical idiosyncrasies reflect Ezra Pound's influence as well as Blake's. Di Prima read this poem aloud when accepting a Lifetime Achievement Award in 2006, in the midst of the Iraq and Afghanistan wars. She read it again in 2009 when she was named San Francisco's Poet Laureate.

Some Lies About the Loba

that she is eternal, that she sings
that she is star-born, that she gathers crystal
that she can be confused with Isis[1]
that she is the goal
that she knows her name, that she swims
in the purple sky, that her fingers are pale & strong

that she is black, that she is white
that you always know who she is

6. Allusion to a passage in William Carlos Williams's "Asphodel, That Greeny Flower" (1955): "It is difficult / to get the news from poems / yet men die miserably every day / for lack / of what is found there."

7. Understanding, intellect (Latin).
8. City-state, society, or community (Greek).
1. Egyptian goddess of maternity and fertility.

when she appears
that she strides on battlements, that she sifts
like stones in the sea
that you can hear her approach, that her jewelled feet
tread any particular measure[2]

that there is anything about her
which cannot be said
that she relishes tombstones, falls
down marble stairs
that she is ground only, that she is not ground
that you can remember the first time you met
that she is always with you
that she can be seen without grace

that there is anything to say of her
which is not truth

1990

This poem and the next are from di Prima's sequence, *Loba,* which undertakes an epic quest to rediscover women's wholeness and power. The Loba is the archetype of the wolf goddess, a figure di Prima derived from various world mythologies.

The Loba Addresses the Goddess / Or the Poet as Priestess Addresses the Loba-Goddess

Is it not in yr service that I wear myself out
running ragged among these hills, driving children
to forgotten movies? In yr service
broom & pen. The monstrous feasts
we serve the others on the outer porch
(within the house there is only rice & salt)
And we wear exhaustion like a painted robe
I & my sisters
        wresting the goods from the niggardly
         dying fathers
healing each other w / water & bitter herbs

     *   *   *

2. Beat, cadence.

that when we stand naked in the circle of lamps
(beside the small water, in the inner grove)
we show
no blemish, but also no superfluous beauty.
It has burned off in watches of the night.
O Nut, O mantle of stars, we catch at you
    lean   mournful
    ragged   triumphant
        shaggy as grass
our skins ache of emergence / dark o' the moon

                            1990

PART TWO

✦

*Late-Twentieth-Century /
Early-Twenty-first-Century Poetry*

INTRODUCTION

It is hard to pin down what writers mean when they use the term "postmodern-ism." Some use it to indicate a spirit of experimentalism: a fragmenting and foregrounding of language, a dismantling of the lyric "I," and a requirement that the reader collaborate in the construction of meaning. Others utilize the term to indicate a critique of social surfaces and the political status quo: a psychological and cultural revisioning that includes the voices of women and people of color as full partners in the poetic project. Still others view postmodernism in more historical terms, as a response to the dislocations of World War II and the Cold War, to the rise of conformity and consumerism, to the pain and disorientation of the Vietnam War, or to the rise of such mass cultural forms as movies, televi-sion, popular music, and even advertising and videos. Some of these versions of postmodernism seek to connect recent poetry back to the experimental fervor of early-twentieth-century modernism, while others reveal closer links between recent poetry and midcentury developments. If the poetry from 1950 to the pres-ent is multiplicitous and at times contradictory, so is the manner in which it has been understood. Yet multiplicity of interpretation may in itself be seen as an intrinsic element of postmodernism. The subtitle of this anthology, *Postmodern-isms, 1950–Present*, employs the term in a nonrestrictive, chronological sense and in plural form to acknowledge the diverse strands that may appropriately be gathered under the postmodernist heading.

Just as World War II (1939–45) seemed to represent a historical breach, mark-ing the end of the modernist era and the beginning of a new ethos, so the Viet-nam War era (1965–1975) caused a further rupture in continuity. The Vietnam War complicated what Tom Engelhardt has termed the "victory culture" of the 1950s. No longer was American military success assured. Yet the Cold War pe-riod ended with something that did indeed appear to be a victory: the fall of the Berlin Wall in 1989 and the crumbling of the Soviet empire in 1991. The emer-gence of an American-led capitalist hegemony, however, created or exacerbated its own set of problems—problems that the more recent poets appearing in this volume have persistently explored. The 1990s and 2000s witnessed additional changes in ways of seeing and knowing. One change grew out of epochal tech-nological developments, such as the rise of the Internet, which provided the human subject with a set of prostheses it had never possessed before, making each individual bionic in a metaphorical (and in some cases literal) sense. Other changes related to the tragedy of 9/11; the seeming fulfillment of Robert Lowell's prophecy (in "Waking Early Sunday Morning") of "small war on the heels of small / war—until the end of time"; and an array of economic, political, medical, and environmental threats. Such developments stripped away the façade of normality from everyday life, leaving individuals uncertain and in special need of empathy, humor, perspective, and wisdom—just the qualities poetry can provide.

One might conceive of poetic postmodernisms since 1975 as shifting back and forth along a spectrum. At one end of the spectrum resides a culturally adventurous poetics, giving voice to alternative subject positions. At the other end resides a linguistically adventurous poetics, juxtaposing words and spaces in radically new ways. Many poets visit multiple points on the spectrum by engaging in both cultural and linguistic adventures. Others remain more or less fixed. But most of the recent poets in this anthology exhibit traits that mark them as postmodern in more than just the chronological sense of the term: a resistance to oppressive norms, a rapprochement with popular culture, and a fascination with phenomena that the larger society might consider unfamiliar or peripheral. Postmodern poets may return to the past, as when they recover or parody an ancestral form, but that return itself represents a break with conventional norms. At the same time, for most of these poets, postmodernism involves a critical engagement with the present moment and an eagerness to remain in the vanguard of change.

Broadly speaking, culturally oriented poets—such as Michael Harper, Frank Bidart, Marilyn Chin, Victor Hernández Cruz, Mark Doty, Naomi Shihab Nye, Li-Young Lee, and Sherman Alexie—emphasize social identity, exploring how interior lives interact with issues of race, ethnicity, gender, sexuality, class, postcoloniality, and traditions of faith. Such poets give voice to the contrasting vocabularies that emerge in a nation that is becoming more diverse in its demography and self-conception. Culturally oriented poets produce a poetics of introspection and empathy, a vision of human vulnerability, and a disturbance in conventional wisdom. Their people-centered poems often critique hegemonic assumptions that keep individuals apart or in hierarchical relation to one another. Rather than relocating their discourse from the margins to the center, they seek to erase the center altogether by creating a new, more egalitarian poetic space. These poets decentralize voice as well, frequently staging a dialogue of self and other. The texts maintain porous borders, through which disparate utterances can be heard, as in Wanda Coleman's "African Sleeping Sickness" or Maurya Simon's "The Bishop of Mysore." The poems often emphasize the presence of difference—within society, and even within the self, which may be cleaved by ambivalence and contradiction. This poetry is frequently one of contact zones and of split identities, languages, and cultures, as exemplified in Lorna Dee Cervantes's use of both English and Spanish in "Freeway 280" or Joy Harjo's use of African-American jazz as the musical setting of her poem of Native American awareness, "Morning Song."

Linguistically oriented poets—such as Susan Howe, Lyn Hejinian, Rae Armantrout, and Amy Gerstler—focus attention on the play of language and questions of form. These poets release language from ordinary uses and formats, exposing the opacity and density of words, reveling in the indeterminacy that is inherent in all language but often disguised in normative usage. They write with a metapoetic dimension, which is to say that the poems reveal awareness of their own artifice. These poets may also have important things to say about culture. Nathaniel Mackey and Harryette Mullen, who are in the forefront of poets playing with language, sensitively explore the African-American experience as well. Charles Bernstein, another leading experimentalist, is one of our most radical thinkers about class disparity. John Yau's and Theresa Cha's poems are consciously avant-garde, yet they also illuminate Asian-American cultural traditions. The common bond among linguistically oriented postmodernists is that they all write texts whose verbal landscapes feature so many fissures, blind alleys, ironies, jokes, and games that they require the reader's energetic participation in ascertaining even the most tenuous of meanings.

Many of these linguistically adventurous poets belong to or are allied with the Language poetry movement, an inheritor of such mid-twentieth-century experimentalists as the Objectivists, the Black Mountain school, and the New York school. Language poetry (or sometimes L=A=N=G=U=A=G=E poetry) is an avant-garde poetic practice that uses language in ways that maximize ambiguity and mystery, often by introducing arbitrary rules or stressing acoustic or visual elements in the text. Despite its occasional inaccessibility, Language poetry maintains close connections with popular culture, thereby suturing poetic language to the vocabulary of the media and the street. This body of poetry challenges the notion of a cohesive, knowable poet naturally speaking or writing the lines of the poem. Instead, the speaking subject is problematized or dispersed, and the poem's "I" exists merely as a textual construct, a grammatical convenience, or an object of verbal play. The poetry frequently uses a form that is either, as Joseph Conte has written in *Unending Design*, serial (seemingly random and provisional) or procedural (regulated by predetermined, arbitrary rules). The poems are puzzles without solutions—or with multiple, partial solutions.

Both cultural and linguistic postmodernisms bear close connections to developments in related art forms such as fiction, film, the visual arts, and music. The prose poem, which straddles the boundary between fiction and poetry, becomes a crucial form in the work of such poets as Forché, Yau, Cha, and Gerstler.

Howe, by writing over her words with different words, turns "Scattering as Behavior Toward Risk" into an abstract graphic design—a visual art form. Other postmodern poets, ranging from Bernstein to Mullen, emphasize the sound elements in their poems, pushing poetry toward the condition of music. Still other poets, such as Harjo, follow Allen Ginsberg's lead in converting their poetic texts into performed and recorded songs. And others, such as Bob Dylan and Queen Latifah, write their poems as song lyrics in the first place, thereby infusing popular music with the verbal concentration and imagery of poetry.

Whereas culturally oriented poetry often provides overt psychological exploration and social criticism, linguistically oriented poetry often works more obliquely, by embedding psychological and social implication into its form. If culturally adventurous postmodernists often emphasize self-examination, communitarian awareness, and political critique, the linguistically adventurous postmodernists employ irony to expose the artificiality of the word, to dismantle the illusory coherence of the speaking subject, and to question the social status quo. Many postmodern poems have traits in common: they portray the present moment without nostalgia for a utopic past, and they engage with social and artistic change. Often controversial and challenging, they provide intellectual stimulation, emotional discovery, and aesthetic pleasure. They invite the reader to see and feel in new ways.

SUSAN HOWE
b. 1937

A LANGUAGE POET AND A FEMINIST, SUSAN HOWE writes poems filled with hesitations, repetitions, ellipses, and unexpected juxtapositions. Reading them, it's often hard to know what is being referred to and who is doing the referring. The poems are inherently mysterious, challenging the reader to make some sort of sense of them or to acknowledge the otherness of language. Some things can only be gotten sideways, by hints and innuendos, by strategically placed silences. Other things cannot be gotten at all. In an interview quoted by scholar Ming-Qian Ma, Howe said that "the poet opens herself. . . . You open yourself and let language enter, let it lead you somewhere . . . let various things—memories, fragments, bits, pieces, scraps, sounds—let them all work into something. This has to do with changing order and abolishing categories. It has to do with sounds in silence."

Poetry has always specialized in such states of indeterminacy and indecision, as the work of Howe's nineteenth-century precursor, Emily Dickinson, exemplifies. Howe's poetry is characterized by its experimental techniques: sentences in fragments, phrases written over each other, lines printed at odd angles, historical quotations run together seamlessly with the poet's own phrases. The reader's first response may be bewilderment, but the second may be fascination. Howe's poems tell us things we want to know about voices of the past, about the strangeness of the present day, and about the potential to question things we take for granted.

Howe moved through several creative careers before settling on writing. First she tried acting and stage design in Dublin and New York. Then she turned to painting, earning a degree from the Boston Museum School of Fine Arts in 1961. Influenced by experimental artists as various as Agnes Martin, John Cage, Andy Warhol, and Richard Serra, she began producing visual collages made up of quotations from artists and others. In effect, she started to draw with words. These graphic designs prefigured the collage texts that would ultimately make her famous. The striking visual design of "Scattering as Behavior Toward Risk" exemplifies her effort to hybridize poetry with the visual arts. Howe boldly destabilizes the poetic line, freeing it to become something new. She changes the face of poetry, and she also defaces it by writing over words, interrogating the iconicity of the printed page. Her postmodern poetry absorbs accidents, fragments, and found texts into a new kind of writing that engages the eye, the ear, and the mind.

Howe has been writing experimental and visionary poetry and prose since the 1970s. A professor of English at the University at Buffalo, she has won many awards and has gained a distinguished international reputation.

FURTHER READING

Rachel Tzvia Back. *Led by Language: The Poetry and Poetics of Susan Howe.* Tuscaloosa: University of Alabama Press, 2002.

Alan Golding. "Drawing with Words: Susan Howe's Visual Poetics." In *We Who Love to Be Astonished: Experimental Women's Writing and Performance Poetics,* ed. Laura Hinton and Cynthia Hogue, 152–64. Tuscaloosa: University of Alabama Press, 2002.

Susan Howe. *The Midnight.* New York: New Directions, 1996.

———. *My Emily Dickinson.* Berkeley, Calif: North Atlantic Books, 1985.

———. *Singularities.* Middletown, Conn.: Wesleyan University Press, 1990.

Ming-Qian Ma. "Poetry as History Revised: "Susan Howe's 'Scattering as Behavior Toward Risk.'" *American Literary History* 6.4 (1994): 716-37.

"Susan Howe." University at Buffalo Electronic Poetry Center website, www.wings.buffalo .edu/epc/.

> I haue determened to scater thē therowout the
> worlde, ād to make awaye the remēbraunce of them
> from amonge men.
>
> *William Tyndale's Pentateuch,*
> *"Deuteronomye," XXXII. 26*

Scattering as Behavior Toward Risk

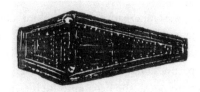

"on a [*p*<suddenly . . . on a>was shot thro with a dyed→<dyed→a soft]"*
(became the vision) (the rea) after Though   [thought]That
Fa

But what is envy [but what is envy]
Is envy the bonfire inkling?

Shackles[(shackles)   ] as we were told the . . . [precincts]

**Billy Budd:* The Genetic Text

A Vengeance must be
a story
Trial and suffering
of Mercy
Any narrative question
away in the annals
the old army
Enlightened rationalism

———

dredful at Hell
bears go in dens
No track by night
No coming out
in the otherday
on wild thoughtpath
Face of adamant
steel of the face
Breast

———

Own political literature

Stoic iconic Collective
Soliloquy and the aside

Suppose finite this is
relect struggle embrace

Violent order of a world

Iconoclastic folio subgenre

a life lived by shifts
evil fortunes of another

Halfway through Wanderings
walks the lean Instaurator

Birth of contemporary thought
Counter thought thought out

———

Loaded into a perfect commonwealth of some idea.

In common.   *Bisket*
                              Risk
                              Herring
More imagined it THE best ordered commonwealth
         VIZE ADMIRAL   Ore   Watchwords
Would have no money no private property no markets.   That open
                 the sayd
Utopian communism comes in pieces while the Narative wanders.
                 aboord
Values in a discourse.   *Shrowds*   Potentiality of sound to directly signal
               To hull in the night
                     Meaning
               wavering   Cape Rase overpast
               wavering   any bruit
               Saxoharmony sparrow or muttering
                              that lamentation
                              The overground level
                         brawling and all that (I) sky
                              Always cutting out

        They do not know what a syllable is   Wading in water
                                   rigor of cold

              The protection of sleep
              The protection of sheep

              Patron of stealthy action
              The stealthy

              Real and personal property

              Paper money and tender acts

              Fiction of administrative law
              Fathers dare not name me

              Chasm dogma scoops out

              The invention of law
              the codification of money

              Democracy and property
              Rules are guards and fences

              In the court of black earth
              to be infinite

———

Consumable commodity

a Zero-sum game
and consequent

spiral haze stricture

Distance or outness

Phrase edged away

Money runs after goods
Men desire money

Wages of labor
Wages in a mother country

Authorial withdrawal

Will as fourth wall

My heavy heavy child

hatchet-heartedness
of the Adversary

On anonimity Anonimity

———

iṇimum
in arm
in ale

s
in tone
open
v e s
i   company
fluent o n

Wedged destiny shed [cancel whole] halter measure mutiny Act Wars

Mute
fluke
squall

Child
regical

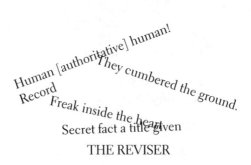

THE REVISER

1990

"Scattering as Behavior Toward Risk" is a visual text as well as a poetic one. At times the words appear as conventional columns of print, but at other times they are printed at strange angles or even over each other. In the more experimental passages, it is difficult to decide the order in which to read the words or the relation of one set of words to another. As the title implies, the poem "scatters" its words on the page, riskily venturing to the edge of chaos. It turns the linearity of the ordinary text into a series of unpredictable designs and meanings that must be inferred. The poem reflects chaos theory in that it represents language as a dynamic system highly sensitive to initial conditions.

The poem's initial conditions are provided by two precursory texts: the book of Deuteronomy (in the Jewish and Christian Bibles) and Herman Melville's novella *Billy Budd*. Howe's poem disarranges those narratives as a way of testing the boundaries between order and disorder. It locates new meanings in old stories, and it tries out new ways of telling stories. Opening itself to multiple interpretations, it allows "feminine" implications to arise from previously "masculine" narratives.

In Deuteronomy (32:26), Moses tells the Israelites that for their sins God would have scattered them "into corners" and made "the remembrance of them to cease from among men" except that he wishes them to make manifest his own enduring presence on earth. Whereas the biblical God rejects scattering as a sign of incoherence, Howe's text purposefully scatters its words on the pages as a way to discover new connections. Ming-Qian Ma suggests that this "scattering" represents Howe's critique of "authorial centering," "patriarchal language," and "authority." On this level, the coffin at the outset may suggest the death of the author, providing a visual image of what the poem itself terms "Authorial withdrawal." Thus, Howe's poem radically revises the biblical text, just as it does the Melvillean one that follows.

In Melville's *Billy Budd*, the innocent, illiterate Billy is falsely charged with conspiring to mutiny, and he is ultimately executed. The first line of the poem reproduces the moment of Billy's execution, as quoted from the "genetic text" of the novella. The "genetic text," annotating every manuscript notation and revision that Melville wrote, was published in 1962 by editors Harrison Hayford and Merton Sealts. Howe's poem, by quoting a sample of Melville's false starts and changes of mind, transforms his focused narrative into a scattering of indeterminate meanings. For example, the finished version of Melville's sentence states that at the moment of execution the fleecy clouds in the East were "shot through with a soft glory as of the fleece of the Lamb of God seen in mystical vision." But the genetic text quoted in line 1 deconstructs this confident narrative. For example, what appears as "soft" was originally "dyed"—a quite different image. In Howe's meditation on this scene in line 2, "the rea" may be short for "the real" or "the reason," but in Latin it means a female defendant in a lawsuit. Perhaps "the rea" implies that the beautiful, inarticulate Billy Budd represents a feminine presence that the masculine law must extinguish. The next phrases, "after Though [though]That" may suggest "after that" or "afterthought"—especially if we view "[though]T" as a single word. Howe's third line, "Fa," may suggest the beginning of "Father" or of "False"—and thereby critique the law that kills Billy Budd. Later in the poem, the text states that administrative law is a fiction and that "Fathers dare not name me." Alternatively, "Fa" may represent a note of music, as in the scale Do Re Mi Fa Sol La Ti Do. Perhaps it is one note in a song of lament.

Howe's poem breaks apart historical narratives to release a myriad of possible new meanings. Ma quotes Howe explaining that her poetry "has involved a breaking of boundaries of all sorts. It involves a fracturing of discourse, a stammering even. Interruption and hesitation used as a force." The "chance meeting of words" that she arranges results in new ways of seeing. As she writes later in her poem, the "best ordered" establishment or codification "comes in pieces while the Narrative wanders." This is the challenge at the heart of Howe's poem. "Scattering as Behavior Toward Risk" invites us to revise the stories we have been told, the concepts that guide us.

LUIS OMAR SALINAS
1937–2008

Luis omar salinas is regarded as one of the founders of contemporary Chicano poetry as well as an important social advocate. His first book, *The Crazy Gypsy*, became an anthem for many Chicano activists and is often considered a landmark in Chicano literature and culture. His poetry is by turns political, introspective, observant, and visionary. Salinas is associated with the Fresno school, which includes Philip Levine and Gary Soto and emphasizes working-class life evoked in free-verse monologues. Salinas's writing has also been discussed in relation to the work of Spanish poet Federico García Lorca and Latin American poets Pablo Neruda and César Vallejo because of its combination of lyricism and surrealism. The poem included here reveals this lyrical voice.

Born along the Texas-Mexico border in Robstown, Salinas lost his mother at the age of four and was adopted by his aunt and uncle. The family moved to Fresno, where he attended public schools. Later he attended Bakersfield City College; California State University, Los Angeles; and California State

University, Fresno. Salinas published ten volumes of poetry in his lifetime. Among his prizes were the Stanley Kunitz Award and a General Electric Foundation Award.

FURTHER READING

Christopher Buckley. "Elegy for Desire: Luis Omar Salinas 1937–2008." *The Writer's Chronicle,* www.awpwriter.org (October/November 2008).
Luis Omar Salinas. *Darkness Under the Trees / Walking Behind the Spanish.* Berkeley: Chicano Library Studies Publications, The University of California, 1982.
———. *Elegy for Desire.* Tucson: University of Arizona Press, 2005.
———. *The Sadness of Days: Selected and New Poems.* Houston: Arte Público Press, 1987.
———, ed. *From the Barrio: A Chicano Anthology.* San Francisco: Canfield Press, 1973.
Gary Soto. "Luis O. Salinas: Chicano Poet." *MELUS* 2 (Summer 1982): 47–82.

My Father Is a Simple Man

I walk to town with my father
to buy a newspaper. He walks slower
than I do so I must slow up.
The street is filled with children.
We argue about the price
of pomegranates. I convince
him it is the fruit of scholars.
He has taken me on this journey
and it's been lifelong.
He's sure I'll be healthy
so long as I eat more oranges,
and tells me the orange
has seeds and so is perpetual;
and we too will come back
like the orange trees.
I ask him what he thinks
about death and he says
he will gladly face it when
it comes but won't jump
out in front of a car.
I'd gladly give my life
for this man with a sixth
grade education, whose kindness
and patience are true . . .
The truth of it is, he's the scholar,

and when the bitter-hard reality
comes at me like a punishing
evil stranger, I can always
remember that here was a man
who was a worker and provider,
who learned the simple facts
in life and lived by them,
who held no pretense,
And when he leaves without
benefit of fanfare or applause
I shall have learned what little
there is about greatness.

1970

Salinas wrote this poem for his adoptive father in *Darkness Under the Trees / Walking
Behind the Spanish.*

MICHAEL S. HARPER
b. 1938

MICHAEL S. HARPER is one of the outstanding voices in contemporary American
poetry. Since the early 1970s, he has eloquently advocated on behalf of the poetry
and culture of African Americans as well as poets who cross cultural boundaries,
such as Elizabeth Bishop and Robert Lowell. While Harper draws heavily on
both jazz and folk traditions, his major goal, as critic Laurence Lieberman has
pointed out, is to foreground excellence. He fills his poetry with such outstanding African-American figures as Jackie Robinson, John Coltrane, and Sterling
Brown; and, as the poem in this entry illustrates, he also extends his philosophy
of excellence to include role models in other cultures. Ernest Smith has written,
"Exploring history, race, art, and kinship, Michael S. Harper's poetry has distinguished itself as both a form of social action and a redemptive balm."

Born in Brooklyn, New York, Harper eventually moved to California, where
he received two degrees. He then was awarded an M.F.A. from the University of
Iowa. Afterward he taught at Reed College and became associated with Lewis &
Clark College, establishing himself in Portland, Oregon, and the Pacific Northwest. Since 1970 he has taught at many colleges and universities but has lived

primarily in Rhode Island. Harper is now a professor of English at Brown University. He was the first Poet Laureate of the State of Rhode Island, serving from 1988 to 1993. Among Harper's dozens of major awards are the Robert Frost Award from the Poetry Society of America, the Robert Hayden Poetry Award from the United Negro College Fund, the Melville-Cane Award, and the Claiborne Pell Award for Excellence in the Arts. He has edited the poetry of Sterling Brown and has co-edited three collections of African-American poetry, including the pathbreaking *Chant of Saints* in 1979.

FURTHER READING

Michael S. Harper. *Songlines in Michaeltree: New and Collected Poems.* Champaign: University of Illinois Press, 2002.
———. *Use Trouble.* Champaign: University of Illinois Press, 2009.
John Hoppenthaler. "Michael S. Harper—Poetry." ConnotationPress.com. December 2009: 1–8.
Ruth Oppenheim. "Fleeing after Kristallnacht: How can I ever explain such fear?" *The Providence Journal,* 10 November 2008:C4.
———. "*Kristallnacht*: How It Was." *MOMENT* 10 (1985): 50–54.
Ernest Smith. "Harper, Michael S." In *The Greenwood Encyclopedia of American Poets and Poetry,* vol. 3, ed. Jeffrey Gray, James McCorkle, and Mary McAleer Balkun, 693–95. Westport, Conn.: Greenwood Press, 2006.

The Ghost of Soulmaking: For Ruth Oppenheim

On that day it was decreed
who shall live and who shall die.

—Yom Kippur prayer[1]

"ART IN ITS ULTIMATE ALWAYS
CELEBRATES THE VICTORY."

The ghost appears in the dark of winter,
sometimes in the light of summer, in the light
of spring, confronts you behind the half-door[2]
in the first shock of morning,
often after hours,[3] with bad memories to stunt

1. Harper features this quotation prominently because, in her 1985 memoir, Oppenheim refers to this prayer when she learns that her favorite uncle has been rejected for immigration by the American consulate just after *Kristallnacht*. See Oppenheim's 2008 article for more information about this family.

2. Refers to the Dutch door of Oppenheim's office in the Horace Mann building, Brown University's English department offices.
3. Dedicated to her work, Oppenheim often stayed late into the evening to complete her tasks.

your day, whines in twilight, whines in the umbrella
of trees.

He stands outside the locked doors, rain or shine;
he constructs the stuntwork of allegiances
in the form of students, in the form of the half-measure
of blankets—he comes to parade rest in the itch of frost
on the maple, on the cherry caught in the open field
of artillery; he remembers the battlefields of the democratic
order; he marks each accent through the gates of the orchard
singing in the cadences of books—
you remember books burned, a shattering of crystals,
prayers for now, and in the afterlife, Germany of the northern
lights[4] of Kristallnacht, the ashes of synagogues.

The ghost turns to your mother as if he believed
in penance, in wages earned, in truth places these flowers
you have brought with your own hands,
irises certainly, and the dalmation rose,
whose fragrance calms every hunger in religious feast or fast.
Into her hands, these blossoms, her fragrant palms.[5]

There is no wedding ring in the life of ghosts,
no sacred asp on the wrist in imperial cool,
but there is a bowl on the reception table,
offerings of Swiss black licorice.[6]
On good days the bowl would entice the dream
of husband, children, and grandchildren;
on good days one could build a synagogue in one's own city,[7]
call it *city of testimony, conscious city of words.*

4. Refers to northern Germany, where Oppenheim lived in the town of Werne. She indicates in her 1985 memoir that her family, the Heimanns, had lived and prospered there for generations. Ashes of synagogues: the local synagogue was in ruins after it was destroyed on *Kristallnacht.* Oppenheim's father, Albert Heimann, was a leader of the congregation. He was able, in spite of brutal beatings, to rescue the synagogue's Torah and later to donate it to The Tabernacle, a New York City synagogue.
5. In this verse, Harper recalls that Oppenheim's 1985 memoir describes how she and her siblings would visit her parents at the synagogue during Yom Kippur, when they prayed and fasted all day. As she states, "we would bring my parents a rose so that the fragrance might sustain them while they fasted."
6. Harper features here Oppenheim's favorite candy, black licorice. Sometimes she kept a bowl of it on her desk.
7. Alludes to Oppenheim's son Jeff, who was instrumental in establishing a synagogue in Falmouth, Massachusetts, on Cape Cod. Previously there had been only one synagogue on the Cape, located in Hyannis. Given the destruction of so many synagogues in Germany on November 9, 1938, his efforts were very meaningful.

In this precinct male and female, the ghost commences, the ghost
disappears.

What of the lady in the half-door of the enlightenment:
tact, and a few scarves,[8] a small indulgence for a frugal
woman; loyalty learned in the lost records of intricate relations:
how to remember, how to forget the priceless injuries
on a steno tablet, in the tenured cabinets of the files.[9]
At birth, and before, the ghost taught understanding:
that no history is fully a record, for the food we will eat
is never sour on the tongue, lethal, or not, as a defenseless
scapegoat, the tongue turned over, as compost is turned over,
to sainthood which makes the palate sing. These are jewels
in the service of others; this is her song. She reaps
the great reward of praise, where answers do not answer,
when the self, unleashed from the delicate bottle,
wafts over the trees at sunrise and forgives the dusk.

1987

Harper wrote this poem for his colleague Ruth Oppenheim at Brown University to celebrate her life, professional achievements, and artistry. She was the academic department
manager of the English department at Brown University when he wrote it. He based the
poem on her memoir "*Kristallnacht*: How It Was." Oppenheim witnessed *Kristallnacht*,
or the Night of Broken Glass, as an eleven-year-old child. On November 9, 1938, German
Nazis destroyed nearly three hundred synagogues, and many Jews, primarily men, were
beaten, tortured, and murdered. Many millions of Jews were ultimately sent to concentration camps, where almost six million of them died. *Kristallnacht* was the beginning of
the Holocaust. Oppenheim's immediate family was able to emigrate to New York City,
though they lost everything they had owned. Many friends and family members, however,
including her Uncle Ernst, her lively Aunt Bertha, and her much-adored cousin Helmut,
died in the camps. This family perished because the American consulate rejected Ernst's
application for immigration due to his knee injury in a motorcycle accident, which the
consulate suspected might cause him to become a financial burden.

As Harper indicates in the poem, Oppenheim transformed her childhood through
her artistry, especially her writing. Harper's poem celebrates Oppenheim while recalling
the horror of *Kristallnacht*. The poem's title is based on a letter by the English poet John
Keats, in which he discusses the world as a "vale of soulmaking." The notes to this poem
are based primarily on an email of November 10, 2005, sent by Ruth Oppenheim to Camille Roman, as well as Oppenheim's two memoirs cited in Further Reading.

8. The scarves suggest Oppenheim's artistic ability to enliven her wardrobe at work.
9. Harper discusses Oppenheim's work in this
section of the poem as well as her ability to write
carefully about faculty meetings and tenure dis-
cussions on her stenographic pad.

KATHLEEN SPIVACK
b. 1938

KATHLEEN SPIVACK brings a unique warmth, passion, and sense of humor to her deeply personal poems about love, family, creativity, and women's experience. Unpretentious in tone, the poems look at the practice of everyday life in original and compelling ways. A friend of Anne Sexton and Sylvia Plath and such senior poets as Robert Lowell and Elizabeth Bishop (all included in this anthology), Spivack extends the autobiographical vein in their work in inventive and humane ways.

Spivack was raised in Bennington, Vermont, and subsequently lived in Montclair, New Jersey, the daughter of Peter and Doris Drucker, refugees from Hitler's Germany and Austria. Her father, an economist who revolutionized business practices, has been termed the inventor of modern management. His daughter, however, inclined in a different way, toward poetry. She obtained her B.A. from Oberlin College and her M.A. from Boston University. She married, had two children, and wrote poetry notable for its immediacy and sensitivity. Influenced by the feminist and countercultural movements of the 1960s, her work also incorporates the poetics of personal experience that Sexton, Plath, and Lowell innovated. Fellow poet Ruth Whitman has observed that Spivack "takes risks which would daunt any poet . . . a real woman emerges, idiosyncratic, domestic, and universal at the same time."

Spivack today divides her time between Boston, where she directs the Advanced Writing Workshop, and Paris, where she teaches at several universities.

FURTHER READING

Kathleen Spivack. *The Beds We Lie In*. Lanham, Md.: Scarecrow Press, 1986.
———. *A History of Yearning*. Milwood, Va.: Sow's Ear Poetry Review, 2010.
———. *The Honeymoon*. St. Paul, Minn.: Graywolf Press, 1986.
———. *Moments of Past Happiness*. Chelsea, Mass.: Earthwinds Editions, 2007.
Cecilia Woloch. "Spivack, Kathleen." In *The Greenwood Encyclopedia of American Poets and Poetry*, vol. 5, ed. Jeffrey Gray, James McCorkle, and Mary McAleer Balkun, 1510–11. Westport, Conn.: Greenwood Press, 2006.

Now the Slow Creation

Now the slow creation of things
comes everywhere:
the warm lapping of petals

in the sun; the leaf that turns
its sticky surface to the air.

Slowly, my pocket opens like an orange,
warm to your touch;
and that five-petaled sun
folds all its fruited segments out.
I turn forever on that bed.

And out of that arc, delicately rising,
children swim like fish
or seahorses; thistle-slim,
their bellies bent,
into the new-rinsed light.

Who put them there, you put
them there, marvelously fat-fingered.
A great soft whoosh of the breath—
they come, endlessly spinning
like soapbubbles through a pipe.

1973

The Eyelid   The Red Tide

she thinks more on the life cycle, that ebb tide—
is it having the baby makes her know it?
the gushing blood-triumphant cry
while her friend lies in hospital, dying?

or is it the yellowing chestnut trees?
body-pain and such pain as she's never known—
the wracked joints cracking, breasts in a bucket,
fall a dark passage whose other end is death?

blindly pressing through blood and bone
jane's baby enters the gates of horn.

1974

The "gates of horn" in this poem is an image of the uterine canal. In Homer's *The Odyssey*, Penelope distinguishes between true dreams, which arrive through a "gate of horn," and deceptive visions, which pass through a "gate of ivory": "Dreams verily are baffling and unclear of meaning, and in no wise do they find fulfillment in all things for men. For two are the gates of shadowy dreams, and one is fashioned of horn and one of ivory. Those dreams that pass through the gate of sawn ivory deceive men, bringing words that find no fullfilment. But those that come forth through the gate of polished horn bring true issues to pass, when any mortal sees them" (19.560–69).

The Insult Sonnet

"We have a short life span," you shrug, "why fight?"
Listen, you bastard, that ain't no excuse.
I'll match you tooth for tooth till you understand
me, understand? Take back, give in, unsay,
let go or face me, snarling on all fours,
my fierce fur flying. Keep your distance please.
I'd rather fight than kiss a guy so rude:
tonight this bed's not big enough for two
so let's go at it. Test me, push for shove,
till I heave you to the floor. You can sleep
on the rug your mother gave you. I will snore
above, in bed, on ironed sheets, and dream
of having you many ways. (Oh, *many* ways.)
And wake to the sound of my own voice crying "More!"

1981

The Moments-of-Past-Happiness Quilt

This square
is made up
of moments of past happiness
duplicated
throughout the entire quilt
and repeated
in random patterns, no order.
This moments-of-past-happiness quilt
was stitched
by many women, each
in her own bright
kitchen, humming:
different rates of speed.
Please note

the individuality of the
stitching: here
the stitchery is tiny;
some of it
is large and bold.
In parts the
stitches cannot even be seen.
Maybe a certain woman
wasn't happy, or maybe moments flowed,
one into another, fluidity like sun
so taken for granted we
can't even see her edges.
Over here
the pattern is uneven:
doubt
took hold, uncertainty
and darkness
and a woman faltered.
Moments of perfect happiness
were past
imperfect, could she remember one?
She sat, she didn't get up,
she didn't turn on the lights.
On this blank part
she stitched her name,
too difficult to read—
it's rather like your own. Here,
look at the rainbow center where
the squares converge,
the color of turning prisms. Yet
the center is most
forgettable, somehow. . . .
So many women worked; they blend. . . .
Don't look so hard, my friend.
You will ruin it.
See, it is fading,
it is fading
even while you watch.
Fold the quilt
quickly;
put it away in its box.

A moments-of-past-happiness quilt
is too delicate.
It won't wash.
It won't wear.
It won't do to wrap babies in.
You are lucky to have touched it,
even once.
It cannot be sold;
it does not last.
Do not hope
to use it on your bed.

2007

FRANK BIDART
b. 1939

FRANK BIDART has written some of the most powerful poems of the postmodern era. Unlike some of his peers, he chooses to make himself vulnerable rather than seeking a cool, ironic perspective. His poems possess a passionate intelligence that is all their own. They have the dignity of tragic drama, the weight of a philosophical meditation, and the complexity of a Tolstoy novel. They immerse us in interior landscapes of desire and regret, blankness and yearning. Suggesting the inability of our culture to sustain and support, they tell of personal and artistic struggle. In a review collected in *On Frank Bidart*, Louise Glück observed that "the importance of Bidart's work is difficult to overestimate; certainly he is one of the crucial figures of our time."

Of Basque-American heritage, Bidart was born in Bakersfield, in California's Central Valley. He received his B.A. in English from the University of California, Riverside, and his M.A. from Harvard, where he studied with Robert Lowell. At Harvard, he developed close friendships with both Lowell and Elizabeth Bishop. His poems reveal the influence of those two poets—and many other American and European writers. Yet as a poet of intricate thought and deep feeling, Bidart is in many ways unique. As critic Lloyd Schwartz noted in *On Frank Bidart*, Bidart's poetry "is characterized by unusual, eccentric, even bizarre punctuation and typography." Bidart's odd punctuation allows us to hear innuendos in the relations between words that the words themselves cannot convey. The punctuation helps produce what Schwartz calls the "tragic power and urgency" of Bidart's verse. Jeffrey Gray adds that Bidart can be grouped with neither the Language poets, who assimilate subjectivity to the status of language, nor the poets who retain a traditional, cohesive lyric voice. Rather, Bidart's poetry explores language and subjectivity at once, exposing the limits and incompleteness of each.

A professor of English at Wellesley College, Bidart has won many prizes, including the Lila Wallace–Reader's Digest Award, the Shelley Award, the Wallace Stevens Award, and the Bollingen Prize for Poetry. Throughout his career, he has written highly original and often disturbing poems. In a style never quite seen before, they plumb the depths of guilt, suffering, passion, remorse, creativity, and love. They interrogate our darkened world, and they pray for insight that often does not come. "The artist's problem," Bidart has said, "is to make life *show* itself. . . . A great deal of Western art has made life *show* itself by dramatizing crisis and disaster." Telling of our failures to fathom the opaque worlds outside of and within ourselves, Bidart's haunting poems come to us, as Herman Melville would have said, with the shock of recognition.

FURTHER READING

Frank Bidart. *Desire*. New York: Farrar, Straus & Giroux, 1997.
———. *In the Western Night*. New York: Farrar, Straus & Giroux, 1990.
———. *Star Dust*. New York: Farrar, Straus & Giroux, 2005.
———. *Watching the Spring Festival*. Farrar, Straus & Giroux, 2008.
Anne Ferry. *The Title to the Poem*. Stanford, Calif.: Stanford University Press, 1996.
Jeffrey Gray. "'Necessary Thought': Frank Bidart and the Postconfessional." *Contemporary Literature* 34.4 (1993): 714–39.
Liam Rector and Tree Swenson, eds. *On Frank Bidart: Fastening the Voice to the Page*. Ann Arbor: University of Michigan Press, 2007.
Alan Williamson. *Eloquence and Mere Life: Essays on the Art of Poetry*. Ann Arbor: University of Michigan Press, 1994.

Self-Portrait, 1969

He's *still* young—; thirty, but looks younger—
or does he? … In the eyes and cheeks, tonight,
turning in the mirror, he saw his mother,—
puffy; angry; bewildered . . . Many nights
now, when he stares there, he gets angry:—
something *unfulfilled* there, something dead
to what he once thought he surely could be—
Now, just the glamour of habits . . .

                              Once, instead,

he thought insight would remake him, he'd reach
—what? The thrill, the exhilaration
unravelling disaster, that seemed to teach
necessary knowledge . . . became just jargon.

Sick of being decent he craves another
crash. What *reaches* him except disaster?

1973

Although "Self-Portrait, 1969" might at first glance be taken as an autobiographical confession, its third-person description and its use of sonnet form complicate any simple
ascription of authenticity to the text. Note, for example, the poem's subtle pattern of slant
rhymes, ending with a couplet that packs a punch. In the collection *On Frank Bidart*,
critic Richard Howard speaks of this poem as a "colonization of inferno," whereas Jonathan Galassi reads the third quatrain as an indication that, for the title character, even
psychoanalysis has become "a mere complex of terms unrelated to truth." Bidart himself
(in an interview printed in *In the Western Night*) said of the relation of artistry and actual-
ity: "All art, of course, is artifice: words . . . don't just 'naturally' happen on paper. . . . But
I think that Frost's statement is also true: 'No tears in the writer, no tears in the reader.'"

To My Father

I walked into the room.
There were objects in the room. I thought I needed nothing
from them. They began to speak,
but the words were unintelligible, a painful cacophony . . .
Then I realized they were saying
                                        the name
of the man who had chosen them, owned them,
ordered, arranged them, their deceased cause,
the secret pattern that made these things order.
I strained to hear: but
the sound remained unintelligible . . .
senselessly getting louder, urgent, deafening.

Hands over my ears, at last I knew
                                        they would remain
inarticulate; your name was not in my language.

1973

Bidart commented in an interview in *In the Western Night*: "I was someone who had
grown up obsessed with his parents. The drama of their lives dominated what, at the

deepest level, *I* thought about. . . . The great model for such poems was of course [Robert Lowell's] *Life Studies*. . . . Lowell's poems were written when he was around forty, and seemed to me to communicate an overwhelmingly grim, helpless sense that the dragons in his life were simply *like that*. . . . But I was twenty-six, not forty—and *my* poems had to be about trying to figure out *why* the past was as it was, what patterns and powers kept me at its mercy (so I could change, and escape)."

The Sacrifice

When Judas[1] writes the history of SOLITUDE,—
. . . let him celebrate

Miss Mary Kenwood; who, without
help, placed her head in a plastic bag,

then locked herself
in a refrigerator.

●

—Six months earlier, after thirty years
teaching piano, she had watched

her mother slowly die of throat cancer.
Watched her *want* to die . . .

What once had given Mary life
in the end didn't want it.

Awake, her mother screamed for help to die.
—She felt

GUILTY . . . She knew that *all* men in these situations felt
innocent—; helpless—; yet guilty.

●

Christ knew the Secret. Betrayal
is necessary; as is woe for the betrayer.

✢   ✢   ✢

---

1. In the New Testament, Judas Iscariot was one of Jesus Christ's twelve apostles. He betrayed Jesus by identifying him to arresting soldiers with a kiss. Jesus was then tried for treason and crucified.

The solution, Mary realized at last,
must be brought out of my own body.

Wiping away our sins, Christ stained us with his blood—;
to offer yourself, yet need *betrayal*, by *Judas*, before SHOULDERING

THE GUILT OF THE WORLD—;
. . . *Give me the courage not to need Judas.*

●

When Judas writes the history of solitude,
let him record

that to the friend who opened
the refrigerator, it seemed

death fought; before giving in.

1983

In the Western Night

1. The Irreparable

First, I was there where unheard
harmonies[1] create the harmonies

we hear—

then I was a dog, sniffing
your crotch.

I asked you why you
were here; your answer was your beauty.

I said I was in need. You said
that the dead

✳   ✳   ✳

1. Possible allusion to John Keats's famous line in "Ode on a Grecian Urn": "Heard melodies are
sweet but those unheard / Are sweeter still." The line may also refer to the Pythagorean idea that the
abstract, unheard harmonies of mathematics produce the heard harmonies of music. Or it may refer
simply to the spiritual or incorporeal aspects of existence.

rule and confuse our steps—

that if I helped you cut your skin
deeply enough

that, at least, was IRREPARABLE. . . .

This afternoon, the clouds
were moving so swiftly—

massed above the towers, rushing.

2. In My Desk

Two cigarette butts—
left by you

the first time you visited my apartment.
The next day

I found them, they were still there—

picking one up, I put my lips where
yours had been . . .

●

Our not-love is like a man running down
a mountain, who, if he dares to try to stop,

falls over—
my hands wanted to touch your hands

because we had hands.

●

I put the two cigarette butts
in an envelope, carefully

taping shut the edges.
At first, the thin paper of the envelope

didn't stop

*   *   *

the stale smell of tobacco . . .
Now the envelope is in my desk.

3. *Two Men*[2]

The man who does not know himself, who
does not know his affections that his actions

speak but that he does not
acknowledge,

      who will SAY ANYTHING

and lie when he does not know that he is
lying because what he needs to believe is true

must indeed
be true,

    THIS MAN IS STONE . . . NOT BREAD.

    STONE. NOT CAKE. NOT CHEESE. NOT BREAD . . .

The man who tries to feed his hunger
by gnawing stone

      is a FOOL; his hunger is

fed in ways that he knows cannot satisfy it.

4. *Epilogue: A Stanza from Horace*[3]

At night in dreams I hold you
    and now I pursue you
fleeing through the grass of the Campus Martius,[4]
you, through the waters (you are cruel) fleeing.

        1990

2. "These lines are indebted to an unpublished lecture by V. A. Kolve, 'Fools In and Out of Motley' (Wellesley 1979)" (Bidart's note).
3. Roman poet (65–8 B.C.E.), author of *Odes*, to which this stanza is indebted. See endnote.
4. The field of Mars, a sunny, open space outside of Rome where athletic competitions took place.

"In the Western Night," which concerns a gay love affair marked by misunderstanding and loss, bears an ironic relation to the final, hopeful lines of Allen Ginsberg's "Howl," from which it takes its title. Ginsberg wrote, "in my dreams you walk dripping from a sea-journey on the highway across America in tears to the door of my cottage in the Western night." Ginsberg's "cottage" was located in Berkeley, California, and Bidart's poem was also written in Berkeley. Ginsberg's final line speaks of "dreams" in which his friend comes to him "dripping from a sea-journey." Conversely, Bidart's poem ends with "dreams" in which his lover is seen *fleeing* "through the waters."

Beyond providing a counterpoint to Ginsberg's text, Bidart's conclusion also echoes the final stanza of Horace's Ode 4.1, "Intermissa, Venus." Horace's aging speaker prays to Venus, the goddess of love, to free him from passion. But he confesses that he still dreams of his young beloved, Ligurinus, running from him across the Campus Martius and then swimming away in the sea. Horace's stanza has been translated thusly by David West in *Horace: The Complete Odes and Epodes*: "At night in my dreams sometimes I catch / and hold you, sometimes I pursue you as you run / over the grass of the Campus Martius / or swim, so hard of heart, the rolling waves."

In the Ruins

1. *Man is a* MORAL *animal.*

2. *You can get human beings to do anything,* — IF
   you convince them it is moral.

3. *You can convince human beings anything is moral.*

●   ●   ●

Oh Night, —

    . . . THE SUN IS DEAD.

           What we dream moves

across our sky by

day, is a CORPSE, —

that sun's day is not the *real* day—;
that day's light is not the *real* light—;

FOR THE SUN IS DEAD . . .

          Now when I learned this,

    ✻   ✻   ✻

I knew the injunction placed upon me.
Before the corpse, I heard: —

RETURN THE DEAD TO LIFE.

1990

Lament for the Makers

Not bird not badger not beaver not bee

Many creatures must
make, but only one must seek

within itself what to make

My father's ring was a *B* with a dart
through it, in diamonds against polished black stone.

I have it. What parents leave you
is their lives.

Until my mother died she struggled to make
a house that she did not loathe; paintings; poems; me.

Many creatures must

make, but only one must seek
within itself what to make

Not bird not badger not beaver not bee

•

Teach me, masters who by making were
remade, your art.

2005

The "masters" in this poem are the great writers who have come before, who have been able to confer meaning. Bidart has commented about making in general: "The desire to make is built into us, its necessities and pleasures and contradictions. . . . Human beings constantly strive to reach the heart of something: when they reach it they find it is only another surface. Art strives to be that center that has reached the light and remains the center."

Curse

May breath for a dead moment cease as jerking your

head upward you hear as if in slow motion floor

collapse evenly upon floor as one hundred and ten

floors descend upon you.

May what you have made descend upon you.
May the listening ears of your victims   their eyes   their

breath

enter you, and eat like acid
the bubble of rectitude that allowed you breath.

May their breath now, in eternity, be your breath.

•

Now, as you wished, you cannot for us
not be. May this be your single profit.

Of your rectitude at last disenthralled, you
seek the dead. Each time you enter them

they spit you out. The dead find you are not food.

Out of the great secret of morals, *the imagination to enter
the skin of another,* what I have made is a curse.

2005

"Curse" refers to the murder of almost three thousand people by al-Qaeda terrorists on September 11, 2001. The speaker pronounces a curse on the violent zealots who inhabited a "bubble of rectitude." But is the speaker cursed as well, in having no language left *but* a curse?

You Cannot Rest

The trick was to give yourself only to what
could not receive what you had to give,

*   *   *

leaving you as you wished, free.
Still you court the world by enacting yet once

more the ecstatic rituals of enthrallment.
You cannot rest. The great grounding

events in your life (weight lodged past
change, like the sweetest, most fantastical myth

enshrining yet enslaving promise), the great
grounding events that left you so changed

you cannot conceive your face without their
happening, happened when someone

could receive. Just as she once did, he did—past
judgment of pain or cost. Could receive. Did.

2008

With Each Fresh Death the Soul Rediscovers Woe

from the world that called you Piñon[1] *not one voice is now not stopped*
Piñon little pine nut sweet seed of the pine tree which is evergreen

Soul that discovered itself as it discovered the irreparable

breaking through ice to touch the rushing stream whose skin
breaking allowed darkness to swallow blondhaired Ramona

in 1944 age six high in the cold evergreen Sierras as you

age five luckily were elsewhere but forever after Soul there
failing to pull her for years of nights from the irreparable

2008

---

1. Piñon was Bidart's familial nickname as a child. The piñon (or pinyon) is a small, fragrant pine
tree that grows in California and surrounding regions. It produces edible, nutritious piñon nuts.

ROBERT PINSKY
b. 1940

ROBERT PINSKY has emerged as one of the most persuasive advocates for poetry on the contemporary American scene. While serving an unprecedented three terms as the nation's Poet Laureate, Pinsky initiated the Favorite Poems Project, which "is dedicated to celebrating, documenting and encouraging poetry's role in Americans' lives." Educated at Rutgers University and Stanford, where he worked with the poet and critic Ivor Winters, Pinsky has an encyclopedic knowledge of poetry. Like many other poets of his generation, he is also drawn to the American jazz masters of the 1950s and 1960s — such as Dizzy Gillespie, Charlie Parker, Sonny Rollins, and John Coltrane — and found a model for his own work in the way these jazz stylists interweave quotation with improvisation. One even detects rapid, staccato bebop rhythms braided with more lyrical passages in the opening and later stanzas of Pinsky's poem "Shirt."

Pinsky was born in Long Branch, New Jersey, then a popular resort town, and was raised in a mixed neighborhood of mostly Jewish and Irish immigrants. He describes his own Jewish upbringing as "nominally Orthodox." His family struggled to make ends meet, especially after his father lost his job as an optician in 1947 and was for a few years unemployed. Yet Pinsky was drawn to the cultural richness and diversity of his community and appreciated his family's support of his development, even on their limited means, as "The Green Piano" somewhat humorously reflects. In his poetry, Pinsky often explores the situations of working people and immigrants who face the anxieties associated with poverty, difficult work conditions, and unemployment but manage to find expression and assert their identity. His poems display great linguistic invention that combines seriousness with a frequent, and often subtle, sense of play.

FURTHER READING

Robert Pinsky. *The Figured Wheel: New and Collected Poems, 1966–1996.* New York: Farrar, Straus & Giroux, 1996.

——— . *Gulf Music: Poems.* New York: Farrar, Straus & Giroux, 2007.

——— and Maggie Dietz. *Americans' Favorite Poems: The Favorite Poem Project Anthology.* New York: W. W. Norton, 1999.

Shirt

The back, the yoke, the yardage. Lapped seams,[1]
The nearly invisible stitches along the collar
Turned in a sweatshop by Koreans or Malaysians[2]

Gossiping over tea and noodles on their break
Or talking money or politics while one fitted
This armpiece with its overseam to the band

Of cuff I button at my wrist. The presser, the cutter,
The wringer, the mangle. The needle, the union,
The treadle, the bobbin.[3] The code. The infamous blaze

At the Triangle Factory in nineteen-eleven.
One hundred and forty-six died in the flames[4]
On the ninth floor, no hydrants, no fire escapes—

The witness in a building across the street
Who watched how a young man helped a girl to step
Up to the windowsill, then held her out

Away from the masonry wall and let her drop.
And then another. As if he were helping them up
To enter a streetcar, and not eternity.

A third before he dropped her put her arms
Around his neck and kissed him. Then he held
Her into space, and dropped her. Almost at once

He stepped to the sill himself, his jacket flared
And fluttered up from his shirt as he came down,
Air filling up the legs of his gray trousers—

❖   ❖   ❖

1. Here, and at several points below, the poem names elements from the construction of a shirt.
2. Shirt manufacturing, a major industry once centered on the Garment District in New York City, had moved by the time this poem was written to developing countries such as Malaysia and Korea, and to the American South.
3. Tools of the shirt-making trade.

4. The 1911 fire in the Triangle Shirt Factory in New York, in which 146 garment workers—mostly young women from immigrant families—died when trapped on the eighth and ninth floors, was an important and tragic incident in the history of American labor relations. The poem provides many historical details about the fire.

Like Hart Crane's Bedlamite, "shrill shirt ballooning."[5]
Wonderful how the pattern matches perfectly
Across the placket and over the twin bar-tacked

Corners of both pockets, like a strict rhyme
Or a major chord. Prints, plaids, checks,
Houndstooth, Tattersall, Madras. The clan tartans[6]

Invented by mill-owners inspired by the hoax of Ossian,[7]
To control their savage Scottish workers, tamed
By a fabricated heraldry: MacGregor,

Bailey, MacMartin. The kilt, devised for workers
To wear among the dusty clattering looms.
Weavers, carders, spinners. The loader,

The docker, the navvy. The planter, the picker, the sorter
Sweating at her machine in a litter of cotton
As slaves in calico headrags sweated in fields:

George Herbert,[8] your descendant is a Black
Lady in South Carolina, her name is Irma
And she inspected my shirt. Its color and fit

And feel and its clean smell have satisfied
Both her and me. We have culled its cost and quality
Down to the buttons of simulated bone,

The buttonholes, the sizing, the facing, the characters
Printed in black on neckband and tail. The shape,
The label, the labor, the color, the shade. The shirt.

2000

---

5. See Hart Crane's "To Brooklyn Bridge": "Out of some subway scuttle, cell or loft / A bedlamite speeds to thy parapets, / Tilting there momently, shrill shirt ballooning."
6. Textile patterns developed in Scottish mills.

7. Supposed author of an ancient Scottish epic; the poem, published in 1760, was in fact a forgery by James MacPherson.
8. George Herbert (1593–1633), Welsh poet and Anglican priest, was the author of "The Collar."

The Green Piano

Aeolian. Gratis. Great thunderer, half-ton infant of miracles[1]
Torn free of charge from the universe by my mother's will.
You must have amazed that half-respectable street

Of triple-decker families and rooming-house housepainters
The day that the bole-ankled oversized hams of your legs
Bobbed in procession up the crazy-paved front walk

Embraced by the arms of Mr. Poppik the seltzer man
And Corydon his black-skinned helper, tendering your thighs[2]
Thick as a man up our steps. We are not reptiles:

Even the male body bears nipples, as if to remind us
We are designed for dependence and nutriment, past
Into future. O Europe, they budged your case, its ponderous

Guts of iron and brass, ten kinds of hardwood and felt
Up those heel-pocked risers and treads splintering tinder.
Angelic nurse of clamor, yearner, tinkler, dominator[3]—

O Elephant, you were for me! When the tuner Mr. Otto Van Brunt
Pronounced you excellent despite the cracked sounding board, we
Obeyed him and swabbed your ivories with hydrogen peroxide.

You blocked a doorway and filled most of the living room.
The sofa and chairs dwindled to a ram and ewes, cowering: now,
The colored neighbors could be positive we were crazy and rich,

As we thought the people were who gave you away for the moving
Out of their carriage house—they had painted you the color of pea soup.
The drunk man my mother hired never finished antiquing you

Ivory and umber, so you stood half done, a throbbing mistreated noble,
Genuine—my mother's swollen livestock of love, lost one, unmastered:
You were the beast she led to the shrine of my genius, mistaken.

    *   *   *

1. A stream of Homeric epithets applied in humorously mock-heroic style to a free ("Gratis") piano acquired by the poet's mother.

2. That is, the legs of the piano.

3. More mock-heroic epithets applied to the piano.

Endlessly I bonged according to my own chord system "Humoresque,"[4]
"The Talk of the Town,"[5] "What'd I Say." Then one day they painted you pink.
Pink is how my sister remembers you the Saturday afternoon

When our mother fell on her head,[6] dusty pink as I turn on the bench
In my sister's memory to see our mother carried moaning up the last
Steps and into the living room, inaugurating the reign of our confusion.[7]

They sued the builder of the house she fell in, with the settlement
They bought a house at last and one day when I came home from college
You were gone, mahogany breast, who nursed me through those

Years of the Concussion, and there was a crappy little Baldwin Acrosonic
In your place, gleaming, walnut shell. You sere, gone, despoiled one
Pink one, forever green one, white-and-gold one, comforter, living soul.

2000

BOB DYLAN
b. 1941

Bob DYLAN is one of the creative giants of the past half century. He has changed
popular music by merging country and folk traditions with electric rock and roll.
He combined musical lyrics with poetry. His lyrics mingle politics, spirituality, surrealism, and psychology with verbal and imaginative play. And he has
produced a seemingly endless supply of memorable songs, lyrics, arrangements,
and performances. At the center of his accomplishment is a huge paradox: he
achieved his individuality by frequently drawing upon songs and poems already
written.

Dylan began as a folk singer, composing lyrics about America, personal relationships, and social injustice. "The Times They Are A-Changin'," released

4. A schmaltzy, and extremely popular, classical piece by Antonín Dvořák.
5. 1933 pop hit by Jerry Livingston, Marty Symes, and Al J. Neiburg. "What'd I Say": 1958 song by Ray Charles, often considered the first example of soul music.
6. When Pinsky was young, his mother fell on

her head and suffered a severe concussion, making her an invalid for two years.
7. See Edwin Arlington Robinson's late-nineteenth-century poem "Eros Turranos": "The falling leaf inaugurates / The reign of her confusion; / The pounding wave reverberates / The dirge of her illusion."

in 1963, epitomizes the political side of this early phase. The song helped to shape the 1960s. Dylan returned to the theme decades later, in "Things Have Changed," released in 2000. In the later song, he seems to express skepticism toward his earlier idealism by adopting a weary, "seen it all" tone.

Soon after the release of "The Times They Are A-Changin'" came Dylan's most revolutionary moment, when, to the distress of some of his fans, he moved from folk music to electric rock and to an even more complex and poetic lyric. "Like a Rolling Stone," released in 1965, exemplifies this stylistic breakthrough. As critic Stephen Scobie puts it, "There's never been a moment in the history of rock and roll to equal the excitement of that first sharp crack of the snare drum. Insistently, arrogantly, authoritatively, it inaugurated a new world. In Bruce Springsteen's words . . . : 'It sounded like somebody'd kicked open the door to your mind.'"

"Like a Rolling Stone" may seem like a vituperative attack on the main character, "Miss Lonely," perhaps an act of revenge based on a personal relationship gone awry. But the song's exuberant feeling indicates that something more is at work. As Scobie says, "There is also a sense that Miss Lonely has liberated herself, and that living 'out on the street' is greatly to be preferred to confinement in 'the finest school.'" Miss Lonely, being on her own and "with no direction home," becomes a kind of existential hero, or a character out of Jack Kerouac, exerting her freedom and independence. She is, perhaps, an image of Dylan himself. "Like a Rolling Stone," in effect, explores all the contemporary resonances, both negative and positive, of the proverb attributed to Erasmus: "A rolling stone gathers no moss." And it does so with passion and imaginative vitality. All three of the songs represented in this selection indicate Dylan's belief in the necessity of mobility and change—his refusal to be just one thing, his unwillingness to be pinned down as a creative artist or as a person, and his ability to transform not only himself but also the culture around him.

Bob Dylan was born Robert Allen Zimmerman in Duluth, Minnesota, and grew up as one of the few Jewish kids in the mining town of Hibbing. As a teenager, he admired such film stars as the rebellious James Dean and such musical performers as the country music singer and composer Hank Williams and the politically engaged folk master Woody Guthrie. He was also fascinated by the emergence of such rock and roll stars as Little Richard and Buddy Holly. He taught himself to play the guitar and other instruments, and he formed rock bands. Attending the University of Minnesota, he discovered contemporary poets, including the Welsh bard Dylan Thomas, after whom he would soon rename himself. He dropped out of the university and moved to New York to pursue a career as a folk singer. As he recounts the story in the first volume of his autobiography, *Chronicles*, he performed in any Greenwich Village nightclub that would employ him, and he immersed himself in music, art, and poetry. The nineteenth-century French symbolist poet Arthur Rimbaud and the American Beat poet Allen Ginsberg in particular strongly affected him. Both poets provided examples of surrealistic, dreamlike imagery, and Ginsberg also modeled a socially conscious poetic. Already Dylan was widening his horizons beyond the traditional folk ballad to the larger world of artistic and cultural expression.

By the early 1960s, Dylan had achieved fame and respect as a folk artist with such politically charged songs such as "Blowin' in the Wind" and "The Times They Are A-Changin'." At the 1965 Newport Folk Festival, however, he introduced an innovative style of electric rock and roll to boos and catcalls. Critics termed the new hybrid folk-rock, but Dylan said, "I don't know what it is. I can't call it folk-rock. It's a whole way of doing things." When, at a subsequent concert in England, an audience member called him Judas, Dylan replied, "I don't believe you." Telling his band to play much louder, he immediately jumped into a raucous, defiant version of "Like a Rolling Stone." The Beats, to whom his new style was indebted, were quick to embrace him. Dylan and Ginsberg began a lifelong friendship that included periodic collaborations; Ginsberg appeared in Dylan's filmed productions and participated in his "Rolling Thunder" tour, and he cited Dylan's songs in his poems. Both Ginsberg and Dylan sought to challenge authority, to foster a more humane society, and to liberate the human spirit. In addition, each wanted to fuse poetry with oral tradition and music, to take poetry from the classroom and put it in the streets.

Dylan continued to refresh his art as his career progressed. In the 1970s he produced an album of country music. Later in the decade, he began a four-year period as a born-again Christian and a gospel singer. The 1990s and 2000s marked another Dylan revival, as a protean artist and as one of the central creative forces of his time. He is perhaps the only individual ever to win multiple Grammy Awards, an Academy Award (for "Things Have Changed"), a Pulitzer Prize (for his autobiography, *Chronicles*), and a Nobel Prize nomination for literature.

FURTHER READING

Bob Dylan. *Chronicles*, vol. 1. New York: Simon and Schuster, 2004.
———. *Tarantula*. New York: Scribner, 2004.
———. www.bobdylan.com.
Clinton Heylin. *Bob Dylan: Behind the Shades Revisited.* New York: HarperEntertainment–HarperCollins, 2001.
Richard E. Hishmeh. "Marketing Genius: The Friendship of Allen Ginsberg and Bob Dylan." *Journal of American Culture,* 29.4 (2006): 395-405.
Greil Marcus. *Bob Dylan: Writings, 1968–2010.* New York: PublicAffairs, 2010.
D. A. Pennebaker, director. *Bob Dylan: Don't Look Back.* DVD. New Video Group, 2007.
Christopher Ricks. *Dylan's Visions of Sin.* New York: Ecco–HarperCollins, 2004.
Stephen Scobie. *Alias Bob Dylan Revisited.* Calgary, Alberta, Canada: Red Deer Press, 2004.
Martin Scorsese, director. *Bob Dylan: No Direction Home.* DVD. Paramount, 2005.

Sam Shepard. *The Rolling Thunder Logbook*. Cambridge, Mass.: Da Capo Press, 2004.
Sean Wilentz. *Bob Dylan in America*. New York: Doubleday, 2010.

The Times They Are A-Changin'

1 Come gather 'round people
2 Wherever you roam
3 And admit that the waters
4 Around you have grown[1]
5 And accept it that soon
6 You'll be drenched to the bone
7 If your time to you is worth savin'
8 Then you better start swimmin' or you'll sink like a stone
9 For the times they are a-changin'

10 Come writers and critics
11 Who prophesize with your pen
12 And keep your eyes wide
13 The chance won't come again
14 And don't speak too soon
15 For the wheel's still in spin
16 And there's no tellin' who that it's namin'
17 For the loser now will be later to win
18 For the times they are a-changin'

19 Come senators, congressmen
20 Please heed the call
21 Don't stand in the doorway
22 Don't block up the hall
23 For he that gets hurt
24 Will be he who has stalled
25 There's a battle outside and it is ragin'
26 It'll soon shake your windows and rattle your walls
27 For the times they are a-changin'

28 Come mothers and fathers
29 Throughout the land
30 And don't criticize

1. Perhaps a reference to the Torah story of Noah and the flood. God, seeing that "the wickedness of man was great in the earth," caused it "to rain upon the earth forty days and forty nights" (Genesis 6:5, 7:4).

31 What you can't understand
32 Your sons and your daughters
33 Are beyond your command
34 Your old road is rapidly agin'
35 Please get out of the new one if you can't lend your hand
36 For the times they are a-changin'

37 The line it is drawn
38 The curse it is cast
39 The slow one now
40 Will later be fast
41 As the present now
42 Will later be past
43 The order is rapidly fadin'
44 And the first one now will later be last[2]
45 For the times they are a-changin'

                                                          1963

"The Times They Are A-Changin'" reveals Dylan's anger about racial segregation and the state and mob violence directed against peaceful protestors. It adopts an apocalyptic tone, drawing from passages in the Old and New Testaments to underline the need for social change. Clinton Heylin observes that the song "was rapidly adopted by causes far wider than the civil rights activists. The rebellious young considered it a song as much about the generation gap as about liberal and conservative forces." Dylan tried to emphasize the song's larger meanings in an interview: "It happened that maybe those were the only words I could find to separate aliveness from deadness. It had nothing to do with age."

Like a Rolling Stone

Once upon a time you dressed so fine
You threw the bums a dime in your prime, didn't you?
People'd call, say, "Beware doll, you're bound to fall"
You thought they were all kiddin' you
You used to laugh about
Everybody that was hangin' out
Now you don't talk so loud
Now you don't seem so proud
About having to be scrounging for your next meal

---

2. Echo of the New Testament: "But many that are first shall be last; and the last shall be first" (Matthew 19:30).

＊　＊　＊

How does it feel
How does it feel
To be without a home
Like a complete unknown
Like a rolling stone?

You've gone to the finest school all right, Miss Lonely
But you know you only used to get juiced[1] in it
And nobody has ever taught you how to live on the street
And now you find out you're gonna have to get used to it
You said you'd never compromise
With the mystery tramp, but now you realize
He's not selling any alibis
As you stare into the vacuum of his eyes
And ask him do you want to make a deal?

How does it feel
How does it feel
To be on your own
With no direction home
Like a complete unknown
Like a rolling stone?

You never turned around to see the frowns on the jugglers and the clowns
When they all come down and did tricks for you[2]
You never understood that it ain't no good
You shouldn't let other people get your kicks for you
You used to ride on the chrome horse with your diplomat
Who carried on his shoulder a Siamese cat
Ain't it hard when you discover that
He really wasn't where it's at
After he took from you everything he could steal

How does it feel
How does it feel
To be on your own

1. Drunk (slang).
2. Compare William Blake's "The Chimney Sweeper": "And because I am happy and dance and sing, / They think they have done me no injury." Also consider Arthur Rimbaud's "Parade" (in his prose-poem sequence "Illuminations"), in which the mad grin ("la grimace enragé") of the swindler and the juggler is linked to both clownishness and terror ("leur raillerie ou leur terreur").

With no direction home
Like a complete unknown
Like a rolling stone?

Princess on the steeple and all the pretty people
They're drinkin', thinkin' that they got it made
Exchanging all kinds of precious gifts and things
But you'd better lift your diamond ring, you'd better pawn it babe
You used to be so amused
At Napoleon in rags and the language that he used
Go to him now, he calls you, you can't refuse
When you got nothing, you got nothing to lose
You're invisible now, you got no secrets to conceal

How does it feel
How does it feel
To be on your own
With no direction home
Like a complete unknown
Like a rolling stone?

1965

Rolling Stone magazine has named "Like a Rolling Stone" the greatest popular song ever written. The song exemplifies Dylan's initially controversial move from folk music to a musical form that blended rock and roll instrumentals with lyrics influenced by such poets as Arthur Rimbaud and Allen Ginsberg. Although much longer than the standard popular song of its time, more caustic in tone, and more surreal in imagery, it rose to number two on the charts. When the song was first released, Dylan performed it on a tour with his band, visiting (among other places) the San Francisco Bay Area. At a press conference, Dylan's friend Ginsberg stood up and asked, "Do you think there will ever be a time when you'll be hung as a thief?" Taken aback, Dylan smiled and replied, "You weren't supposed to ask that." The next day, he attended a Beat gathering and was photographed alongside Ginsberg and other Beat poets. According to biographer Sean Wilentz, the widely reproduced photo affirmed "Dylan's place among the poets and theirs with him."

Dylan's vision of strangeness and rootlessness undoubtedly owes something to Rimbaud's "The Drunken Boat," "Illuminations," and "A Season in Hell," and something to Ginsberg's "Howl." All of these texts mingle despair and exultation, and they use dreamlike imagery to portray the driftings of loners. Like Rimbaud's speaker in "The Drunken Boat," Miss Lonely is a wanderer without rudder or anchor. Like Rimbaud's speaker in "A Season in Hell," she is on the run, without country or friends. As a female version of Ginsberg's hipsters, who "wandered around and around," Miss Lonely can be seen alternatively as an injured soul, a monster, an artist, a saint, or an everyperson.

Things Have Changed

1 A worried man with a worried mind
2 No one in front of me and nothing behind
3 There's a woman on my lap and she's drinking champagne
4 Got white skin, got assassin's eyes
5 I'm looking up into the sapphire-tinted skies
6 I'm well dressed, waiting on the last train

7 Standing on the gallows with my head in a noose
8 Any minute now I'm expecting all hell to break loose

9 People are crazy and times are strange
10 I'm locked in tight, I'm out of range
11 I used to care, but things have changed

12 This place ain't doing me any good
13 I'm in the wrong town, I should be in Hollywood
14 Just for a second there I thought I saw something move
15 Gonna take dancing lessons, do the jitterbug rag
16 Ain't no shortcuts, gonna dress in drag
17 Only a fool in here would think he's got anything to prove

18 Lot of water under the bridge, lot of other stuff too
19 Don't get up gentlemen, I'm only passing through

People are crazy and times are strange
I'm locked in tight, I'm out of range
I used to care, but things have changed

20 I've been walking forty miles of bad road[1]
21 If the Bible is right, the world will explode[2]
22 I've been trying to get as far away from myself as I can
23 Some things are too hot to touch

1. "Forty Miles of Bad Road" was the title of a guitar instrumental in the 1950s by the legendary Duane Eddy; an album in the 1980s by the Lee Thomas Band; and a song by the Bruisers in 1996 that included the lines, "It's forty miles of bad road / And I got troubles on my mind." After Dylan's song appeared, another band, Dead Moon, also produced a song called "40 Miles of Bad Road."

2. End-of-the-world prophecies occur in Judaic, Christian, and Islamic holy books. For example, the New Testament states, "And this gospel of the kingdom shall be preached in all the world for a witness unto all nations; and then shall the end come" (Matthew 24:14).

24 The human mind can only stand so much
25 You can't win with a losing hand

26 Feel like falling in love with the first woman I meet
27 Putting her in a wheelbarrow and wheeling her down the street

> People are crazy and times are strange
> I'm locked in tight, I'm out of range
> I used to care, but things have changed

28 I hurt easy, I just don't show it
29 You can hurt someone and not even know it
30 The next sixty seconds could be like an eternity
31 Gonna get low down, gonna fly high
32 All the truth in the world adds up to one big lie
33 I'm in love with a woman who don't even appeal to me

34 Mr. Jinx and Miss Lucy, they jumped in the lake
35 I'm not that eager to make a mistake

> People are crazy and times are strange
> I'm locked in tight, I'm out of range
> I used to care, but things have changed

2000

"Things Have Changed" was written for the film *The Wonder Boys* (2000) and won an Academy Award for best song. Reviewing the song, Greil Marcus commented that it borrows phrases from such country songs as the Carter Family's "Worried Man Blues" and Duane Eddy's "Forty Miles of Bad Road." He interprets the lyric as transmitting the "I been all around the world, boys" mood of many old mountain songs and white blues. Scholar Stephen Scobie notes that because the song expresses the jaded perspective of the film's main character, played by Michael Douglas, "it can't be taken *simply* as an expression of Dylan's own opinions. Rather, it has to be seen indirectly, as another alias, another mask. He is in effect 'quoting' a fictional character. . . . The language is by turns direct, imagistic, and whimsical, but it is always full of the implications of quotation (not least the self-citation by which it irresistibly calls to mind the much younger and more idealistic 'The Times They Are A-Changin'")."

LYN HEJINIAN
b. 1941

Lyn hejinian is one of the founders of the Language poetry movement, in which poetry engages with contemporary ideas about discourse and subjectivity. Language poetry seeks to disturb the social and political status quo by using language in a radically nonnormative fashion. It defies assumptions that the relation of word to referent—or poetic "I" to subjectivity—is in any way simple. In Hejinian's practice, the texts hint at an autobiographical subject but in an elusive and perhaps illusory fashion, so that the vagaries of language get emphasized instead. Everything you think you know about reading, about placing yourself in the world, gets questioned in the space of one of Hejinian's poems. The poems challenge the reader to collaborate with the poet in constructing their meaning. As Hejinian writes in *The Language of Inquiry*, poetry is not the telegraphing of a message but rather an "inquiry" into linguistic theory and practice.

When reading the poems of *My Life*, for example, the reader cannot take for granted that they are actually about either "my" or "life" or even that they are poems. Instead, the text is a sea of floating signifiers, visually designed to resemble neither lineated poetry nor paragraphed prose but to appear similar to and different from both. Moreover, each "poem" arbitrarily has a number of sentences that conforms to the poet's age when writing—forty-five in the revised version. Thus, each poem seems less directly concerned with the poet's life or with fitting into the traditions of poetry than with containing a certain number of sentences. Nevertheless, the sentences hint at events and feelings that might be autobiographical, and the qualities of indirection and complexity manifest the spirit, if not the letter, of traditional poetry. Hejinian's poems soon disabuse you of any temptation to feel that poetry is easy. Instead, they introduce you to the pleasure of what's difficult.

Born in San Francisco, Hejinian graduated from Harvard in 1963, the first year women were eligible to receive Harvard degrees. Returning to the Bay Area in 1968, she married jazz saxophonist and composer Larry Ochs and had two children. In this same period, she began publishing her experimental poems, along with such fellow Language poets as Charles Bernstein and Rae Armantrout. She received particular recognition for the poems in *My Life* and *The Cell*. Living in Berkeley, she codirects the literary project Atelos and is a professor of English at the University of California, Berkeley.

In her "Poetic Statement" in *The Language of Inquiry*, Hejinian writes that she espouses "a poetics of uncertainty, of doubt, difficulty, and strangeness." But she makes clear that hers is also "a poetics of affirmation." She believes that the task of poetry is to produce "a sensation of newness, yes, and of renewedness . . . an acknowledgment of the liveliness of the world." Poetry should remind us of "the sheer bliss of simply being alive."

FURTHER READING

Craig Dworkin. "Penelope Reworking the Twill: Patchwork, Writing, and Lyn Hejinian's *My Life*." *Contemporary Literature* 36 (1995): 58–81.
Lyn Hejinian. *The Cell*. Los Angeles: Sun & Moon Press, 1992.
———. *The Fatalist*. Richmond, Calif.: Omnidawn Publishing, 2003.
———. *The Language of Inquiry*. Berkeley: University of California Press, 2000.
———. *My Life*. Expanded edition. Los Angeles: Sun & Moon Press, 1987.
Laura Hinton. "Postmodern Romance and the Descriptive Fetish of Vision in Fanny Howe's *The Lives of a Spirit* and Lyn Hejinian's *My Life*. In *We Who Love to Be Astonished*, ed. Laura Hinton and Cynthia Hogue, 140–151. Tuscaloosa: University of Alabama Press, 2002.
Marjorie Perloff. *Radical Artifice: Writing Poetry in the Age of Media*. Chicago: University of Chicago Press, 1991.
Juliana Spahr. "Resignifying Autobiography: Lyn Hejinian's *My Life*." *American Literature* 68:1 (March 1996): 139–59.

A pause, a rose, something on paper

A moment yellow, just as four years later, when my father returned home from the war,[1] the moment of greeting him, as he stood at the bottom of the stairs, younger, thinner than when he had left,[2] was purple—though moments are no longer so colored. Somewhere, in the background, rooms share a pattern of small roses. Pretty is as pretty does.[3] In certain families, the meaning of necessity is at one with the sentiment of pre-necessity.[4] The better things were gathered in a pen.[5] The windows were narrowed by white gauze curtains which were never loosened. Here I refer to irrelevance, that rigidity which never intrudes. Hence, repetitions, free from all ambition. The shadow of the redwood trees, she said, was oppressive. The plush must be worn away. On her walks she[6] stepped into

1. World War II, which dates the poem to about 1945, when the poet was four. The passage recalls the charged feeling when the absent father returns.
2. Perhaps an adult's interpretation she overheard.
3. A cliché the speaker perhaps remembers from childhood.
4. "The remark is gently satiric, pointing to the family's need to predict what will happen, to control future events" (Perloff).
5. Perhaps the better toys were kept in the playpen, the better dishes were stacked in a cabinet, or the better memories were remembered through writing.
6. Perhaps, but not certainly, the "she" is the mother, and perhaps it the same "she" who found the shadow of redwoods oppressive.

people's gardens to pinch off cuttings from their geraniums and succulents. An occasional sunset is reflected on the windows. A little puddle is overcast.[7] If only you could touch, or, even, catch those gray great creatures.[8] I was afraid of my uncle with the wart on his nose, or of his jokes at our expense which were beyond me, and I was shy of my aunt's deafness who was his sister-in-law and who had years earlier fallen into the habit of nodding, agreeably. Wool station.[9] See lightning, wait for thunder. Quite mistakenly, as it happened. Long time lines trail behind every idea, object, person, pet, vehicle, and event. The afternoon happens, crowded and therefore endless.[10] Thicker, she agreed. It was a tic, she had the habit, and now she bobbed like my toy plastic bird on the edge of its glass, dipping into and recoiling from the water. But a word is a bottomless pit.[11] It became magically pregnant and one day split open, giving birth to a stone egg, about as big as a football. In May when the lizards emerge from the stones, the stones turn gray, from green. When daylight moves, we delight in distance. The waves rolled over our stomachs, like spring rain over an orchard slope. Rubber bumpers on rubber cars. The resistance on sleeping to being asleep.[12] In every country is a word which attempts the sound of cats, to match an inisolable portrait in the clouds to a din in the air. But the constant noise is not an omen of music to come. "Everything is a question of sleep," says Cocteau,[13] but he forgets the shark, which does not. Anxiety is vigilant. Perhaps initially, even before one can talk, restlessness is already conventional, establishing the incoherent border which will later separate events from experience. Find a drawer that's not filled up. That we sleep plunges our work into the dark. The ball was lost in a bank of myrtle. I was in a room with the particulars of which a later nostalgia might be formed, an indulged childhood.[14] They are sitting in wicker chairs, the legs of which have sunk unevenly into the ground, so that each is sitting slightly tilted and their postures make adjustment for that. The cows warm their own barn. I look at them fast and it gives the illusion that they're moving. An "oral history" on paper. *That* morning this morning. I say it about the psyche because it is not optional. The overtones are a denser shadow in the room characterized by its habitual readiness, a form of charged waiting,

---

7. Perhaps a memory of rainy days.
8. Perhaps the clouds mentioned in the preceding sentence or the remembered relatives mentioned in the succeeding sentence.
9. Perhaps a reference to the aunt's knitting.
10. Endless, perhaps, in memory.
11. This meta-comment about words implies both their emptiness and their reverberance.
12. Perhaps the child's disinclination to go to sleep; or perhaps the power of dreams.

13. Jean Cocteau (1889–1963), French poet, novelist, playwright, and filmmaker. Shark: the ambiguous last clause could mean that the shark does not sleep or that the shark does not forget itself.
14. A meta-comment implying a contrast between the concrete particulars of a childhood and what memory makes of those particulars—for example, a narrative of an "indulged childhood."

a perpetual attendance, of which I was thinking when I began the paragraph, "So much of childhood is spent in a manner of waiting."

1987

"A *pause, a rose, something on paper*" is the first poem in Hejinian's autobiographical poetic sequence, *My Life*. The poem that follows, "*As for we who 'love to be astonished,'*" is the second. These poems adhere to what is often called procedural form, in which the form is arbitrary and predetermined. Each poem has forty-five sentences, the number of years old the poet was when she revised it; when she composed the first version at age thirty-seven, each poem had thirty-seven sentences. The poems expose language's dual capacity to be both referential and nonreferential, and they immerse us in that tension rather than striving to be either perfectly clear or perfectly opaque. The poems concern the interplay of autobiographical memory and self-enclosed language—free association and verbal play. By employing discontinuous sentences, the poems insist that the reader take an active role in the text. And by subverting our regular ways of understanding, they put into question all our assumptions about reality.

About the title, Marjorie Perloff asks: "Are the 'pause' and the 'rose' nouns in apposition or do they refer to the same thing? The consonantal endings (z) link the two monosyllabic words, but even then, we can't specify their meaning or relate them with certainty to the 'something on paper.'" Later she suggests that "it is the poet herself who is pausing to put 'something on paper,' something that is her written offering, her 'rose.'" But according to Perloff, in Hejinian's poem, "secrets seem about to be revealed, enigmas about to be clarified, but the moment of revelation never comes. . . . Hers is autobiography that not only calls attention to the impossibility of charting the evolution of a coherent 'self' . . . but one that playfully deconstructs the packaged model crowding the bookstore shelves today."

As for we who "love to be astonished"

You spill the sugar when you lift the spoon. My father had filled an old apothecary jar with what he called "sea glass," bits of old bottles rounded and textured by the sea, so abundant on beaches. There is no solitude.[1] It buries itself in veracity. It is as if one splashed in the water lost by one's tears. My mother had climbed into the garbage can in order to stamp down the accumulated trash, but the can was knocked off balance, and when she fell she broke her arm. She could only give a little shrug. The family had little money but plenty of food. At the circus only the elephants were greater than anything I could have imagined. The egg of Columbus,[2] landscape and grammar. She wanted

1. Perhaps an intimation of crowded memory.
2. The phrase commonly refers to a brilliant idea that seems simple after the fact. It is based on an apocryphal story about Christopher Columbus. Responding to critics, he challenged them to make an egg stand on its tip; when they could not, he tapped the egg to flatten its tip and then did it easily.

one where the playground was dirt, with grass, shaded by a tree, from which would hang a rubber tire as a swing, and when she found it she sent me.[3] These creatures[4] are compound and nothing they do should surprise us. I don't mind, or I won't mind, where the verb "to care" might multiply. The pilot of the little airplane had forgotten to notify the airport of his approach, so that when the lights of the plane in the night were first spotted, the air raid sirens went off, and the entire city on that coast went dark.[5] He was taking a drink of water and the light was growing dim. My mother stood at the window watching the only lights that were visible, circling over the darkened city in search of the hidden airport. Unhappily, time seems more normative than place.[6] Whether breathing or holding the breath, it was the same thing, driving through the tunnel from one sun to the next under a hot brown hill. She sunned the baby for sixty seconds, leaving him naked except for a blue cotton sunbonnet. At night, to close off the windows from view of the street, my grandmother pulled down the window shades, never loosening the curtains, a gauze starched too stiff to hang properly down.[7] I sat on the windowsill singing sunny lunny teena,[8] ding-dang-dong. Out there is an aging magician who needs a tray of ice in order to turn his bristling breath into steam. He broke the radio silence. Why would anyone find astrology interesting when it is possible to learn about astronomy.[9] What one passes in the Plymouth.[10] It is the wind slamming the doors. All that is nearly incommunicable to my friends. Velocity and throat verisimilitude. Were we seeing a pattern or merely an appearance of small white sailboats on the bay,[11] floating at such a distance from the hill that they appeared to be making no progress. And for once to a country that did not speak another language.[12] To follow the progress of ideas, or that particular line of reasoning, so full of surprises and unexpected correlations, was somehow to take a vacation. Still, you had to wonder where they had gone, since you could speak of reappearance. A blue room is always dark. Everything on the boardwalk was shooting toward the sky.[13] It was not specific to any year, but very early. A German goldsmith covered a bit of metal with cloth in the 14th century and

3. The "she" is perhaps the speaker's mother, and the "one" is a school.
4. Perhaps a reference to the remembered figures of childhood.
5. Apparently a World War II story, perhaps one told to the speaker by her mother.
6. Perhaps a complaint against the universal power of time.
7. Perhaps a suggestion of domestic propriety, and seemingly an echo of the "white gauze curtains which were never loosened" that appear in "A *pause, a rose, something on paper.*"
8. Nonsense words, chosen for their sound

repetitions, perhaps recalled from childhood and prefiguring the speaker's poetic vocation. Alternatively, they may be a version of "Sonnez les matines" from the French children's song "Frcre Jacques."
9. Perhaps something the speaker remembers hearing or saying.
10. Popular automobile of the 1940s and 1950s.
11. San Francisco Bay.
12. Perhaps a reference to a trip to an English-speaking country, or to the intellectual "vacation" described in the next sentence.
13. Perhaps an early memory of fireworks.

gave mankind its first button. It was hard to know this as politics,[14] because it plays like the work of one person, but nothing is isolated in history—certain humans are situations. Are your fingers in the margin. Their random procedures make monuments to fate.[15] There is something still surprising when the green emerges. The blue fox has ducked its head. The front rhyme of harmless with harmony.[16] Where is my honey running. You cannot linger "on the lamb."[17] You cannot determine the nature of progress until you assemble all of the relatives.[18]

1987

"As for we who 'love to be astonished,'" like the poem that precedes it, focuses on the speaker's early childhood, beginning with memories of the father and mother. The poem dwells on the multiplications, disjunctions, and uncertainties inherent in both memory and language. Scholar Laura Hinton comments: "Hejinian's insistently language-invented speaker is among those who love to astonish, as well as 'love to be astonished.'. . . In *My Life*, any momentary reflection upon the self or characterization external to this wall of words is immediately absorbed back into a wordplay."

[It is the writer's object]

It is the writer's object
    to supply the hollow green
    and yellow life of the
    human I
It rains with rains supplied
    before I learned to type
    along the sides who when
    asked what we have in
    common with nature replied opportunity
    and size
Readers of the practical help
They then reside
And resistance is accurate—it
    rocks and rides the momentum

14. Perhaps a meta-comment on the political implications of the poem.
15. Perhaps a meta-comment on the random procedures of the poem.
16. That is, the beginnings of these words repeat or rhyme, as they do in "honey" and "running" in the next sentence.
17. "Lamb" may be conceived of as a living animal or as food; "on the lam" refers to those, like fugitives, who flee the policy or make a hasty departure.
18. "Relatives" may mean family members, or it may mean any phenomenon having a relation to progress.

Words are emitted by the
   rocks to the eye
Motes, parts, genders, sights collide
There are concavities[1]
It is not imperfect to
   have died

October 6, 1986

1992

"It is the writer's object" is the first poem in Hejinian's poetic sequence *The Cell*. The following three poems are also from this sequence, composed between October 1986 and January 1989, the final years of Ronald Reagan's presidency, and published in 1992. Like the poems in *My Life*, these pieces both employ and parody the genre of life writing, in this case achieving the effect of a diary through the use of composition dates. Also like the earlier poems, these poems are marked by ambiguity and what Hejinian calls "strangeness." The book's back cover indicates that the title, *The Cell*, connotes several contradictory things at once: biological life, imprisonment, closure, and circulation.

[In the dark sky there]

In the dark sky there
   are constellations, all of them
   erotic and they break open
   the streets
The streets exceed the house
On occasion the body exceeds
   the self
Everyday someone replaces someone and
   someone's mother is sad so
   as to exceed
The bed is a popular
   enclosure from which to depart
Outside the stars are stunning
   —touching
It is a question of
   scale

1. Hollowed-out shapes, perhaps suggesting the hollowness of words, or of the "human I" mentioned earlier.

It is erotic when parts
    exceed their scale

November 15, 1986

1992

[At x o'clock I shook]

At x o'clock I shook
    the radio
It is a fixed point
    and a great sentinel
The assistance that society was
    made for
And alpha prospects require alpha
    patrol
The noisy whispers of an
    open faucet, a boiling egg,
    and an electric clock come
    from the next room
The sound of withdrawal when
    the front door is being
    unlocked
The way gulls pump themselves
    up in the air they
    look like they're waving a
    thick magazine left in the
    sun
An idea left in a
    crate
I've thought that many times
    —myopia is psychosomatic
The universe pours through a
    funnel whose spout wobbles
The universe is endless but
    it splashes out unexpectedly
And my fate is convex
    like an eyeball

November 29, 1986

1992

The refusal to identify the time more specifically than "x o'clock" reflects the poem's inclination to mock rather than to produce traditional narrative. Nevertheless, the text soon becomes a testimony to the sensuous richness of everyday life—the "noisy whispers / of an open faucet" or a boiling egg, the way the universe "splashes out unexpectedly." In her "Poetic Statement," Hejinian advocates "an art that heightens perceptibility."

[Unorganized octave ashes scattered in]

> Unorganized octave ashes scattered in
>   the humid light
> The unblinking ears[1] are their
>   damp confidant
> The poem is not natural,[2]
>   unnaturally desired and saturated
> The relentless obligation of seductive,
>   descriptive, and corrupting perceptions
> Of some eternal, never-ending, everyday
>   task

> *December 13–14, 1986, January 6, 1987*
> *1992*

"Unorganized octave ashes scattered in" constitutes a kind of poetics or theory of poetry. Although the ending can be read in different ways, it seems to envision poetry as an "everyday task," a relevant assertion considering that the poems in this sequence are dated on an almost daily basis.

[A permanent sense of weirdness is the precursor]

> A permanent sense of weirdness is the precursor
> to mental life. As in going from "shallow" to "wool" or "weed"
> to "welcome" first you say "that's not what I wanted" and then
> you think. Hikers experience this
> in the mountains where the distance is near. The eye is always close
> to the ear. We go from "the wave" to "lapping" and from "lapping"
> to "mapping" and from there we go to the potluck feast
> celebrating collaboration with the so-called "Persian

1. A completely impossible figure of speech, a catachresis, like John Milton's "blind mouths" in his poem "Lycidas."

2. Perhaps a riposte to Robert Duncan's "Poetry, A Natural Thing."

rice." One's purported destination
when traveling is not actually that at all. We meet
at the café on the corner called La Strada[1]
where T might stand for time or for a road that divides
in two and the process requires that "one" is one again
and again, which is evidence of one's engagement with the present
or presents. To remember would be to turn back
and hence to turn away but not for me. The tag team nannies
are mostly playing (which is a lot of work) and but for footnote 10
I probably wouldn't know there was a process of substitution
going on. The bands of pink roosters signal the sunrise as the sun
melts the horizon—just think of the "incomprehensibility"
or "impenetrability" I keep attributing
with praise to Beethoven's late work.[2] Relationships can be
described as forming associations. Failing to call them passions
would have been, without some help, a huge mistake.

2003

This poem is from a sequence of untitled poems called *The Fatalist*. The poem invites the reader to enter into its poetics of "incomprehensibility," and to encounter some pleasingly bent epigrams and verbal surprises. Moving through its verbal leaps and swerves, one gains a sense of why "one's purported destination / when traveling is not actually that at all."

ALEX KUO
b. 1941

ALEX KUO, best known for his fiction, was an American Book Award winner for *Lipstick and Other Stories* in 2002. But he is also a major Chinese-American poet and one of the first Chinese American to have published a book of poetry. Born in Boston, he received his B.A. from Knox College in Galesburg, Illinois, and his M.F.A. from the University of Iowa. He has lived most of his adult life

1. "The Street" (Italian); also the title of a realistic film (1954) directed by Federico Fellini.
2. Composer Ludwig van Beethoven (1770–1827), ill and deaf, composed quartets toward the end of his life that were considered bewildering at the time but are now landed as towering musical achievements.

in the American West, beginning in 1956 when he took a job as a firefighter for the U.S. Forest Service. Kuo has taught creative writing and ethnic studies for the past forty-five years at universities and colleges in both China and the United States. At Washington State University, where he is now writer in residence, he has nurtured several generations of writers, including Sherman Alexie (included in this anthology). Kuo has also taught at Peking University, Beijing Forestry University, Jilin University, and Fudan University in China as well as at the University of Colorado. In the United States, he has been a major advocate on behalf of multiethnic writers and anthologies.

FURTHER READING

Alex Kuo. *A Chinaman's Chance: New and Selected Poems. 1960–2010*. La Grande, Ore.: Wordcraft of Oregon, 2011.

————. *This Fierce Geography*. Boise, Idaho: Limberlost Press, 1999.

————. *The Man Who Dammed the Yangtze: A Mathematical Novel*. Hong Kong: Haven Books, 2011.

————. www.alexkuo.org.

Coming into Beijing, 1997

for Moling[1]

Don't tell anyone about this
But I feel as if I'm coming home
Grass browning, coal smoke drifting
In this even November sunlight.

Concrete block buildings in all colors
Dark figures in narrow hutongs[2]
With less than a little money to spend
They have been here for generations, sweeping

Everywhere the carefully planted trees
Tendered rows of elms, willows and locusts
Above them the flitting magpies and higher
Always the crows that have witnessed all

And all have come to this, like me
Stones and people from every province
Still able to be astonished
Still doing wrong or right in different directions

---

1. Chinese cinematographer.   2. Streets or alleys.

*   *   *

Did I arrive with the right currency?
And enough cigarettes for everyone?
Unlike the Hong Kong I've just left
My Chinese is better understood here

The familiar, differing warm expressions
Their all-day tea jars warming in the sun
In the shadow of another Mao talisman
Or any other remediable mistake

I enter the city writing this poem
That has become important to remember
Holding back tears the entire ride
A 30-km trip I used to bicycle everyday

At every intersection hundreds of bicyclists
Negotiate past truckloads of cabbage
Testament to another government surplus
Distributed free to every work unit

The same traffic signs are still cautious
Saying the exact same thing to cyclists
And the working horses that have refused
To pay attention for centuries in their toil

Next morning I will watch early dancers
Face the rising sun at the pavilion
As if they've just jumped out of prison
Onto the back of a dragon vexing everywhere

Early next morning I will also pick up
A fallen gingko leaf, wipe off the dew with my fingers
And press it deep into my passport
So dear, where it will stay, where I am not

1999

WANDA COLEMAN
b. 1946

Wanda Coleman writes poems notable for both their pride and their introspection. She is, as she once called herself, "the warrior queen," avidly asserting her solidarity with other African Americans and women, and indeed with all people who fight injustice. She has said that "my anger knows no bounds. . . . Maybe the word 'perceptive' has to be wedded to the concept of anger." At the same time, she is a poet of remarkable sensitivity, eager to explore her endangered identity, to consider human frailty, to trace connections between her work and that of poets who have inspired her, and to ponder the threads tying her lived experience to her words on the page.

Coleman has been called an "Afro-Angelino." As a voice of urban, black Los Angeles, she focuses on working-class issues as well as racism and sexism. She states that "the hunger was always there to present my worldview, because my worldview didn't exist—it didn't even exist when Simone de Beauvoir wrote *The Second Sex*. She wrote about women all right, but what she wrote didn't apply to *me*." Coleman tries to preserve a black woman's sanity, besieged by larger social systems and caught in the maze of big-city life. She practices a kind of "glocalism," in which local issues combine with global awareness. In "African Sleeping Sickness," for example, she portrays African consciousness as suffering from a prolonged, dream-filled illness from which it is trying to awaken. In "Dear Mama," she contemplates the fragile ties that bind the self to a beloved other. In "Disconnections," she exposes the self-doubts that persist beneath the "warrior" persona, while in "Supermarket Surfer," she explores an everyday experience with good humor.

Coleman's poems often work in circular or repetitive ways rather than through a straight linear progression. The influence of blues, jazz, and ordinary conversation is felt in her innovative, postmodern forms. Her poems proceed not from a single logic or vantage point but from multiplicitous, sometimes contradictory ones. In her writing, urban speech and sounds become a new poetic diction, often layered with echoes of prior texts written by poets ranging from Langston Hughes to Allen Ginsberg. Formally innovative and socially activist, Coleman's poems meditate on marginalization and survival, inwardness and politics, the burden of history and the necessity of change. Above all, the poems use language in a daring fashion, inventing new ways—sometimes blunt and sometimes elliptical—to evoke a contemporary urban consciousness.

Coleman was born in the working-class neighborhood of Watts in Los Angeles. Her mother was a domestic worker once employed by Ronald Reagan, and her father worked in journalism and advertising. Coleman went to college for several years, and then she joined Studio Watts, a program for bringing about social change through art. She spent the 1960s living in two worlds: "the world of the Black militants" and "the world of the hippies." That period ended when she decided she "wanted to become an artist." Married thrice (presently and for nearly thirty years to poet and artist Austin Straus), and the mother of three, she has held a wide variety of jobs, including medical secretary, waitress, magazine editor, script writer, journalist, radio host, and college lecturer. She won an Emmy as staff writer for the television soap opera *Days of Our Lives*, the only poet in this anthology to have garnered that award. Her poetry has earned her a Guggenheim Fellowship and the Lenore Marshall Poetry Prize.

Famed for her poetry readings, Coleman spontaneously broke into verse in 2006 while attending an exhibition in Paris called "Los Angeles 1955–85." "I love it," said one young Frenchwoman as she listened to the improvised performance by the older African-American poet. She added that it reminded her of "what I see in American cinema about the '60s."

FURTHER READING

Priscilla Ann Brown. "What Saves Us: An Interview with Wanda Coleman." *Callaloo* 26:3 (Summer 2003): 635–62.

Wanda Coleman. *African Sleeping Sickness: Stories and Poems*. Santa Rosa, Calif: Black Sparrow Press, 1990.

———. *Bath Water Wine*. Santa Rosa, Calif.: Black Sparrow Press, 1998.

———. *Mercurochrome: New Poems*. Santa Rosa, Calif.: Black Sparrow Press, 2001.

———. *The Riot Inside Me: More Trials & Tremors*. Boston: David R. Godine/Black Sparrow, 2005.

Dear Mama (4)

when did we become friends?
it happened so gradual i didn't notice
maybe i had to get my run out first
take a big bite of the honky[1] world and choke on it
maybe that's what has to happen with some uppity youngsters
if it happens at all

and now
the thought stark and irrevocable
of being here without you
shakes me

*   *   *

1. African-American slang for a white person, usually used disparagingly.

beyond love, fear, regret or anger
into that realm children go
who want to care for/protect their parents
as if they could
and sometimes the lucky ones do

into the realm of making every moment
important
laughing as though laughter wards off death
each word given
received like spanish eight[2]

treasure to bury within
against that shadow day
when it will be the only coin i possess
with which to buy peace of mind

1987

This is the fourth in a series of intimate poems, written at different periods in Coleman's career, addressed to her mother.

African Sleeping Sickness

for Anna Halprin[1]
even my dreams have dreams

1
four centuries of sleep they say
i've no memory
say they say they i talked quite coherently
i don't remember
four centuries gone[2]

i walk eternal night/the curse of ever-dreaming

sing me a lullaby

2. The old Spanish piece of eight, or *el real de la ocho*, was a silver coin minted in Spain from 1497 into the nineteenth century. Widely used, it became the first world currency. Pieces of eight often served as buried treasure in pirate stories, such as Robert Louis Stevenson's *Treasure Island*.

1. A San Francisco choreographer, one of the pioneers of postmodern dance, born in 1920.
2. Reference to the enslavement of Africans and a lingering aftermath of racial discrimination.

2
my father hoists me over his shoulder, holds me
snug to him. i cannot walk
we move thru the sea of stars in blue
i love my father's strength
i love how blue the blue is
and the coolness of stars against my face
he sings me "my blue heaven"[3]

3
i am tied hand and foot
astraddle the gray county hospital bed on the basement floor
my scream smothered in 4×4 adhesive
nothing on but the too short too thin cotton gown
above a naked saffron bulb in socket
nothing else in the ward but empty beds row upon row
and barred windows

i do not know why i'm here or who I am
i see my wounds
they belong to the black child

4
giant green leech-dinosaurs invade the city
superman flies to rescue but weakened by kryptonite
can't stop the havoc
the slug creatures destroy the city, ooze into the Sierras/
along my back into my spinal cord leaving a trail
of upper Jurassic slime

(it gets down to skin and bones, skin/the body's last line
of defense. when awakened the impulse to become—a
cavernous hunger unfillable unsated

                        bones/the minimal elements
                        of survival)

         *   *   *

3. Popular song written by Walter Donaldson and George Whiting in 1927, and popularized by Gene Austin in 1928 and by Fats Domino in 1956.

"who am i?"[4]
the physician observes my return to consciousness
the petite white man with sable hair and clark kents[5]
makes note. he is seated in front of a panorama
hills and A-frames sloping to the sea

"who am i," i ask again
"who do you think you are?" he asks
"i'm not myself," i say

5
the encephalopathy[6] of slavery—trauma to racial cortices
resulting in herniated[7] ego/loss of self
rupture of the socio-eco spleen and
intellectual thrombosis[8]

(*terminal*)

sing me rivers[9] the anthem of blue waters the hymn of
genesis

6
lift up your voice and[10]

the tympanic[11] reverberation of orgasmic grunt
               ejaculatio praecox[12]
traumatized. infected. abrupt behavioral changes
               the vomitus/love-stuff[13]

          *   *   *

4. Awakening from surgery, the African-American protagonist of Raph Ellison's 1952 novel, *Invisible Man*, asks this same question.
5. Glasses like those worn by Clark Kent, the mild-mannered alter ego of the comic-book hero Superman.
6. A disease of the brain, especially one involving alterations of brain structure. Cortices: the outer layer of the cerebrum and cerebellum, responsible for the interpretation and correlation of sensory impressions.
7. Broken apart.
8. Life-threatening clot.
9. Perhaps a multiplicitous reference to Langs-ton Hughes's 1921 poem, "The Negro Speaks of Rivers," Hughes's 1945 poem, "I, Too, Sing America," and Arthur Hamilton's 1953 blues ballad, "Cry Me a River," originally sung by Ella Fitzgerald.
10. Reference to the poem and gospel song "Lift Every Voice and Sing," written by poet James Weldon Johnson in 1900 and now often termed the black national anthem.
11. Relating to a drum or an eardrum.
12. "Premature ejaculation" (Latin).
13. Vomitus: medical term for matter from the stomach that has come up into the mouth. Love-stuff: semen.

he watches me masturbating with the Jamaican dancer
whose hand is up my womb to the elbow
and starts to cry

the weight swells my heart/cardiopulmonary edema[14]
doubled in size it threatens to pop

i ask the doctor why things are so distorted

"we've given you morphine
for the pain of becoming"

7
chills. sing to me fever. sing to me. myalgia.[15] sing to me
delirium. sing to me. fluid filled lungs
i walk eternal night

in the room done in soft maroon warm mahogany amber gold
we disrobe to the dom-dom-dom a heady blues suite[16]

i pity the man his 4-inch penis
then am horrified as it telescopes upward becoming a
2-quart bottle of Coca-Cola

i talk quite coherently they say

8
fucking in the early dark of evening
mid-stroke he's more interested in being overheard
i go back into my trance as we resume the
6 o'clock news

> the car won't start. the mechanic is drunk
> i can't break his snore. the engine whines sputters
> clunks shutters in the uncanny stillness
> they're coming for me. i've got to escape
> angry, i lash out at the steering wheel, strike
> my somnambulate lover in his chest
> he jumps out of bed yelling
> "what's wrong?"

---

14. Abnormal accumulation of fluid in a bodily   15. Muscular pain.
organ, causing swelling.   16. Series of blues compositions.

*   *   *

the curse of ever-dreaming

sing to me, i say. sing to me of rivers

1990

The "African sleeping sickness" of the title is literally a brain disease characterized by fever, prolonged lethargy, tremors, and weight loss. Metaphorically, the term has both historical and personal dimensions. The poem combines cultural history, autobiography, and meditations on the spirit and the body. In an interview printed in *The Riot Inside Me*, Coleman explains her willingness to use shocking words and imagery: "I'm about *communicating*. I'm not about shock. . . . I want freedom when I write, I want the freedom to use any kind of language — whatever I feel is appropriate to get the point across."

African Sleeping Sickness (3)

after Theodore Roethke[1]

i sleep to wake and take my sleeping slow
i feel my fate in what i fear
i learn my feelings as i go

there's too much to learn and infinity to know
i dance my dance from tear to tear
i sleep to wake and take my snoring slow

of those so near outside me who are you?
Asmodeus[2] blisters this ground! i shall stomp mightily
here and be lost by going where? nowhere to go

night take the sun! but who can tell me how?
o lowly servant scours crystal stair[3]
dares dream to wake and takes that dreaming slow

great nation has nothing to do but dally with
my life/pollute the air and dastardly i'm spun
in circles round and round up and down i go

*   *   *

---

1. American poet (1908–1963).
2. The king of demons in Jewish legend.
3. An echo of Langston Hughes's 1922 poem,

"Mother to Son," which contains the line "Life for me ain't been no crystal stair."

my shaking heart's unsteady i should know
what rises rises always, and is near
i sleep to wake and take my rimming[4] slow
i learn by groping where i'm damned to go

1998

The third in Coleman's series of "African Sleeping Sickness" poems, this one echoes—
and significantly departs from—Theodore Roethke's poem "The Waking," which is also
included in this anthology. For additional examples of postmodern revision (or sampling),
see "Supermarket Surfer" below and Lorna Dee Cervantes's "In the Waiting Room," also
in this anthology.

Disconnections

1
i was not born. i was invented

stark & raving
relying heavily upon my cultural heritage
of poverty & bad grammar

my stumblings across the human landscape

(i didn't start out
                to be an ink spot)

all my loves massacred (mother, 'no hawk's blood was e'er
so red') in an unseemly rush to dignity

my identity as a speaker of dreams
& ceremonies in dark cold thoughts[1]

words like wild ponies freed to roam southwestern plains

sympathy reserved for the prophets, profligates
and pollyannas touting false positives

while my cruel & perverse sense of justice
incites riots of exoticism—broken minds, shattered fictions

✻   ✻   ✻

4. Vulgar slang for anal sex.
1. Allusion to the title of Lonne Elder's play

about black male relationships, *Ceremonies in
Dark Old Men* (1969).

living in a white sensibility
(there are no dirty sentences here)

blues (my deep sense of inexorable limitations)
expressed in my will to conquer
this nationally sanctioned villainy
spirited to the weary-witty last

i too have cried I am,[2] but have gathered nothing
but a strange unforgiving silence

2

of an unfortunately undereducated caste
self-cultivated and self-promoted
too thick to surrender (bullhearted)
this lightness and basin spell the tomb.
what am i to say when my temple is desecrated
and the shitter goes unclean and unpunished?
i am cut off from friends & fans, locked
in the ghetto of my extra-societal failures
ill-supported in my apostolic depression
unpatronized & unpampered, rags-to-rags
an unconventional American (skkkugly)
sardonic & powerless in my empty purse
eyes ogleless, flesh violating the limits of nylon.
nothing here but the rubble of high hopes
the dust of collapse choking off breath.
i am slipping from my own grasp
there rises a soul-sickening despair
and i pray that i will not survive the fall

3
imprisoned in the sugar bowl

ant.[3] i couldn't keep the job i thought i wanted. ant.
what does an angelic shade like me do in Hades?
(i felt moved by my own sense of life. was that
irrational?)

2. Allusion to the title of John Williams's auto-biographical novel, *The Man Who Cried I Am* (1985).
3. Possibly an allusion to Ezra Pound's *Pisan Cantos* (1948), in which the poet accuses himself of being antlike: "The ant's a centaur in his dragon world. Pull down thy vanity" (Canto 81).

*   *   *

antantant. true ant

trapped in an adolescent fantasyland where
garbage is plentiful as evidence of gluttony yet legions starve

(it took godzillion[4] years for that pissant to notice me
sitting on his face, and now
all he can do is express the silly regret that he
didn't bother to notice me before my cherry was popped)

in this strange revolt where i loot sentences
for sustenance

ant. and more ant

"we cannot escape our organs no matter how hard we try," said The Gypsy

mediocrity & cowardice of barbaric proportions
occlude the consciousness of my generation. ant.

beware any tendency to substitute kneejerk approval
for a profound if exothermic[5] understanding

red ant

unfulfilled. wasted. sweet as raw sugar. untasted

wham. blue ant

2001

Supermarket Surfer

after Allen Ginsberg[1]

what bohunkian[2] images i have of you
crash against my niggernoggin[3] as i shiver and stroll
long air-conditioned aisles at 2 a.m. the liquor

4. Verbal play on god, Godzilla, and zillion. Pissant: slang for ant.
5. Releasing energy in the form of heat, light, electricity, or sound.

1. American poet (1926–1997), author of "A Supermarket in California."
2. "Bohunk" is a slang term of derision for Eastern European Caucasians.
3. "Noggin" is slang for the human head.

under lock and key, the lettuce full and moist with
a fresh spray of mist and neon
my cart wobbles giddily on crooked wheels as i sputter
between the confused and the absurd as i cruise for pudding
and citrus-free hand lotion. there's plenty of disabled
parking outside. it is lonely here though the
automatic doors never close and a bleak phosphorescence
never dims and bananas are going at two pounds for
the price of one. the bin of avocados is small
and most of them more like plankton-stained golf balls
or too rotten. somewhere, i am detected via camera
lens while picking over pepper mills between
the spice racks and the baking soda

hang ten[4] toward checkout is a certainty

the only Walt[5] here is Disney
the pork chops are killing me
i am a nobody angel[6]
my heart is a frozen delicacy

2001

This poem echoes and condenses Allen Ginsberg's "A Supermarket in California" (also
included in this anthology). While Coleman perpetuates Ginsberg's theme of loneliness,
note the expanded role that fruit, vegetables, and other supermarket products play in
Coleman's retelling.

4. Surfer slang for a maneuver in which the surfer, riding a wave, manages to hang all ten toes over the front of the board and holds two "high fives" up in the air as a celebratory gesture.
5. In Ginsberg's poem, the speaker is accompanied by the spirit of Walt Whitman. Here it appears to be Walt Disney—the person or the corporation.
6. "Nobody's Angel" was the name of a novel by Thomas McGuane (1982) and a briefly sensational young women's pop band of the late 1990s.

RAE ARMANTROUT
b. 1947

RAE ARMANTROUT explores the ironies of contemporary life in an elliptical style, speaking as much through what is unsaid as what is said. Interested in what happens around her in small moments rather than in extended periods of time, she locates the humor, loneliness, and menace in the way we live now—the suburban paradise dusted by freeway exhaust in "Necromance," the fear of touch in "Sit-Calm." Her poems breach the pretty surface of things to probe the power relations, the pain, the dissonances beneath. They probe satirically, but with a light touch. Composed of hints and implications, they reveal their insights in glimmers, in single strange words placed next to white space, and in what Hank Lazar calls "wacky" juxtapositions. This is an art of social observation, subtly feminist and coolly alert but never polemical. At the same time, it is a minimalist art, suspicious of the elaborate narratives we spin in our own heads and in conversation with others. Less, in Rae Armantrout's poetry, is definitely more.

Armantrout explains (in her *Collected Prose*) that "various voices speak in my poems. I code-shift. I am many things: a white person, a working-class person with roots in the South, a woman, an academic of sorts, a '60s person who still likes rock and roll, someone who was raised on the Bible, a skeptic, etc. My voices manifest their own social unrest." She adds that, in looking over her work, she was struck by "how often my poems parody and undermine some voice of social control." Armantrout writes poems that, despite their detached demeanor, are inherently rebellious. They assume that language is always involved in pre-existent structures of dominance and subordination. Through their strategic deployment of silences and disjunctures, their refusal to cohere in any obvious way, Armantrout's poems explore what she calls "the fissures in identity and ideology." Yet at the same time, the poems are held together by artful sonic structures and by clusters of associations that take the place of linear narratives.

Armantrout, a single child, was raised in San Diego in a fundamentalist Christian household. Her father was a naval officer, and her mother managed a candy store. At the age of twelve, she stopped considering herself a believer and began to develop an interest in poetry instead. She was also a loner, nursing a plan to be a bandit in Mexico when she grew up. As a teenager, she was particularly drawn to the poetry of William Carlos Williams and Emily Dickinson, influences still visible in her poetry today. She loved the "poignancy" of the gap between perception and thing. Hearing "Satisfaction" by the Rolling Stones on the car radio was a turning point; reading Betty Friedan's *The Feminine Mystique* and joining the antiwar movement were two more. In her senior year, Armantrout transferred from San Diego State to the University of California, Berkeley, where she studied with Denise Levertov and came into contact with some of the founders of Language poetry—"the biggest turning point" in her life. The move gave her the impetus she needed to become a poet. She informally joined the Language poetry movement, attracted by its progressive approach to gender and its refusal to pass along fabricated, coherent stories as truth.

After receiving an M.A. at San Francisco State and teaching there for several years, Armantrout returned to San Diego, where she and her husband raised a son. She is now a professor of literature at the University of California, San Diego. A cancer survivor, she is increasingly interested in biology, physics, and the other natural sciences. Her poetry has won various recognitions, including the Pulitzer Prize in 2010. Armantrout describes her poetry by referring to Lewis Carroll's Cheshire cat, who appears and vanishes at will: "It's a Cheshire poetics, one that points two ways then vanishes in the blur of what is seen and what is seeing, what can be known and what it is to know."

FURTHER READING

Rae Armantrout. *Collected Prose.* San Diego: Singing Horse Press, 2007.
———. *Money Shot.* Middletown, Conn.: Wesleyan University Press, 2011.
———. *Next Life.* Middletown, Conn.: Wesleyan University Press, 2007.
———. *Veil: New and Selected Poems.* Middletown, Conn.: Wesleyan University Press, 2001.
———. *Versed.* Middletown, Conn.: Wesleyan University Press, 2009.
Nicole E. Cortz. "Rae Armantrout." In *Encyclopedia of American Poetry: The Twentieth Century,* ed. Eric Haralson, 22–23. Chicago: Fitzroy Dearborn, 2001.
Fanny Howe. "The Garden of Even." In *A Wild Salience: The Writing of Rae Armantrout,* ed. Tom Beckett, 51–54. Cleveland, Ohio: Burning Press, 1999.
Hank Lazar. "The Poetry of Rae Armantrout." In *American Women Poets in the 21st Century: Where Lyric Meets Language,* ed. Claudia Rankine and Juliana Spahr, 27–52. Middletown, Conn.: Wesleyan University Press, 2002.
Christina J. Mar. "Rae (Mary) Armantrout." In *Contemporary American Women Poets: An A-to-Z Guide,* ed. Catherine Cucinella, 18–22. Westport, Conn.: Greenwood Press, 2002.
Ron Silliman. "Asterisk: Separation at the Threshold of Meaning in the Poetry of Rae Armantrout." In *We Who Love to Be Astonished,* ed. Laura Hinton and Cynthia Hogue, 28–40. Tuscaloosa: University of Alabama Press, 2002.

Necromance

Poppy under a young
pepper tree, she thinks.
The Siren[1] always sings

1. A creature in Greek myth, having the head of a woman and the body of a bird, that was believed to lure mariners to their death by singing. Odysseus has a memorable encounter with two Sirens in Homer's *The Odyssey.*

like this. Morbid
glamour of the singular.
Emphasizing correct names
as if making amends.

Ideal
republic of the separate
dust motes
afloat in abeyance.
Here the sullen
come to see their grudge
as pose, modeling.

The flame trees[2] tip themselves
with flame.
But in that land
men prized
virginity. She washed
dishes in a black liquid
with islands of froth—
and sang.

Couples lounge
in slim fenced yards
beside the roar
of a freeway. Huge pine
a quarter mile off
floats. Hard to say where
this occurs.

Third dingy
bird-of-paradise[3]
from right. Emphatic
precision
is revealed as
hostility. It is
just a bit further.

        ✳   ✳   ✳

2. Any of several different species of tree, all of which have scarlet leaves.
3. A bananalike plant (*Strelitzia reginae*) that has orange and purple flowers suggestive of a bird; widely planted as an ornamental in Southern California.

The mermaid's[4]
privacy.

1991

The title of "Necromance," which combines the words "necromancy" and "romance," implies a number of possibilities. "Necromancy" means the art of magically revealing the future, magically influencing the course of events, or magically conjuring up the souls of the dead. "Romance" means a medieval tale involving adventure, legend, the super-natural, and chivalric love, and it also means a love affair. The prefix "necro-" refers to corpses, so one meaning of the title might be the romance of death, and another might be the death of romance. It is hard to pin down the resonances of "Necromance." As Ron Silliman has said, each Armantrout poem "resonates with the undecidable." Fanny Howe connects Armantrout's poetry to the postmodern, postsuburban cityscape of San Diego and comments, "If San Diego is a possible model for the rest of the developing world, then Rae's work anticipates the way it feels to inhabit the world."

Attention

Ventriloquy
is the mother tongue.

Can you colonize rejection
by phrasing your request,
                              "Me want?"

Song: "I'm not a baby.
        Wa, Wa, Wa.

        I'm not a baby.
        Wa, Wa, Wa.

        I'm crazy
        like you."

The "you"
in the heart of
molecule and ridicule.

Marks resembling
the holes

---

4. A mythical aquatic creature with a female human head and torso and the tail of a fish, sometimes related visually to the Sirens.

＊　＊　＊

in dead leaves
define the thing (moth wing).

That flutter
of indifference,
                feigned?

But if lapses
are the dens

strategy aims
to conceal,

then you don't know
what you're asking.

                1991

"Attention" concerns a difficult, conflicted bond—perhaps between mother and child, two would-be lovers, or a poet and poetry. Hank Lazar suggests that the ambiguity and humor of Armantrout's writing grows out of its "gap-and-connection" style, its "wacky" juxtapositions, and its pattern of "intensifying brevities."

Sit-Calm

In the excitement phase
we think we want something
we're made up to seem
exaggeratedly unfit for,
say, touch.

This is the funny part,
but also the dangerous
moment. Right away
we're talked out of it—
no harm done—
by a band of wise-acre friends.

"I don't know
what I'm thinking," we say,
to a spike of merriment.
Here is the warm,

human part
which dissipates tension
1995

The ending of "Sit-Calm," which lacks a final period, exemplifies what Armantrout calls in *Collected Prose* a "false bottom, which gives way on second thought. . . . Mine is a poetics of the double take, the crossroads."

Reversible

1

Try this.

Shadow of leaves
between shadows of venetian blinds

bounce

like holes

across the scroll of a
player piano.

But are similes reversible?

Try this.

Trunk of a palm tree
as the leg

of a one-legged ballerina.

2

That's a bad
Sean Connery,[1] but
a good Prince.[2]

＊   ＊   ＊

1. Sean Connery (b. 1930), a Scottish actor, portrayed a king who blessed the prince-like Robin Hood in the film *Robin Hood: Prince of Thieves* (1991).

2. Perhaps a reference to Robin Hood, a "prince of thieves" in the film of that name; or perhaps a reference to Prince (b. 1958), a noted singer, songwriter, and musician.

We wake up to an empty room
addressing itself in scare quotes.[3]

"Happen" and "now"
have been smuggled out,

to arrive safely in the past tense.

We come home to a cat
made entirely of fish.

2007

A Resemblance

As a word is
mostly connotation,

matter is mostly
aura?

Halo?

(The same loneliness
that separates me

from what I call
"the world.")

*

Quiet, ragged
skirt of dust

encircling a ceramic
gourd.

*

Look-alikes.
"Are you happy now?"

*   *   *

3. Quotation marks used to express skepticism or derision concerning the use of the enclosed word
or phrase.

＊

Would I like
a vicarious happiness?

Yes!

Though I suspect
yours of being defective,

forced

2009

Fellow poet Ron Silliman comments about Armantrout's later style: "Armantrout's use of silence, of gaps, breaks and the unsaid over time has evolved. Her poems today are more apt to come in numbered sections or with the not quite ubiquitous asterisk that leaps out from her books, cleaving segment from segment. . . . The first thing one notices about a poem that arrives at its conclusion in segments, particularly when it is short, is its constructedness. It is difficult to feign the simple, single voice of the writing workshop monologue if in fact the work in front of the reader arrives visibly in pieces."

Scumble

What if I were turned on by seemingly innocent words such as "scumble,"[1] "pinky," or "extrapolate"?

What if I maneuvered conversation in the hope that others would pronounce these words?

Perhaps the excitement would come from the way the other person touched them lightly and carelessly with his tongue.

What if "of" were such a hot button?

"Scumble of bushes."

＊   ＊   ＊

1. To make a painting's color less brilliant by covering it with a thin coat of opaque color applied with a nearly dry brush; to soften the lines or colors of a drawing by rubbing it slightly; the color applied in this manner. Pinky: the little finger. Extrapolate: to project or extend known data into an area not known so as to arrive at a usually conjectural knowledge of the unknown area.

What if there were a hidden pleasure
in calling one thing
by another's name?

2009

Sway

Caught up
in the leaf,
entranced,
the carbon atom
gets a life—
but whose life is it?

*

A slender whirlpool,
momentary poppy,
sways
over a drain.
Forget her.
She doesn't love you.
You will never have
such grace.

2011

LINDA HOGAN
b. 1947

LINDA HOGAN, along with other such major poets as Joy Harjo and Sherman
Alexie, addresses the complex history of Native American rooted existence and
diaspora. Equally important, she has established herself as a leading ecofeminist.
Suffused with Native American spirituality and feminist awareness, her writing
seeks to heal cultural wounds and reunite human beings with their natural sur-
roundings. Her desire to serve as a record keeper of her paternal family as well
as to explore her maternal family's history has led to her outstanding literary

career as not only a poet but also a novelist, essayist, memoirist, playwright, and environmental activist. She has won many prizes, including the American Book Award, the Lannan Prize, and the Lifetime Achievement Award from the Native Writers' Circle of the Americas.

Born in Denver, Colorado, Hogan received her bachelor's and master's degrees from the University of Colorado and has taught at many schools, including her alma mater. She now considers Oklahoma, her father's home state, to be her home as well. Her father, a Chickasaw, pursued a career in the military; her mother was a Nebraskan European immigrant. As a result, Hogan's poetry often focuses on Chickasaw history as well as European immigration culture. In an interview, she stated that "from my family I have learned the secrets of never having a home," a reflection of her experience with her father's frequent moves in the military and her family's history of continual movement in diaspora.

Hogan's characteristic interplay of home and homelessness—a sense of place and displacement—has led to her deep reading of international and transcultural writing. She has cited both Pablo Neruda and Elizabeth Bishop as inspirational transnational writers. Such global poets have allowed her, she has commented, to view the world holistically.

FURTHER READING

Kay Bonetti et al., eds. *Conversations with American Novelists*. Columbia: University of Missouri Press, 1997.
Andrea Campbell. *New Directions in Ecofeminist Literary Criticism*. Newcastle, Eng.: Cambridge Scholars Publishing, 2008.
Linda Hogan. *The Book of Medicines*. Minneapolis: Coffee House Press, 1993.
———. *Dwellings: A Spiritual History of the Living World*. New York: W. W. Norton, 2007.
Linda Hogan and William Kittredge. *Rounding the Human Corners*. Minneapolis: Coffee House Press, 1993.

The History of Red

First
there was some other order of things
never spoken
but in the dreams of darkest creation.

Then there was black earth,
lake, the face of light on water.
Then the thick forest all around
that light,
and then the human clay
whose blood we still carry

rose up in us
who remember caves with red bison
painted in their own blood,
after their kind.

A wildness
swam inside our mothers,
desire through closed eyes,
a new child
wearing the red, wet mask of birth,
delivered into this land
already wounded,
stolen and burned
beyond reckoning.

Red is the yielding land
turned inside out
by a country of hunters
with iron, flint and fire.
Red is the fear
that turns a knife back
against men, holds it at their throats,
and they cannot see the claw on the handle,
the animal hand
that haunts them
from some place inside their blood.

So that is hunting, birth,
and one kind of death.
Then there was medicine, the healing of wounds.
Red was the infinite fruit
of stolen bodies.
The doctors wanted to know
what invented disease
how wounds healed
from inside themselves
how life stands up in skin,
if not by magic.

They divined the red shadows of leeches
that swam in white bowls of water;
they believed stars

in the cup of sky,
They cut the wall of skin
to let
what was bad escape
but they were reading the story of fire
gone out
and that was science.

As for the animal hand on death's knife,
knives have as many sides
as the red father of war
who signs his name
in the blood of other men.
And red was the soldier
who crawled
through a ditch
of human blood in order to live.
It was the canal of his deliverance.
It is his son who lives near me.
Red is the thunder in our ears
when we meet.
Love, like creation,
is some other order of things.

Red is the share of fire
I have stolen
from root, hoof, fallen fruit.
And this was hunger.

Red is the human house
I come back to at night
swimming inside the cave of skin
that remembers bison.
In that round nation
of blood
we are all burning,
red, inseparable fires
the living have crawled
and climbed through
in order to live
so nothing will be left
for death at the end.

* * *

This life in the fire, I love it,
I want it,
this life.

1993

"The History of Red" addresses the colonial violence visited on Native Americans as well
as environmental issues, Western medicine, and tribal healing practices. The poem also
points beyond the two traditional ways of viewing nature—as either sublime or alienat-
ing—to a vision of Native Americans integrated with the natural environment.

YUSEF KOMUNYAKAA
b. 1947

ALTHOUGH THE VIETNAM WAR is usually dated from 1965 to 1975, historians
continue to grapple with the provisionary dating of this historical "moment" as
well as the outcome of the war and its legacy. When we examine the poetry of
the Vietnam era, many divergent and often contradictory perspectives emerge.
With hundreds of books of poetry about the war available at this time, the poetic
narrative has become heterogeneous and sometimes diffuse and fragmented.
Nevertheless, Yusef Komunyakaa has emerged as probably the best known of
these war poets. His collection *Dien Cai Dau* is the most acclaimed book of
American poetry about the war. His poems have a notable immediacy and
thoughtfulness that have made the war, its confusions, and its horrors real for
readers who never experienced it.

The son of a carpenter, Komunyakaa grew up in Bogalusa, Louisiana. Born
James Brown, Komunyakaa chose his present name as a tribute to his African
ancestors, who bore the name Komunyakaa in their homeland. After graduating
from high school, Komunyakaa enlisted in the military and was sent to Vietnam
in 1969. Working as a journalist for the army, he witnessed many deaths and was
in frequent danger himself. Returning to the United States, he received his B.A.
from the University of Colorado, Boulder, and his M.F.A. from the University of
California, Irvine. Having published many notable volumes of poems, he now
teaches at Princeton University. He has won both a Pulitzer Prize and a Ruth
Lilly Poetry Prize.

FURTHER READING

Yusef Komunyakaa. *Dien Cai Dau*. Middletown, Conn.: Wesleyan University Press, 1988.
———. *Neon Vernacular: New and Selected Poems*. Middletown, Conn.: Wesleyan University Press, 1993.
———. *Warhorses: Poems*. New York: Farrar, Straus & Giroux, 2008.
Joyce Pettis. *African American Poets: Lives, Works, and Sources*. Westport, Conn.: Greenwood Press, 2002.

Thanks

Thanks for the tree
between me and the sniper's bullet.
I don't know what made the grass
sway seconds before the Viet Cong[1]
raised his soundless rifle.
Some voice always followed,
telling me which foot
to put down first.[2]
Thanks for deflecting the ricochet
against that anarchy of dusk.
I was back in San Francisco
wrapped up in a woman's wild colors,
causing some dark bird's love call
to be shattered by daylight
when my hands reached up
& pulled a branch away
from my face. Thanks
for the vague white flower
that pointed to the gleaming metal
reflecting how it is to be broken
like mist over the grass,
as we played some deadly
game for blind gods.
What made me spot the monarch
writhing on a single thread
tied to a farmer's gate,
holding the day together

1. The political and military organization that fought against U.S. and South Vietnamese forces in the Vietnam War.
2. To avoid a land mine.

like an unfingered guitar string,
is beyond me. Maybe the hills
grew weary & leaned a little in the heat.
Again, thanks for the dud
hand grenade tossed at my feet
outside Chu Lai.[3] I'm still
falling through its silence.
I don't know why the intrepid
sun touched the bayonet,
but I know that something
stood among those lost trees
& moved only when I moved.

                                    1988

During the Vietnam War, Yusef Komunyakaa served as a reporter and editor for the military newspaper *The Southern Cross.* "Thanks" reveals the dangers that military reporters faced at the warfront. It provides a bewildered, bleak, and pained perspective on the war. One might consider the speaker's "thanks" as being directed toward God for permitting him to survive. Conversely, one might consider his thanks for random good fortune an indication that the speaker believes that God is absent or indifferent. The "blind gods" mentioned in the poem may be a version of that absent divinity, or they may be the American, Vietnamese, and Chinese leaders who authorized the war. You may wish to consider this poem in the context of other poems about the Vietnam War by Denise Levertov, Adrienne Rich, Gerald McCarthy, W. D. Ehrhart, Ray A. Young Bear, and Bao-Long Chu.

NATHANIEL MACKEY
b. 1947

A POET INFLUENCED BY JAZZ, NATHANIEL MACKEY creates improvised, rhythmic poems that evoke the sense of being far from home, on an immense journey from somewhere to somewhere else. His texts create dreamscapes of language, in which words are in close touch with their sounds, and in which African-American characters are adrift in language, music, dreams, and history. In "On

3. Chu Lai means "harbor of big ships" in Vietnamese. It was a Marine Corps base from 1965 to 1971.

Antiphon Island," the characters dance on a ship whose origination point and destination are unclear. In "Song of the Andoumboulou: 51," the speaker and his imaginary companions make an endless car trip through surreal landscapes.

Mackey's work reflects the inheritance of the "world poem" as written by such cross-cultural predecessors as Ezra Pound, H.D., William Carlos Williams, Charles Olson, Robert Duncan, and Robert Creeley (the latter three included in this volume). Mackey is also associated with such African-American synthesizers of jazz and poetry as Melvin Tolson and Amiri Baraka (the latter included in this volume). Employing African, Caribbean, and African-American folkloric and musical traditions, Mackey provides a particularly challenging and rewarding instance of multiethnic avant-garde postmodernism at work. Matthew Lavery summarizes Mackey's poetic aims: "Besides his fervent invocation of the necessity of cohering language, which cannot be seen as grounded in referentiality to anything 'real,' in some sort of other, 'real' artifice, there is his astute shaping of that artifice according to a device that coheres language's multiplicity . . . , no less than the inevitability of this coherence resulting in political commentary."

Born in Florida, Mackey moved to California when he was four. He received his B.A. from Princeton and his Ph.D. in English from Stanford, where he wrote his dissertation on Robert Duncan's Vietnam War poetry. He has taught at the University of California, Santa Cruz, since 1979.

FURTHER READING

Norman Finkelstein. "Nathaniel Mackey and the Unity of All Rites." *Contemporary Literature* 49.1 (Spring 2008): 24–55.

Alan Gilbert. "A Review of *Splay Anthem*." *Believer* magazine (March 2007). www.believer mag.com/issues/200703/?read=review_mackey.

Matthew Lavery. "The Ontogeny and Phylogeny of Mackey's Song of the Andoumboulou." *African American Review* 38.4 (Winter 2004).

Nathaniel Mackey. *Bass Cathedral*. New York: New Directions, 2008.

———. *Discrepant Engagement: Dissonance, Cross-Culturality, and Experimental Writing*. New York: Cambridge University Press, 1993.

———. *Splay Anthem*. New York: New Directions, 2006.

Paul Naylor, ed. "Nathaniel Mackey: A Special Issue." *Callaloo* 23.2 (Spring 2000).

On Antiphon Island

— *"mu" twenty-eighth part* —

On Antiphon Island they lowered
the bar and we went back. It
wasn't limbo we were in albeit

we limbo'd.[1] Everywhere we
went we
limbo'd, legs bent, shoulder
blades grazing the dirt,
donned
andoumboulouous[2] birth-shirts,
sweat salting the silence
we broke . . . Limbo'd so low we
fell and lay looking up at
the clouds, backs embraced by
the
ground and the ground a fallen
wall
we were ambushed by . . . Later we'd
sit, sipping fig liqueur, beckoning
sleep, soon-come somnolence nowhere
come as yet. Where we were, not-
withstanding, wasn't there . . .

Where we
were was the hold of a ship we were
caught
in.[3] Soaked wood kept us afloat . . . It
wasn't limbo we were in albeit we
limbo'd our way there. Where we
were was what we meant by "mu."
Where
we were was real, reminiscent
arrest we resisted, bodies briefly
had,
held on
to

●

1. Pun on two different senses of the word "limbo." In Christian theology, Limbo is a region existing on the border of hell as the abode of souls barred from heaven through no fault of their own; hence a place of confinement, transition, or oblivion. Limbo is also a form of contra dancing from Trinidad in which the dancer, moving to a Caribbean beat, leans backward and tries to dance under a horizontal pole without touching it.
2. That is, relating to or recalling the Andoumboulou, a group of migrant humanoids in West African Dogon mythology.
3. Perhaps an allusion to the Middle Passage.

* * *

"A Likkle Sonance"[4] it said on the
record. A trickle of blood hung
overhead I heard in spurts. An
introvert trumpet run, trickle of
sound . . .
A trickle of water lit by the sun
I saw with an injured eye, captive
music ran our legs and we danced . . .
Knees
bent, asses all but on the floor, love's
bittersweet largesse . . . I wanted
trickle turned into flow, flood,
two made one by music, bodied
edge
gone up into air, aura, atmosphere
the garment we wore. We were on
a ship's deck dancing, drawn in a
dream
above hold . . . The world was ever after,
elsewhere.
Where we were they said likkle for little, lick
ran with trickle, weird what we took it
for . . . The world was ever after, elsewhere,
no
way where we were
was there

2006

An "antiphon" is a response. More specifically, it is a devotional verse sung alternately
by two choirs, similar to the African oratorical and musical pattern of call-and-response.
"On Antiphon Island" is one poem in a long sequence called "Mu" that Mackey has been
writing for decades. According to Mackey, "Mu" signifies music, myth, mouth, and muse.
Alan Gilbert has written of "Mu" (and of the related *Song of the Andoumboulou*) that,
unlike traditional epic poems, which are oriented toward place and home, Mackey's work
records "an experience of diasporic restlessness among African American subjects, a tidal
ebb and flow of unrecuperating hope." He also observes that Mackey's poems draw on "a
vast range of materials and knowledge: like epic poems, they universalize from mythic
sources. However, Mackey's project differs in being cross-culturally adrift between traditions and civilizations, which helps explain all the references to water, edges, and boats."

4. Sound or tune.

Song of the Andoumboulou: 51

—cargo cult[1]—

Took the wheel, put in a cassette
and we pulled out. We bid the Inn
of Many Monikers[2] goodbye, pulled
                                        away
        wanting never to come back . . .
        Nunca[3] was at the wheel, namesake
            chauffeur we made-believe
        we believed in, stiff-backed
            ecstatics that we were . . .
                                        Something
        new was on the tape so we perked
    up. What we heard stole tone from
        arrival, the where we'd eventually
    be. It wasn't limbo what we did,
                                        we
sat up straight, backs ironing-board
                                        stiff
        not limbo where we were, a kind of
    loop we were in . . . It wasn't lost we'd
        have said we were, we reconnoitered,[4]
                                        Lone
    Coast itineracy[5] long since understood,
    iffed and averred,[6] we called it verge . . .

We were inland. Crab amble called out
from hills we saw in the distance,
        implicate sound sewn into Nunca's
        cassette . . . Morning light lit the
                                        plain,
        a boon to the yet-to-awaken. Verge
    gave way to green, green que te quiero

---

1. Religious movements, especially common in South Pacific islands before and after World War II, that resulted from the encounter with technologically advanced visitors or military. Cargo cults were characterized by a messianic expectation that ancestors or gods would return in ships or planes carrying cargoes of the products of modern civilization.

2. Names; nicknames.
3. "Never" (Spanish), a symbol of impossibility that has supplanted promise.
4. Made a preliminary survey or examination.
5. Action of traveling from place to place.
6. Acknowledged as true; asserted.

verde,[7] Spain it suddenly was we were
   in… No sooner Spain than it was
   somewhere known as Adnah[8] we came to
                     next
everyone went around on all fours. Animal
   surmise local parlance proclaimed it.
No sooner were we there than we moved on…

   Erstwhile[9] Anuncia was at the wheel,
                  albeit
of what began to change. What had been a
   car became a van became a bus ad infinitum,
                 an
   ambulance whatever it otherwise was, wounded
                     crew
     that we were, an ambulance notwithstanding we
   sat up straight … We rounded the bend and what
   we wanted was there, satiety's rival tone a
rendition of soul we were slow to accept …

   Leaned inward, sat up straight, crab
auspices' outward list compensated, Nunca's
   demiurgic[10] wheel Anuncia's long remembered
     kiss gone south . . . Crash we'd have
   remembered gone blank . . . Anansic[11]
                 bend
   we'd have been caught in, webbed
               had we
   not leaned
   in

2006

This poem is one part of *Song of the Andoumboulou,* an epic of bodily mobility and dispersed awareness based on West African Dogon creation myth. The epic traces the waking and dreaming travels of a pre-human underground people who inhabit holes in

---

7. "How I want you green" (Spanish). An allusion to the first line of Federico García Lorca's poem "Romance Sonámbulo."

8. "Pleasure" or "delight" (Hebrew). In the Jewish and Christian Bibles, Adnah was a chief of the tribe of Manasseh who joined David's army at Ziklag (1 Chronicles 12:20).

9. Former or onetime. Anuncia: one who announces (Spanish), the promise banished by the figure of Nunca (never).

10. Like a subordinate god.

11. Anansi is a trickster spider in West African and Caribbean folklore.

the earth. Mackey explains in the introduction to *Splay Anthem*, from which this poem derives, "I couldn't help thinking of the Andoumboulou as not simply a failed or flawed, earlier form of human being but a rough draft of human being, the work-in-progress we continue to be."

GERALD MCCARTHY
b. 1947

GERALD MCCARTHY is best known for his spare, devastating poems about the Vietnam War and its aftermath. McCarthy was born in upstate New York, the eldest son of an Italian-American mother and a working-class Irish-American father. He joined the U.S. Marines at the age of seventeen and served in Vietnam from 1965 to 1968. After questioning the war at length, he decided to desert. Following his release from military prison and civilian jail, he worked as a stonecutter, a factory hand, and an antiwar activist. He then studied at SUNY Geneseo and the University of Iowa's Writers' Workshop and began to write full time. Having taught at prisons and migrant labor camps, he is presently a professor of English at St. Thomas Aquinas College in Sparkill, New York. He lives with his wife and sons in Nyack, New York. He is now writing a memoir about his wartime experiences.

FURTHER READING

W. D. Ehrhart, ed. *Unaccustomed Mercy: Soldier-Poets of the Vietnam War*. Lubbock: Texas Tech University Press, 1989.

Philip Mahoney, ed. *Both Sides Now: The Poetry of the Vietnam War and Its Aftermath*. New York: Scribner's, 1998.

Gerald McCarthy. *Trouble Light*. Albuquerque, N.M.: West End Press, 2008.

———. *War Story*. Langhorne, Penn.: Crossing Press, 1977.

The Hooded Legion

Let us put up a monument to the lie.

—Joseph Brodsky[1]

There are no words here
to witness why we fought,
who sent us or what we hoped to gain.

There is only the rain
as it streaks the black stone,[2]
these memories of rain
that come back to us—
a hooded legion reflected in a wall.

Tonight we wander weaponless and cold
along this shore of the Potomac
like other soldiers who camped here
looking out over smoldering fires into the night.

What did we dream of
the summer before we went away?
What leaf did not go silver
in the last light?
What hand did not turn us aside?

1992

In "The Hooded Legion," McCarthy suggests that no words can adequately describe the war and its motives as he examines the Vietnam Veterans Memorial in Washington, D.C. The "other soldiers" may refer to troops camped along the Potomac River during the U.S. Civil War. You may wish to consider this poem in the context of other Vietnam War poems and antiwar protest poems, such as those by Denise Levertov, Allen Ginsberg, Adrienne Rich, Yusef Komunyakaa, W. D. Ehrhart, Ray A. Young Bear, and Bao-Long Chu. Young Bear's and Chu's poems, for example, also allude to the Vietnam Veterans Memorial. While Ehrhart's "A Relative Thing" offers a soldier's view, which many consider the most telling perspective on war, McCarthy's "The Hooded Legion" complicates a combatant's story, adding the dimensions of ethical and psychological questioning as well as the decision to desert the military.

1. Russian-American Nobel Prize winner in literature. In 1972 Brodsky (1940–1996) became an involuntary exile from Soviet Russia and emigrated to the United States. He had been convicted in the Soviet Union of treason for his dissident writings.

2. Reference to the Vietnam Veterans Memorial in Washington, D.C., as is the later "wall" in this stanza.

W. D. EHRHART
b. 1948

W. D. EHRHART grew up in rural Pennsylvania, the son of a Protestant minister and a special education teacher. Upon graduating from high school, he enlisted in the U.S. Marine Corps and served for three years, including thirteen months in Vietnam during the Tet Offensive of 1968. Subsequently he received a B.A. from Swarthmore, an M.A. from the University of Illinois, Chicago, and a Ph.D. from the University of Wales. He has earned his living as a writer and a high school teacher. He was a U.S. delegate to the First Conference of U.S. and Vietnamese Veteran-Writers in Hanoi. Ehrhart is married, has a daughter, and lives in Philadelphia.

FURTHER READING

Kevin Bowen, Nguyen Ba Chung, and Bruce Weigl, eds. *Mountain River: Vietnamese Poetry from the Wars, 1948–1993*. Amherst: University of Massachusetts Press, 1998.

W. D. Ehrhart. *Beautiful Wreckage: New & Selected Poems*. Easthampton, Mass.: Adastra Press, 1999.

———. *The Bodies Beneath the Table*. Easthampton, Mass.: Adastra Press, 2010.

———. *Ordinary Lives: Platoon 1005 and the Vietnam War*. Philadelphia: Temple University Press, 1999.

W. D. Ehrhart, ed. *Unaccustomed Mercy: Soldier-Poets of the Vietnam War*. Lubbock: Texas Tech University Press, 1989.

H. Bruce Franklin, ed. *The Vietnam War in Stories, Poems & Songs*. New York: St. Martin's Press, 1995.

Philip Mahoney, ed. *Both Sides Now: The Poetry of the Vietnam War and Its Aftermath*. New York: Scribner's, 1998.

Relative Thing

We are the ones you sent to fight a war
you didn't know a thing about.

It didn't take us long to realize
the only land that we controlled
was covered by the bottoms of our boots.

When the newsmen said that naval ships
had shelled a VC[1] staging point,

---

1. VC stands for Viet Cong, the political and military organization that fought the U.S. and South Vietnamese forces during the war.

we saw a breastless woman
and her stillborn child.

We laughed at old men stumbling
in the dust in frenzied terror
to avoid our three-ton trucks.

We fought outnumbered in Hue City[2]
while the ARVN[3] soldiers looted bodies
in the safety of the rear.
The cookies from the wives of Local 104[4]
did not soften our awareness.

We have seen the pacified supporters
of the Saigon[5] government
sitting in their jampacked cardboard towns,
their wasted hands placed limply in their laps,
their empty bellies waiting for the rice
some district chief has sold
for profit to the Viet Cong.

We have been Democracy on Zippo[6] raids,
burning houses to the ground,
driving eager amtracs[7] through new-sown fields.

We are the ones who have to live
with the memory that we were the instruments
of your pigeon-breasted fantasies.
We are inextricable accomplices
in this travesty of dreams:
but we are not alone.

We are the ones you sent to fight a war
you did not know a thing about—
those of us that lived
have tried to tell you what went wrong.
Now you think you do not have to listen.

2. Hue City is located in South Vietnam in Hue Province, near the border with North Vietnam. In the Tet Offensive of 1968, the Battle of Hue occurred in the city. Hue City is now a UNESCO World Heritage Site.
3. ARVN refers to the Army of the Republic of Vietnam (that is, South Vietnam).
4. A labor union.
5. Saigon was the capital of South Vietnam; it is now known as Ho Chi Minh City.
6. Metal cigarette lighter.
7. U.S. amphibious assault vehicles.

*   *   *

Just because we will not fit
into the uniforms of photographs
of you at twenty-one
does not mean you can disown us.

We are your sons, America,
and you cannot change that.
When you awake,
we will still be here.

1975

A comparatively early Vietnam War poem, still raw with emotion, "A Relative Thing" offers a soldier's view of the war. Ehrhart expresses anger about the wartime horrors he has seen and about the lack of understanding soldiers received from the homefront. Compare this poem to the later Vietnam War poems by Yusef Komunyakaa, Gerald McCarthy, Ray A. Young Bear, and Bao-Long Chu.

CAROL FROST
b. 1948

CAROL FROST creates poems of a sometimes painful beauty, poems that often dramatize moments of displacement or metamorphosis, when the observer's sense of reality undergoes a profound and disturbing challenge. In some cases, as in her poem of the dream life, "A Good Night's Sleep," that change might be temporary. In others, such as "Pure," the change might be forever. Frost's poems are often set in nature. However, as in the work of Elizabeth Bishop (whose presence is reflected in "The Poet's Black Drum"), Frost's poems inhabit a natural world haunted by human consciousness and—more so than in Bishop's—haunted also by the lingering or unsatisfied spirits of the past, spirits who make their presence felt in poems such as "Chimera" and "Lucifer in Florida."

Born Carol Perrins in Lowell, Massachusetts, she lived as a child for a year in her mother's native city of Vienna. She studied French literature and art at the Sorbonne before earning a bachelor's degree at the State University College at Oneonta, New York. She married the poet and jazz drummer Richard Frost in 1969. After receiving a master's from Syracuse University, Frost began teaching in 1981 at Hartwick College, where she became writer-in-residence and founded the Catskill Poetry Workshop. She now holds an endowed chair in creative writing at Rollins College in Winter Park, Florida. Many of Frost's poems explore poles of north and south, their settings either in the rural farming and hunting culture of upstate New York or in the shorelines and fishing lore of coastal Florida.

In recent years, confronted by her mother's growing dementia, Frost has examined, in such poems as "(For the ones," the challenging alterations in consciousness experienced by the elderly in the grip of Alzheimer's, and even here her poetry is marked by the freshness, surprise, acuity of perception, and resilience in the face of loss that are among its signal characteristics.

FURTHER READING

Carol Frost. *Chimera*. Salt Lake City: Peregrine Smith, 1990.
———. *I Will Say Beauty*. Evanston, Ill.: TriQuarterly Books, 2003.
———. *Love and Scorn: New and Selected Poems*. Evanston, Ill.: TriQuarterly Books, 1998.
———. *Pure*. Evanston, Ill.: TriQuarterly Books, 1994.
———. *The Queen's Desertion*. Evanston, Ill.: TriQuarterly Books, 2006.

Chimera

By the verge of the sea a man finds a gelatinous creature,
parching, thick as a shoe, its head a doubtful dark green
that leans toward him as he bends near in some dark
wonderment of his own. The sky is haunted by pure light,

the sea a rough mixture of blue, and green, and black. Suddenly
he hears the air rent with loud cries and looks to see
pelicans on the piers raising their wings then falling, changing shape
to dive into the sea. He thinks of Bosch's rebellious angels[1]
changing shape as they are pursued out of the immaculate sky.

Who are they? Angels who accept the hideous
and monstrous. Fallen, they make up a nightmare fauna.
Say the sea is to be questioned. Below the bounds
of this estate, through rainbowed cold, the rockheaded and cored

of bone, the chimera our madness does not cease to reinvent
and which we dare not think alive, crawls in a thick ooze.
Yet even this one, torn to the plain insides and leaking dyes,

---

1. *The Fall of the Rebel Angels* (ca. 1504), a painting by Hieronymus Bosch.

exudes a gentle unrest of the soul. Is it not good? The man pauses,
looks around—the sea undulated, sharpening and smoothing

all the grooves that history has graven on the sand—
then he puts his hands under the terrible flesh and heaves it
as far as he can back into the Atlantic, as if it were the mirror
of a lost estate, the dawn-time of the world's first season.

1990

Pure

He saw that the white-tailed deer he shot was his son;
it filled his eyes, his chest, his head, and horribly it bent on him.
The rest of the hunting party found him hunkered down in the grass,
spattered like a butcher, holding the body as it kept growing colder in his arms.
They grasped his elbows, urging him to stand, but he couldn't. He screamed
    then
for Mary and Jesus, who came and were present. Unable to bear
his babbling, and that he might no longer have to be reproached, the men
    went to get help.
He only had left to him his pure hunter's sense, still clean under his skin,
a gun, the example of wounds, a shell's ease in the chamber, as he loaded,
the speed of the night chill, while his mind like a saint's tried to bear
that which God took from His own mind when he could not, not for another
    moment. . . .

1994

A Good Night's Sleep

Reassured that we return as before, we enter
a land where everything changes, densities, colors,
rhythms of breathing, and we meet the dead.

What sort of name might turn up inside our pockets
if we remained there? The hair stands on end.
The repose around the eyes can't wash off;
it only becomes a little cleaner.

And the ones we did not know we loved
we follow down the nights

in cities half-built of where we've been, half-
built of ribbons.

. . . the body itself divine and absent, the lineaments
of beauty stored even more powerfully in thought:
the ankle's pale butterfly in a chrysalis.

What would we know of this going-hence
but the occasional fissure of light?

Ai, the divine ignorance of closed eyes.

. . . missing only that moment of coming to,
as if giant hands extracted from a small rip in fate and placed you,
who counted for so little when liberated in sleep, where you last stood.

2000

The Poet's Black Drum

Come in the silent acting in a dream now wayfarer
come back from that deepest paradise
where all that haven't breath the breathless mouth
may summon: Tell us about your journey fishing::
barbels: stony teeth in the throat: aching shoulders:
and what Florida locals call tailing[1] (the drifting fleece)—
drum underneath the flutter—: fecund
with slender parasites: beauty's flesh::
tasting of waters you taste and you say light dyed.

2004

Frost has suggested that the black drum, an ocean fish that can weigh as much as ninety
pounds, may have been a model for Elizabeth Bishop's "The Fish" (also included in this
anthology).

1. According to Frost, "'Tailing' refers to the feeding habit of the drum (red and black) in shallow
water. When its head is down—the fish nosing
oyster beds for small blue crabs, its favorite food, and anything else—the tail is exposed to the air.
By careful observation the angler knows where
the prize fish is, where it is headed, and where
to cast."

Lucifer in Florida

I Lucifer, cast down from heaven's city which is the stars,
soar darkly nights across the water to islands
and their runway lights—after sunset burning petals;
sights, sorrows, all evils become the prolonged shadows
and lightning through palm trees and the ancient oaks.
. . . And ride with darkness, dark below dark, uttermost
as when the cormorant dives and the fish dies, eye-deep
in hell;[1] the bird is I, I hide in its black shining
spread of wings raised drying afterward on a tree bough.
Nothing more onyx or gold than my dark wings.
Yet Venus rising, the off chords and tender tones
of morning birds among the almonds, small flames
of lemon flowers, phosphorus on the ocean,
all I've scorned, all this lasts whether I leave or come.
The garden fails but the earth's garden lives on
unbearable—elusive scent on scent from jasmine
mixed with brine, the smell of marshes, smells of skin
of fisherman, burned rose and a little heroic
while leviathan winds rise and darkness descends.
Sin and death stay near, black with serenity,
calm in dawn's light suggestions. If the future is
a story of pandemonium,[2] perfection's close—
from the sea the islands at night, from the island
the sea at night with no lights rest equally, lit by
a wanderer's memory bringing dark and light to life,
luminous and far as dreams endure, charcoal and flame
in a fire, the embers of pride and pain in each breath.

2006

Among the devil's many names, Lucifer (Latin for "light-bearer") connotes his identity as the chief of the fallen angels who were driven out of heaven following their failed rebellion against God. Here, Lucifer looks down from the night sky over modern Florida in a scene reminiscent of his first glimpse of Eden in Milton's *Paradise Lost*. Recognizing that he can never enjoy Edenic bliss, Satan faces "infinite despair" because "'Which way I fly is hell; myself am hell" (*Paradise Lost* 4.74–75).

1. Ezra Pound, in "Hugh Selwyn Mauberley," section IV, describes soldiers in the trenches of World War I as having "walked eye-deep in hell."

2. Pandemonium: literally, "all the demons"; Milton's coinage for the "Palace of Satan" erected by the recently fallen devils in Book I of *Paradise Lost*.

(For the ones

who line the corridors and sit
silent in wheelchairs
before the television with the volume off,
whose cares
are small and gray and infinite,
time as ever to be faced . . .
Methuselahs the nurses wash
and dress without haste—
none needed . . .
this one has drunk from the poppy-cup
and drowses in her world of dream . . .
Heliotrope,
carnations, wakeful violets, and lilies in vases—
masses of flowers—wrap
the urine-and-antiseptic air in lace . . .
Please wake up; it is morning;
robins whistle; the bees dance.
Isn't this other one listening
from her shell of silence,
and shouldn't she smile at the green return
and dappled light through windows?
As earth orbits the corridor
clocks are wound . . .
The last hour is a song or wound . . .
Except in this corridor—mother's—
where finity's brainless wind
blows ash, and ash again
blows through their cells:
So much silence, so little to say in the end.)

2007

The poem's setting is a nursing home.

VICTOR HERNÁNDEZ CRUZ
b. 1949

VICTOR HERNÁNDEZ CRUZ writes exuberant poems that often mix English, Spanish, and other languages in what he has termed "linguistic stereo." A Nuyorican poet—born in Puerto Rico but raised in New York—Cruz also mixes diverse cultural references, ranging from the Americas to Europe and Africa. His themes are cultural hybridity, political and spiritual liberation, and the joys of living. His poems possess enormous verbal gusto, employing remarkable rhythms and repetitions that link them to oratory and music. They are made to be spoken aloud—even to be sung or to accompany a dance. In an essay in his volume *Red Beans*, he writes: "We can walk the planet with our genes, imagine ourselves in the Sevilla of the Arabs holding court with ibn Arabi and al-Ghazálí, quickly switch over to the halls of Tenochtitlán, then once again wake up in our contemporary reality dancing Yoruba choreography in some club in Manhattan." He gives his English some "spice" and "Hispanic mobility" so as to resonate with Anglo, Latino, and all other sorts of readers.

Cruz's poems often follow a fragmented, unpredictable course. They suggest an aesthetic of movement and music while adhering to a conception of the socially engaged, prophetic poet. Cruz was influenced by a wide variety of cultural sources: Latino folk and popular music as well as U.S. jazz and rock and roll; Latin American poets such as Ernesto Cardenal and Octavio Paz as well as U.S. poets ranging from Walt Whitman and William Carlos Williams to Allen Ginsberg and Amiri Baraka. Ginsberg called Cruz an "original soul looking out intelligent Bronx windows." Whether Cruz is evoking a Caribbean folk dance (as in "Areyto") or contemplating red beans and white rice (as in "Red Beans"), he discovers verbal pleasure and cultural complexity while seeking, as he says, "the essence of things."

Cruz was born in a small mountain town in Puerto Rico, but because of difficult financial circumstances his family moved to New York when he was five. He grew up in Manhattan and started to write poetry when he was fourteen. Beginning to publish his work at the age of eighteen, he quit high school months before graduation and became a cofounder of the East Harlem Gut Theater and an editor of a magazine called *Umbra*. Well known as a poet and essayist, he has taught at a variety of universities, including the University of California, Berkeley. He presently divides his time between Puerto Rico, New York, and Morocco.

FURTHER READING

Frances Aparicio. "On Subversive Signifiers." In *Tropicalizations: Transcultural Representations of Latinidad*, ed. Frances Aparicio and Susana Chávez-Silverman. Hanover: Dartmouth University Press, 1997.

Victor Hernández Cruz. *Maraca: New and Selected Poems, 1965–2000*. Minneapolis: Coffee House Press, 2001.

———. *The Mountain in the Sea*. Minneapolis: Coffee House Press, 2006.

———. *Panoramas*. Minneapolis: Coffee House Press, 1997.

———. *Red Beans*. Minneapolis: Coffee House Press, 1991.

Bruce Allen Dick. *A Poet's Truth: Conversations with Latino/Latina Poets*. Tucson: University of Arizona Press, 2003.

Areyto

My empire of flamboyans[1]
Through boulevards made of mountains
Dressed green to the heavens
As voices circulate the hymns
of our history
From the dancers of the round
serpent formed at the center of
Life[2]
This is Americas Areyto
This is Americas Areyto

In cities mountains of flying metallic
cars and consumer junk/
Nerves pile up upon horizons
of progress
That whisper inside/
Mira[3] look
Look mira that whisper inside
Is the old calendar ticking
The Areyto is still swinging:
The Gods said they would take
us back and deliver us from

---

1. Puerto Rican tree with red or orange flowers.
2. Perhaps a reference to the Ouroboros, an ancient Egyptian symbol that represented a serpent swallowing its own tail and forming an eternal circle. Possibly also a reference to the Mayan deity Kukulcan and the Aztec deity Quetzalcoatl, both of which were feathered serpents associated with rebirth and art.
3. "Look" (Spanish).

Plush media inventions
From racket and industrial tension
From textbooks that are lying
tongues of pretensions
The river on the other side
of English is carrying the message
Yukiyu⁴ has not abandoned you
The quetzals⁵ are still flying
Quetzalcóatl⁶ is on the phone
Be cool Roberto and José
Carmen and María
Just go horizontal into the circle
Areyto

The current will take you

America that Betances,⁷ José Martí
That Hostos⁸ wanted all together as
ONE
Vasconcelos⁹ said RAZA CÓSMICA
Seeing red mixed with black
And black with white
Rhythms united married in history
This is the greatest flavor
The earth has to offer

Marimba¹⁰ tango samba
Danza¹¹ Mambo bolero

*   *   *

4. Primary god of the Taíno people, indigenous inhabitants of Puerto Rico.
5. Brightly colored tropical birds noted for their striking reds and greens.
6. Aztec feathered-serpent god.
7. Ramón Emeterio Betances (1827–1898) founded the Puerto Rican independence movement. José Martí (1853–1895): a Cuban poet, political theorist, and independence advocate who died in a battle with Spanish troops.
8. Eugenio María de Hostos (1893–1903) was a Puerto Rican–born revolutionary who fought for independence and equal rights throughout the Caribbean and South America.

9. José Vasconcelos Calderón (1882–1959) was a Mexican writer, politician, and political philosopher known for his advocacy for indigenous peoples. RAZA CÓSMICA: "Cosmic Race" (Spanish), the title of an essay by Vasconcelos foreseeing the eventual unification of all races.
10. Percussion instrument developed in Guatemala and Mexico, with African origins. Tango: dance originating in Argentina and Uruguay. Samba: Brazilian dance with African roots.
11. Ballroom dance originating in Puerto Rico. Mambo: Cuban dance. Bolero: a kind of dance and song with both Cuban and Spanish forms.

Linda[12] America just rise and take
off your clothes[13]
Your age is so old that
Giants appear out of trees as tobacco
smoke takes photographs of the wind
Directing itself into a voice
Where salt pebbles dance guaguancó[14]
Something so good that it became
blueprints for legs
That moved with such precision
That ten thousand appear to be one
In the Areyto where you hear the drum
As the knees and the legs
describe an area between two stars

Old fire of agricultural guitar
spreading North
Trio Los Diamantes[15] sunrise moving
through silk on slow tropical wind
Johnny Albino[16] Trio San Juan
Making an escalator of sound
Into your hearts that grow feathers
To fly toward the desert to enter
The la'uds[17] invasion of Iberian perfume
To land upon the shoulders of the Gypsies
and Mayas[18] as a fan from Granada cools
our Amerindians features of the love
That comes of the love that goes

America is our belly
Our abdomen of spirit
We grew out of the plants
It knows who we are
Linda America that Betances

12. "Pretty, lovely" (Spanish).
13. See Allen Ginsberg's "America": "America
when will you be angelic? / When will you take
off your clothes?"
14. A kind of Cuban rumba, a style of dance and
music.
15. Musical group that performed Afro-Cuban
bolero in the 1940s.

16. Puerto Rican bolero singer (1919–2011) who
in the 1940s was the lead voice in the popular
Trio San Juan.
17. Egyptian stringed instrument, forerunner of
the lute.
18. Indigenous people of present-day Guatemala,
Honduras, and southern Mexico. Granada: city
in Spain.

José Martí to Hostos us up UNIDOS[19]
As único[20] one (JUAN)

America sur[21] south
America norte[22]
Juan America
Two America Juan
Juan America one
Then America blend
Give the idea roots of
harmonious peace serene/
Sí[23] and yes it is possible for the
Snake of heart and mind to
grow quetzal feathers and fly
Out of the Areyto circle
Areyto circle
Areyto circle

Possible to be possible
Possible to be
A whole unto one
A nation with lots of fish to
eat
And fruit that offers itself
it is possible to be
it is possible to
Struggle against blocks
of inertia
Against conquistadors'[24] wishes
lurking in blood nervous systems
Nightmaring dreams/
Dogs that come bark at the
beautiful dance
It is possible to be
pure fresh river water
We are bird that sings
Free

19. "United" (Spanish).
20. "Unique" (Spanish). One (JUAN): bilingual pun.
21. "South" (Spanish).
22. "North" (Spanish).
23. "Yes" (Spanish).
24. "Conquerors" (Spanish).

✳   ✳   ✳

Areyto
Maraca²⁵ güiro and drum
Quicharo²⁶ maraca y tambor
Who we are
Printed in rhythm and song

Areyto south
Areyto north
Two America Juan
One America One
America that Bolívar²⁷ Betances
to José Martí Us to Hostos who wanted
us to be one único Unidos

Areyto güiro and drum
Quicharo maraca y tambor

Areyto song
Areyto song
AREYTO.

1991

The word "areyto" refers to a traditional festival of the indigenous Taíno people of Puerto Rico and other Caribbean islands. The areyto is a folk dance accompanied by music and by songs that pass down historical knowledge from one generation to another. Many Puerto Ricans and Dominicans today identify themselves as descendants of the Taínos. Cruz's poem celebrates Native American myths and customs as well as Pan-American unity and cultural hybridity. The poem combines English with Spanish and indigenous languages because, as Cruz explains in an essay in *Red Beans*, "The earth is migration, everything is moving, changing interchanging, appearing, disappearing. National languages melt, sail into each other. . . ."

25. Dried gourd containing seeds or pebbles, used as a percussion instrument, often in pairs (Spanish). Güiro: Puerto Rican hollowed gourd, used as a percussion instrument (Spanish).
26. A kind of gourd (Spanish). Tambor: "drum" (Spanish).

27. Simón Bolívar (1783–1830) was a political and military leader who spearheaded Latin America's successful struggle for independence from Spain.

Dimensions of a Linguist

I felt it in Taino[1]
I thought about it in Spanish
I wrote it in English.

1993

Red Beans

Next to white rice
it looks like coral[1]
sitting next to snow

Hills of starch
Border
The burnt sienna[2]
of irony

Azusenas[3] being chased by
the terra cotta[4] feathers
of a rooster

There is a lava flow
through the smoking
white mounds

India red
spills on ivory

Ochre cannon balls
falling
next to blanc pebbles

Red beans and milk
make burgundy wine

✻   ✻   ✻

1. The indigenous people of Puerto Rico, with whom many of their mixed-heritage descendants identify.
1. Stony substance secreted by marine animals; also a tree with red flowers. Generally, anything bright red in color.
2. An iron oxide pigment and famous crayon color, a mid-brown.
3. "Lilies" (Spanish).
4. Glazed or unglazed ceramic material colored red, brown, or orange.

Violet pouring
from the eggshell
tinge of the plate.

1993

The title "Red Beans" may be a pun on "red beings," suggesting the contribution of indigenous peoples to Latina/o and world cultures.

CHARLES BERNSTEIN
b. 1950

CHARLES BERNSTEIN writes what he calls "impermeable" texts. That is, as a
founder and practitioner of Language poetry, he writes poems that highlight
the density of language and invite the reader to collaborate in the construction
of the text's meanings. If his language were made of glass, it would be stained
glass, not a transparent pane. One notices the patterns in the words, the stains
in the glass, while the things that the words refer to—the sights to be seen beyond the glass—remain obscure. Bernstein's style is discontinuous, distracted,
and self-aware. His poems are often collages of parodied discourses, and they are
frequently hilarious. It is difficult to locate a stable, autobiographical "I" anchor-
ing the perspective. The poems thus pose a challenge but always a fascinating,
and often amusing, one.

Bernstein's language aims at "a recharged use of the multivalent referential
vectors that any word has," as he writes in *Content's Dream*. In Bernstein's work,
the referential aspect of language, deprived of its automatic reflex reaction,
roams freely over the range of associations suggested by each word, becoming an
energy field. Writing becomes "maximally open in vocabulary, forms, shapes."
Whereas standard grammatical patterns narrow possibilities, Bernstein uses
quick cuts, gaps, and jumps to widen possibilities and to let the reader experience the poem individually, without needing to find a single, author-determined
meaning. The poems, therefore, are part of a libratory, empowering project.
They aim, as Bernstein writes in *A Poetics*, to "wake / us from the hypnosis" of
more realistic and authoritarian forms of writing.

Typical Bernstein poems, such as "Ballet Russe" or "Social Pork," are, as the
poet writes in *My Way*, "aversive to cultural and linguistic norms" but nevertheless "committed to exchange, interaction, communication, and community."

Bernstein uses discontinuity as a new way of producing meaning. In "Of Time and the Line," he assumes the role of comedian-philosopher, using jokes and puns to make serious points. In "every lake . . . ," a verbal substitution game generates the text. Bernstein's poems also have a critical social perspective. In *My Way* he asserts, "Poetry can interrogate how language constitutes, rather than simply reflects, social meaning and values. You can't fully critique the dominant culture if you are confined to the forms through which it reproduces itself." He believes that by writing idiosyncratically, "we confer political value on the odd, eccentric, different, opaque, maladjusted—the non-conforming. We also insist that politics demands complex thinking and that poetry is an arena for such thinking."

Bernstein was born and raised in New York City, and his poetry retains a patina of urban wit and sophistication. The youngest of three children, he was the son of a self-made businessman and his wife. He studied philosophy at Harvard, where he wrote his senior thesis on Gertrude Stein and Ludwig Wittgenstein. He married the visual artist Susan Bee (Laufer), with whom he had gone to high school, and together they had a daughter, Emma, and a son, Felix. His choice of a life in the arts seemed to his father an exercise in "downward mobility." In the late 1970s Bernstein cofounded a small, innovative literary journal called *L=A=N=G=U=A=G=E*, which helped revolutionize poetry by rejecting received notions of voice, self, and poetic form. The title of the journal supplied the name for what subsequently became known as the Language poetry movement, which includes among its members Susan Howe, Lyn Hejinian, and Rae Armantrout (all included in this anthology). Bernstein has continued to live in New York, even while holding professorships at the University at Buffalo and now at the University of Pennsylvania.

In *A Poetics*, Bernstein registered his passion "for poetry that insists on running its own course, finding its own measures, charting worlds otherwise hidden or denied or, perhaps best of all, never before existing." His poetry has run its own course with serious purpose and great good humor.

FURTHER READING

Bruce Andrews and Charles Bernstein, eds. *The L=A=N=G=U=A=G=E Book*. Carbondale: Southern Illinois University Press, 1984.
Charles Bernstein. *All the Whiskey in Heaven: Selected Poems*. New York: Farrar, Straus & Giroux, 2010.
———. *Content's Dream: Essays 1975–1984*. Los Angeles: Sun & Moon Press, 1986.
———. *Girly Man*. Chicago: University of Chicago Press, 2006.
———. *My Way: Speeches and Poems*. Chicago: University of Chicago Press, 1999.
———. *A Poetics*. Cambridge, Mass.: Harvard University Press, 1992.
———. *Republics of Reality, 1975–1995*. Los Angeles: Sun & Moon, 2000.
Linda Reinfeld. *Language Poetry: Writing as Rescue*. Baton Rouge: Louisiana State University Press, 1992.

Ballet Russe

Every person has feeling.
    It is all the same.
I will travel.
    I love nature.
I love motion & dancing.
        I did not understand God.
I have made mistakes.
Bad deeds are terrible.
    I suffered.
My wife is frightened.
    The stock exchange is death.
I am against all drugs.
    My scalp is strong & hard.
I like it when it is necessary.
It is a lovely drive.
    A branch is not a root.
Handwriting is a lovely thing.
I like tsars & aristocrats.
    An aeroplane[1] is useful.
One should permanently help the poor.
    My wife wants me to go to Zurich.
Politics are death.
            All young men do silly things.
The Spaniards are terrible people because they murder bulls.
My wife suffered a great deal because of her mother.
    I will tell the whole truth.
I love Russia.
    I am nasty.
I am terrified of being locked up & losing my work.
    Mental agony *is* a terrible thing.
        I pretend to be a very nervous man.

                                    1978

The title of this poem means "Russian ballet" in French. Les Ballets Russes (the Russian Ballets) was a famous Russian ballet company that performed in Paris and other cultural capitals between 1909 and 1920 under the direction of Sergei Diaghilev. The company combined dance, music, and visual art in notably innovative and influential ways. After the company dissolved, it was succeeded by two competing offshoots: the Ballet Russe de

1. British spelling of "airplane."

Monte Carlo and the Original Ballet Russe. The connection between this title and the poem itself is enigmatic. The poem comprises a series of sentences that lack apparent relationship. Some of the sentences resemble self-descriptions or confessions ("I have made mistakes"), whereas other sentences seem to be general assertions ("Every person has feeling"). Deprived of context, the sentences hover uncertainly between the profound and the ridiculous, unsettling the way we habitually respond to the performance and meaning of utterance.

Autonomy Is Jeopardy

I hate artifice. All these
contraptions so many barriers
against what otherwise can't
be contested, so much seeming
sameness in a jello of
squirms. Poetry scares me. I
mean its virtual (or ventriloquized)
anonymity—no protection, no
bulwark to accompany its pervasive
purposivelessness,[1] its accretive
acceleration into what may or
may not swell. Eyes demand
counting, the nowhere seen everywhere
behaved voicelessness everyone is clawing
to get a piece of. Shudder
all you want it won't
make it come any faster
last any longer: the pump
that cannot be dumped.

1990

The title, "Autonomy Is Jeopardy," parodies Sigmund Freud's infamous phrase about gender, "anatomy is destiny." The poem's word "purposivelessness" alludes to the philosopher Immanuel Kant (1724–1804), who associated the quality of purposivelessness with the sublime and the beautiful in his *Critique of Judgment.* Thus, "Autonomy Is Jeopardy" juxtaposes Freud's discourse on sexuality with Kant's philosophy of aesthetic objects. Using irony, it may defend poetry in the act of ostensibly complaining about it. Whereas the speaker of the poem may claim to *"hate artifice,"* Bernstein himself maintains (in *The*

---

1. Whereas *purposive* means "serving a useful function," *purposivelessness* implies the lack of a practical purpose in aesthetic language, as opposed to more informational or utilitarian uses of language.

L=A=N=G=U=A=G=E Book) that "there is no natural look or sound to a poem. Every element is intended, chosen. That is what makes a thing a poem."

Precisely and Moreover

I died in chance abandon, made the clearing
tough to take, or went to meet a bleat of
feigning belly crates, to fly by number to
render coil. By bait the trough is
ridden, hung tanks upon a top of
toil, or tender mute the silent, shrill
the shorn, and bear a coal to castle's
glare. Less 'parent than 'prehended
shakes time to bugger oil (the bellicosity out
(of). Sponge season, or fretful tongs with
claws.

1991

Of Time and the Line

George Burns[1] likes to insist that he always
takes the straight lines; the cigar in his mouth
is a way of leaving space between the
lines for a laugh. He weaves lines together
by means of a picaresque narrative;
not so Henny Youngman,[2] whose lines are strictly paratactic.[3] My father pushed a
line of ladies' dresses—not down the street
in a pushcart but upstairs in a fact'ry
office. My mother has been more concerned
with her hemline. Chairman Mao[4] put forward

---

1. Masterful comedian born in New York (1896–1996) who often played straight man to his wife and partner, Gracie Allen. He performed while holding a cigar, taking a puff to punctuate the joke.
2. British-born American comedian (1906–1998), known for his rapid-fire one-liners and his verbal wit.
3. Designating a style in which sentences or elements within sentences are set down suc-

cessively with little or no indication of their relationship. Often applied to passages of poetry or prose, the term here suggests Youngman's method of telling a succession of brief jokes, each taking only a sentence or two.
4. Mao Zedong (or Tse-tung; 1893–1976), Communist revolutionary, political theorist, and Chairman of the People's Republic of China from 1949 to 1976. Many of his policies were reversed by his successors.

Maoist lines, but that's been abandoned (mostly) for the East-West line of malarkey
so popular in these parts. The prestige
of the iambic line has recently
suffered decline, since it's no longer so
clear who "I" am, much less who *you* are. When
making a line, better be double sure
what you're lining in & what you're lining
out & which side of the line you're on; the
world is made up so (Adam didn't so much
name as delineate). Every poem's got
a prosodic lining, some of which will
unzip for summer wear. The lines of an
imaginary are inscribed on the
social flesh by the knifepoint of history.
Nowadays, you can often spot a work
of poetry by whether it's in lines
or no; if it's in prose, there's a good chance
it's a poem. While there is no lesson in
the line more useful than that of the picket line, the line that has caused the most adversity is the bloodline. In Russia
everyone is worried about long lines;
back in the USA, it's strictly soup-
lines.[5] "Take a chisel to write," but for an
actor a line's got to be cued. Or, as
they say in math, it takes two lines to make
an angle but only one lime to make
a Margarita.

1991

"Of Time and the Line" is written in syllabic verse. Every line has ten syllables, except the last, which has five. The poem, following in the tradition of comedians George Burns and Henny Youngman, makes a series of jokes and puns based on the word "line." The poem thus locates Bernstein in a long line of Jewish humorists, but one who is concerned with poetic lines as well as punchlines. The poem also offers a rare glimpse into the poet's personal past. Bernstein tells us in *My Way* that his father "worked in the garment industry,

---

5. Depression-era term for lines of hungry people waiting for a free meal at a meal center, usually located in Skid Row. "Take a chisel to write": compare Exodus 34:1, "And the Lord said unto Moses, Hew thee two tables of stone like unto the first: and I will write upon these tables the words that were in the first tables, which thou breakest."

eventually as co-owner of Smartcraft Corporation, a medium-size manufacturer of ladies' dresses." The poem similarly attests that the father's "fact'ry" produced "ladies' dresses" and "summer wear," while the mother was a fashionable housewife.

"Of Time and the Line" makes salient points about both politics and poetry. In keeping with Bernstein's egalitarian perspective, it affirms that "the picket line" is useful, whereas "the bloodline" causes adversity. The poem also highlights the danger that art can unwittingly reinforce oppression: "The lines of an / imaginary are inscribed on the / social flesh." The poem dissolves its artifice and its complex meditation on art and life with a final verbal jest worthy of George Burns or Henny Youngman.

Under the Pink Tent

Focus
& the light under the shade
begins to focus
back, the
sand underneath,
with a runcible[1]
grin, denotes
what's out past scrambles —
the lost wax of the module
I
had never been,
nor adhered to —
percolations of silhouette
projection, slurred by
ruinous ridges, rumpled
privileges.

1995

Social Pork

What a flimsy excuse for denial —
The whole hog attenuates the ceremonial
Blotted artery of common fork[1]
Or wheel and be spun

---

1. A nonsense word invented by English writer Edward Lear (1812–1888), used most famously in his poem, "The Owl and the Pussycat": "They dined on mince and slices of quince, / which they ate with a runcible spoon."

1. Perhaps a pun on "common folk" or on "common pork."

Over the mountains of dilapidating
Incorrigibilities till the twine
Warps the broken hearts in
Bundles for periods well in excess of
Berserk Baalzebubs,[2] bickering balks—
Deriding only the fuel gage never the
Fire raging inside or crushed
In a regime of ice.

1995

"every lake . . ."

every lake has a house
& every house has a stove
& every stove has a pot
& every pot has a lid
& every lid has a handle
& every handle has a stem
& every stem has an edge
& every edge has a lining
& every lining has a margin
& every margin has a slit
& every slit has a slope
& every slope has a sum
& every sum has a factor
& every factor has a face
& every face has a thought
& every thought has a trap
& every trap has a door
& every door has a frame
& every frame has a roof
& every roof has a house
& every house has a lake

2006

2. *Baalzebub* means "lord of the flies" in Hebrew and Arabic. Originally a Semitic deity worshiped in the Philistine city of Ekron, he appears as a rival to God in the Second Book of the Kings in the Hebrew Bible (1:2). He later appears as Beelzebub, the prince of the devils, in the New Testament (Matthew 12:24; Mark 3:22).

This poem is generated through a substitution game, whereby the last noun in one line becomes the first noun in the next. The series ends in a circle, but one in which the final assertion reverses the initial one and in which both assertions are manifestly at odds with material reality.

All the Whiskey in Heaven

Not for all the whiskey in heaven
Not for all the flies in Vermont
Not for all the tears in the basement
Not for a million trips to Mars

Not if you paid me in diamonds
Not if you paid me in pearls
Not if you gave me your pinky ring
Not if you gave me your curls

Not for all the fire in hell
Not for all the blue in the sky
Not for an empire of my own
Not even for peace of mind

No, never, I'll never stop loving you
Not till my heart beats its last
And even then in my words and my songs
I will love you all over again

2010

"All the Whiskey in Heaven" is a defiant elegy for the lost beloved. Bernstein wrote it after the death in Venice of his daughter, Emma Bee Bernstein (1985–2008), a budding photographer and writer.

CAROLYN FORCHÉ
b. 1950

CAROLYN FORCHÉ has innovated the concept of a "poetry of witness." A former journalist for Amnesty International, she brings the news of political injustice from around the world. Her poetry continues a tradition of moral awareness that includes such European poets as Anna Akhmatova and Paul Celan, and such Latin American poets as Claribel Alegría and Pablo Neruda. Her transnational concerns can also be connected to the work of many contemporary U.S. poets, such as Adrienne Rich, Nathaniel Mackey, Victor Hernández Cruz, Joy Harjo, and Lorna Dee Cervantes (all included in this anthology).

Forché has explained that the poetry of witness is neither wholly personal nor wholly political but occupies a "social space" where affairs of state and the havens of the personal meet. She argues that the injustices, exiles, and mass murders that pockmark recent history require a poetry that records such events and stands against them: "The poem might be our only evidence that an event has occurred." Forché not only writes such poems herself; she also has translated such poems, and she has collected examples from around the world in her anthology, *Against Forgetting: Twentieth-Century Poetry of Witness.* As Forché's work bears witness to inhumanity, it also exhorts its readers to turn "against despair" and toward "the spirit of communality."

Forché was born to a working-class family in Detroit, Michigan. Her father was a tool-and-die maker and her mother a homemaker. Forché received a B.A. in international relations and creative writing from Michigan State University and an M.F.A. in creative writing from Bowling Green State University. Although she began as a self-described "introspective poet," her experiences as a human rights worker and journalist in Central America, the Middle East, and Africa turned her toward poems that "bear the trace of extremity within them." Forché has a husband and son, and she is presently a professor of poetry at George Mason University in Virginia.

FURTHER READING

Forché, Carolyn. *The Angel of History.* New York: Harper & Row, 1994.
———. *The Country Between Us.* Port Townsend, Wash.: Copper Canyon Press, 1981.
———. "El Salvador: An Aide-Memoire." *American Poetry Review* 10.4 (July–August 1981): 3–7.
——— ."The Poetry of Witness." In *The Writer in Politics,* ed. William H. Gass and Lorin Cuoco, 135–47. Carbondale: Southern Illinois University Press, 1996.
———. "Twentieth-Century Poetry of Witness." *American Poetry Review* 22.2 (March–April 1993): 17.

Forché, Carolyn, ed. *Against Forgetting: Twentieth-Century Poetry of Witness*. New York: Norton, 1993.
Moyers, Bill. *The Language of Life: A Festival of Poets*, 129–41. New York: Doubleday, 1995.

The Colonel

What you have heard is true. I was in his house. His wife carried a tray of coffee and sugar. His daughter filed her nails, his son went out for the night. There were daily papers, pet dogs, a pistol on the cushion beside him. The moon swung bare on its black cord over the house.[1] On the television was a cop show. It was in English. Broken bottles were embedded in the walls around the house to scoop the kneecaps from a man's legs or cut his hands to lace. On the windows there were gratings like those in liquor stores. We had dinner, rack of lamb, good wine, a gold bell was on the table for calling the maid. The maid brought green mangoes, salt, a type of bread. I was asked how I enjoyed the country. There was a brief commercial in Spanish. His wife took everything away. There was some talk of how difficult it had become to govern. The parrot said hello on the terrace. The colonel told it to shut up, and pushed himself from the table. My friend said to me with his eyes: say nothing. The colonel returned with a sack used to bring groceries home. He spilled many human ears on the table. They were like dried peach halves. There is no other way to say this. He took one of them in his hands, shook it in our faces, dropped it into a water glass. It came alive there. I am tired of fooling around he said. As for the rights of anyone, tell your people they can go f— themselves. He swept the ears to the floor with his arm and held the last of his wine in the air. Something for your poetry, no? he said. Some of the ears on the floor caught this scrap of his voice. Some of the ears on the floor were pressed to the ground.[2]

1981

This prose poem derived from the year Forché spent in El Salvador in 1978. General Carlos Humberto Romero had ascended to the presidency in 1977 and instituted a military dictatorship. Reports of murder, rape, and torture earned the government the condemnation of the Inter-American Commission on Human Rights, Amnesty International, and the U.S. State Department. Working with Amnesty International, Forché investigated what happened to people who had disappeared. Her work brought her into contact with Archbishop Oscar Romero, a human rights advocate who was assassinated in 1980,

1. "I thought the moon in the poem was just the moon until someone pointed out that it seems to be a white lamp shining in a box in an interrogation room" (Forché's comment).

2. "There's an expression, 'ear to the ground,' you know the way you can hear a train coming if you put your ear to the ground?" (Forché's comment).

and with people working for the military dictatorship, such as the high-ranking military officer of this poem.

Forché commented to Bill Moyers that the colonel "got a little intoxicated and angry, and he wanted to send a message to the Carter administration. He wanted me to go back to Washington and tell President Carter, 'We've had enough of this human rights policy,' and his actions were his way of demonstrating his contempt. . . . I remember feeling sick and dizzy, but nothing happened to me. Everything was fine. His wife brought us out into the living room for coffee and tried to make everything better because she felt the dinner party was ruined. But he was not the worst man I met, not even the worst officer. In fact, this officer tried to warn priests when they were in danger."

MAURYA SIMON
b. 1950

MAURYA SIMON'S POETRY conveys a persistent effort to achieve spiritual and imaginative insight. At the same time, her work is intensely connected to the things of this world—sights to be seen, sufferings to be imagined, the existential "tunnels" and "windows" to be experienced (as she writes in "Enough"). In "The Bishop of Mysore," the speaker moves through geographical and cultural space in a manner that recalls the poems of Elizabeth Bishop. In "Enough" and "Benediction," we encounter sonic repetitions that may remind us of early Renaissance poetry or of prayer. But Simon's poems swerve sharply enough from all predecessors to be unique. They possess what poet and critic Carol Frost has called "reverence, wonder, and 'razzamatazz,'" a sense of "magic, awe, epiphany, and the ineffable." Simon's poems go their own way, carving out interior and verbal spaces that seem entirely new. She has said in an interview that "poetry can show us how to better understand and enjoy our lives—or how to endure them."

The daughter of visual artist Baila Goldenthal and ethnomusicologist Robert Simon, Maurya Simon was raised in the Los Angeles area after a four-year family sojourn in London and Paris. As she has said, she felt "seduced by the creative life because of the milieu in which my family moved." She studied at the University of California, Berkeley, and then, after a hiatus, received her B.A. in English from Pitzer College in Claremont, California. She then received her M.F.A. in creative writing from the University of California, Irvine. Since 1997 she has taught at the University of California, Riverside, where she is a professor of creative writing. Simon has won many fellowships and recognitions, including awards from the Poetry Society of America and the Academy of American

Poets. Married, with children, She lives in the San Gabriel Mountains, northeast of Los Angeles.

FURTHER READING

Carol Frost. "Simon, Maurya." In *The Greenwood Encyclopedia of American Poets and Poetry*, vol. 5, ed. Jeffrey Gray, James McCorkle, and Mary MacAleer Balkun, 1476–78. Westport, Conn.: Greenwood Press, 2006.
Dominique McCafferty. "Interview of Maurya Simon." www.mauryasimon.com/Publications/interviews.html.
Maurya Simon. *Cartographies: Uncollected Poems 1980–2005*. Los Angeles: Red Hen Press, 2008.
———. *Ghost Orchid*. Los Angeles: Red Hen Press, 2004.
———. *The Golden Labyrinth*. Columbia: University of Missouri Press, 1995.

The Bishop of Mysore

At dusk we follow the empty, twisting road that
rises skyward, Rao at the helm, our Ambassador[1]
coughing and tacking like an asthmatic sailor.
Past one curve, a blur: a pair of wild dogs
quickly disappears into a well of underbrush.

I want to stop to see the winking city lights
below, where tiny, smoky trails filament the sky.
Elene points out the sloping plains' opalescent gem,
the Lalitha Mahal Hotel,[2] blazing like an open lotus.
Too polite to hurry us, Rao fidgets with his pen.

When we park near the Bull Temple[3] stairs, a man
in starched white cassock[4] comes to shake our hands.
"I'm the Bishop of Mysore,"[5] he happily explains.
"How I love America, Americans, hot dogs, and Coke!"
Rao is impatient; we must hurry on now to reach

       ✳   ✳   ✳

1. "An Ambassador is an Indian-made car" (Simon's note).
2. The Lalitha Mahal Palace Hotel in Mysore, India, a large and opulent hotel. Lotus: water lily represented in ancient Hindu art and religious symbolism.
3. Hindu shrine built in 1537 and dedicated to Lord Shiva. Located on Bungle Hill in the outskirts of Bangalore, Karnataka, in southern

India, the temple features a large granite statue of Nandi, a sacred bull said to have been mounted by the Hindu deity Shiva.
4. Long robe or coat worn by clergy in the Roman Catholic Church and several other Christian churches.
5. A town about 140 kilometers southwest of Bangalore.

the great Chamundeswara Temple[6] for evening puja.
Except for a Brahmin priest[7] blessing a motorcycle,
the parking lot is ghostly: all the hangers-on and
trinket peddlers have wandered home at last—
a lone girl sells us an arm's length of jasmine,[8]

then Rao leads us past her to the sanctum sanctorum,[9]
where incense interweaves itself with wisps of prayer.
Here the air gathers into a stilled fullness that
encircles our bodies slowly, so we become awash
now in a reverence so resonant it stings our skin.

But too soon the spell is broken; we emerge slowly
from the labyrinthine chambers, out into a cobalt[10] night,
a spattering of stars flickering overhead, oil lamps
scattering their drops above the blackened plains.
"Don't forget to write," the smiling Bishop calls out,

as he stiffly climbs back into his chauffeured Cadillac
and rolls down his window with a gloved hand so the girl
can kiss his satin fingertip. Rao frowns just slightly
as he leans against our car, but his gaze is softened
by the moon, is gilded by some grace I know I lack,

by a holiness that barely grazed our senses, by a spirit
so subtle, it embraced and entered him effortlessly.
We begin our gradual descent down the hilly slope;
Rao stares out beyond the glassy night, a mute calm
relaxing his face. Each small world transforms itself.

—for Elene Kallimanis

1995

"The Bishop of Mysore" derives from a period Simon spent in Bangalore, India, on a Fulbright/Indo-American Fellowship. The poem recalls an incident that occurred while the poet was touring with Elene Kallimanis, a friend from Southern California, and Rao, an Indian guide.

6. The most famous Hindu temple in Mysore, dedicated to the Goddess Chamundeswara. Puja: "a Hindu devotional rite" (Simon's note).
7. Priest in the Hindu religion.

8. Asian, warm-weather shrub with extremely fragrant blossoms.
9. Most holy place.
10. Dark greenish blue.

Enough

Heaven has enough windows for everyone,
Yet there's a secret wedged behind each pane.
God seals His lips with paraffin,[1] but
The devil knows how to speak in tongues.

There's a secret wedged behind each pain
A mortal man or woman feels; we're dumb,
But the devil knows how to speak in tongues:
He voices our longings in wind and rain.

Each mortal man and woman feels numb
When gazing through the windows of heaven,
Where our longings are voiced in windy rain.
(Hell has no windows, only endless tunnels.)

Still gazing up to the windows of heaven,
We search for God, but He's not there.
In windowless Hell, beyond the tunnels,
We'll find him at last, burning the air.

We search for God, but He's not where
We thought we'd find Him — burning the air
In Hell's kitchen, beyond our tunnel vision.
Instead, He's gazing into our earthly windows,

Watching as flesh-bound men and women drown
In longing for that primal garden, where God
Rained down in a golden silence, and was nowhere
And everywhere at once, housed in each breast.

2004

"Enough" is rhythmically and sonically complex, in a way that coincides with the speaker's struggle to find God. Note that each stanza (except the first) includes an end-word identical (or nearly so) to one in the preceding stanza. Many contraries resound through the poem as well, such as windows and tunnels, burning and drowning, man and woman, heaven and hell, and the devil and God.

---

1. A waxy substance used in sealing and coating.

Benediction

Bless the man with the torturer's mouth,
bless the woman with the fossil soul,

bless the man with the storm in his groin,
bless the woman whom no one loves,

bless the man with a skull made of iron,
bless the woman who dreams of great kingdoms,

bless the man who's strange and swift to anger,
bless the woman whose habit is silence,

bless the man who surrenders nothing,
bless the woman who's a martyr to pigeons,

bless the man who lurks in the tower,
bless the woman of no conscience, no armor,

bless the man who nightly cries "Wolf,"
bless the woman who blushes and stutters,

bless the man who subdues the trees,
bless the woman who curses the rainbow,

bless the man who is a slave to pity,
bless the woman who delights in nakedness,

bless the man who is broken by love,
bless the woman who heals herself in greed,

bless the man whose grip is slipping,
bless the woman who is dangerous with pride,

bless the man on the threshold of jumping,
bless the woman newly born into pain,

bless the man be he murderer or thief,
bless the woman drooling in her cup,

bless the man with a worm for a tongue,
bless the woman with a shadow for a heart,

   ✻ ✻ ✻

bless the man who forgives only himself
bless the woman who shoulders the world,

bless them all who are nameless and mad,
oh bless the man, yes, bless the woman.

2004

Simon noted that "'Benediction' is for Allen Ginsberg, in memoriam, April 5, 1997."

JOHN YAU
b. 1950

JOHN YAU writes poetry that challenges habitual ways of perceiving and communicating. His poems have a brilliant but elusive quality, often giving way to
wordplay. They hint at autobiography, social analysis, and ideas without going
beyond innuendo. They show no interest in abstract statement or precise description. These are works of shimmering surfaces that imply but don't explore
the depths below. On the one hand, they avoid reducing human beings and
material reality to language. On the other hand, they resist the illusion that they
can ever go beyond language, that they can absorb reality. They demonstrate the
ways that language is both a vital source of meaning and an inevitable obstacle
to it. Witty, serious, beautiful, and unsettling, Yau's poems stretch and breach
the borders of poetry, making it subtly new.

Yau was born in Lynn, Massachusetts, shortly after his parents emigrated from
China. His mother belonged to a prominent Chinese family from Shanghai,
and his father was of mixed Chinese and English ancestry. Growing up on Beacon Hill in Boston and then in suburban Brookline, Yau experienced a sense
of diasporic "betweenness" as a Chinese American who did not fit comfortably
into any mold. He received his B.A. from Bard College in upstate New York and
his M.F.A. from Brooklyn College, where he studied with John Ashbery (also
included in this anthology). An art critic, editor, and fiction writer as well as a
poet, Yau has published many volumes and has received numerous awards and
grants. Married, with one child, he is now a professor at the Mason Gross School
of the Arts at Rutgers University.

Yau's poetry was influenced by the surrealists and other experimental groups
of the 1920s as well as John Ashbery's New York school of poets and artists in the

1970s. It bears some relation to that of contemporary Language poets such as Susan Howe, Charles Bernstein, and Amy Gerstler as well as to Asian-American poets such as Theresa Cha, Marilyn Chin, and Li- Young Lee (all included in this anthology). Yet his work is singular as well. Its probing of Chinese-American subjectivity, American identity, and personhood in general through disconnected images, narrative disruptions, parodies of popular culture, language games, visual-arts techniques, and free associational riffs results in texts that are alternatively inspiring, puzzling, anxiety-producing, and amusing. Always a step ahead of the reader, they suggest new ways of thinking, feeling, and communicating in the twenty-first century.

FURTHER READING

Edward Foster. "An Interview with John Yau." *Talisman* 5 (1990): 31–50.
Christina Mar. "John Yau's Poetry and the Ethnic/Aesthetic Divide." In *Literary Gestures: The Aesthetic in Asian American Writing*, ed. Rocio Davis and Sue-Im Lee, 70–85. Philadelphia: Temple University Press, 2005.
John Yau. *Borrowed Love Poems*. London: Penguin, 2002.
———. *Forbidden Entries*. Santa Rosa, Calif.: Black Sparrow Press, 1996.
———. *Ing Grish*. Philadelphia: Saturnalia Books, 2005.
———. *Radiant Silhouette: New and Selected Work, 1974–1988*. Santa Rosa, Calif.: Black Sparrow Press, 1994.
Xiaojing Zhou. "Postmodernism and Subversive Parody: John Yau's 'Genghis Chan: Private Eye' Series." *College Literature* 31.1 (Winter 2004): 73–102.

Chinese Villanelle

I have been with you, and I have thought of you
Once the air was dry and drenched with light
I was like a lute filling the room with description

We watched glum clouds reject their shape
We dawdled near a fountain, and listened
I have been with you, and I have thought of you

Like a river worthy of its gown
And like a mountain worthy of its insolence
Why am I like a lute left with only description

How does one cut an axe handle with an axe?
What shall I do to tell you all my thoughts
When I have been with you, and thought of you

   ✳ ✳ ✳

A pelican sits on the dam, while a duck
Folds its wings again; the song does not melt
I remember you looking at me without description

Perhaps a king's business is never finished,
Though "perhaps" implies a different beginning
I have been with you, and I have thought of you
Now I am a lute filled with this wandering description

1979

This poem uses the villanelle form, which originated in sixteenth-century France and requires five tercets and a quatrain in which the first and third lines of the initial tercet alternately repeat as the closing lines of the later tercets and then appear as the final two lines of the quatrain. Yau, however, forgoes the rhyme scheme that is also a feature of the traditional villanelle. The poet has said that "to write about one's life in terms of a subjective 'I' . . . is to fulfill the terms of the oppressor." Yet this poem includes many hints of his subjectivity: its conflation of Chinese and Western culture in the title, the implications of love and loss in the poem, and the suggestion of diasporic displacement from China as well.

Electric Drills

I used to have a fear of tools, largely because of my father. When I was three, and he, my mother, and I lived in a basement apartment on Beacon Hill, my father developed a ritual to scare me when I misbehaved. Somewhere, he had acquired a beautiful set of tools, each of them red and shiny like a child's fire truck. I don't know why or where he got them, since I have never seen him use them again. I remember the apartment as industrial green. There were lots of pipes overhead, and linoleum seems to have been on all the floors. I also remember the high chair, and the arm chair I had to sit in, when my father was mad at me. It faced the closet. While I was sitting there, feeling smaller than I should have in this chair for adults, my father would get out the electric drill, plug it in, and open the closet door until I could see both him and it in profile. He would then drill some holes in the door, while telling me I had been "bad," and the possible consequences that might result. The insistence of his voice competing with the whining of the electric drill was always what frightened me the most.

Eighteen years later, when I was a student at Bard College, I got into a car accident. I was admitted to Northern Dutchess Hospital on May 29th, 1971 and left for the first time on January 15th. I had forty-seven roommates, and watched two of them die. There were four of us in the car, a baby blue '65 Chevy sedan, we had borrowed from a friend who had passed out on the floor of his room, after extolling the poems of Pushkin in Russian. I bent down, took the keys from his pocket, flipped them in the air, and said to the other three in my best Randolph Scott–James Dean voice[1]—"Let's go for a ride."

At the time of the accident, the two with driver's licenses were sitting in the back. The one who was driving, had never driven before, and hasn't since. The car hit a tree head on. I was lying under the car, near the rear wheel, when I regained consciousness. Both my legs (right tibia, left femur) were broken, as well as my pelvis and nose. I required stitches in my tongue and on my face. My right ring finger was dislocated. I was awake for most of the operation, since the amount of liquor and drugs I had taken eliminated the possibility of anesthesia. While I was lying in the Pre-Op room, they began giving me morphine to ease the pain.

For most of the time, when I was under morphine, I felt like America while a lot of riots were taking place in Canada. I knew it was going on, but I didn't particularly care. I tore out my stitches, undid my bandages, ripped the tubes for the plasma and glucose out of my arms, and called the nurses names that, as one of them said with a smile months later, she didn't know existed. I don't remember any of these things, since they all took place at night, and I was supposedly asleep. Eventually, I would light my bed on fire because, as I told my roommate, I wanted to see what it was like. The morphine was then discontinued, though I would be given it for five more periods, each lasting up to a week, and I would refine the possibilities of how I felt with liquor, grass and valiums I had saved up.

When the doctors set my right leg, I remember feeling the warmth of the plaster-soaked bandage, and being surprised. It felt invigorating, and I told the doctors they "should set the rest of me like that." I don't remember the whine of the electric drill, as much as the realization something was happening to me. I was tied to the operating table. I managed to sit up and see one of the doctors drilling through my left leg, just below the knee. The drill was green, like the living room of the apartment on Beacon Hill. The pin would remain there, attached to weights, nearly the whole time I was in the hospital. I was taken out of traction when the decision was made to put a stainless steel plate in my left leg, from my hip to just above my knee. The doctor showed me the plate from a catalog that reminded me of Sears. Beneath the picture was a

---

1. Randolph Scott (1898–1987) and James Dean (1931–1955) were charismatic movie stars who achieved great acclaim in films of the 1950s.

list of its vital dimensions. They probably used a drill to attach it to my femur which, as the doctor said, "looked like a stack of marbles." A month later the doctors inserted two pins into my right leg, after re-setting it. It seems they hadn't done it correctly on that first morning.

A couple of months after I got out of the hospital, I was sitting in Adolph's, the Bard campus bar, drinking with a friend. I had been thinking of electric drills, and the part they played in my life—both in the psychological development and the physical reconstruction of my body. At that point, I had not yet moved to Manhattan, bought a loft, and built a lot of bookcases and furniture—all with a gray electric drill I had bought as a gift for the sculptor I was living with. According to my friend, I had a bemused smile on my face when I turned to him and said, "Do you want to hear a funny story?" Recently I called him up. We haven't seen much of each other in the last seven years, but we manage to keep in touch. He asked me if I ever thought about writing down the story I told him.

1980

This text can be viewed as a prose poem, which combines the concision of poetry with the rhythmic and narrative freedom of prose. The border between prose poetry and short fiction or memoir, however, is an ambiguous and permeable one. For other examples of the genre, see "Cenotaph" below, as well as Theresa Cha's "Dead time" and "Dead words" and Amy Gerstler's "White Marriage" and "An Unexpected Adventure" (all included in this anthology). Although Yau has resisted writing about a "subjective 'I'"—and he does refuse to explore the thoughts and feelings of the "I" in this text—he nevertheless includes apparently autobiographical details here: the apartment on Beacon Hill, the dorm room at Bard College, and the exact dates of his hospitalization.

Avenue of Americans

The audience cheers as the monkey correctly
identifies their desire by curling his lips
around the statue of a cigarette.[1]
Stretching from knee to shiny knee,[2]
somehow it made sense.
Nurses attended to his every skid.
She woke up, remembering the miles of empty sky
unfurling from banner to banner.

1. Perhaps a linguistic revision or echo of the Statue of Liberty.
2. A parodic reference to the phrase "from sea to shining sea" in the song "America the Beautiful."

*　*　*

The woman skidded to a halt when she saw a monkey
climb onto her windshield with a letter clamped firmly in his mouth.
The plane stretched beside the mountain,
its seats bubbling with cheers that faded
only as night demanded its portion of the rent.
The highway leading to the statue's permanent shrug.

The monkeys arranged themselves in alphabetical order.
To convert failure into success, the president was advised
to stop scratching his nose with his thumb.
She woke up and was rewarded
with questions leading to questions.

Each street is named after a country
that does not return its mail.
The president of the monkeys corrected his audience
by adjusting his smile from moment to moment.
Permanent shrug of her cigarette.

Inside the letter was the map of the highway
leading to the correct audience.
A response is not necessarily an answer.
Minutes arrange themselves in a circular alphabet;
statue first, shrug second.
Success was as simple.
But whose angel was perched on the smiling monkey's shoulder?

> His hand held all the answers to some of the questions.
> I learned to accommodate your doubts by lying.

> His answers held hands with some of the questions.
> I learned to accommodate myself by doubting my own lies.

The president's smile faded only when it made sense.
On the bus, the monkey sat next to a man smoking a pipe.

Each street is named after a shrug.

The highway fades into the side of a night scarred by mountains.
The echo of the president's smile is carried from promise to promise.
The boy hides the answers in his mouth, his elbows scratching his knees.
If he is lucky, amnesia will be his reward.

1981

This surrealist poem, its title punning on New York City's Avenue of the Americas, satirizes American public rhetoric by fragmenting and deforming it. The work suggests a landscape of clichés and insincerity through its repeated use of evocative or apparently inappropriate nouns, such as monkeys, smiles, lies, and shrugs. Christina Mar argues that the poem registers the danger that an ideology of sameness may elide ethnic and cultural difference.

Cenotaph

I

The clues to what they remembered had been pasted into an album. Photographs of her family and friends, snapshots he had taken during the war. The album was packed neatly in a trunk, which was then stored in the ship's hold. It was nearly spring when they sailed
from Shanghai to San Francisco.

II

The album was not, as the word suggests, white. Its pages were black—the time inside the camera before light casts its shadows on the wall. What were white were the words, the laconic summations printed along the bottom of every page.

III

The album was divided into two parts, his and hers. In the second part, his part, someone (most likely her) had carefully removed the snapshots. It was here I always slowed down and inspected the pages. The place where the words were lined up beneath black rectangles.

IV

What had reflected the light was gone. Only the rows of white letters remained. Only the faded rectangles framing empty black spaces.

V

I would spin in my room until I was too dizzy to stand. Then, lying on the bed with my eyes closed, I would pretend the plane was about to crash.

VI

Those black rectangles surrounded by faded black almost blue frames. The words were arranged neatly along the bottom of every page. My father was an accountant, this was his ledger.

VII

I understood someone had tried to erase this history of excerpts. The words continued echoing long after I returned the album to its place on the shelf.

VIII

The hospital was next to the jail. From the roof I could see the inmates playing basketball, the interns practicing their serves.

IX

I tried imagining the pictures the black triangles once held. *Mound of Heads, Shanghai, 1946*[1] was my favorite. Movies showed me everything but this.

X

At the beach I saw the words transformed by the sun. Saw them become hills of bleached skulls. Now they were smooth and round, white as the words describing them.

XI

Lying beside the sagging castles, watching the sand trickle through my fingers. Tiny examples of what I read. All afternoon I played beneath the sun with the skulls, molding them into little mountains.

1984

This poem, which evokes the traumatic knowledge of mass murder in the twentieth century, employs a fragmentary style to suggest the fragmentation of historical knowledge. The speaker's memories circle around an absence—the never-seen photos of skulls mentioned in section IX. His elliptical memories of the photo album are interrupted by tangential memories in sections V and VIII.

Red Fountain

When the last mirage
evaporates, I will be
the sole proprietor of this voice
and all its rusted machinery.
I have reread the instructions.

---

1. The Japanese military occupation of China from 1937 to the end of World War II in 1945 was particularly bloody. It has been estimated that up to 3,000,000 Chinese were killed; up to 300,000 died in the 1937 Nanking Massacre alone. In Shanghai, untold thousands of Chinese—along with interned Jewish, American, British, and Dutch refugees—died of hunger and infectious diseases. U.S. air raids on Shanghai in 1944 and 1945 killed thousands more.

I have hidden the limelight vapors
and flowers of memory.
By tomorrow or the day after,
I will have collected enough
gasoline and lightning.
Do you remember the lipstick imprint?
Is it true he has my name
stamped on his identity card?
The leaves are whiter this year
and another boat has capsized on the lake.
Did I tell you I delivered the letter?
Your eyes are green sometimes blue or brown.
I have mowed the lawn and fed the chickens.
The wind is spinning, but air has settled into the locks.[1]

1988

Genghis Chan

Private Eye XXIV

Grab some
Grub sum

Sub gum
machine stun

Treat pork
pig feet

On floor
all fours

Train cow
chow lane

Dice played
trade spice

Makes fist
first steps

1996

1. Air locks, door locks, and locks of hair are three of the potential references here.

This poem combines—and parodies—two different Asian figures who have held key places in popular culture: Genghis Khan (the warlike founder of the Mongol Empire in the twelfth and thirteenth centuries) and Charlie Chan (a benevolent Chinese-American detective who first appeared in stories by Earl Biggers and then in films and TV shows, usually played by a European-American actor). The poem has a good deal of fun with language, cross-cultural references, and the names of Chinese dishes such as "dim sum," "subgum," and "chow mein." The next poem continues the Genghis Chan sequence.

Genghis Chan

Private Eye XXVII

Moo goo
Milk mush

Guy pan[1]
Piss pot
1996

Borrowed Love Poem 1

What can I do, I have dreamed of you so much
What can I do, lost as I am in the sky

What can I do, now that all
the doors and windows are open

I will whisper this in your ear
as if it were a rough draft

something I scribbled on a napkin
I have dreamed of you so much

there is no time left to write
no time left on the sundial

for my shadow to fall back to the earth
lost as I am in the sky

2002

This poem is the first of ten in a series called "Borrowed Love Poems."

---

1. Moo goo gai pan is a Cantonese stir-fry dish with chicken and vegetables.

RAY A. YOUNG BEAR
b. 1950

Rᴀʏ ᴀ. ʏᴏᴜɴɢ ʙᴇᴀʀ, a member of the Meskwaki tribe, was raised on the Meskwaki Tribal Settlement in central Iowa, where he lives today with his wife and collaborator, Stella Young Bear. He is a poet, novelist, and performance artist who has toured with his performance group, Black Eagle Child. A native speaker of Meskwaki, Young Bear began writing in English in his teens. He has taught creative writing and Native American literature at numerous institutions, including the University of Iowa and Iowa State University. He writes to correct misrepresentation of Native American culture and to express his sense of sharing the universe with all other beings. Patricia Ploesch has written that Young Bear's poetry "engages historical and contemporary political issues and employs dream sequences with which he is able to explore the ephemeral boundaries between reality and dreams, between the past and present, and between ancestors and progeny."

FURTHER READING

Duane Niatum, ed. *Harper's Anthology of 20th Century Native American Poetry*. New York: HarperCollins, 1988.
Patricia Ploesch. "Young Bear, Ray." In *The Greenwood Encyclopedia of American Poets and Poetry*, vol. 5, ed. Jeffrey Gray, James McCorkle, and Mary McAleer Balkun, 1752–53. Westport, Conn.: Greenwood Press, 2006.
Ray A. Young Bear. *Black Eagle Child*. New York: Grove Press, 1996.
———. *Invisible Musician*. Duluth, Minn.: Holy Cow! Press, 1990.

Wa ta se Na ka mo ni, Vietnam Memorial

Last night when the yellow moon
of November broke through the last line
of turbulent Midwestern clouds,
a lone frog, the same one
who probably announced
the premature spring floods,
attempted to sing.
Veterans' Day, and it was
sore-throat weather.
In reality the invisible musician
reminded me of my own doubt.
The knowledge that my grandfathers

were singers as well as composers—
one of whom felt the simple utterance
of a vowel made for the start
of a melody—did not produce
the necessary memory or feeling
to make a Wadasa Nakamoon,[1]
Veteran's Song.
All I could think of
was the absence of my name
on a distant black rock.[2]
Without this monument
I felt I would not be here.
For a moment, I questioned
why I had to immerse myself
in country, controversy and guilt,
but I wanted to honor them.
Surely, the song they presently
listened to along with my grandfathers
was the ethereal kind which did not stop.

1990

Young Bear memorializes the Native Americans who served in the Vietnam War, and he reflects on his alienation as well as his desire to respect the tribal men. His bilingual title uses the language of the Meskwaki tribe. You may wish to consider this poem in the context of poems by poets who experienced the Vietnam War firsthand, such as Yusef Komunyakaa, Gerald McCarthy, W. D. Ehrhart, and Bao-Long Chu. You may also wish to relate it to other poems by Native American poets, such as Joy Harjo, Linda Hogan, and Sherman Alexie.

THERESA HAK KYUNG CHA
1951–1982

THERESA HAK KYUNG CHA was born in Pusan, Korea, the middle child of five siblings. Her mother was a teacher and her father a merchant. In 1962, the family left Korea for the United States. After the family settled in San Francisco, Cha

1. A term from the Meskwaki language for a veteran's song.   2. The Vietnam Veterans Memorial in Washington, D.C.

attended Catholic school, where she studied French, music, and the classics. She received dual B.A.'s in comparative literature and art and an M.F.A in art from the University of California, Berkeley. She also studied film in Paris and began winning awards for her videos, films, and art pieces. After becoming an American citizen in 1977, Cha made return visits to Korea in 1979 and 1981. In 1980, she moved to New York, where she worked at the Metropolitan Museum of Art and continued to produce performance pieces, art installations, films, and written texts. In 1982, she married artist Richard Barnes and published her masterpiece *Dictée*, a collage of poems, autobiography, history, film theory, and other genres. In November of that same year she was murdered by a stranger while on her way to meet her husband.

The two prose poems presented below both derive from *Dictée*, a book that defies categories. It includes photographs and other visual representations, a memoir of Cha's mother, parodies of language lessons, lyric meditations, and much, much more. The book is a postmodern icon—fragmented, haunted, strange, and beautiful. It is written at the intersection of feminist, Korean-American, global, and experimental discourses. Its narratives and lyrics are often interrupted and undermined, a display of the author's distrust of master narratives and uncritical writing. *Dictée* assumes that one cannot critique the status quo in the language of the status quo. It foregrounds language play, while it ruminates on the need for an adequate language in a social regime that wants to silence and disguise individual difference.

The two prose poems printed below require metaphorical or creative thinking on the part of the reader. They do not give the expected cues about meaning. They have something to say about speech and silence, memory and identity, women's identity, and feelings of depression, displacement, and aspiration. They have a profound way of intimating new perspectives on these enduring topics.

FURTHER READING

Theresa Hak Kyung Cha. *Dictée*. 1982; reprint, Berkeley and Los Angeles: University of California Press, 2001.

———. *Exilée and Tempo Morts: Selected Works*. Berkeley: University of California Press, 2009.

Anne Anlin Cheng. *The Melancholy of Race: Psychoanalysis, Assimilation, and Hidden Grief*, 139–68. New York: Oxford University Press, 2001.

Eric Hayot. "Immigrating Fictions: Unfailing Mediation in *Dictée* and *Becoming Madame Mao*." *Contemporary Literature* 47 (Winter 2006): 601–35.

Elaine H. Kim. "Poised on the In-between: A Korean American's Reflections on Theresa Hak Kyung Cha's *Dictée*." In *Writing Self, Writing Nation*, ed. Elaine H. Kim and Norma Alarcon, 3–34. Berkeley: Third Woman Press, 1994.

Lisa Lowe. "Unfaithful to the Original: The Subject of *Dictée*." In *Writing Self, Writing Nation*, ed. Elaine H. Kim and Norma Alarcon, 35–72. Berkeley: Third Woman Press, 1994.

[Dead time]

Dead time. Hollow depression interred   invalid[1]
to resurgence, resistant to memory. Waits. Apel.[2]
Apellation.[3] Excavation. Let the one who is
diseuse.[4] Diseuse de bonne aventure. Let her call
forth. Let her break open the spell cast upon time
upon time again and again. With her voice,
penetrate earth's floor, the walls of Tartaurus[5] to
circle and scratch the bowl's surface. Let the
sound enter from without, the bowl's hollow its
sleep. Until.

1982

This prose poem, the first written text in the "Lyric Poetry" section of *Dictée*, evokes the poet's struggle to plumb the self, to challenge the silence and speak. More specifically, it suggests the need for women and Korean Americans to allow their voices to emerge in a culture dominated by others.

[Dead words]

Dead words. Dead tongue. From disuse.[1] Buried in
Time's memory. Unemployed. Unspoken. History.
Past. Let the one who is diseuse, one who is mother
who waits nine days and nine nights be found.
Restore memory. Let the one who is diseuse, one
who is daughter restore spring with her each appearance from beneath the earth.
The ink spills thickest before it runs dry before it
stops writing at all.

1982

1. The word has a double meaning. As an adjec-
tive, it means indefensible, weak, inadequate, or
untrue. As a noun, it refers to a person who is
sick, injured, or disabled.
2. This word is not in any dictionary, but in
French, the very similar word "appel" means
call, appeal, summons, name, or telephone
ring.
3. Not a correctly spelled word, but in both English and French, the noun "appellation" indicates the name or title of a person, thing, clan,
or vintage of wine.

4. A rarely used French word, indicating a female speaker or performer of monologues. The
word may also suggest such English words as
"disease" and "disuse." Disuse de bonne aventure: "female fortune-teller" (French); literally,
a speaker of good adventures or experiences.
5. "Hell" (Latin).
1. As in "[Dead time]" above, this prose poem
plays on similarities among the words "disuse,"
"disease," and "diseuse" (French for female
speaker). See also "diseuse" in lines 3 and 5.

The last written text in the "Lyric Poetry" section of *Dictée*, this prose poem returns to some of the themes of "[Dead time]" above, including the birth of language from silence and a woman's reemergence from depression, grief, despair, or self-censorship. Note also the tension in both prose poems between language and death.

JOY HARJO
b. 1951

JOY HARJO'S VISIONARY POETRY transforms the contemporary world with Native American wisdom. It fully acknowledges the harsh realities of contemporary culture, such as environmental depredation, commercial superficiality, and urban alienation. "We are all strange in this place," as she says in "The Path to the Milky Way Leads through Los Angeles." Yet her poetry suggests that Native American concepts and values still survive, against the odds, to help us steer our course and find comfort.

Harjo's poems envision a circle of life in which the seen coexists harmoniously with spirit that is unseen but powerful. Like Walt Whitman and many Native American poets of old, Harjo postulates a continuum of spiritual existence after death and between all beings. Like Adrienne Rich and Carolyn Forché, she writes from a woman-centered political position. She grieves the losses that Native American have suffered—for example, the expulsion of the Creek Nation from Alabama to Oklahoma in 1832, a policy to which her ancestor Monahwee led the opposition. But Harjo finds sustenance in the spiritual realm, in the belief that we all are "truly blessed," as she says in "Eagle Poem."

These poems vividly infuse Native American beliefs into everyday existence. They put Native American ways of seeing into fruitful contact with postmodern conditions. They urge us to recover a sense of wholeness, to close the gap between ourselves and the other beings and objects of this world, to overcome separateness within a "circle of motion." Harjo's work discovers beauty in nature and even in the surreal contemporary cityscapes in which many of us live. It posits the presence, as she said in an interview, of "dynamic possibility."

Joy Harjo was born and raised in Tulsa, Oklahoma. Her mother was of mixed Cherokee and European background, and her father was of Muskogee (or Creek) descent. Her grandmother, Naomi Harjo, was a noted painter. Harjo herself is an enrolled member of the Muskogee tribe. She studied at the Institute of American Indian Art in Santa Fe, New Mexico, and then received her B.A. from the University of New Mexico in Albuquerque (where the novelist Leslie Marmon Silko gave her her first typewriter) and her M.F.A. from the University of Iowa. A single mother with two children, she has lived in New Mexico, Arizona, Colorado, and California, and she now resides in Hawaii. She has published many books of award-winning poetry. She is also a jazz-inflected musician, with several CDs to her credit. On her CD *Winding through the Milky Way*, which includes a musical version of the poem "Morning Song," she describes her songs as "a little road music to accompany us as we make the timeless journey between earth and sky. We're in a story that will always include the ancient while riding to the outer edge."

FURTHER READING

Jenny Goodman. "Politics and Personal Lyric in the Poetry of Joy Harjo." *MELUS* 19 (1994): 35–56.
Janice Gould. "An Interview with Joy Harjo." *Western American Literature* 35.2 (2000): 131–42.
Joy Harjo. *How We Became Human: New and Selected Poems, 1975–2001.* New York: W. W. Norton, 2002.
———. *Native Joy for Real.* Audio CD. Mekko Productions. www.joyharjo.com. 2004.
———. *She Had Some Horses: Poems.* New York: W. W. Norton, 2008.
———. *The Spiral of Memory: Interviews.* Ed. Laura Coltelli. Ann Arbor: University of Michigan Press, 1996.
———. *Winding through the Milky Way.* Audio CD. Mekko Productions. www.joyharjo.com. 2008.
Azfar Hussain. "Joy Harjo and Her Poetics as Praxis: A 'Postcolonial' Political Economy of the Body, Land, Labor, and Language." *Wicazo Sa Review* 15.2 (Fall 2000): 27–61.

Eagle Poem

To pray you open your whole self
To sky, to earth, to sun, to moon
To one whole voice that is you.
And know there is more
That you can't see, can't hear,
Can't know except in moments
Steadily growing, and in languages
That aren't always sound but other
Circles of motion.
Like eagle that Sunday morning
Over Salt River.[1] Circled in blue sky
In wind, swept our hearts clean

1. River in Arizona that flows southwest from the White Mountains along Indian reservations and the Tonto National Forest and through a series of dams and the Phoenix-Tempe metropolitan area, where it usually runs dry.

With sacred wings.
We see you, see ourselves and know
That we must take the utmost care
And kindness in all things.
Breathe in, knowing we are made of
All this, and breathe, knowing
We are truly blessed because we
Were born, and die soon within a
True circle of motion,
Like eagle rounding out the morning
Inside us.
We pray that it will be done
In beauty.
In beauty.[2]

1990

Infused with Native American spirituality, "Eagle Poem" uses the image of a circling eagle to suggest the unity of human beings and nature, and of life and death. Harjo performs the poem as a song lyric on her *Native Joy for Real* CD and on a YouTube video.

Harjo comments on the poem's river setting: "The *Salt River* or Río Salado flows through Tempe, Arizona. Josiah Moore, an O'odam and Pima educator, leader, and friend, told me that the river was an historical gathering place for his people. He remembered when the banks were lined with cottonwoods. He remembered horses and wagons lined up along the river, enjoying the cool oasis. When he told me this in the early eighties the river had been dammed and was kept in Lake Roosevelt. What remained was a winding dusty ditch that became an angry river after the urgent rainstorms that arrived every rainy season. Now, I've heard, there is water again because the City of Tempe businesses wanted the water to flow again through the city." The river, which supplies drinking and irrigation water to the area, runs dry by the time it reaches Tempe and Phoenix, except at Tempe Town Lake, a city reservoir.

The Path to the Milky Way Leads through Los Angeles

There are strangers above me, below me and all around me and we are all
    strange in this place of recent invention.

This city named for angels appears naked and stripped of anything resembling
    the shaking of turtle shells, the songs of human voices on a summer night
    outside Okmulgee.[1]

2. An echo of the conclusion of the Navajo "Night Chant" or "Night Way": "It is finished in beauty, / It is finished in beauty."

1. City in Oklahoma, population of about 13,000, the capital of the Muskogee Creek Nation since the Civil War.

✳   ✳   ✳

Yet, it's perpetually summer here, and beautiful. The shimmer of gods is easier
   to perceive at sunrise or dusk,

when those who remember us here in the illusion of the marketplace turn
   toward the changing of the sun and say our names.

We matter to somebody,
   We must matter to the strange god who imagines us as we revolve together
   in the dark sky on the path to the Milky Way.

We can't easily see that starry road from the perspective of the crossing of
   boulevards, can't hear it in the whine of civilization or taste the minerals of
   planets in hamburgers.

But we can buy a map here of the stars' homes, dial a tone for dangerous
   love, choose from several brands of water, or a hiss of oxygen for gentle
   rejuvenation.

Everyone knows you can't buy love[2] but you can still sell your soul for less than
   a song, to a stranger who will sell it to someone else for a profit
   until you're owned by a company of strangers
   in the city of the strange and getting stranger.

I'd rather understand how to sing from a crow
   who was never good at singing or much of anything
   but finding gold in the trash of humans.

So what are we doing here I ask the crow parading on the ledge of falling that
   hangs over this precarious city?

Crow[3] just laughs and says *wait, wait and see* and I am waiting
   and not seeing anything, not just yet.

But like crow I collect the shine of anything beautiful I can find.

                                                                2000

"The Path to the Milky Way Leads through Los Angeles" evokes Native American myths
and perspectives, especially the Lenape legend of the Rainbow Crow, who brought fire to
earth from the Sky Spirit. By carrying the fire in his beak, the crow scorched his feathers
and lost his beautiful singing voice, so the Sky Spirit compensated him with shiny black

2. Allusion to the Beatles song "Can't Buy Me   3. The crow often plays a role in Native Ameri-
Love," composed by Paul McCartney in 1964.   can stories and myths as a messenger to and
                                             from the Creator.

feathers that reflect the rainbow colors of the world or, as Harjo's poem says, "anything beautiful." At the same time, the poem is in conversation with other poems about urban scenes, such as Allen Ginsberg's "Howl."

Harjo has commented about the poem's reference to Okmulgee: "*Okmulgee* is the capital of the Creek nation west of the Mississippi. It is said that my family once owned most of the town. And there's a story told me by my Aunt Lois Harjo who talked of the appearance of the first traffic light in town. She and her mother and sisters stood at the corner waiting for the signal to cross. When the light turned green they tentatively started across, then the light turned yellow. 'My mother was so nervous,' she said, 'she turned around and slapped your grandmother.' I think about this every time I drive through Okmulgee and pass by the traffic light that still dangles above the street. It is probably the original one."

Morning Song

The red dawn now is rearranging the earth
Thought by thought
Beauty by beauty
Each sunrise a link in the ladder
Thought by thought
Beauty by beauty
The ladder the backbone
Of shimmering deity
Thought by thought
Beauty by beauty
Child stirring in the web of your mother
Do not be afraid
Old man turning to walk through the door
Do not be afraid

2000

Joy Harjo sings a version of this poem, in both Creek and English, on her CD *Winding through the Milky Way*. In the song, she repeats and expands the poem's concluding lines:

> The red dawn will carry you home
> Cover you with a blanket of beauty
> Child stirring in the web of your mother
> Don't be afraid
> Old man turning to walk through the door
> Don't be afraid
> Do not be afraid.

RITA DOVE
b. 1952

RITA DOVE'S POETRY is remarkable for its nuanced and beautifully observed exploration of the lives of ordinary people. She is drawn toward what she calls "'the underside of history,' the dramas of ordinary people—the quiet courage of their actions, all which buoy up the big events." Dove was for many years a student of the cello (she now plays viola da gamba), and her poems have a graceful musicality that, combined with her quietly inventive approach to metaphor and her deftly suggestive hand at characterization and storytelling, lends a luminous aura to the scenes of daily life and family intimacy that are the frequent subjects of her verse. She has often been praised for the skill with which she weaves African-American experience into the broader fabric of American life.

Dove was born in Akron, Ohio, and she continues to identify with what she terms "a certain attitude and inflection—that Midwestern, flat, no-nonsense tone—that's part of me, too." She grew up in a supportive family, and both her father, Ray Dove, a chemist, and her mother, Elvira, a homemaker, encouraged Dove's early tendency toward voracious reading and intellectual discovery. Dove's three-part sequence "Adolescence" explores a teenage girl's dawning awareness of her emerging womanhood. An outstanding student, Dove received a B.A. from Miami University and was awarded a Fulbright Fellowship to attend the University of Tübingen in West Germany before completing an M.F.A. at the University of Iowa Writers' Workshop in 1977. She married the German-born writer Fred Viebahn in 1979. In 1987, Dove won the Pulitzer Prize—only the second such award for an African-American poet—for her breakthrough volume *Thomas and Beulah* (1986), a book-length poetic sequence based on the lives of her maternal grandparents, who settled in Akron and began to raise a family early in the twentieth century. The first part of the sequence, "Mandolin," offers glimpses of the life of Thomas, the poet's maternal grandfather. The second and final segment of the sequence, "Canary in Bloom," explores moments in the life of her maternal grandmother, Beulah.

From 1993 to 1995, Dove was the first African-American poet to serve as the nation's Poet Laureate (although Gwendolyn Brooks had served in 1985–86 under the earlier, less euphonious title Poetry Consultant to the Library of Congress). From 1981 to 1989, Dove taught at Arizona State University. In 1989 she took a teaching post at University of Virginia, where she currently holds an endowed chair as Commonwealth Professor of English.

FURTHER READING

Rita Dove. *American Smooth*. New York: Norton, 2004.
———. *Mother Love*: New York: Norton, 1995.
———. *On the Bus with Rosa Parks*. New York: Norton, 1999.
———. *Selected Poems*. New York: Vintage, 1993.
———. *Sonata Mulattica*. New York: Norton, 2009.
———. *Thomas and Beulah*. Pittsburgh: Carnegie Mellon Press, 1986.

Adolescence—I

In water-heavy nights behind grandmother's porch
We knelt in the tickling grass and whispered:
Linda's face hung before us, pale as a pecan,
And it grew wise as she said:
        "A boy's lips are soft,
        As soft as baby's skin."
The air closed over her words.
A firefly whirred in the air, and in the distance
I could hear streetlamps ping
Into miniature suns
Against a feathery sky.

Adolescence—II

Although it is night, I sit in the bathroom, waiting.
Sweat prickles behind my knees, the baby-breasts are alert.
Venetian blinds slice up the moon; the tiles quiver in pale strips.

Then they come, the three seal men with eyes as round
As dinner plates and eyelashes like sharpened tines.
They bring the scent of licorice. One sits in the washbowl,
One on the bathtub edge; one leans against the door.
"Can you feel it yet?" they whisper.
I don't know what to say, again. They chuckle,

Patting their sleek bodies with their hands.
"Well, maybe next time." And they rise,
Glittering like pools of ink under moonlight,

        ✳   ✳   ✳

And vanish. I clutch at the ragged holes
They leave behind, here at the edge of darkness.
Night rests like a ball of fur on my tongue.

Adolescence—III

With Dad gone, Mom and I worked
The dusky rows of tomatoes.
As they glowed orange in sunlight
And rotted in shadows, I too
Grew orange and softer, swelling out
Starched cotton slips.

The texture of twilight made me think of
Lengths of Dotted Swiss. In my room
I wrapped scarred knees in dresses
That once went to big-band dances;
I baptized my earlobes with rosewater.
Along the window-sill, the lipstick stubs
Glittered in their steel shells.

Looking out at the rows of clay
And chicken manure, I dreamed how it would happen;
He would meet me by the blue spruce,
A carnation over his heart, saying,
"I have come for you, Madam;
I have loved you in my dreams."
At his touch, the scabs would fall away.
Over his shoulder, I see my father coming toward us:
He carries his tears in a bowl,
And blood hangs in the pine-soaked air.

1980

FROM Thomas and Beulah

The Event

Ever since they'd left the Tennessee ridge
with nothing to boast of
but good looks and a mandolin,

the two Negroes leaning
on the rail of a riverboat
were inseparable: Lem plucked

to Thomas' silver falsetto.
But the night was hot and they were drunk.
They spat where the wheel

churned mud and moonlight,
they called to the tarantulas
down among the bananas

to come out and dance.
You're so fine and mighty; let's see
what you can do, said Thomas, pointing

to a tree-capped island.
Lem stripped, spoke easy: Them's chestnuts,
I believe. Dove

quick as a gasp. Thomas, dry
on deck, saw the green crown shake
as the island slipped

under, dissolved
in the thickening stream.
At his feet

a stinking circle of rags,
the half-shell mandolin.
Where the wheel turned the water

gently shirred.

1986

The Zeppelin Factory

The zeppelin factory
needed workers, all right—
but, standing in the cage
of the whale's belly, sparks
flying off the joints
and noise thundering,
Thomas wanted to sit
right down and cry.

That spring the third
largest airship was dubbed
the biggest joke
in town, though they all
turned out for the launch.
Wind caught,
"The Akron" floated
out of control,

three men in tow—
one dropped
to safety, one
hung on but the third,
muscles and adrenalin
failing, fell
clawing
six hundred feet.

Thomas at night
in the vacant lot:
     Here I am, intact
     and faint-hearted.

Thomas hiding
his heart with his hat
at the football game, eyeing
the Goodyear blimp overhead:
     Big boy I know
     you're in there.

1986

Akron, Ohio, is the home of the Goodyear Company. Dove's grandfather, Thomas, worked at the factory on the famous blimps.

Weathering Out

She liked mornings the best—Thomas gone
to look for work, her coffee flushed with milk,

outside autumn trees blowsy and dripping.
Past the seventh month she couldn't see her feet

so she floated from room to room, houseshoes flapping,
navigating corners in wonder. When she leaned

against a door jamb to yawn, she disappeared entirely.

Last week they had taken a bus at dawn
to the new airdock. The hangar slid open in segments

and the zeppelin nosed forward in its silver envelope.
The men walked it out gingerly, like a poodle,

then tied it to a mast and went back inside.
Beulah felt just that large and placid, a lake;

she glistened from cocoa butter smoothed in
when Thomas returned every evening nearly

in tears. He'd lean an ear on her belly
and say: *Little fellow's really talking,*

though to her it was more the *pok-pok-pok*
of a fingernail tapping a thick cream lampshade.

Sometimes during the night she woke and found him
asleep there and the child sleeping, too.

The coffee was good but too little. Outside
everything shivering in tinfoil—only the clover

between the cobblestones hung stubbornly on,
Green as an afterthought. . . .

1986

The House on Bishop Street

No front yard to speak of,
just a porch cantilevered on faith
where she arranged the canary's cage.
The house stayed dark all year
though there was instant light and water.
(No more gas jets hissing,

their flicker glinting off
Anna Rettich's midwife spectacles
as she whispered *think a baby*
and the babies came.) Spring
brought a whiff of cherries, the kind
you boiled for hours in sugar and cloves

from the yard of the Jewish family next door.
Yumanski refused to speak so
she never bought his vegetables
at the Canal Street Market. Gertrude,
his youngest and blondest,
slipped by mornings for bacon and grits.
There were summer floods and mildew

humming through fringe, there was
a picture of a ship she passed
on her way to the porch, strangers calling
from the street *Ma'am, your bird
shore can sing!* If she leaned out she could glimpse
the faintest of mauve—no more than an idea—
growing just behind the last houses.

                                    1986

Daystar

She wanted a little room for thinking:
but she saw diapers steaming on the line,
a doll slumped behind the door.

So she lugged a chair behind the garage
to sit out the children's naps.

             *   *   *

Sometimes there were things to watch—
the pinched armor of a vanished cricket,
a floating maple leaf. Other days

she stared until she was assured
when she closed her eyes
she'd only see her own vivid blood.

She had an hour, at best, before Liza appeared
pouting from the top of the stairs.
And just what was mother doing
out back with the field mice? Why,

building a palace. Later
that night when Thomas rolled over and
lurched into her, she would open her eyes
and think of the place that was hers
for an hour—where
she was nothing,
pure nothing, in the middle of the day.

1986

CHERRÍE MORAGA
b. 1952

A POET, PLAYWRIGHT, AND ESSAYIST, CHERRÍE MORAGA has helped found the
Chicana literary tradition in the United States. Her poems are at once deeply
personal and highly aware of their political and cultural significances. They con-
tribute to the developing body of writing by radical and queer women of color.
Early in her career, Moraga succeeded in inserting a strong Chicana voice into
a U.S. poetic tradition that had been dominated by white males. She also helped
break the silence about lesbian sexuality pervading a traditional Latino culture
that generally adhered to heterosexual norms. Moraga's poems are intensely introspective, exploring feelings of strangeness, exclusion, and frustration, as in
"The Slow Dance," and romantic joy, as in "Poema como Valentín." Moreover,
Moraga has blazed a new path in the discourse of race, class, gender, and sexuality. Her texts thus function as both a moving and revealing inward journey and
an effective agent of social change.

Moraga was born in Whittier, California, a suburb of Los Angeles. Her mother was a Chicana, with indigenous roots, and her father an Anglo. Brought up within her mother's extended family, she located herself culturally within the Chicana/o community. After receiving her B.A. in Los Angeles and working as a teacher for several years, she moved to San Francisco, where she devoted herself to creative and political writing. Moraga received her M.A. from San Francisco State University and edited, with Gloria Anzaldua, *This Bridge Called My Back*, a pioneering collection of essays by radical women of color. Moraga went on to publish numerous volumes of poems, essays, plays, and memoirs. She has taught at the University of California, Berkeley, and presently teaches creative writing and Chicana/o culture at Stanford. Her work has won numerous awards, including the Before Columbus American Book Award and the Fund for New American Plays Award. She lives in San Francisco with her son.

FURTHER READING

Bridget Kevane and Juanita Heredia. "City of Desire: An Interview with Cherríe Moraga." In *Latina Self-Portraits*, ed. Bridget Kevane and Juanita Heredia, 97–108. Albuquerque: University of New Mexico Press, 2000.

Yvonne Marbro-Bejarano. "Deconstructing the Lesbian Body: Cherríe Moraga's *Loving in the War Years*." In *Chicana Lesbians: The Girls Our Mothers Warned Us About*, ed. Carla Trujillo, 143–55. Berkeley: Third Woman Press, 1991.

Cherríe Moraga. *The Hungry Woman*. Albuquerque: West End Press, 2001.

———. *The Last Generation: Prose & Poetry*. Cambridge, Mass.: South End Press, 1993.

———. *Loving in the War Years*. Expanded edition. Cambridge, Mass.: South End Press, 2000.

Cherríe Moraga and Gloria Anzaldua, eds. *This Bridge Called My Back: Writings by Radical Women of Color*. Berkeley: Third Woman Press, 2002.

Rosemary Weatherston. "An Interview with Cherríe Moraga: Queer Reservations; or, Art, Identity, and Politics in the 1990s." *Queer Frontiers*, ed. Joseph A. Boone et al., 64–83. Madison: University of Wisconsin Press, 2000.

The Slow Dance

Thinking of Elena, Susan—watching them dance together. The images return to me, hold me, stir me, prompt me to want *something*.

Elena moving Susan around the floor, so in control of the knowledge: how to handle this woman, while I fumble around them. When Elena and I kissed, just once, I forgot and let too much want show, closing my eyes, all the eyes around me seeing me close my eyes. I am a girl wanting so much to kiss a woman. She sees this too, cutting the kiss short.

✼   ✼   ✼

But not with Susan, Susan's arm around Elena's neck. Elena's body all leaning into the center of her pelvis. *This is the way she enters a room*, leaning into the body of a woman.

The two of them, like grown-ups, like women. The women I silently longed for. Still, I remember after years of wanting and getting and loving, still I remember the desire to be that *in sync* with another woman's body.

And I move women around the floor, too—women I think enamored with me. My mother's words rising up from inside me—"A *real* man, when he dances with you, you'll know he's a *real* man by how he holds you in the back." I think, *yes*, someone who can guide you around a dance floor and so, I do. Moving these women kindly, surely, even superior. *I can handle these women*. They want this. And I do too.

Thinking of my father, how so timidly he used to take my mother onto the small square of carpet we reserved for dancing, pulling back the chairs. She really leading the step, him learning to cooperate so it *looked* like a male lead. I noticed his hand, how it lingered awkwardly about my mother's small back, his thin fingers never really getting a hold on her.

I remember this as I take a woman in my arms, my hand moving up under her shoulder blade, speaking to her from there. It is from *this* spot, the dance is directed. From *this* place, I tenderly, with each fingertip, move her.

I am my mother's lover. The partner she's been waiting for. I can handle whatever you got hidden. I can provide for you.

But when I put this provider up against the likes of Elena, *I* am the one following/falling into her. Like Susan, taken up in the arms of this woman. *I want this.*

Catching the music shift; the beat softens, slows down, I search for Elena— the bodies, the faces. *I am ready for you now.* I want age, knowledge. *Your body that still, after years, withholds and surrenders—keeps me there, waiting, wishing.* I push through the bodies, looking for her. Willing. Willing to feel *this time* what disrupts in me. Girl. Woman. Child. Boy. Willing to embody what I will in the space of her arms. Looking for Elena. I'm willing, wanting.

And I find you dancing with this other woman. My body both hers and yours in the flash of a glance.

* * *

I can handle this.

I am used to being an observer.
I am used to not getting what I want.
I am used to imagining what it must be like.

1983

Poema como Valentín

(or a San Francisco Love Poem)

An artist friend
once showed me how to see

color as a black & white
phenomenon.

Look. See that broad-faced glistening leaf?
Look. See where it is white, a light
magnet to the sun?
Look. See where it is black?

The eye narrows into a pinpoint focus
of what was never
green, really
only light condensing
into dark.

You could paint a portrait
this way, seeing
from black to white.

Her mouth would still
be rose and round
but less tired of explaining

itself

and as I pressed mine to it
it could remember no mouth
even vaguely reminiscent
no mouth with this particular
blend of wet and warm

in the darkest and fullest
place that sustains me

while all the world of this city weeps
beneath a blanket
of intercepted

light.

1993

The title of this love poem, which is in Spanish, might be translated, "Poem as valentine,"
though there is no exact equivalent of the word *valentine* in Spanish.

NAOMI SHIHAB NYE
b. 1952

ONE OF THE MAJOR VOICES in contemporary American literature, Naomi
Shihab Nye is renowned for her fiction, songs, and videos as well as her poetry.
She is often compared with Gary Snyder as a poet of spirituality and nature.
Nye's mentor, the poet William Stafford, has praised her poetry for its "transcen-
dent" vividness, warmth, and human insight. Her poems celebrate dailiness,
cultural hybridity, and the inner life.

Nye is a notable peace activist and has been named a peace hero by Peaceby
Peace.com. Currently a chancellor of the American Academy of Poets, she has
traveled extensively in the Middle East and Asia. In addition to reflecting on her
long residence in Texas and the American Southwest, her poetry also negotiates
Palestinian, German, and Swiss cultures. Nye has received many awards and
honors, including the Isabella Gardner Poetry Award, four Pushcart Prizes, a
Guggenheim fellowship, and the Academy of American Poets' Lavan Award.

Nye was born in St. Louis, Missouri, to a Palestinian-American father and
a German-Swiss-American mother. Her father, Aziz Shihab, is the author of *A
Taste of Palestine: Menus and Memories*. She spent much of her adolescence
in Ramallah, Jordan; the Old City in Jerusalem; and San Antonio, Texas. She
received her bachelor's degree from Trinity University in San Antonio, where
she lives now. Nye's creative productions often meditate on her Palestinian-
American heritage and on a multicultural, multinational awareness of the contemporary world.

FURTHER READING

Ibis Gomez-Vega. "Extreme Realities: Naomi Shihab Nye's Essays and Poems." *Alif: Journal of Comparative Poetics* 30 (2010): 109–33.
Bill Moyers. "NOW Transcript: Naomi Shihab Nye: A Bill Moyers Interview." www.pbs.gov.
Naomi Shihab Nye. *Honeybee! Poems & Short Prose*. New York: HarperCollins, 2008.
———. *There Is No Long Distance Now: Very Short Stories*. Greenwillow Books, 2011.
Gregory Orfalea. "Doomed by Our Blood to Care: The Poetry of Naomi Shihab Nye." *Paintbrush* 18.35 (Spring 1991): 56–66.

The Small Vases from Hebron

Tip their mouths open to the sky.
Turquoise, amber,
the deep green with fluted handle,
pitcher the size of two thumbs,
tiny lip and graceful waist.

Here we place the smallest flower
which could have lived invisibly
in loose soil beside the road,
sprig of succulent rosemary,
bowing mint.

They grow deeper in the center of the table.

Here we entrust the small life,
Thread, fragment, breath.
And it bends. It waits all day.
As the bread cools and the children
open their gray copybooks
to shape the letter that looks like
a chimney rising out of a house.

And what do the headlines say?

Nothing of the smaller petal
perfectly arranged inside the larger petal
or the way tinted glass filters light.
Men and boys, praying when they died,
fall out of their skins.
The whole alphabet of living,
heads and tails of words,

sentences, the way they said,
"Ya'Allah!" when astonished,
or "ya'ani" for "I mean"—
a crushed glass under the feet
still shines.
But the child of Hebron sleeps
with the thud of her brothers falling
and the long sorrow of the color red.

1998

In "The Small Vases from Hebron," Nye draws upon her Palestinian family background as well as her time spent in the Middle East. Hebron, an ancient city in the West Bank of the Palestinian territories and a place sacred to both Muslims and Jews, has been the focus of tension between the Israelis and Palestinians since the 1967 Arab-Israeli War.

ALBERTO RÍOS
b. 1952

A<small>LBERTO</small> R<small>ÍOS</small> was raised in Nogales, Arizona, on the U.S.–Mexican border in the Sonoran Desert. His poetry recreates what he has called "a place of exchange," a threshold space that "reckons with the world a little differently." His poems of childhood memory evoke various kinds of "in-between" states—between the English and Spanish languages, American and Mexican cultures, childhood and puberty (in "Madre Sofía"), and life and death (in "Mi Abuelo"). Ríos is a famously close observer of people and places, but he also departs from everyday reality to suggest eerie, haunted experiences. He employs a style of "magical realism," a Latin American mode of combining empirically accurate detail with dreamlike ones to locate imaginative and emotional truths that lie hidden beneath surfaces. Ríos's memory poems—on the border between fantasy and reality, between inward consciousness and outward appearance—transform childhood experience into a realm that is rich and strange.

Ríos's father was born in Chiapas, Mexico, and his mother immigrated to the United States from Lancashire, England. His paternal grandfather, whose presence is recalled in "Mi Abuelo," participated in the struggle for democracy during the Mexican revolution of 1910–20. Ríos initially spoke both English and Spanish, but he lost much of his Spanish in grade school, only relearning it later on. He received bachelor's degrees in English and psychology, and an M.F.A. in creative writing, all from the University of Arizona. He is now Regents Professor of English at Arizona State University. In addition to poetry, Ríos writes short fiction and memoir. His writing has won the Walt Whitman Award, the Western Literature Association's Distinguished Achievement Award, and the Latino Hall of Fame Award. His work has been adapted to both dance and music.

FURTHER READING

Sheilah Britton. "Discovering the Alphabet of Life." *Research magazine* 11.2 (1997); http://researchmag.asu.edu/articles/alphabet.html.
Susan McInnis. "Interview with Alberto Rios." *Glimmer Train* 26 (1998): 105–21.
Alberto Ríos. *Capirotada: A Nogales Memoir.* Albuquerque: University of New Mexico Press, 1999.
———. *The Curtain of Trees: Stories.* Albuquerque: University of New Mexico Press, 1999.
———. *The Dangerous Shirt.* Port Townsend, Wash.: Copper Canyon Press, 2009.
———. *The Smallest Muscle in the Human Body.* Port Townsend, Wash.: Copper Canyon Press, 2002.
———. *Whispering to Fool the Wind.* New York: Sheepmeadow Press, 1982.

Mi Abuelo

Where my grandfather is is in the ground
where you can hear the future
like a movie Indian with his ear at the tracks.
A pipe leads down to him so that sometimes
he whispers what will happen to a man
in town or how he will meet the best
dressed woman tomorrow and how the best
man at her wedding will chew the ground
next to her. Mi Abuelo[1] is the man
who speaks through all the mouths in my house.
An echo of me hitting the pipe sometimes
to stop him from saying *my hair is a*
sieve is the only other sound. It is a phrase
that among all others is the best,
he says, and *my hair is a sieve* is sometimes
repeated for hours out of the ground
when I let him, which is not often.
An abuelo should be much more than a man
like you! He stops then, and speaks: *I am a man*

---

1. "My Grandfather" (Spanish).

who has served ants with the attitude
of a waiter, who has made each smile as only
an ant who is fat can, and they liked me best,
but there is nothing left. Yet I know he ground
green coffee beans as a child, and sometimes
he will talk about his wife, and sometimes
about when he was deaf and a man
cured him by mail and he heard groundhogs
talking, or about how he walked with a cane
he chewed on when he got hungry.
At best, mi abuelo is a liar.
I see an old picture of him at nani's[2] with an
off-white yellow center mustache and sometimes
that's all I know for sure. He talks best
about these hills, *slowest waves*, and where this man
is going, and I'm convinced his hair is a sieve,
that his fever is cooled now underground.
Mi Abuelo is an ordinary man.
I look down the pipe, sometimes, and see a
ripple-topped stream in his best suit, in the ground.

1982

Ríos told a student asking about the poem that "my grandfather, whose name was Margarito, had quite a history, fighting in the Mexican Revolution on the side of Álvaro Obregón." He also explained, "This poem is really a personal poem, and the references in it—for example, to the ants—come from when I first visited his grave as a child. He is buried in San Luis Potosí, in Mexico, and when I stood at this gravesite with my parents, from my child's eye view I saw an anthill right on the top of his grave. It made me think that the ants were going down into his grave and, who knows, maybe eating him. As a child it made quite an impression on me."

Madre Sofía

My mother took me because she couldn't
wait the second ten years to know.
This was the lady rumored to have been
responsible for the box-wrapped baby
among the presents at that wedding,
but we went in, anyway, through the curtains.

2. "Grandma's" (Spanish).

Loose jar-top, half turned
and not caught properly in the threads,
her head sat mimicking its original intention
like the smile of a child hitting himself.
Central in that head grew unfamiliar poppies
from a face mahogany, eyes half yellow
half gray at the same time, goat and fog,
slit eyes of the devil, his tweed suit, red
lips, and she smelled of smoke, cigarettes,
but a diamond smoke, somehow; I inhaled
sparkles, I could feel them, throat, stomach.
She did not speak, and as a child
I could only answer, so that together
we were silent, cold and wet, dry and hard:
from behind my mother pushed me forward.
The lady put her hand on the face
of a thin animal wrap, tossing that head
behind her to be pressured incredibly
as she sat back in the huge chair and leaned.
And then I saw the breasts as large as her
head, folded together, coming out of her dress
as if it didn't fit, not like my mother's.
I could see them, how she kept them
penned up, leisurely, in maroon feed bags,
horse nuzzles of her wide body,
but exquisitely penned up
circled by pearl reins[1] and red scarves.
She lifted her arm, but only with the tips
of her fingers motioned me to sit opposite.
She looked at me but spoke to my mother
words dark, smoky like the small room,
words coming like red ants stepping occasionally
from a hole on a summer day in the valley,
red ants from her mouth, her nose, her ears,
tears from the corners of her cinched[2] eyes.
And suddenly she put her hand full on my head
pinching tight again with those finger tips
like a television healer, young Oral Roberts[3]

1. Straps.
2. Tightened, bound.

3. Television evangelist and faith healer (1918–
2009).

A triangle of sunlight
Was stretched out
On the floor
Like a rug
Like a tired cat.
It flared in
From the window
Through a small hole
Shaped like a yawn.
Strange I thought
And placed my hand
Before the opening,
But the sunlight
Did not vanish.
I pulled back
The shutters
And the room glowed,
But this pyramid
Of whiteness
Was simply brighter.
The sunlight around it
Appeared soiled
Like the bed sheet
Of a borracho.[2]
Amazed, I locked the door,
Closed the windows.
Workers, in from
The fields, knocked
To be let in,
Children peeked
Through the shutters,
But I remained silent.
I poured a beer,
At a table
Shuffled a pack
Of old cards,
And watched it
Cross the floor,
Hang on the wall

2. "Drunkard" (Spanish).

Like a portrait
Like a calendar
Without numbers.
When a fly settled
In the sunlight
And disappeared
In a wreath of smoke,
I tapped it with the broom,
Spat on it.
The broom vanished.
The spit sizzled.
It is the truth, little one.
I stood eye to blank eye
And by misfortune
This finger
This pink stump
Entered the sunlight,
Snapped off
With a dry sneeze,
And fell to the floor
As a gift
To the ants
Who know me
For what I gave.

1978

"The Tale of Sunlight" comes from a sequence of poems spoken by a character named Manuel Zaragoza, a bartender at a village cantina in the state of Guerrero, Mexico. Manuel has suffered loss and pain in his life, including the death of his wife in childbirth, but he remains perceptive and hopeful. This poem may be regarded as an example of either "magical realism" or psychological realism. "Magical realism" is a term associated with such Latin American fiction writers as Jorge Luis Borges and Gabriel García Márquez. In such writing, supernatural or mythic elements coexist with a realistic atmosphere in order to reach a deeper plane of reality.

A Red Palm

You're in this dream of cotton plants.
You raise a hoe, swing, and the first weeds
Fall with a sigh. You take another step,

———. *Sweet Machine.* New York: HarperCollins, 1998.
David R. Jarraway. "Creatures of the Rainbow: Wallace Stevens, Mark Doty, and the Poetics of Androgyny." *Mosaic* 30.3 (September 1997): 169–83.

A *Display of Mackerel*

They lie in parallel rows,
on ice, head to tail,
each a foot of luminosity

barred with black bands,
which divide the scales'
radiant sections

like seams of lead
in a Tiffany window.
Iridescent, watery

prismatics: think abalone,
the wildly rainbowed
mirror of a soapbubble sphere,

think sun on gasoline.
Splendor, and splendor,
and not a one in any way

distinguished from the other
—nothing about them
of individuality. Instead

they're *all* exact expressions
of the one soul,
each a perfect fulfillment

of heaven's template,
mackerel essence. As if,
after a lifetime arriving

at this enameling, the jeweler's
made uncountable examples,
each as intricate

*   *   *

in its oily fabulation
as the one before.
Suppose we could iridesce,

like these, and lose ourselves
entirely in the universe
of shimmer—would you want

to be yourself only,
unduplicatable, doomed
to be lost? They'd prefer,

plainly, to be flashing participants,
multitudinous. Even now
they seem to be bolting

forward, heedless of stasis.
They don't care they're dead
and nearly frozen,

just as, presumably,
they didn't care that they were living:
all, all for all,

the rainbowed school
and its acres of brilliant classrooms,
in which no verb is singular,

or every one is. How happy they seem,
even on ice, to be together, selfless,
which is the price of gleaming.

                                            1995

The Embrace

You weren't well or really ill yet either;
just a little tired, your handsomeness
tinged by grief or anticipation, which brought
to your face a thoughtful, deepening grace.

I didn't for a moment doubt you were dead.
I knew that to be true still, even in the dream.

You'd been out—at work maybe?—
having a good day, almost energetic.

We seemed to be moving from some old house
where we'd lived, boxes everywhere, things
in disarray: that was the story of my dream,
but even asleep I was shocked out of narrative

by your face, the physical fact of your face:
inches from mine, smooth-shaven, loving, alert.
Why so difficult, remembering the actual look
of you? Without a photograph, without strain?

So when I saw your unguarded, reliable face,
your unmistakable gaze opening all the warmth
and clarity of you—warm brown tea—we held
each other for the time the dream allowed.

Bless you. You came back, so I could see you
once more, plainly, so I could rest against you
without thinking this happiness lessened anything,
without thinking you were alive again

1998

HARRYETTE MULLEN
b. 1953

Harryette mullen's poetry explores the cultural politics of language. Her poems often juxtapose words according to an arbitrary formula, such as a letter of the alphabet ("I've just returned from Kenya and Korea"), or they tear words apart to reveal new words within ("yell ow"). These juxtapositions and deconstructions expose new social resonances and ideological links. The poems display humor and sparkle as well as an aura of foreboding and discontent. They avoid the autobiographical "I" of traditional lyric poetry, and yet a personal perspective definitely arises amid the verbal play.

Mullen's work bears comparison to that of other postmodernist poets influenced by the Language poetry movement, such as Lyn Hejinian, Rae Armantrout,

Charles Bernstein, and Amy Gerstler. Her work also bears comparison to the projects of other feminists and poets of color, such as Gwendolyn Brooks, Adrienne Rich, Michael Harper, Wanda Coleman, Nathaniel Mackey, and Lorna Dee Cervantes. Mullen's poetry exposes a range of multiple meanings within each verbal unit while maintaining a critical perspective on social and cultural phenomena. It plays with language and form to refresh poetic practice and to get at issues of gender, race, and sexuality that otherwise remain hidden.

Mullen has described her desires as a poet as being contradictory: "I aspire to write poetry that would leave no insurmountable obstacle to comprehension and pleasure other than the ultimate limits of the reader's interest and linguistic competence. However, I do not necessarily approach this goal by employing a beautiful, pure, simple, or accessible literary language, or by maintaining a clear, consistent, recognizable, or authentic voice in my work. . . . One reason I have avoided a singular style or voice for my poetry is the possibility of including a diverse audience of readers attracted to different poems and different aspects of the work."

Mullen was born in Florence, Alabama, and raised in Fort Worth, Texas. She received a B.A. in English from the University of Texas in 1975 and a Ph.D. in literature from the University of California, Santa Cruz, in 1990. Early in her career, she worked in the Artists in Schools program sponsored by the Texas Commission on the Arts. For six years she taught African-American and other U.S. ethnic literatures at Cornell University. Now residing in Los Angeles, she is a professor of English at UCLA. The author of critical essays as well as poetry, Mullen has won many awards, including the Gertrude Stein Award, in acknowledgment of her witty and original work.

FURTHER READING

Calvin Bedient. "The Solo Mysterioso Blues: An Interview with Harryette Mullen." *Callaloo* 19.3 (1996): 651–69.

Elizabeth A. Frost. "*Sleeping with the Dictionary*: Harryette Mullen's 'Recyclopedia.'" In *American Women Poets in the 21st Century: Where Lyric Meets Language*, ed. Claudia Rankine and Juliana Spahr, 405–24. Middletown, Conn.: Wesleyan University Press, 2002.

Harryette Mullen. "African Signs and Spirit Writing." *Callaloo* 19.3 (1996): 670–89.

———. "Imagining the Unimagined Reader." In *American Women Poets in the 21st Century: Where Lyric Meets Language*, ed. Claudia Rankine and Juliana Spahr, 403–5. Middletown, Conn.: Wesleyan University Press, 2002.

———. *Recyclopedia: Trimmings, S*PeRM**K*T, and Muse & Drudge*. Minneapolis: Graywolf Press, 2006.

———. *Sleeping with the Dictionary*. Berkeley: University of California Press, 2002.

Amy Moorman Robbins. "Harryette Mullen's *Sleeping with the Dictionary* and Race in Language/Writing." *Contemporary Literature* 51.2 (Summer 2010): 341–70.

All She Wrote

Forgive me, I'm no good at this. I can't write back. I never read your letter. I
can't say I got your note. I haven't had the strength to open the envelope. The
mail stacks up by the door. Your hand's illegible. Your postcards were defaced.
"Wash your wet hair"? Any document you meant to send has yet to reach me.
The untied parcel service[1] never delivered. I regret to say I'm unable to reply
to your unexpressed desires. I didn't get[2] the book you sent. By the way, my
computer was stolen. Now I'm unable to process words. I suffer from aphasia.[3]
I've just returned from Kenya and Korea. Didn't you get a card from me yet?
What can I tell you? I forgot what I was going to say. I still can't find a pen that
works and then I broke my pencil. You know how scarce paper is these days.
I admit I haven't been recycling. I never have time to read the *Times*.[4] I'm out
of shopping bags to put the old news in. I didn't get to the market. I meant to
clip the coupons. I haven't read the mail yet. I can't get out the door to work,
so I called in sick. I went to bed with writer's cramp.[5] If I couldn't get back to
writing, I thought I'd catch up on my reading. Then *Oprah* came on with a
fabulous author plugging her best-selling book.[6]

2002

"All She Wrote" sympathetically yet mockingly expresses contemporary failures of contact. In the first part of this prose poem, the speaker cannot or will not receive communications from others. She then begins to lose the ability to communicate herself, suffering
from broken writing implements, a scarcity of paper, and writer's cramp. By the end, she
can neither read nor write, preferring to watch an author plug her book on TV than to
actually read a book. Mullen has commented on the linguistic and cultural context for
much of her writing: "It would be accurate to say that my poetry explores the reciprocity
of language and culture."

Coo-Slur

da red
yell ow
bro won t
an orange you

1. Verbal play on United Parcel Service (UPS).
2. A pun on two senses of the word: receive and understand.
3. The loss of the ability to use words as symbols of ideas, often resulting from a brain injury.
4. Note the pun on time and *Times*.
5. Part of the joke is that writer's cramp doesn't require bed rest like some other "diseases," and part is the double entendre of the phrase "went to bed with."
6. Oprah Winfrey featured many authors in the "Book Club" segment of her television show between 1996 and 2011.

bay jaun[1]
pure people
blew hue
a gree gree in
viol let
purepeople
be lack
why it
pee ink

2002

The title "Coo-Slur" indicates that this poem may have some connection to "color," "coo-ing" (sounds of affection), the "slurring" (or blurring) of speech, and the racial "slur" (or insult). Elizabeth Frost has written that Mullen "asserts the power of language to shape the subject and examines the politics of race through the history and evolution of words." In this case, Mullen examines racial issues through the words that accidentally reside in or near other words. For example, "da red" may be interpreted as "the red" in African-American dialect or as a broken version of the word "dared." "Brown" turns into such variants as "bro won," "bro won't," "brown not," and "brownout." "Black," "white," and "pink" acquire cultural complexities when revised as "be lack," "why it," and "pee ink."

Natural Anguish

Every anguish is arbitrary but no one is neuter.[1] Bulldozer can knock down dikes.[2] Why a ragged bull don't demolish the big house? The fired cook was deranged.[3] On the way back when I saw red I thought ouch. Soon when I think colored someone bleeds. The agency tapping my telephone heard my pen drop. Now I'm walking out[4] of pink ink. We give microphones to the voice-less to amplify their silence. The complete musician could play any portion of the legacy of the instrument. My ebony's under the ocean.[5] Please bring back my bone (sic) to me. Once was illegal for we to testify. Now all us do is testify.

---

1. *Jaune* is French for "yellow." San Juan Bay is a coastal feature in Puerto Rico.
1. Perhaps a pun on "neutral."
2. Earthen barriers, stone walls, or levees; but also possibly a pun on the slang term "dykes," indicating self-assertive lesbians.
3. Mentally unbalanced, but also a joke referring to a cooking range.
4. As one walks out of a play or performance, but also perhaps a twist on the phrase "running out."

5. Perhaps a reference to the Middle Passage of African people from Africa to the New World as part of the Atlantic slave trade. This sentence and the next also parody the traditional Scottish folk song "My Bonnie Lies over the Ocean," which begins, "My Bonnie lies over the ocean / My Bonnie lies over the sea / My Bonnie lies over the ocean / Please bring back my Bonnie to me."

We's all prisoners of our own natural anguish. It's the rickety rickshaw[6] that will
drive us to the brink.

2002

"Natural Anguish" casts an ironic light on social iniquities while illustrating the poet's
avoidance of a consistent voice or a continuous argument.

GJERTRUD SCHNACKENBERG

b. 1953

GJERTRUD SCHACKENBERG'S POETRY offers a poignant exploration of lost
worlds, a probing into the partly forgotten, partly remembered world of private
and public history. Her work explores memory, surviving artifacts, documents,
published accounts, and other myths and records to recover that which is recoverable from the "lost world" of the past, and to contemplate the problem of that
which is not recoverable. For her, the death of loved ones, the loss and potential
recovery of religious faith, isolation, death, and the sheer destructive weight of
time are the forces against which her poetry struggles while trying to create what
Robert Frost termed "a momentary stay against confusion." Her work tends to
exist in a natural or architectural space that helps to define and circumscribe
each poem's quest. It is largely through her epistemologically sophisticated engagement with the gap between the past and the present, and all the crowded
information, activity, and emotion that exists (or may once have existed) on both
sides of that ever-moving dividing line, that her work derives its power and rel-
evance. In this way her poetry, despite its frequently traditional or formal look, is
powerfully contemporary.

Schnackenberg was born in Tacoma, Washington, where her father, Walter
Charles Schnackenberg (1917–1973), a noted scholar, taught Russian and medieval history at Pacific Lutheran University. An outstanding student, Schnackenberg graduated from Mount Holyoke College in 1975. She has lived in Italy (a
significant locale for her later poetry) and Tacoma, and she currently resides in
Cambridge, Massachusetts. In 1987, she married the eminent Harvard philosophy professor Robert Nozick, who died in 2002. Critic Rachel Wetzsteon has
described Schnackenberg as "a poet of great emotional power, immense formal
skill, and formidable learning."

6. Nineteenth-century Japanese vehicle for one passenger pulled by a man.

FURTHER READING

Gjertrud Schnackenberg. *Portraits and Elegies*. Boston: Godine, 1982; revised edition, New York: Farrar, Straus & Giroux, 1986.
———. *Supernatural Love: Poems, 1976–1992*. New York: Farrar, Straus & Giroux, 2000.
———. *The Throne of Labdacus*. New York: Farrar, Straus & Giroux, 2000.
Rachel Wetzsteon. "Schnackenberg, Gjertrud." In *The Greenwood Encyclopedia of American Poets and Poetry*, vol. 5, ed. Jeffrey Gray, James McCorkle, and Mary McAleer Balkun, 1427–29. Westport, Conn.: Greenwood Press, 2006.

FROM "Laughing with One Eye"

Nightfishing

The kitchen's old-fashioned planter's clock portrays
A smiling moon as it dips down below
Two hemispheres, stars numberless as days,
And peas, tomatoes, onions, as they grow
Under that happy sky; but though the sands
Of time put on this vegetable disguise,
The clock covers its face with long, thin hands.
Another smiling moon begins to rise.

We drift in the small rowboat an hour before
Morning begins, the lake weeds grown so long
They touch the surface, tangling in an oar.
You've brought coffee, cigars, and me along.
You sit still, like a monument in a hall,
Watching for trout. A bat slices the air
Near us, I shriek, you look at me, that's all,
One long sobering look, a smile everywhere
But on your mouth. The mighty hills shriek back.
You turn back to the lake, chuckle, and clamp
Your teeth on your cigar. We watch the black
Water together. Our tennis shoes are damp.
Something moves on your thoughtful face, recedes.
Here, for the first time ever, I see how,
Just as a fish lurks deep in water weeds,
A thought of death will lurk deep down, will show
One eye, then quietly disappear in you.
It's time to go. Above the hills I see
The faint moon slowly dipping out of view,
Sea of Tranquility, Sea of Serenity,

Ocean of Storms . . .[1] You start to row, the boat
Skimming the lake where light begins to spread.
You stop the oars, midair. We twirl and float.

I'm in the kitchen. You are three days dead.
A smiling moon rises on fertile ground,
White stars and vegetables. The sky is blue.
Clock hands sweep by it all, they twirl around,
Pushing me, oarless, from the shore of you.

1982

"Nightfishing" is the first poem in Schnackenberg's sequence "Laughing with One Eye," and the poem that follows, "'There are no dead,'" is the twelfth and final poem in the sequence. "Laughing with One Eye" is a poignant memorial tribute to the poet's beloved father, who died at age fifty-six when the poet herself was twenty. In these elegiac poems, Schnackenberg's contemplation of time, history, and loss emerges naturally out of a consideration of her father's own engagement with history and of his disquieting mortality.

"There are no dead"

Outside, a phoebe whistles for its mate,
The rhododendron rubs its leaves against
Your office window: so the spring we sensed
You wouldn't live to see comes somewhat late.
Here, lying on the desk, your reading glasses,
And random bits of crimped tobacco leaves,
Your jacket dangling its empty sleeves—
These look as if you've just left for your classes.
The chess game is suspended on the board
In your mind's pattern, your wastebasket
Contains some crumpled papers, your filing cabinet
Is packed with years of writing working toward
A metaphysics of impersonal praise.
Here students came and went, here years would draw
Intensities of lines until we saw
Your face beneath an etching of your face.
How many students really cared to solve
History's riddles?—in hundreds on the shelves,
Where men trying to think about themselves
Must come to grips with grief that won't resolve,

1. The names of three *lunar maria*, which to the naked eye resemble the earth's seas.

Blackness of headlines in the daily news,
And buildings blown away from flights of stairs
All over Europe, thanks in empty squares,
The burning baby carriages of Jews.

Behind thin glass, a print hangs on the wall,
A detail from the Bayeux Tapestry.
As ignorant women gabbled incessantly,
Their red, sore hands stitched crudely to recall
Forests of ships, the star with streaming hair,
God at Westminster blessing the devout,[1]
They jabbed their thousand needles in and out,
Sometimes too busy talking to repair
The small mistakes; now the centuries of grease
And smoke that stained it, and the blind white moths
And grinning worm that spiraled through the cloth,
Say death alone makes life a masterpiece.

There[2] William of Normandy remounts his horse
A fourth time, four times desperate to drive
Off rumors of his death. His sword is drawn.
He swivels and lifts his visor up and roars,
Look at me well! For I am still alive!
Your glasses, lying on the desk, look on.

1982

ELMAZ ABINADER
b. 1954

ELMAZ ABINADER is a major poet, playwright, performer, and activist who currently lives and works in Oakland, California. In her work, she focuses on bringing Islamic and Christian cultures together, often focusing on the values of compassion, equity, and respect for the earth. While her poems are often a

1. Scenes from the Bayeux Tapestry, which provides a contemporary account of William of Normandy's quest for the English throne, his decisive victory at the Battle of Hastings in 1066, and his subsequent coronation at Westminster Abbey. The tapestry was stitched by seamstresses in Normandy and displayed annually in the cathedral in the Norman town of Bayeux.
2. That is, in the Bayeux Tapestry.

political intervention, they also address the divisions between private and public lives. Abinader won a PEN Award for her first volume of poetry, *In the Country of My Dreams*, and her book *Children of the Roojme* was the first memoir about Arab Americans to be published by a major press in the United States. In addition, she has written and performed plays and monologues such as *Country of Origin*, *The Torture Quartet*, and *Voice from the Siege*, accompanied by music by Tony Khalife.

Abinader was born and raised in a Lebanese family and community in the coal mining region near Pittsburgh, Pennsylvania. She earned her B.A. in writing from the University of Pittsburgh, her M.F.A. in poetry from Columbia University, and her Ph.D. in fiction from the University of Nebraska. While living in New York City, she taught and also worked in advertising. She is presently W. M. Keck Foundation Professor at Mills College in Oakland, California.

Abinader cofounded and works for the Voices of Our Nations Arts Foundation, a workshop for writers of color held on the campus of the University of San Francisco. In addition to a PEN award, she has also received a Schweitzer Postdoctoral Fellowship in the Humanities, two Drammies (Oregon Drama Critics Award), and a Goldies Award for Literature.

FURTHER READING

Elmaz Abinader. *Children of the Roojme: A Family's Journey from Lebanon.* Madison: University of Wisconsin Press, 1997.
———. *In the Country of My Dreams.* New York: Sufi Warrior Publishing, 1999.

In the Country of My Dreams

For Marcel Khalife and Khalil Gibran[1]

The tales my mother and father told me
are true: the apricots are as big
as oranges and bright as the sun.
Grapes stay on the vine from the wealth
of wine already inside them. The figs burst
as you walk through the groves,
begging for you to hold one
and admire the milk cracking their skin.
In the country of my dreams, my sixth grade
geography book explained: Long haired sheep

---

1. Marcel Khalife (b. 1950) is a Lebanese composer, singer, and oud player who is a UNESCO Artist for Peace. Khalil Gibran (1883–1931) was a Lebanese-American poet and author of *The Prophet* (1920). One of the first Arab-American poets, he was a founder of the Arab Renaissance and of modern Arabic literature.

roam the rocky terrain of Mt. Lebanon
and Mt. Sannin.[2] Oranges in huge bundles
are thrown onto carts pulled by donkeys
to travel west from the Bekaa Valley.[3]
Silk spins on spools and every woman's
fingers are blistered from piercing
her intricately embroidered fabric.

A 1945 *National Geographic* described it as
a small country bordered by Palestine
to the south, Syria to the north
and east. Peopled by Arabs, Christians,
Muslims, Jews, Druse,[4] Kurds, Armenians,
Bedouins, Europeans, everyone is welcome.
A tourist economy with a multi-lingual population.
Christ once walked its hillsides.

In the country of my dreams, the guide books
tell me, the ancients left their treasures
at Sido and Tyre,[5] that the Romans landed
their temples in Ba-albek,[6] that the sea
is the color of the finest jewels, lapis
and turquoise. Gold can be found
in the shops, on the arms of women,
in the teeth of men, hanging from the tiny
lobes of daughters, like pieces of stars.

Now the newspapers say, a fire burns
in the country of my dreams, wicked and consuming,
flying from the hands of soldiers, from the mouths
of children who have been raised by war. Smoldering
on the lips of mothers, heads bent praying
to God, to Allah, to anyone who will listen.
That we cannot travel freely and sanctioned.
We are dangerous to ourselves
and our friends.

2. Mountain in the Mount Lebanon Range, which bisects Lebanon on a north–south axis, dividing the port city of Beirut to the east from the Bekaa Valley to the west.
3. Valley in Lebanon, source of agricultural products.
4. Religious community located primarily in Syria, Lebanon, Israel, and Jordan.
5. Sido is south of Beirut, Lebanon. Tyre, the fourth largest city in Lebanon, is also south of Beirut.
6. Town in the Bekaa Valley, famous for its ruins of immense Roman temples.

✻   ✻   ✻

But they are not listening. In the country
of my dreams, no one plots invasions with
armies of soldiers. From the edge
of the sea, it's our poets who set sail,
mouths full of music, our painters and musicians,
artists and philosophers. Armed
with an infantry of voices, people rise
and sing, clap their hands and whirl
in circles and stamp,
shouting their name,
their country, signifying their cause.

At the beginning of the century, it is you,
Khalil,[7] who wracks our bodies
so completely, generations clutch
your words to steady their bosoms, year
after year, whisper your phrases at their weddings,
and cultivate gardens to commemorate your name
and no other's. At the end of the century, it is you,
Marcel,[8] who makes them leap up shouting in gospel,
clutching the hands of their children, dancing
with abandon, and calling out listen, we
are not alone, we do not forget.

To produce such warriors as these:
Gibran and Khalife, take a soil luscious
and fertile. A fact the books overlooked;
the newspapers failed to see. What we have
to fear from this country is the note held strong,
the stroke of the painter, the string of the oud,[9]
the beat of the drum, hand on skin, fingers
on flute, bells, language that sears our temples
and shakes the silence of memory, agitates
the stillness of history. And we have heroes,
whose instruments are aimed directly
at our hearts, who do not kill us,
but keep us alive.

1999

7. Khalil Gibran.   9. Arabic lute.
8. Marcel Khalife.

"In the Country of My Dreams" praises poet Khalil Gibran and musician Marcel Khalife for playing heroic roles in Lebanese culture, and it honors the beauty of the Lebanese nation. The poem also laments the violence and war that have periodically plagued Lebanon since 1975. Viewing Gibran and Khalife as countervailing forces who "keep us alive," the poem implicitly protests the prosecution of Khalife by Lebanese authorities in both 1996 and 1999 (and again in 2003, after this poem was written). Khalife, who faced up to three years in prison, was accused of "insulting religious values by using a verse from the chapter of Joseph [Yousef] from the Qur'an in a song." The accusation concerned Khalife's well-known song, "I am Joseph, O Father," based on a poem by Palestinian poet Marhoud Darwish. Defended by human rights organizations, writers, intellectuals, and many ordinary citizens, Khalife was ultimately found innocent.

LORNA DEE CERVANTES
b. 1954

A LEADING CONTEMPORARY POET, LORNA DEE CERVANTES writes poems that explore culture, language, and personal experience in complex and imagistic ways. Employing Spanish as well as English, she engages in an intertextual conversation with writers throughout the Americas. Her books bear epigraphs from cultural figures as diverse as Sylvia Plath (included in this anthology), Frida Kahlo (a Mexican visual artist), Violeta Parra (a Chilean poet), and T. S. Eliot (an Anglo-American poet). Although she has overcome economic, ethnic, and gender barriers, the memory of those struggles remains embedded in her work. Her vision encompasses past and present, intellect and feeling, feminism and multiculturalism, local concerns and global awareness.

Of mixed Mexican and Native American ancestry, Cervantes grew up with her brother and their single mother in a poor Mexican-American community near San Jose, California. Her mother cleaned houses for a living and brought home discarded books for her daughter to read. Cervantes began writing poems as a child, eventually publishing them in newspapers and magazines, and publishing her first book at twenty-seven. To protect her daughter from discrimination, her mother had forbidden her to speak Spanish as a child, and Cervantes's poems often reveal her wish to recover her linguistic and cultural legacy. Her poems also reflect the devastation she felt when her mother was brutally murdered in 1982.

Cervantes received her B.A. from San Jose State University and did graduate study at the University of California, Santa Cruz. After decades of teaching in the creative writing program at the University of Colorado, Boulder, she returned to California, where she directs writing workshops in Berkeley and Santa Cruz. Although "a terror of rejection" has limited her publishing to only three books, her poetry has won many awards, including the American Book Award, the Paterson Poetry Prize, and a Lila Wallace–Reader's Digest Award.

Founded in memory and social observation, Cervantes's early poems, such as "Freeway 280," recall childhood landscapes, frustrated desires, and unrecognized moments of joy. Her later poems, such as "Drawings: For John Who Said to Write About True Love" and "For My Ancestors Adobed in the Walls of the Santa Barbara Mission," reveal a more densely textured, allusive, and wide-ranging approach. "Pleiades from the Cables of Genocide," for example, delves into a variety of stories and myths, revealing the cultural fusions that inevitably follow social change.

Cervantes's poems explore social and psychological borders. They alternately focus on love and loss, contemplation and activism, history and language. They create a new cultural vocabulary out of the social rifts and mergings that mark our time. Engaged with the personal life as well as with social realities, Cervantes's work aims to construct a new poetic identity and tradition.

FURTHER READING

Cordelia Candelaria. *Chicana Poetry: A Critical Introduction.* Westport, Conn.: Greenwood Press, 1986.
Lorna Dee Cervantes. Blog. http://lornadice.blogspot.com/.
———. *Drive: The First Quartet.* San Antonio: Wings Press, 2006.
———. *Emplumada.* Pittsburgh: University of Pittsburgh Press, 1981.
———. *From the Cables of Genocide: Poems on Love and Hunger.* Houston: Arte Público Press, 1991.
Sonia V. González. "Poetry Saved My Life: An Interview with Lorna Dee Cervantes." *MELUS* 32.1 (Spring 2007): 163–80.
Tey Diana Robelledo. *Women Singing in the Snow: A Cultural Analysis of Chicana Literature.* Albuquerque: University of New Mexico Press, 1995.
Edith Vasquez. "Poetry as Survival of and Resistance to Genocide in Lorna Dee Cervantes's *Drive: The First Quartet.*" *Journal of International Women's Studies* 10.4 (May 2009): 290–300. http://www.bridgew.edu/SOAS/jiws/May09/index.htm.

Freeway 280

Las casitas[1] near the gray cannery,
nestled amid wild abrazos[2] of climbing roses
and man-high red geraniums

---

1. Little houses (Spanish). 2. Embraces, bear hugs (Spanish).

are gone now. The freeway conceals it
all beneath a raised scar.

But under the fake windsounds of the open lanes,
in the abandoned lots below, new grasses sprout,
wild mustard remembers, old gardens
come back stronger than they were,
trees have been left standing in their yards.
Albaricoqueros, cerezos, nogales . . .[3]
Viejitas[4] come here with paper bags to gather greens.
Espinaca, verdolagas, yerbabuena . . .[5]

I scramble over the wire fence
that would have kept me out.
Once, I wanted out, wanted the rigid lanes
to take me to a place without sun,
without the smell of tomatoes burning
on swing shift in the greasy summer air.

Maybe it's here
en los campos extraños de esta ciudad[6]
where I'll find it, that part of me
mown under
like a corpse
or a loose seed.

1981

In this poem, the autobiographical speaker returns to the barrio where she grew up, which was then adjacent to a tomato canning factory but more recently has deteriorated beneath the shadow of a new freeway. In this changed yet familiar landscape, the speaker contemplates both loss and potential revival.

Meeting Mescalito at Oak Hill Cemetery

Sixteen years old and crooked
with drug, time warped blissfully
as I sat alone on Oak Hill.

*   *   *

3. Apricot, cherry, and walnut trees (Spanish).
4. Little old women (Spanish).

5. Spinach, purselane, mint (Spanish).
6. In the strange lands of this city (Spanish).

The cemetery stones were neither erect
nor stonelike, but looked soft and harmless;
thousands of them rippling the meadows
like overgrown daisies.

I picked apricots from the trees below
where the great peacocks roosted and nagged
loose the feathers from their tails.
I knelt to a lizard with my hands
on the earth, lifted him and held him in my palm—Mescalito
was a true god.

Coming home that evening
nothing had changed. I covered Mama on the sofa

with a quilt I sewed myself, locked my bedroom
door against the stepfather, and gathered
the feathers I'd found that morning, each
green eye in a heaven of blue, a fistful
of understanding;

and late that night I tasted
the last of the sweet fruit, sucked the rich pit
and thought nothing of death.

1981

Mescalito is slang for mescaline or peyote, an herbal medicine made from a Mexican cactus. It is used ceremonially by some Native American groups to produce visions and ecstatic feelings. The drug, which has some dangerous side effects, achieved wider popularity after the publication of Carlos Castaneda's *The Teaching of Don Juan: A Yaqui Way of Knowledge* (1968), in which the figure of Mescalito appears in visions as a kind and gentle "protector" god.

The Body as Braille

He tells me, "Your back
is so beautiful." He traces
my spine with his hand.

*   *   *

I'm burning like the white ring
around the moon. "A witch's moon,"
dijo mi abuela.[1] The schools call it

"a reflection of ice crystals."
It's a storm brewing in the cauldron
of the sky. I'm in love

but won't tell him
if it's omens
or ice.

                                        1981

Drawings: For John Who Said to Write About True Love

"The writer. It's a cul-de-sac," you wrote that
winter of our nation's discontent.[1] That first time
I found you, blue marble lying still in the trench, you, staked
in waiting for something, anything but the cell of your small
apartment with the fixtures never scrubbed, the seven great
named cats you gassed in the move. *I couldn't keep them.*
You explained so I understood. And what cat never loved
your shell-like ways, the claw of your steady fingers, *firme*[2]
from the rasping of banjos and steady as it goes
from the nose to the hair to the shaking tip. My favorite
tale was of the owl and the pussycat in love in a china cup[3]
cast at sea, or in a flute more brittle, more lifelike
and riddled with flair, the exquisite polish of its gaudy
glaze now puzzled with heat cracks, now foamed
opalescent as the single espresso dish you bought from
Goodwill. What ever becomes of the heart our common
child fashioned, red silk and golden satin, the gay glitter
fallen from moves, our names with *Love* written in black
felt pen? Who gets what? Who knows what becomes of the
rose you carried home from Spanish Harlem that morning
I sat waiting for the surgeon's suction. What ever becomes
of waiting and wanting, when the princess isn't ready and

1. My grandmother told me (Spanish).
1. Allusion to the opening lines of Shakespeare's
Richard III: "Now is the winter of our discontent
/ Made glorious summer by this son of York"
(1.1.1–2).

2. Firm or hard (Spanish).
3. Allusion to Edward Lear's nonsense song,
"The Owl and the Pussycat."

the queen has missed the boat, again? Do you still write
those old remarks etched on a page of Kandinsky's[4] ace
letting go? Like: *Lorna meets Oliver North[5] and she
kicks his butt.* The dates are immaterial to me as
salvation or a freer light bending through stallions
in an air gone heavy with underground tunnels. Do you
read me? Is there some library where you'll find me, smashed
on the page of some paper? *Let it go* is my morning mantra
gone blind with the saved backing of a clock, now dark
as an empty womb when I wake, now listening for your tick
or the sound of white walls on a sticky street. Engines out
the window remind me of breathing apparatus at the breaking
of new worlds, the crash and perpetual maligning of the sand
bar where sea lions sawed up logs for a winter cabin. I dream
wood smoke in the morning. I dream the rank and file of used
up chimneys, what that night must have smelled like, her mussed
and toweled positioning, my ambulance of heart through stopped
traffic where you picked the right corner to tell me: *They think
someone murdered her.* You were there, all right, you were
a statue carved from the stone of your birth. You were patient
as a sparrow under leaf and as calm as the bay those light
evenings when I envisioned you with the fishwife you loved.
And yes, I could have done it then, kissed it off, when the scalpel
of single star brightened and my world blazed, a dying bulb
for the finger of a socket, like our sunsets on the Cape, fallen
fish blood in snow, the hearts and diamonds we found and left
alone on a New England grave. Why was the summer so long
then? Even now a golden season stumps me and I stamp
ants on the brilliant iced drifts. I walk a steady mile
to that place where you left it, that solid gold band
thrown away to a riptide in a gesture the theatrical
love—so well. What was my role? Or did I leave it
undelivered when they handed me the gun of my triggered
smiles and taught me to cock it? Did I play it to the hilt
and bleeding, did I plunge in your lap and wake to find you
lonely in a ribbon of breathing tissue? Does this impudent
muscle die? Does love expire? Do eternal nestings mean much
more than a quill gone out or the spit? I spy the bank

4. Wassily Kandinsky (1866–1944), Russian abstract artist.

5. An American Marine involved in the Iran-Contra scandal of the late 1980s.

of frothed fog fuming with airbrushed pussies on a pink
horizon. I score my shoes with walking. My skill is losing.
It's what we do best, us ducks, us lessons on what not
to do.
Thanks for the crack,
you wrote
in my O.E.D.[6] that 30th renewal when the summer snapped
and hissed suddenly like a bullet of coal flung from a fire
place or a dumb swallow who dove into the pit for pay. Kiss
her, and it's good luck. I palm this lucky trade but the soot
never sells and I never sailed away on a gulf stream that divides
continents from ourselves. But only half of me is cracked, the
other is launched on a wild bob, a buoy, steadfast in storm. I may
sail to Asia or I might waft aimlessly to Spain where my hemp
first dried from the rain. My messages wring from the line,
unanswered, pressed sheets from an old wash or the impression
of a holy thing. But don't pull no science on this shroud, the
date will only lie. She'll tell you it's sacred, even sell you
a piece of the fray. She appears on the cracked ravines of this
country like a ghost on the windshield of an oncoming
train. She refuses to die, but just look at her nation
without a spare penny to change. My wear is a glass made
clean through misuse, the mishandling of my age as revealing
as my erased face, Indian head of my stick birth, my battle
buried under an island of snow I've yet to get to. What could I do
with this neighborhood of avenues scattered with empty shells
of mailboxes, their feet caked with cement like pulled up
pilings? Evidently, they haven't a word
for regret
full heart.
Someday, I said, I can write us both from this mess. But the key
stalls out from under me when I spell your name. I have to fake
the O or go over it again in the dark, a tracing of differences
spilled out on a sheet. If I could stick this back
together, would it stay? It's no rope, I know, and no good
for holding clear liquid. I gather a froth on my gums, and grin
the way an old woman grimaces in the morning mirror. I was never
a clear thing, never felt the way a daughter feels, never lost
out like you, never drove. My moon waits at the edge

6. *Oxford English Dictionary.*

of an eagle's aerie, almost extinct and the eggs are fragile
from poisoned ignitions. I'm never coming out from my cup
of tea, never working loose the grease in my hair, the monkey
grease from my dancing elbows that jab at your shoulder.
But I write, and wait for the book to sell, for I know
nothing comes of it but the past with its widening teeth,
with its meat breath baited at my neck, persistent as the smell
of a drunk. Don't tell me. I already know. It's just the rule of
the game for the jack of all hearts, and for the queen of baguettes;[7]
it's a cul-de-sac for a joker drawing hearts.

1991

The title of this divorce poem echoes that of Anne Sexton's "For John, Who Begs Me Not to Enquire Further" (included in this anthology). The text of the poem may also contain echoes of Elizabeth Bishop's "One Art" and Sylvia Plath's "Poppies in October," "Lady Lazarus," and "Edge" (all four also included in this anthology).

Pleiades from the Cables of Genocide

for my grandmother and against the budgets of '89[1]

Tonight I view seven sisters
As I've never seen them before, brilliant
In their dumb beauty, pockmarked
In the vacant lot of no end winter
Blight. Seven sisters, as they were before,
Naked in a shroud of white linen, scented angels
Of the barrio,[2] hanging around for another smoke,
A breath of what comes next, the aborted nest.
I'll drink to that, says my mother within. Her mother[3]
Scattered tales of legendary ways when earth
Was a child and satellites were a thing of the
Heart. Maybe I could tell her this. I saw them
Tonight, seven Hail Marys, unstringing;

viewed Saturn

---

7. An ornamental molding, a rectangular gem, a wand or baton, or a loaf of French bread.
1. The California state budget of 1989 was marked by what the *Los Angeles Times* called "cuts and omissions." At the federal level, President George H. W. Bush responded to a budget deficit by calling for cuts in almost every category of domestic spending.
2. A Spanish-speaking neighborhood in a U.S. city or town.
3. That is, the speaker's grandmother.

Through a singular telescope. Oh wonder
Of pillaged swans! oh breathless geometery
Of setting! You are radiant in your black light
Height, humming as you are in my memory.
Nights as inked as these, breathless
From something that comes from nothing.
Cold hearts, warm hands in your scuffed
Up pockets. I know the shoes those ladies[4] wear,
Only one pair, and pointedly out of fashion
And flared-ass breaking at the toes, at the point
Of despair. Those dog gone shoes. No repair
For those hearts and angles, minus of meals, that
Flap through the seasons, best in summer, smelling
Of sneakers and coconuts, armpits steaming
With the load of the lording boys who garnish
Their quarters: the gun on every corner,
A chamber of laughter as the skag[5]
Appears—glossed, sky white and sunset
Blush, and incandescence giving out, giving up
On their tests, on their grades, on their sky
Blue books, on the good of what's right. A star,
A lucky number that fails all, fails math, fails
Street smarts, dumb gym class, fails to jump
Through the broken hoop, and the ring
Of their lives wounds the neck not their
Arterial finger. Seven sisters, I knew them
Well. I remember the only constellation
My grandmother could point out with the punch
Of a heart. My grandma's amber stone
Of a face uplifts to the clarity of an eaglet's
Eye—or the vision of an águila[6]
Whose mate has succumbed, and she uplifts
Into heaven, into their stolen hemispheres.
                                        It is true.
When she surrenders he will linger by her leaving,
Bringing bits of food in switchblade talons, mice
For the Constitution, fresh squirrel for her wings

4. The seven stars imagined as antisocial women—and perhaps, metaphorically, as energy corporations.
5. Slang for heroin or a derogatory term for a person, usually a woman.
6. Eagle (Spanish).

The length of a mortal. He will die there, beside
Her, belonging, nudging the body into the snowed
Eternal tide of his hunger. Hunters will find them
Thus, huddled under their blankets of aspen
Leaves. Extinct. And if she lives who knows what
Eye can see her paused between ages and forgotten
Stories of old ways and the new way
Of ripping apart. They are huddled, ever squaring
With the division of destiny. You can find them
In the stars, with a match, a flaring of failure,
That spark in the heart that goes out with impression,
That thumb at the swallow's restless beating.
And you will look up, really to give up, ready
To sail through your own departure. I know.
My grandmother told me, countless times, it was all
She knew to recite to her daughter of daughters,
Her Persephone[7] of the pen.
                        The Seven Sisters
Would smoke in the sky in their silly shoes
And endless waiting around doing nothing,
Nothing to do but scuff up the Big Bang[8] with salt
And recite strange stories of epiphanies of light,
Claim canons, cannons and horses, and the strange
Men in their boots in patterns of Nazis and Negroes.
I count them now in the sky on the abacus[9] of spun duck
Lineage, a poison gas. There, I remind me, is the nation
Of peace: seven exiles with their deed of trust
Signed over through gunfire of attorney.
                              She rides
Now through the Reagan Ranch[10] her mothers owned.
I know this—we go back to what we have loved
And lost. She lingers, riding in the pied pinto gauchos,[11]
In her hat of many colors and her spurs, her silver

7. Goddess of spring, renewal, and fertility in Greek myth.
8. A cosmological theory postulating that in a singular event the universe rapidly expanded from a dense, compact initial condition and that it continues to expand today.
9. A calculating tool used primarily in parts of Asia for performing arithmetic processes.
10. "Rancho del Cielo," or Sky Ranch, is a 688-acre ranch northwest of Santa Barbara, California, once owned by President Ronald Reagan and First Lady Nancy Reagan. It was built on land originally belonging to the Chumash Indians.
11. Spotted or multicolored trousers in the style worn by Argentine cowboys of mixed Spanish and Indian descent.

Spurs. She does not kick the horse. She goes
Wherever it wants. It guides her to places where
The angry never eat, where birds are spirits
Of dead returned for another plot or the crumb
Of knowledge, that haven of the never to get.
And she is forever looking to the bare innocence
Of sky, remembering, dead now, hammered as she is
Into her grave of stolen home. She is singing
The stories of Calafia[12] ways and means, of the nacre
Of extinct oysters and the abalone I engrave
With her leftover files. She knows the words
To the song now, what her grandmother sang
Of how they lit to this earth from the fire
Of fusion, on the touchstones of love tribes. *Mira,*[13]
She said, *This is where you come from.* The power
                  peace
Of worthless sky that unfolds me—now—in its greedy
Reading: Weeder of Wreckage, Historian of the Native
Who says: *It happened. That's all. It just happened.*
And runs on.

                                       1991

Cervantes commented on this poem: "The Chumash who inhabited the Santa Barbara coast may have believed that they descended to earth from the Pleiades, also known as The Seven Sisters. The Seven Sisters also refers to the seven big oil companies." The Pleiades are a conspicuous cluster of stars in the constellation Taurus. In Greek myth, they were originally the seven daughters of Atlas. The "cables of genocide" in the poem's title may mean wire ropes or cords; ropelike assemblies of electrical conductors; cable-grams or telegraphic messages; or knitting stitches that resemble the twist of a cable. "Genocide," the extermination of a social group or the destruction of a group's language and culture, may refer to destructive acts visited on Native Americans, Latinos, and other ethnic populations. The poem uses a surreal style to meld together myths, astronomy, memories of the speaker's grandmother, and present-day political realities.

12. A legendary warrior queen, associated with the mythical Pacific island of California. Some think that California in the United States and Baja California in Mexico were named after her. Nacre: mother-of-pearl.
13. Look (Spanish).

For My Ancestors Adobed in the Walls
of the Santa Barbara Mission

after Phil Goldvarg[1]

The bones that hold the holy.
Bones, grafted from bailing
and tar. The feathers
of a sleeker bird
resting in the nest.
The wry sense of autumn
calling like a winning smile.

The rapid fire. The wind
laid rest. The certainty
of servitude. The last ash
for the piki.[2] Petals of a lost
desire. A woman's breast
releasing a flower of milk
on her dress. Buckskin bark
carpets the forests. Manzanita[3]
swirls its own polish, her old bone
gleam. Her steady burn. The burl.

Bones weighed in at market.
The single bones, the married
bones with bands on bones.
Bones of a bonsai rectitude,
a fortitude of factories
on the horizon. Bones to raise
a Nation. An axe. An awl.

Bones stripped of their acorns.
Bones nipped from the grave.
Baskets of mourning
foreign to the settlers.
Baskets of bones
with rattlers inside.

1. California poet and Chicano activist (1932–2004), author of *What Makes Bones Talk*.
2. Maize bread baked in thin sheets by the Indians of the southwestern United States.
3. A native California shrub with gleaming, dark red bark.

Baskets of bones
with the teeth in hide.
Bounties of bones
with the people inside.

For every sale
there is a bone.
For every bone
there is a home
and a prayer
calling out the human heart,
chants on a drum
of human hide
with the bill of sale
still inside. And a brand
name still entails
a tag on the toe, a museum
label, a designer death
for you who were buried
with the names inside.

I say this peace, purple dove
of passion for you
who were robbed as bones.
For you who were stripped
of your meat. For you who were
worked to death grinding corn
at the metate[4] you toted
for their feed, the sweet
smoke of age barely at your tail
when they packed you up for good
rebar for the reinforcement.

Oh, Savior of the Mission of Bones,
Oh, Designer Death for the Architect,
Pope of the Bones
and the sainted orders—
the sainted terrorists.

*   *   *

---

4. A mortar or stone tool used, typically by women, for grinding maize, acorns, or seeds.

Bones that hold,
the Holy.

Amen
     d.

2006

This poem laments the deaths of Native Americans baptized in the Franciscan mission at Santa Barbara, California. Founded in 1786, the mission was completely rebuilt following an earthquake in 1812. The Chumash Indians associated with the mission steadily declined in number between 1803 and 1830, either fleeing or dying of infection, impoverishment, or overwork.

In the Waiting Room

A dead man, yellow margins
and a date, lamps and magazines,
rivulets of fire. It got dark,
the inside of a volcano. Over
people, photographs
full of ashes, 'round and 'round
a waiting room, an appointment
slung on a wire. Too long
to stop that nothing stranger,
a big black slush, the fifth
of falling, those awful similarities,
a different pair of hands.
Then, I was back in it, of falling off.
The room was bright. War,
a loud cold wait.

2006

This poem is based on Elizabeth Bishop's "In the Waiting Room" (included in this anthology). Cervantes is engaging in a postmodern procedure she calls "a 'Deconstruction' Exercise." This procedure involves taking someone else's poem "and selecting words in order of their appearance, making a 'new' text or poem." She thereby condenses the original text so as to release a new play of meanings and to initiate an intertextual conversation.

MARILYN CHIN
b. 1955

CALLING HERSELF A "CHINESE-AMERICAN POET," MARILYN CHIN has said that her poetry "both laments and celebrates my 'hyphenated' identity." "How I Got That Name," for example, tells how her father changed her name from "Mei Ling" to "Marilyn," for the iconic American movie star Marilyn Monroe. In her witty, sometimes sardonic poems, she presents identity as mobilized, dynamic, and a subject of wonderment and humor. She employs her ironic perspective on both personal and cultural stories, which tend to overlap and merge in her texts.

Chin was born in Hong Kong and raised in Portland, Oregon. She received her B.A. from the University of Massachusetts, Amherst, and her M.F.A. from the University of Iowa. She is now a professor at San Diego State University, where she codirects the M.F.A. program. She has published four books of her own poetry and has translated poems from Chinese and Japanese.

Although humorous and unpretentious, Chin's poetry is fundamentally serious. Considering the question "What is American about American poetry?," she has written that her work "is seeped with the themes and travails of exile, loss and assimilation." It includes "a delicate and apocalyptic melding of east and west," as she mixes a variety of dialects and dictions, preserving both halves of her Chinese-American identity while at the same time asking what it means to have a global consciousness. Influenced by the work of feminist poet Adrienne Rich, Chin's poems reflect the viewpoint of a woman struggling to maintain her independence and sanity in a society with which she is frequently at odds. As a "hyphenated American poet," Chin seeks "to hammer the rich virtues and contradictions of my adopted country into a fusionist's delight."

FURTHER READING

Marilyn Chin. *The Phoenix Gone, the Terrace Empty*. Minneapolis: Milkweed Editions, 1994.
———. *Rhapsody in Plain Yellow*. New York: W. W. Norton, 2002.
———. "What is American about American Poetry?" Poetry Society of America website, www .poetrysociety.org/chin.html.
Catherine Cucinella. "Marilyn Chin." In *Contemporary American Women Poets: An A-to-Z Guide*, ed. Catherine Cucinella, 55–60. Westport, Conn.: Greenwood Press, 2002.
———. *Poetics of the Body: Edna St. Vincent Millay, Elizabeth Bishop, Marilyn Chin, and Marilyn Hacker*. New York: Palgrave Macmillan, 2010.
Bill Moyers. "Marilyn Chin." In *The Language of Life: A Festival of Poets*, 67–80. New York: Doubleday, 1995.

How I Got That Name

an essay on assimilation

I am Marilyn Mei Ling Chin.
Oh, how I love the resoluteness
of that first person singular
followed by that stalwart indicative
of "be," without the uncertain i-n-g
of "becoming." Of course,
the name had been changed
somewhere between Angel Island[1] and the sea,
when my father the paperson[2]
in the late 1950s
obsessed with a bombshell blonde[3]
transliterated "Mei Ling" to "Marilyn."
And nobody dared question
his initial impulse—for we all know
lust drove men to greatness,
not goodness, not decency.
And there I was, a wayward pink baby,
named after some tragic white woman
swollen with gin and Nembutal.
My mother couldn't pronounce the "r."
She dubbed me "Numba one female offshoot"
for brevity: henceforth, she will live and die
in sublime ignorance, flanked
by loving children and the "kitchen deity."
While my father dithers,
a tomcat in Hong Kong trash—
a gambler, a petty thug,
who bought a chain of chopsuey joints
in Piss River, Oregon,
with bootlegged Gucci cash.
Nobody dared question his integrity given

1. Island in San Francisco Bay where about one million Asian-American immigrants were registered and/or detained on their journey to the United States between 1910 and 1940. Chin's father could not literally have passed through this immigration center (now a California state park), because it was closed in 1940.
2. Chinese immigrants using false papers to claim that they were sons of American citizens. The practice resulted from the discriminatory Chinese Exclusion Act of 1882, which was repealed in 1943, more than a decade before Chin's father immigrated to the United States.
3. Marilyn Monroe (1926–1962), a celebrated Hollywood movie actress who died from an overdose of the sleeping pill Nembutal.

his nice, devout daughters
and his bright, industrious sons
as if filial piety were the standard
by which all earthly men were measured.

*

Oh, how trustworthy our daughters,
how thrifty our sons!
How we've managed to fool the experts
in education, statistics and demography—
We're not very creative but not adverse to rote-learning.
Indeed, they can *use* us.
But the "Model Minority" is a tease.
We know you are watching now,
so we refuse to give you any!
Oh, bamboo shoots, bamboo shoots!
The further west we go, we'll hit east;
the deeper down we dig, we'll find China.
History has turned its stomach
on a black polluted beach—
where life doesn't hinge
on that red, red wheelbarrow,[4]
but whether or not our new lover
in the final episode of "Santa Barbara"[5]
will lean over a scented candle
and call us a "bitch."
Oh God, where have we gone wrong?
We have no inner resources![6]

*

Then, one redolent spring morning
the Great Patriarch Chin
peered down from his kiosk in heaven
and saw that his descendants were ugly.[7]
One had a squarish head and a nose without a bridge.
Another's profile—long and knobbed as a gourd.
A third, the sad, brutish one
may never, never marry.

4. A reference to William Carlos Williams's poem "The Red Wheelbarrow."
5. Soap opera on American television (1984–93).
6. See John Berryman's Dream Song 14: "I conclude now I have no / inner resources, because I am heavy bored."
7. See Genesis 1:31: "And God saw every thing that he had made, and, behold, it was very good."

And I, his least favorite—
"not quite boiled, not quite cooked,"
a plump pomfret[8] simmering in my juices—
too listless to fight for my people's destiny.
"To kill without resistance is not slaughter"
says the proverb. So, I wait for imminent death.
The fact that this death is also metaphorical
is testament to my lethargy.

*

So here lies Marilyn Mei Ling Chin,
married once, twice to so-and-so, a Lee and a Wong,
granddaughter of Jack "the patriarch"
and the brooding Suilin Fong,
daughter of the virtuous Yuet Kuen Wong
and G. G. Chin the infamous,
sister of a dozen, cousin of a million,
survived by everybody and forgotten by all.
She was neither black nor white,
neither cherished nor vanquished,
just another squatter in her own bamboo grove
minding her poetry—
when one day heaven was unmerciful,
and a chasm opened where she stood.
Like the jowls of a mighty white whale,[9]
or the jaws of a metaphysical Godzilla,[10]
it swallowed her whole.
She did not flinch nor writhe,
nor fret about the afterlife,
but stayed! Solid as wood, happily
a little gnawed, tattered, mesmerized
by all that was lavished upon her
and all that was taken away!

1994

When Bill Moyers asked Chin, "Where do you most belong?," she replied: "I believe I belong with my passport. I see myself and my identity as nonstatic. I see myself as a frontier, and I see my limits as limitless. Somebody once accused me of being a leftist radical

8. Spiny-finned fish of the northern oceans, valued for food.
9. See the whales in the biblical book of Jonah and in *Moby Dick*.
10. Lead character in a series of twenty-nine Japanese monster films beginning with *Godzilla* in 1954. The name derives from the Japanese words for "gorilla" and "whale."

feminist, West Coast, Pacific Rim, socialist, neo-Classical Chinese-American poet. And I say, 'O yes, I am all of those things.' Why not? I don't believe in static identities. I believe that identities are forever changing." Moyers then asked Chin about the "elegiac quality" of the last lines of "How I Got That Name." She replied: "There's a doubleness to nearly all my work, to how I feel about things, and perhaps especially about assimilation. As I've said, my family's past is irretrievable, but assimilation *must* happen. . . . I think *everything* must merge, and I'm willing to have it merge within me, in my poetry."

Blues on Yellow (#2)

for Charles

Twilight casts a blue pall on the green grass
　　The moon hangs herself on the sickly date palm near the garage

Song birds assault a bare jacaranda,[1] then boogy toward Arizona
　　They are fewer this year than last

Sadness makes you haggard and me fat
　　Last night you bolted the refrigerator shut

X-tra, X-tra, read all about it
　　Chinese girl eats herself to death

Kiss a cold banquet and purge the rest
　　There's room in the sarcophagus if you want it

I keep my hair up in a bereavement knot
　　Yours grow thinner, whiter, a pink skullcap

My Levi's hang loosely and unzipped
　　You won't wash, won't shave or dress

I am your rib, your apple, your adder
　　You are my father, my confessor, my ox, my draft

Heartbreak comes, again, when does it come?
　　When your lamp is half dim and my moon is half dark

2002

---

1. Tree with lacy green foliage and blue or lavender trumpet-shaped flowers. Originally from Brazil and Argentina, the trees are now commonly seen in Southern California and other parts of the world. Boogy: dance to rock and roll music (derived from African-American slang).

Folk Song Revisited

(to the tune of "Her Door Opens to White Waters")[1]

My friend Mieko Ono bought a condo
Over a brand-new wooden footbridge
In Miami University, Oxford, Ohio
She teaches Japanese to Business Minors
Each night she dims the stone lanterns
She lives there alone without a lover

2002

Ohio/Ohio

for Mieko

There is a spot near your broken heart
    Stupid pupils, they're blind
You teach them the Kanji[1] for love
    The tenth stroke is the great aorta
Only one girl saw your terror

Ten thousand in this village, but you're unloved
    Breasts should be kissed
Not lopped
    A cold bed of chemo awaits
No sister to hold you, no lover

A surgeon's knife is not love
    That which won't kill us will maim us
Fifty, you're still chasing love
    Time's running out, the clock drips regret
Let's cruise the websites for a savior

2002

1. Apparently a nonexistent song.
1. Adopted Chinese written characters that are used in the modern Japanese writing system along with native Japanese characters and in some cases the Latin alphabet.

CATHY SONG
b. 1955

Cᴀᴛʜʏ sᴏɴɢ writes poems of exquisite observation and reflection. Her work belongs to the venerable tradition of the personal lyric, based in perception and memory, and anchored in a stable but responsive "I." Each poem tells a story of human development and relationship, with subtle nuances of individual, interpersonal feeling. Each highlights Song's powers of attention and empathy.

Many of Song's poems explore what it is like to inhabit a human world. Pieces such as "The Youngest Daughter" and "Leaving" focus on family conflicts and the possibility or impossibility of reconciliation. This dynamic often merges with a meditation on gender issues: a young woman's interior tension between passive subordination and active agency, between fear and creativity. The poems pay heed to natural landscapes as well—most typically, the impact of Hawaii on the mind's eye, as in "Leaving," but also the impact of the New England environment, as in "School Figures."

Writing in free verse, Song reveals the vulnerability of the individual in relation to others, as do such earlier poets as Theodore Roethke, Elizabeth Bishop, Robert Lowell, Anne Sexton, and Sylvia Plath. Song situates this personal vulnerability in a new cultural context—in multicultural Hawaii seen from the perspective of the grandchild of Asian immigrants. Her poems, always refined in thought and emotion, put Western and Eastern styles into conversation. In so doing, they freshen long-standing lyric traditions and bring them into the twenty-first century.

Cathy Song was born in Honolulu to a Chinese-American mother and a Korean-American father. Her paternal grandmother was a mail-order bride from Korea. Song grew up first in Wahiawa, a rural village near Honolulu, and then in Honolulu itself. After graduating from high school, she attended the University of Hawaii at Manoa for two years and then Wellesley College, near Boston, where she received her B.A. in 1977. She then earned her M.A. in creative writing from Boston University. Her first poetry collection, *Picture Bride*, won the Yale Younger Poets competition and was published in 1983. Several years later, Song returned to Honolulu, where she married, had three children, and helped found Bamboo Ridge Press to give local writers a publication outlet. She has continued to publish volumes of poetry, which have won awards and been well reviewed. She teaches at the University of Hawaii at Manoa, and she conducts poetry workshops in the Hawaiian public schools.

FURTHER READING

Elaine Kim. "Asian American Writers: A Bibliographical Review." *American Studies International* 22.2 (1984): 41–78.

Lee Kyhan. "Korean-American Literature: The Next Generation." *Korea Journal* 34.1 (1994): 20–35.

Cathy Song. *Cloud Moving Hands*. Pittsburgh, Penn.: University of Pittsburgh Press, 2007.

———. *Picture Bride*. New Haven, Conn.: Yale University Press, 1983.

———. *School Figures*. Pittsburgh, Penn.: University of Pittsburgh Press, 1994.

Cathy Song and Juliet S. Kono, eds. *Sister Stew: Fiction and Poetry by Women*. Honolulu: Bamboo Ridge Press, 1991.

Stephen Sumida. *And the View from the Shore: Literary Traditions of Hawaii*. Seattle: University of Washington Press, 1991.

Patricia Wallace. "Divided Loyalties: Literal and Literary in the Poetry of Lorna Dee Cervantes, Cathy Song, and Rita Dove." *MELUS* 18.3 (1993): 3–19.

The Youngest Daughter

The sky has been dark
for many years.
My skin has become as damp
and pale as rice paper[1]
and feels the way
mother's used to before the drying sun
parched it out there in the fields.

Lately, when I touch my eyelids,
my hands react as if
I had just touched something
hot enough to burn.
My skin, aspirin colored,
tingles with migraine. Mother
has been massaging the left side of my face
especially in the evenings
when the pain flares up.

This morning
her breathing was graveled,
her voice gruff with affection
when I wheeled her into the bath.
She was in a good humor,

---

1. Paper made from parts of the rice plant, used for centuries in China for painting, printing, and calligraphy.

making jokes about her great breasts,
floating in the milky water
like two walruses,
flaccid and whiskered around the nipples.
I scrubbed them with a sour taste
in my mouth, thinking:
six children and an old man
have sucked from these brown nipples.

I was almost tender
when I came to the blue bruises
that freckle her body,
places where she has been injecting insulin[2]
for thirty years. I soaped her slowly,
she sighed deeply, her eyes closed.
It seems it has always
been like this: the two of us
in this sunless room,
the splashing of the bathwater.

In the afternoons
when she has rested,
she prepares our ritual of tea and rice,
garnished with a shred of gingered fish,
a slice of pickled turnip,
a token for my white body.
We eat in the familiar silence.
She knows I am not to be trusted,
even now planning my escape.
As I toast to her health
with the tea she has poured,
a thousand cranes[3] curtain the window,
fly up in a sudden breeze.

1983

"The Youngest Daughter" is a monologue spoken by an Asian immigrant's daughter, consigned to the caretaker role. The daughter carries out her tasks dutifully, perhaps

2. A hormone essential for the metabolism of carbohydrates, used in the treatment and control of diabetes.
3. In Asian countries, the crane is a symbol of peace, health, and prosperity. It is commonly said that folding one thousand origami paper cranes makes a person's wish come true.

even lovingly, but she dreams of "escape." Lee Kyhan comments that "next generation writers" such as Cathy Song, who belongs to the third generation of her family to live in the United States, "share a common project to somehow weave together the various life stories of their elders in a biographical novel, in the hopes that the experiences of first generation immigrants could somehow help them to better deal with their agonizing ambivalence toward their own hybrid identity." Kyhan adds that in this poem, the restrictions of the older generations "are mind-forged manacles of filial obligations dictated by the Confucian tradition. The young daughter is physically and emotionally drained by the never ending chores involved in nursing her ailing mother."

Leaving

Wahiawa[1] is still
a red dirt town
where the sticky smell
of pineapples
being lopped off
in the low-lying fields
rises to mix
with the minty leaves
of eucalyptus
in the bordering gulch.

We lived there
near the edge
where the orchids grew huge
as lanterns overnight
and the passion fruits rotted
on the vines
before they could be picked.

We grew there
in the steady rain
that fell like a gray curtain
through which my mother peered:
patches of depression.
She kept the children under cover.
We built houses within houses,
stripping our parents' bed

1. "Small town on the island of Oahu, Hawaii" (Song's note). Song spent her early years there.

of pillows and sheets,
erecting walls out of
The National Geographic[2]
which my father had subscribed to
for years. We feasted
on those pictures of the world,
while the mud oozed
past the windows
knocking over the drab green leaves
of palm fronds
as we ate our spinach.
The mildew grew in rings
around the sink
where centipedes came
swimming up the pipes
on multiple feet
and the mold grew
around our small fingers
making everything slippery
to touch.
We were squeamish and pale.

I remember one night
my sister screamed.
All the lights blinked on
in the house.
In the sudden brightness,
we rushed to her room
and found her crumpled
in the far corner of the bed,
her nightgown twisted in a strange shape;
her eyes were as huge as mine,
staring into the eyes of the bat
that clung to the screen.
Its rodent fingers
finally letting go
as my father jabbed its furry body
with the end of a broom.

1983

2. Popular magazine with a trademarked yellow border around its cover, containing articles and photographs of places and people all over the world.

"Leaving" appears to be based on a childhood memory. The title invokes the dream of "escape" also articulated in "The Youngest Daughter." Elaine Kim has attributed to Song's poetry what she calls the "consummately Korean-American theme" of "exploring the relationship between the persona and her family, from whom she ventures forth and with whom she is eventually reconciled." One might also note the similarities between this poem and others based on family memories by such poets as Elizabeth Bishop, Robert Lowell, Anne Sexton, and Sylvia Plath. The poem moves from a description of landscape to a specific remembered event, ending in a moment of fear and horror.

School Figures

The boundaries were there, the orchard,
where in spring we would climb
down from our windows, shake clean
our hair, and offer ourselves to the sky,
framed by the branches, a lesson in perspective—
the apple trees' congested blossoms
against the Constable[1] clouds,
English and majestic,
like the poems we were happy to abandon.

Views of Mt. Fuji[2] our devotion might have seemed,
persistent as Hokusai's fine gradations of seeing,
intent on exactitude, replication,
students of nature uncovering
the mineral world,
the invisible fire beneath the ice.
The days were diligently divided
into books of hours, each hour
a season, a state of mind illuminated differently.
We studied the decline of beauty,
admired Mondrian's[3] strict view of the world—
how the black lines stabilized the colors,
the gridiron of discipline
like a dancer's training barre

1. John Constable (1776–1837), English painter noted for the realism and freshness of his landscapes.
2. *Thirty-six Views of Mount Fuji* is a series of large, color woodblock prints by the Japanese visual artist Katsushika Hokusai (1760–1849), depicting Mount Fuji from various perspectives in different seasons.
3. Piet Mondrian (1872–1944), Dutch painter noted for his nonrepresentational forms, which typically consisted of a grid of vertical and horizontal black lines occasionally filled in with red, yellow, or blue.

did not imprison:
the colors leaped, became more efficient.

Patience and Restraint were the names of our daughters.
We yearned to be virtuous,
to embody an ideal.
Thin as Audrey Hepburn[4] in *Roman Holiday*,
you belonged to Ingres,[5]
to the architectural lines
of his furniture, crisp, classical,
more so than the serpentine women
who lounged upon them,
their necks and arms as thick as pythons.
White hands, white face,
anorexic, a black rose in the snow,
you made a minimalist statement toward a metaphor.
Like the chilled orchid, seeded in science,
a distillation unfolding, you resembled
a fabulous, futuristic bird.

So practice would make us perfect
in the repetition of school figures,
obedience traced into the crystalline structure,
unadorned and essential as numbers—
the reclining nude,
the twentieth-century novel,
the irreducible core of Cézanne's[6] monumental apples.

In the afternoons Brueghel[7]
became our patron saint.

4. The lithe, ballet-trained Hepburn (1929–1993) was one of the most popular actresses of her time, winning an Academy Award for *Roman Holiday* (1953) and nominations as Best Actress for four other roles.
5. Jean-August-Dominique Ingres (1780–1867) was a French painter noted for his portraits and his depictions of historical and literary scenes. Among his paintings of romantically portrayed women who "lounged" on neoclassical furniture were *La Grande Odalisque* (The Great Concubine) (1814) and *Odalisque with a Slave* (1840).
6. Paul Cézanne (1839–1906) was a French Post-impressionist painter noted for his innovative use of color and design. Among his many paintings of apples are *Still Life with Apples* (1890) and *The Basket of Apples* (1894).
7. Pieter Brueghel the Elder (1525–1569) was a painter and printmaker from the Netherlands. He is famous for his detailed, vivid scenes of common folk at work and play.

This the hour of the magnifying glass,
the small detail, and the postage stamp,
multiplied until there were a dozen
of us at the lake's edge, lacing our skates.
The lake that in November saw
the wind's agitated brush strokes
rip its surface by February felt
the stark calligraphy of skaters
gliding by in figure eights,
a loose confederacy of ducklings and swans
linked by an unselfconscious grace.
We felt the pull of the ice
as we moved in silence across the lake.

So quiet when the first snow fell,
when you were walking back at twilight,
a pair of skates slung over your shoulder
the way Brueghel's hunters might have carried
home a dead rabbit, trapped in the black forest,
the odor of fur sharp and warm.
There was beauty in your flight.
You walked in quick strides,
as if you knew something about yourself was fleeting
and inconsequential in the wheel of lights
beginning to spin across the sky.
The stars yielded to the pull of their own fire,
that long infinite perfection,
and, like skaters,
traced the daily recital toward oblivion
etched in ice.
The black and white of it,
you knew about it then.

1994

"School Figures" provides an autobiographical or fictional account of student life at a
northern U.S. college such as Wellesley, from which Song received her B.A. The poem
indirectly approaches such issues as the preciousness of life in the shadow of eternity and
the complex relations between art and life, Eastern and Western cultural traditions, and
masculine and feminine ways of knowing.

The Day Has Come When My Mother

The day has come when my mother
no longer knows me.
It comes on a day of dying
paperwhites,[1] crumpled
like words from a typewriter.
Weightless, they scatter, generous
as sighs, across the table, the patio,
where the attendant wheels her,
leaning into the dead
weight of her,
through so many
blossoms it actually
looks like snow.

2007

AMY GERSTLER
b. 1956

A LEADING LOS ANGELES POSTMODERNIST, AMY GERSTLER writes witty yet unsettling accounts of contemporary emotional life. Her poems flash with the glamour of the popular culture texts they often parody. Below the seductive surface, however, the reader comes into contact with some of the less attractive components of the postmodern world, including alienation, loneliness, and frustrated desire. Like other poets in the New York school and the Language poetry movement, both of which have influenced her, Gerstler produces poems that are funny and racy. Within their hip style, they generate profound social and psychological insights.

Born in San Diego, Amy Gerstler grew up in a family that was oriented toward the performing arts, especially musical comedy. After receiving a B.A. in psychology at Pitzer College in 1978, she transitioned into the poetry and visual

---

1. Paperwhites are daffodil bulbs with brilliant white flowers noted for their fragrance. Native to both Asia and Europe, they include the Chinese Sacred Lily among their varieties. Once they blossom, they do not bloom again.

arts scenes in Los Angeles. Since the 1980s she has produced avant-garde poems and prose poems as well as art installations and art criticism. She lives in Los Angeles with her husband, the short-story writer Benjamin Weissman, and teaches at the Art Center College of Design in Pasadena.

Gerstler has spoken of being influenced by comic books, the thesaurus, recipes, and old science textbooks "where people try to explain the world, but they explain it wrong." Her poems subversively plumb the bottomless gulfs just below the seemingly placid surface of our culture: the haunting presences of separation, loss, and grief, the things that "are dark, in the head." As Amy Moorman Robbins was first to note, Gerstler also provides vivid "portrayals of women" and of homophobia, childhood sexuality, and hierarchically gendered power relations. Although Gerstler's work evokes the rhythms of Los Angeles domestic life and cultural productions, the poet downplays the impact that location makes. She doesn't see "much difference between one place or the other" except that in Los Angeles the scenes are more spread out, providing a sense of "privacy" in which to do one's work.

Sven Birkerts has commented that Gerstler's poems capture "the surrealism of everyday life." Laurence Goldstein has similarly observed that the poet internalizes the abundance of what she sees "and converts it to autonomous images fit for enumeration as an imaginary city of words." Gerstler spins popular culture, high art, folklore, science, and objects and events personally encountered into a textual world that is by turns enjoyable and disturbing. She combines a gift for insight with a love of verbal experiment and an irreverent spirit.

FURTHER READING

Rise B. Axelrod and Steven Gould Axelrod. "Amy Gerstler's Rhetoric of Marriage." *Twentieth Century Literature* 50.1 (Spring 2004): 88–105.
Sven Birkerts. "Prose ~~Poetry~~." *Parnassus* 15 (1989): 163–84.
Amy Gerstler. *Bitter Angel.* 1990. Reprint. Pittsburgh: Carnegie Mellon Press, 1997.
——— . *Dearest Creature.* New York: Penguin, 2009.
——— . *Medicine.* New York: Penguin, 2000.
——— . "What is American about American Poetry?" Poetry Society of America website, www .poetrysociety.org/gerstler.html.
Laurence Goldstein. "Looking for Authenticity in Los Angeles." *Michigan Quarterly Review* 30 (1991): 717–31.
"Ignition Magazine Interviews Amy Gerstler." *Ignition* 1 (2000): 1–8.
Amy Moorman Robbins. "Amy Gerstler." In *Contemporary American Women Poets: An A-to-Z Guide*, ed. Catherine Cucinella. 138–41. Westport, Conn.: Greenwood Press, 2002.

I Fall to Pieces

What does a kiss mean in our kind of relationship?
A truce of lips? That though we're both animals,
you won't bite? After necking in the cemetery,
I felt scattered as that married couple's ashes.
You read their plaque aloud: TOO BAD, WE HAD FUN.
Hope my crumbs and dust wind up feeding a cactus
whose fruit becomes your tequila. You'd drink me,
and I'd enter your temple: an ever-faithful headache.
But I wouldn't be able to see your Adam's apple jump
when you swallowed. Glug glug. So let's walk upright
awhile, keep paradise at bay, OK? Kiss me again,
breathe your little ills and weird fear into me.
Erase my name, leave me speechless..

1986

The title of "I Fall to Pieces" alludes to Patsy Cline's 1961 country-pop song hit of the same name, written by Harlan Howard and Hank Cochran. Cline's song tells of a rejected lover's inability to stop loving her ex. It begins, "I fall to pieces / Each time I see you again. / I fall to pieces. / How can I be just your friend?" In Gerstler's retelling, the speaker seems to "fall to pieces" in the sense of mentally unraveling.

White Marriage

1. The keeper's daughter, I grew up in a lighthouse, pale as an iceberg, surrounded by water, and father's groggy demands. No mother to teach me to blush.[1] We had a small orchard, in the midst of a wicked reef, prey to wind, wave and quake. I was constantly wet, had occasional chest pains, no visitors. Father laced his oatmeal with cognac that washed up in crates on our beach. He stayed drunk and silent for days. I was permitted to walk as far as the sea wall. One sunset, while collecting mussels for supper, I saw a young couple under the dock. Two dark postures, heads bent together like animals drinking, or grazing.[2] The girl's back was against a piling. I thought "Those barnacles are sharp," but perhaps she didn't feel it. They couldn't see me. They were busy, feeding. From the pit of my stomach, a burning sensation radiated out to my limbs, and my joints went watery. Father had lied to me: that action was no

---

1. That is, as a motherless child, the speaker had no one to guide her into the functions of female modesty central to American cultural ideology.

2. Feeding, like an animal nibbling on grass; also rubbing, like a sharp object scratching the skin.

lullaby. At home, I couldn't stop staring at my father's bald spot. He was yawning. An aging tattooed man, with little understanding of life on dry land. Could I imagine my hair being smoothed by any other hand? He said, "Come here, Celeste. You look feverish." He made me lie down. Not even sleep shields me from the power of his frown.

2.   I only hold still for this because you're named for my favorite angel . . . the one who protects others with no thought for himself. One who thirsts for deeper knowledge of me. One who was raised on a small estate by the river. One who's seen too much and so bites his tongue, bides his time. One who recovered from scarlet fever, and ever since understands the animals' language. One who cultivates plants with sword-shaped leaves and plots rebellions. One who experiences the "joy-on-awakening" that field workers feel returning home. We see them from our bedroom window, shouldering their picks and rakes, as we spend another Christmas together, locked in this brothel. I'm sorry I socked you. I know this arrangement protects me from worse enslavements.[3] You and I were in the same orphanage, in another life. Don't laugh, I'm psychic. Stale bread, ugly nuns, and a game we played: queen and slave. One night you pulled aside my covers, pretending to hold the royal tent-flap open for me, just as you're doing now. Why, sometimes, in this palace of strangers,[4] I'm almost homesick for that miserable place.

3.   *Why so quiet, dear?*[5] Just thinking. Remember shortly after we met, when you put your foot down and decreed: NO MORE KISSING? I lifted my skirt, so you'd see what you were talking about going without. But you were right. Who needs that salad of wilted limbs, followed by a procession of whimpering, living misgivings? Bless the oak board that divides our bed. A wave of vapor, really a family of white herons,[6] rises from the weedy marsh to settle on our evergreen lake. Each evening they make this short migration, from where they feed to where they'll sleep. It's comforting to have a routine. Once I ventured out. A man left his purple mark on my neck, below the collarbone. Luckily, my husband and I always undress in the dark, so no explanation was necessary. And the blemish, sin's grape colored stain, went away.

1986

3. Perhaps an allusion to the daughter's situation in part 1 and the wife's in part 3.
4. In the book of Isaiah, God's power is thusly acknowledged: "For thou hast made of a city a heap: of a defensed city a ruin: a palace of strangers to be no city" (25:2).
5. This may be a husband's question to his wife, initiating the wife's spoken or unspoken response.
6. A species of bird that lives near lakes and wetlands.

504 ◆ *Amy Gerstler*

The title, "White Marriage," uses a common term for a marriage without sexual relations, though it may have a racial implication as well. This three-part prose poem (or sequence of three poems) mocks traditional imagery of the family by suggesting its unequal power relations and a sense of discord and lovelessness. It also undermines the norms of lyric poetry by appearing in prose, and it subverts narrative expectations through its discontinuities. Rise and Steven Axelrod explain that the first part of the text "parodies a wide variety of cultural sources that use the lighthouse keeper and his daughter as a trigger for sentimentality, idealization, and ultimately consumer desire. Perhaps the most famous among these sources is the story of the aptly named Grace Darling, who rescued five survivors from a shipwreck off England's Northumberland coast in 1838. She thereby became what Jessica Mitford called 'the first media heroine,' celebrated in news story, legend, and song. . . . More recently, the Disney film, *Pete's Dragon* (1977), tells the story of a lighthouse keeper's kindly daughter who befriends a runaway orphan named Pete. A Norman Rockwell painting, reproduced on dishes and mugs and available for purchase on the web, pictures a lighthouse keeper's young daughter faithfully mending her father's old jacket."

An Unexpected Adventure

Driving home to River Heights after a hard day's work on a new mystery, Nancy Drew's dark blue roadster lurches and slows. "A flat, I'll bet." Nancy's hunches are spooky; she's almost always right. The young sleuth pulls onto the gravel shoulder, removes her gloves, places her handbag on the seat beside her. Night is falling. Cunningly attired in a simple two-piece linen sports frock with matching sweater, the girl detective changes the tire easily. Though she doesn't relish the work, she's no shirker, and the convertible is soon repaired. Nancy's pooped, so at first she doesn't notice the short, heavy-set man with a large nose approaching. But nothing escapes Nancy's keen gaze for long. "That fellow acts as if he's being pursued," Nancy notes. Her eyes sparkle with anticipation. Her intuition tells her she may be on the threshold of another mystery! As the man draws closer, Nancy controls her excitement, and speaks in a calm, casual voice: "Sir, may I offer you some assistance?" she asks sincerely.

Even after repairing her car, Nancy looks incredibly clean. Her sports frock is perfectly tailored to her trim figure. The color suits her complexion exactly. The creamy pallor of her skin contrasted with the healthy flush of recent exertion still fresh on her cheeks is very becoming. The stranger's face descending toward hers and his unpleasant breath are the last items to register clearly on the amateur detective's mind as his stout, chapped hands find her sweater clasp. Nancy's miffed when she comes to, lying alone in the road. The culprit's vanished. She notices immediately her purse is gone, and with it, her car keys.

Her intuition clicking like a geiger counter, she has a revelation she may have lost more than her compact and billfold to this ruffian, as, with leaden feet, she begins the long walk home.

1990

"An Unexpected Adventure" parodies the popular series of detective novels for children and teens featuring Nancy Drew. First conceived by Edward Stratemeyer in 1930, the books have been written by a variety of ghostwriters, all using the pen name Carolyn Keene. Nancy Drew has contradictory traits of optimism, fearlessness, docility, and passivity, making her an iconic representation of mixed feelings about femininity.

A Love Poem

Me Jerusalem, you Kansas City.
You fifth,[1] me jigger.
Me fork, you can opener.
You sweetmeat,[2] me bean-cake.
Me zilch,[3] you nada.

1990

The Bride Goes Wild

You Can't Run Away from It and You Can't Take It
With You, Man of a Thousand Faces: The Children
Upstairs, Brats; All These Women Up in Arms—
Misunderstood Husband Hunters. It Started in Paradise—
The Best of Everything: Ten Nights in a Bar Room, Men
Without Names, The Exquisite Sinner High and Dizzy—
Long Legs, Dimples, The Velvet Touch. Foolin' Around,
Just This Once, She Had to Say Yes. A Night to Remember.
Don't Tell. I Confess—I'm No Angel, I Am the Law!
The Fiend Who Walked West, Breathless, Accused
My Foolish Heart. The Pleasure of His Company
Changes White Heat to a Cold Wind in August.
But One Night in the Tropics, I Saw What You Did.

---

1. A bottle of liquor holding one-fifth of a gallon. Jigger: a measuring glass used in mixing drinks and holding one and a half ounces.
2. A food rich in sugar; candy. Bean-cake: sweet cake in China and Japan; spicy dish in Latin America.
3. Zero, nil (slang). Nada: nothing (Spanish).

Ready, Willing and Able, Naughty but Nice, She Wore
a Yellow Ribbon. Miles from Home, Living It Up,
She Couldn't Say No—My Sister Eileen—Too Young to Kiss,
Each Pearl a Tear. The Awful Truth: Ladies Love Brutes.
The Good News: The Devil Is a Sissy. So Tickle Me,
Doctor X, Truly Madly Deeply. Keep Laughing. You Gotta
Stay Happy. Naked, the Invisible Woman Cries and Whispers
Nothing but the Truth, Too Scared to Scream.

2000

"The Bride Goes Wild" is composed of nothing but the titles of Hollywood films. *You Can't Run Away from It*, for example, was a 1956 musical comedy in Technicolor and CinemaScope, directed by Dick Powell and starring June Allyson and Jack Lemmon. *You Can't Take It with You* was a comedy film of 1938, adapted from the play of the same name by George S. Kaufman and Moss Hart, directed by Frank Capra and starring James Stewart and Jean Arthur. Beginning with comedy titles, the poem ends with one from a low-budget horror film. *Too Scared to Scream*, appearing in 1985, starred Mike Connors and Anne Archer and was directed by Tony Lo Bianco. Gerstler has commented that one reason she feels "drawn to the packed, colorful titles of American films is that so many of them seem to present the funny, irrepressible melodramatics of American English in a nutshell—our language with its distinctive mixture of slang and preachiness, the elevated and the silly."

Advice from a Caterpillar

Chew your way into a new world.
Munch leaves. Molt. Rest. Molt
again. Self-reinvention is *everything*.
Spin many nests. Cultivate stinging
bristles. Don't get sentimental
about your discarded skins. Grow
quickly. Develop a yen for nettles.[1]
Alternate crumpling and climbing. Rely
on your antennae. Sequester poisons
in your body for use at a later date.
When threatened, emit foul odors
in self-defense. Behave cryptically
to confuse predators: change colors, spit,
or feign death. If all else fails, taste terrible.

2009

1. Prickly or stinging plants.

LI-YOUNG LEE
b. 1957

LI-YOUNG LEE writes autobiographical poems that explore the complexities of ethnicity and the immigrant experience. The memory poem included here, "The Gift," recalls the father's love, and it also makes a connection between the "gift" of care that the father gave to the speaker and the similar "gift" that the speaker bestows on his wife. Although the poem pays tribute to the father's "tenderness," it also includes dark undertones in the father's associations with pain and the "flames of discipline." "The Gift" suggests that love exists despite impediments, and it creates meaning in the shadow of fear and death. Emotional openness combines with an apparently casual but precise, classical style in Lee's work. His poems are influenced by both traditional Chinese poetry and the family studies of poets such as Theodore Roethke, Robert Lowell, and Sylvia Plath. Lee's work reveals the deep resonances to be found in human relationships and ordinary occurrences.

Lee was born in Jakarta, Indonesia, the son of Chinese parents who had fled from Communist rule in China. After his father was imprisoned for nineteen months as a target of the anti-Chinese sentiment of Indonesian President Sukarno, the family fled again, to Hong Kong and Japan. The family ultimately settled in rural Pennsylvania, where Lee's father, who had been a physician in China, became a Presbyterian minister. Lee received his B.A. from the University of Pittsburgh, where he discovered his passion for poetry. Now married, with two children, he lives in Chicago.

FURTHER READING

Dianne Bilyak. "Interview with Li-Young Lee." *Massachusetts Review* 44.4 (Winter 2003–4): 600–612.
Li-Young Lee. *Behind My Eyes: Poems*. New York: W. W. Norton, 2008.
———. *Rose*. Rochester, N.Y.: BOA Editions, 1986.
———. *The Winged Seed: A Remembrance*. New York: Simon & Schuster, 1995.
Wenying Xu. "Transcendentalism, Ethnicity, and Food in the Work of Li-Young Lee." *Boundary 2* 33.2 (Summer 2006): 129–57.
Xiaojing Zhou. "Inheritance and Invention in Li-Young Lee's Poetry." *MELUS* 21.1 (Spring 1996): 113–32.

The Gift

To pull the metal splinter from my palm
my father recited a story in a low voice.
I watched his lovely face and not the blade.
Before the story ended, he'd removed
the iron sliver I thought I'd die from.

I can't remember the tale,
but hear his voice still, a well
of dark water, a prayer.
And I recall his hands,
two measures of tenderness
he laid against my face,
the flames of discipline
he raised above my head.

Had you entered that afternoon
you would have thought you saw a man
planting something in a boy's palm,
a silver tear, a tiny flame.
Had you followed that boy
you would have arrived here,
where I bend over my wife's right hand.

Look how I shave her thumbnail down
so carefully she feels no pain.
Watch as I lift the splinter out.
I was seven when my father
took my hand like this,
and I did not hold that shard
between my fingers and think,
Metal that will bury me,
christen it Little Assassin,
Ore Going Deep for My Heart.
And I did not lift up my wound and cry,
Death visited here!
I did what a child does
when he's given something to keep.
I kissed my father.

1986

Lee wrote "The Gift" in the aftermath of his father's death in 1981.

JUAN DELGADO
b. 1960

JUAN DELGADO'S POETRY portrays the lives of those on social and economic margins. His characters are often immigrants who inhabit the cultural border zone between Mexico and the United States. They live on the edge of things—in impoverished neighborhoods, in the desert, in places that others avoid. Ordinary people, they make their way unaided through life, dealing with their deprivations and losses. They are sustained by their courage, faith, wariness, and often a rich inner life. Attentive to small but resonant details, Delgado's poems paint realistic portraits of common people who live in challenging circumstances.

Delgado was born in Guadalajara, Mexico. His family recrossed the border many times before settling down in Southern California. His father and grandfather were migrant farmers, and his childhood was spent in poverty. Although Delgado was at one point forced to drop out of college to support his family through manual labor, he returned and received his B.A. from California State University, San Bernardino. At the university he was mentored by poet and English professor Larry Kramer, who persuaded him to apply to the M.F.A. program at the University of California, Irvine. Armed with his advanced degree, Delgado returned to California State University, San Bernardino, as an English professor himself. He has published four books of poetry, all of which depict human beings who strive for human connection and a place in the world.

Delgado lives in Southern California with his wife and three children. He regularly reads his poems in unusual locales such as retirement homes, factories, community centers, and general stores. He explains, "While most people would say it's crazy to do a reading in the middle of an office, I say it's crazy not to. By performing in places typically not used as art venues, you have the power to raise questions and educate an overlooked population on the importance of art. . . . While every community is different, I tend to find that the audiences at these offbeat locations are more willing to share their own stories and emotions."

FURTHER READING

Juan Delgado. *El Campo*. Santa Barbara, Calif.: Capra Press, 1998.
———. *Green Web*. Athens: University of Georgia Press, 1994.
———. *A Rush of Hands*. Tucson: University of Arizona Press, 2003.
Craig Svonkin. "Delgado, Juan." In *The Greenwood Encyclopedia of American Poets and Poetry*, vol. 2, ed. Jeffrey Gray, James McCorkle, and Mary McAleer Balkun, 372–73. Westport, Conn.: Greenwood Press, 2006.
Rosa Martha Villareal. "The Poetry of Passages." *Tertulia* 2.1 (July 2004): 23–24.

The House in El Monte

He was not surprised the ivy grew
Where the chicken-wire fence once stood,
And a stump still marked the yard's end.
He stared at the rusty hinges of a screen door,
The screen grim as his aunt's death veil,
And recalled a room shrunk to a mattress
That pressed against a wall of stains.
His finger would follow a crack on the stucco,
Then another until he found a route out.
The stains on the ceiling grew into islands,
And the lumpy raft he shared with his sisters
Drifted while roaches squirmed around them.
He wormed between his sisters and slept.
The house was chicken-bone brittle
And had a creaking voice until dawn.

After his second knock a woman appeared,
Tilting her head to one side to see around him.
While he told her in his choppy Spanish
He had once lived in her house, she ordered
The two children hiding behind her legs
And peering at him to return to the kitchen.
When she turned her head to call her husband,
He said, "Mire, señora,"[1] pulling out a photo.
She reached for it, studying the family
Standing in front of her house, the same
Tilting TV antenna, the paint flaking off the door,
And at the bottom the dog's scratches.
She waited on her side of the threshold,
Scrutinizing a boy's face, then his,
Trying to match what in him had not changed,
But before he could see the bedroom wall
Where he had scratched with his fingernails,
She turned him away, closing the door,
Suspicious he was eyeing their belongings,
And locking the door latch as if to say,
"Déjenos en paz. No tenemos nada."[2]

2003

---

1. "Look, ma'am" (Spanish).   2. "Leave us alone. We don't have anything" (Spanish).

"The House in El Monte" is set in a working-class suburb of Los Angeles. The poem's use of both English and Spanish emphasizes the community's multicultural nature. The main character attempts to come to terms with his memories of impoverishment—a house with "rusty hinges," cracked stucco, "lumpy" bed, and "roaches." But he is denied admittance to his past, which remains opaque and elusive to him. Craig Svonkin comments, "Delgado describes his visit to his childhood home, where he tried unsuccessfully 'in his choppy Spanish' to communicate with the Mexican woman now living there. His failure demonstrates the challenges facing those striving to connect."

St. Francis

In a desert too hot and cold for most,
Where winds send trailer homes rolling
And drifting into sand dunes, you dug
And cemented a stand for your saint
Who protects all living creatures, even me
Who says deserts are only good for buzzards.

"Here the dust gathers everywhere,
And there is no avoiding it," you say
As you sweep your trailer's doorway clean,
Inviting me, your cousin, to stay for supper.

When I ask you why you put up your saint
And your house on its blocks here, you say:
"I step into this vista like a prayer.
I was just rehearsing before—I was like
A waiting suitor whose finger hovers
Over the doorbell, afraid to go on in."

2003

St. Francis of Assisi (1181–1226), a simple man who followed Christ's example, is known in the Roman Catholic church as the patron saint of animals and the environment.

BAO-LONG CHU
b. 1965

Bᴀᴏ-ʟᴏɴɢ ᴄʜᴜ was a child in Vietnam during the Vietnam War and moved to
the United States as an immigrant afterward. He earned his M.F.A. in poetry at
the University of Houston. He now works as associate director of the Writers in
the Schools organization in Houston. His work has been anthologized in such
collections as *Both Sides Now* and *Bold Words*.

FURTHER READING

Philip Mahoney, ed. *Both Sides Now: The Poetry of the Vietnam War and Its Aftermath.* New
York: Scribner, 1998.
Rajini Srikanth and Esther Y. Iwanaga, eds. *Bold Words: A Century of Asian American Writing.*
New Brunswick, N.J.: Rutgers University Press, 2001.

My Mother's Pearls

Broken shadow gestured winter
trees in Maine, black on white
I thought of my mother's pearls,
ebony seeds, old as the sea
They lie
suspended from her white ao dai[1]
    The color of mourning
    or of mornings in 1975
    unbroken, silent
    after a rain of bombs
    except for the tears of women
    crying for broken temples against green
    sky; fallen idols
    with carved breasts,
    jade, I think, in the black earth,
    in the twisted vines

Last summer, in Washington
I saw the black wall[2]

1. "Ao dai" refers to Vietnamese traditional dress.   2. The Vietnam Veterans Memorial in Washington, D.C.

My shadow reflected
the names of faceless men.
I traced the ruins
carved in stone but did not find
Mother's name
or the names of other women
who stood against the wall of a temple
garden, parting leaves, weeping
napalm tears
     Sandalwood incense
     sweet crooked smoke
they drove all things
out of mind.
And the pearls
forty seeds, black and unruly,
I thought they were beautiful against
my mother's carved breasts.

They lie now,
I think, on a sloping knoll
farther than Maine

or Washington.
                1998

In "My Mother's Pearls," Chu reflects upon the death of his mother as well as the deaths of other civilian Vietnamese women, and he draws attention to the destruction of Buddhist temples in the Vietnam War. You may wish to compare this poem to other poems about the Vietnam War in this anthology by such writers as Denise Levertov, Adrienne Rich, Yusef Komunyakaa, Gerald McCarthy, W. D. Ehrhart, and Ray A. Young Bear. Or you may wish to consider it in relation to Asian-American poetic tradition, as exemplified by the work of such poets as Carlos Bulosan, Mitsuye Yamada, Alex Kuo, John Yau, Theresa Cha, Marilyn Chin, Cathy Song, and Li-Young Lee.

SHERMAN ALEXIE
b. 1966

ONE OF THE LEADING WRITERS and cultural figures on the contemporary
American scene, Sherman Alexie is a cutting-edge poet, fiction writer, and
screenwriter. Whether dressed in U.S. colonial costume with long pink evening
gloves and mimicking Martha Washington telling the audience "Feed me," or
using a more understated style, Alexie draws in his audience with humor and
then delivers a resounding, acerbic attack against such problems as imperialism
and genocide. His extraordinary gifts in storytelling, mimicry, burlesque, and
stand-up comedy draw attention to the long-overlooked Native American traditions of performance that include such artists as twentieth-century comedian
Will Rogers and poet Alexander Posey. Married, with two children, Alexie has
won dozens of awards, including the National Book Award, the American Book
Award, the Shelley Memorial Award in Poetry, and the Lifetime Achievement
Award from the Native Writers' Circle of the Americas.

Alexie spent his childhood in Wellpinit, a small town in eastern Washington on his father's Coeur d'Alene tribal lands. His experiences with the Coeur
d'Alene as well as his mother's Spokane tribe shaped his awareness of the genocide as well as other hardships and injustices suffered by Native Americans. The
ancestral lands of the Coeur d'Alene once covered thousands of acres in Idaho,
eastern Washington, and western Montana, encompassing major rivers, lakes,
and mountain ranges. The Spokanes settled along the Spokane River and Falls
and were split up by the U.S. government. The Grand Coulee Dam was built
on their lands.

Alexie's lifetime struggle with living as a Native American male in a white-
dominated culture increased greatly when he left the reservation to attend high
school. During these years, he started playing basketball and felt that he had
found himself on the court and with his team. Because of his interest in basketball, he decided to attend Gonzaga University in Spokane, but he became
disenchanted with the university's rigid social structure. Transferring after two
years to Washington State University in Pullman, Alexie enrolled in a pre-med
program and then moved into the American studies program. He recognized
himself more fully in this environment, and he began developing his writing
talents in poet Alex Kuo's class, which included many Native American poems
on the syllabus. Alexie studied tribal poets alongside Walt Whitman and Emily
Dickinson. He also started to think seriously about popular film and television.
Not surprisingly, then, his poetry is filled with national cultural icons such as
James Dean and Marilyn Monroe.

Alexie's career in writing did not begin immediately after graduation. When his first book of poetry was published, he was serving as a secretary in a high school exchange program in Spokane. Recently, he has been focusing increasingly on developing programs for young adults when he is not writing or performing. In 2005 he became a founding board member of Longhouse Media, which teaches filmmaking to tribal youths. He has described writing as both a cultural privilege and a responsibility. He uses writing as a way to negotiate his pain and anger about being caught in a mainstream-dominated world that is prone to misrepresent his tribal cultures. His poetry explores the defeats and triumphs of Native American life.

FURTHER READING

Sherman Alexie. *The Absolutely True Diary of a Part-Time Indian*. Boston: Little, Brown, 2007.
———. *Face*. New York: Hanging Loose Press, 1996.
———. *The Lone Ranger and Tonto Fistfight in Heaven*. New York: Vintage, 1993.
———. *The Summer of Black Widows*. Brooklyn, N.Y.: Hanging Loose Press, 1996.
———. *War Dances*. New York: Grove Press, 2009.
———. www.fallsapart.com.
Jeff Berglund and Jan Roush, eds. *Sherman Alexie: A Collection of Critical Essays*. Salt Lake City: University of Utah Press, 2010.
Nancy Peterson, ed. *Conversations with Sherman Alexie*. Oxford: University Press of Mississippi, 2009.

Defending Walt Whitman

Basketball is like this for young Indian[1] boys, all arms and legs
and serious stomach muscles. Every body is brown!
These are the twentieth-century warriors who will never kill,
although a few sat quietly in the deserts of Kuwait,[2]
waiting for orders to do something, to do something.

God, there is nothing as beautiful as a jumpshot
on a reservation summer basketball court
where the ball is moist with sweat,
and makes a sound when it swishes through the net
that causes Walt Whitman[3] to weep because it is so perfect.

There are veterans of foreign wars here
although their bodies are still dominated
by collarbones and knees, although their bodies still respond

---

1. Alexie prefers the term "American Indian" to "Native American."

2. During the Gulf War of 1991–92.

3. American poet (1819–1892).

in the ways that bodies are supposed to respond when we are young.
Every body is brown! Look there, that boy can run
up and down this court forever. He can leap for a rebound
with his back arched like a salmon, all meat and bone
synchronized, magnetic, as if the court were a river,
as if the rim were a dam, as if the air were a ladder
leading the Indian boy toward home.[4]

Some of the Indian boys still wear their military hair cuts
while a few have let their hair grow back.
It will never be the same as it was before!
One Indian boy has never cut his hair, not once, and he braids it
into wild patterns that do not measure anything.
He is just a boy with too much time on his hands.
Look at him. He wants to play this game in bare feet.

God, the sun is so bright! There is no place like this.
Walt Whitman stretches his calf muscles
on the sidelines. He has the next game.
His huge beard is ridiculous on the reservation.

Some body throws a crazy pass and Walt Whitman catches it
with quick hands. He brings the ball close to his nose
and breathes in all of its smells: leather, brown skin, sweat,
black hair, burning oil, twisted ankle, long drink of warm water,
gunpowder, pine tree. Walt Whitman squeezes the ball tightly.
He wants to run. He hardly has the patience to wait for his turn.
"What's the score?" he asks. He asks, "What's the score?"

Basketball is like this for Walt Whitman. He watches these Indian boys
as if they were the last bodies on earth. Every body is brown!
Walt Whitman shakes because he believes in God.
Walt Whitman dreams of the Indian boy who will defend him,
trapping him in the corner, all flailing arms and legs
and legendary stomach muscles. Walt Whitman shakes
because he believes in God. Walt Whitman dreams
of the first jumpshot he will take, the ball arching clumsily
from his fingers, striking the rim so hard that it sparks.

---

4. The reference to the life cycle of the salmon—which returns up river ladders toward ancestral breeding grounds—reflects Alexie's Pacific Northwest tribal experiences with fish as a food and a source of income as well as the ongoing struggle to maintain the supply of salmon in the rivers.

Walt Whitman shakes because he believes in God.
Walt Whitman closes his eyes. He is a small man and his beard
is ludicrous on the reservation, absolutely insane.
His beard makes the Indian boys righteously laugh. His beard
frightens the smallest Indian boys. His beard tickles the skin
of the Indian boys who dribble past him. His beard, his beard!

God, there is beauty in every body. Walt Whitman stands
at center court while the Indian boys run from basket to basket.
Walt Whitman cannot tell the difference between
offense and defense. He does not care if he touches the ball.
Half of the Indian boys wear t-shirts damp with sweat
and the other half are bareback, skin slick and shiny.
There is no place like this. Walt Whitman smiles.
Walt Whitman shakes. This game belongs to him.

1996

"Defending Walt Whitman," one of Alexie's most anthologized poems, focuses on tribal
veterans who served in Kuwait. The poem also reflects Alexie's intimate knowledge of
basketball. See his treatment of his high school years in *The Absolutely True Diary of a
Part-Time Indian*. Finally, the poem resonates Whitman's sympathetic treatment of Native Americans, his interest in the body, and his compassion toward the victims of war in
Leaves of Grass.

QUEEN LATIFAH [DANA OWENS]
b. 1970

QUEEN LATIFAH—sometimes comic, often bold, always spontaneous—is one
of popular culture's major contemporary icons. Whether dressed as a campy
vamp or a defiant rapper, she asserts her strength in a musical and film culture
that the media often presents as male-dominated. Queen Latifah has been compared to such modernist African-American performers and lyricists as Josephine
Baker, Billie Holliday, Ma Rainey, and Bessie Smith, who were also compelling creative figures in their day. Unlike them, however, she has been able to
amass control over her creative work by becoming a record label president and
entrepreneur. With more than eight CDs, forty-three films, and three television
series, Queen Latifah has won many awards, including a Golden Globe Award, a

Grammy Award, and two Screen Actors Guild Awards. She also was nominated for an Academy Award for her role as "Mama" Morton in the musical *Chicago*. Among her other nominations are six Grammy nominations and one Emmy Award nomination.

Born in Newark, New Jersey, Dana Elaine Owens adopted the stage name of "Queen Latifah." *Latifah* in Arabic means "delicate" and "very kind." Queen Latifah has devoted her career to foregrounding issues of women—especially black women. She also is a strong advocate of education and has been serving as co-chair of the Lancelot H. Owens Scholarship Foundation.

FURTHER READING

Ann M. Ciasullo. "Making Her (In)Visible: Cultural Representations of Lesbianism and the Lesbian Body in the 1990s." *Feminist Studies* 27.3 (2001): 577–608.
Cheryl L. Keyes. *Rap Music and Street Consciousness*. Champaign: University of Illinois Press, 2004.
Linda Mizejewski. "Queen Latifah, Unruly Women, and the Bodies of Romantic Comedy." *Genders* 46 (2007). www.Genders.org, www.queenlatifah.com.
Queen Latifah. *The Evil Men Do*. CD. WB Music, 1989.

The Evil Men Do

You asked, I came, so behold the Queen
Let's add a little sense to the scene
I'm living positive, not out here knocked up
But the lines are so dangerous; I ought to be locked up
This rhyme doesn't require prime time
I'm just sharing thoughts of mine
Back again cause I knew you wanted it
From the Latifah with the Queen in front of it
Dropping bombs, you're up in arms, you're puzzled
The lines will flow like fluid while you're guzzling
The sip I drop you on a BDP-produced track[1]
From KRS[2] to be exact
It's a flavor unit quest that today has me speaking
Cause it's knowledge I'm seeking
Enough about myself, I think it's time that I tell you
About the evil that men do

---

1. The song was produced by Boogie Down Productions, a company owned by rapper KRS-One, who also contributes to this lyric.

2. Lawrence "Kris" Parker, rap artist who participates on this track, using his stage name of KRS-One (or KRS-1).

* * *

Situations, reality, what a concept![3]
Nothing ever seems to stay in step
So today, here is a message to my sisters and brothers
Here are some things I want to cover
A woman strives for a better life, but who the hell cares?
Because she's living on welfare
The government can't come up with a decent housing plan
So she's in no man's land
It's a sucker who tells you you're equal

[KRS-One:]
You don't need him, Johannesburg's[4] crying for freedom!

[Queen Latifah:]
We the people hold these truths to be self-evident[5]

[KRS-One:]
But there's no response from the president

[Queen Latifah:]
Someone's living the good life, tax-free
Except for a girl, can't find a way to be crack free
And that's just part of the message
I thought I had to send you about the evil that men do

Tell me, don't you think it's a shame?
When someone can put a quarter in a video game
But when a homeless person approaches you on the street
You can't treat him the same
It's time to teach the def, the dumb, the blind
That black-on-black crime only shackles and binds
You to a doom, a fate worse than death
But there's still time left
Stop putting your conscience on cease
And bring about some type of peace
Not only in your heart, but also in your mind
It will benefit all mankind

3. Echo of a joke by comedian Robin Williams: "Reality, what a concept!"
4. Largest city in South Africa.
5. Conflation of introductory sentences in the U.S. Constitution ("We the people") and the Declaration of Independence ("We hold these truths to be self evident").

Then there will be one thing that will never stop
And it's the evil that men do

1989

Officially a collaboration between Queen Latifah (Dana Owens) and KRS-One (Law-rence "Kris" Parker), this lyric has been described by Cheryl Keyes as Queen Latifah's strong affirmation on behalf of young black women on welfare, encouraging them to remain strong as they face political and economic challenges. Queen Latifah also can be viewed, as Ann Ciasullo has pointed out, as a forceful, self-confident lesbian voice repre-senting the desires of women for independence and social justice. With this rap, Queen Latifah broke into a rap field that was itself male-dominated (and frequently sexist and heterosexist). However, she urges women to focus on making peace.

ABOUT THE EDITORS

Steven Gould Axelrod is Distinguished Professor of English at the University of California, Riverside. Among his books are *Robert Lowell: Life and Art* (Princeton University Press, 1978), which was nominated for a Pulitzer Prize, and *Sylvia Plath: The Wound and the Cure of Words* (Johns Hopkins University Press, 1990). Books he has edited include *Robert Lowell: New Essays on the Poetry* (Cambridge University Press, 1986), *Critical Essays on Wallace Stevens* (G. K. Hall, 1988), *Critical Essays on William Carlos Williams* (G. K. Hall/Macmillan, 1995), and *The Critical Response to Robert Lowell* (Greenwood Press, 1999). Recently he has published recent articles on Elizabeth Bishop, Robert Lowell, Gwendolyn Brooks, Allen Ginsberg, Sylvia Plath, Frank Bidart, Yusef Komunyakaa, and Amy Gerstler. He has won his university's Distinguished Teaching Award and has held the McCauley Chair in Teaching Excellence. He is president of the Robert Lowell Society.

Camille Roman is currently a visiting scholar at Brown University. Emeritus Professor at Washington State University in English, Women's Studies, and American Studies, she has published more than a dozen books including *Elizabeth Bishop's World War II-Cold War View*. Coeditor of *The Women and Language Debate: A Sourcebook* with Suzanne Juhasz and Cristanne Miller, she is also the founding coeditor of the Twayne Medical Arts Series for Twayne Publishers with Chris Darwin Frigon. She is the individual volume coeditor of books on musicians such as the Beatles, Lester Young, Sonny Rollins, Carlos Chavez, and Claude Debussy. Her many journal and newspaper essays and reviews focus on diverse writers and poets, including Frank O'Hara, Sylvia Plath, Elizabeth Bishop, Andre Norton, Billie Holiday, Robert Frost, Ernest Hemingway, F. Scott Fitzgerald, Zelda Fitzgerald, Amy Lowell, Edna Millay, Louise Bogan, and D. H. Lawrence. She is a former president of The Robert Frost Society and a current member of the advisory board of The Elizabeth Bishop Society; in addition to receiving several teaching awards, she has won the national John Cotton Dana Library Public Relations Award and the Jean Starr Untermeyer Poetry Award.

Thomas Travisano is Professor of English and Chair of English and Theatre Arts at Hartwick College, Oneonta, New York, where he also currently serves as Wandersee Scholar in Residence. He is the author of *Elizabeth Bishop: Her Artistic Development* (University of Virginia, 1988) and *Midcentury Quartet: Bishop, Lowell, Jarrell, Berryman, and the Making of a Postmodern Aesthetic* (University of Virginia, 1999); the coeditor of *Gendered Modernisms: American Women Poets and Their Readers* (University of Pennsylvania Press, 1996); and the principal editor of *Words in Air: The Complete Correspondence of Elizabeth Bishop and Robert Lowell* (Farrar, Straus & Giroux, 2008). He is the founding president of the Elizabeth Bishop Society and Senior Advisor to the Robert Lowell Society.

COPYRIGHTS AND PERMISSIONS

Anthem; copyright 2002 by Nathaniel Mackey. Reprinted with permission of New Directions Publishing Corp.

Gerald McCarthy: "The Hooded Legion" from *Shoetown*; copyright 1992 by Gerald McCarthy. Reprinted with permission of the author, Gerald McCarthy.

James Merrill: "The Victor Dog" and "Self-Portrait in Tyvek™ Windbreaker" from *Collected Poems* by James Merrill, edited by J. D. McClatchy and Stephen Yenser; copyright 2001 by the Literary Estate of James Merrill at Washington University. Used by permission of Alfred A. Knopf, a division of Random House, Inc.

Cherríe Moraga: "The Slow Dance" from *Loving in the War Years*; copyright 1983 by Cherríe Moraga. "Poema como Valentín" from *The Last Generation*; copyright 1999 by Cherríe Moraga. All reprinted with permission from the author, Cherríe Moraga.

Harryette Mullen: "All She Wrote," "Coo-Slur," and "Natural Anguish" from *Sleeping with the Dictionary*; copyright 2002 Regents of the University of California. All reprinted with permission of University of California Press.

Naomi Shihab Nye: "The Small Vases from Hebron" from *Fuel*; copyright 1999 by Naomi Shihab Nye. Reprinted with permission of BOA Editions, Ltd. (www.boaeditions.org).

Frank O'Hara: "The Day Lady Died" from *Lunch Poems*; copyright 1964 by Frank O'Hara. Reprinted with permission of City Lights Books. "Autobiographia Literaria," "Avenue A," and "Having a Coke with You" from *The Collected Poems of Frank O'Hara* by Frank O'Hara, edited by Donald Allen; copyright 1971 by Maureen Granville-Smith, Administratrix of the Estate of Frank O'Hara; renewed in 1999 by Maureen O'Hara Granville-Smith. Introduction by Donald Allen; copyright 1971 by Alfred A. Knopf, a division of Random House, Inc. The above reprinted with permission of Alfred A. Knopf, a division of Random House, Inc.

Charles Olson: "As the Dead Prey Upon Us" from *Selected Writings of Charles Olson*; copyright 1960 by Charles Olson. "The Distances" and from *Selected Writings of Charles Olson*; copyright 1966 by Charles Olson. "The Songs of Maximus" from *Selected Writings of Charles Olson*; copyright 1966 by Charles Olson. All reprinted with permission of New Directions Publishing Corp.

George Oppen: "Tug against the river" and "She lies, hip high" from *New Collected Poems*; copyright 1934 by The Objectivist Press. "Eclogue," "Birthplace: New Rochelle," "O Western Wind," "Squall," "Time of the Missile," and "Still Life" from *New Collected Poems*; copyright 1962 by George Oppen. "Of Being Numerous #7" from *New Collected Poems*; copyright 1968 by George Oppen. "Anniversary Poem" from *New Collected Poems*; copyright 1972 by George Oppen. "Till Other Voices Wake Us" from *New Collected Poems*; copyright 1978 by George Oppen. All reprinted with permission of New Directions Publishing Corp.

Robert Pinsky: "Shirt" and "The Green Piano" from *Jersey Rain*; copyright 2000 by Robert Pinsky. Reprinted with permission of Farrar, Straus, and Giroux, LLC.

Sylvia Plath: "The Moon and the Yew Tree," "Elm," "Daddy," "Medusa," "Lady Lazarus," "Poppies in October," "Kindness," "Words," and "Edge" from *Ariel: Poems by Sylvia Plath*; copyright 1961, 1962, 1963, 1964, 1965, 1966 by Ted Hughes. "The Jailer" from *The Collected Poems of Sylvia Plath*; copyright 1963 by Ted Hughes. "'Context'" from *Johnny Panic and the Bible of Dreams*; copyright 1952, 1953, 1954, 1955, 1956, 1957, 1960, 1961, 1962, 1963 by Sylvia Plath; copyright 1977, 1979 by Ted Hughes. All reprinted with permission of Harper-Collins Publishers.

Queen Latifah: "The Evil Men Do." Words and music by Queen Latifah. Copyright 1989 WB Music Corp. and Queen Latifah Music Inc. All rights administered by WB Music Corp.; all rights reserved. Used with permission of Alfred Music Publishing Company, Inc.

Adrienne Rich: "The Burning of Paper Instead of Children," "Diving into the Wreck,"

"Power," "Twenty-One Love Poems" (Poems I, III, IX, XIII, XX, and XXI), "Tattered Kaddish," and Part XIII: "(Dedications)" from "An Atlas of the Difficult World" from *The Fact of a Doorframe: Selected Poems, 1950–2001*; copyright 2002 by Adrienne Rich; copyright 2001, 1999, 1995, 1991, 1989, 1986, 1984, 1981, 1967, 1963, 1962, 1961, 1960, 1959, 1958, 1957, 1956, 1955, 1954, 1953, 1952, 1951 by Adrienne Rich; copyright 1978, 1975, 1973, 1971, 1969, 1966 by W. W. Norton & Company, Inc. All reprinted with permission of the author, Adrienne Rich, and the publisher, W. W. Norton & Company, Inc.

Alberto Ríos: "Mi Abuelo" and "Madre Sofía" from *Whispering to Fool the Wind*; copyright 1982 by Alberto Ríos. All reprinted with permission of the author, Alberto Ríos.

Theodore Roethke: "Cuttings" copyright 1948 by Theodore Roethke; "Cuttings (Later)" copyright 1948 by Theodore Roethke; "My Papa's Waltz" copyright 1942 by Hearst Magazines, Inc.; "The Waking" copyright 1953 by Theodore Roethke; "In a Dark Time" copyright 1960 by Beatrice Roethke, Administratrix of the Estate of Theordore Roethke. All from *Collected Poems of Theodore Roethke* by Theodore Roethke. Reprinted by permission of Doubleday, a division of Random House Inc.

Muriel Rukeyser: "To Enter That Rhythm Where the Self Is Lost," "The Poem as Mask," "Poem (I lived in the first century of world wars)," "The Speed of Darkness," "Waking This Morning," "Myth," and "St. Roach" from *Out of Silence*; copyright 1994 by Muriel Rukeyser. All reprinted with permission of International Creative Management, Inc.

Luis Omar Salinas: "My Father Is a Simple Man" from *The Sadness of Days*; copyright 1987 by Arte Público Press–University of Houston. Reprinted with permission of the publisher, Arte Público Press–University of Huston.

Gjertrud Schnackenberg: "Nightfishing" and "'There are no dead'" from *Supernatural Love: Poems, 1976–1992*; copyright 2000 by Gjertrud Schnackenberg. All reprinted with permission of Farrar, Straus, and Giroux, LLC.

Anne Sexton: "You, Doctor Martin," "Music Swims Back to Me," "Her Kind," and "For John, Who Begs Me Not to Enquire Further" from *To Bedlam and Part Way Back*; copyright 1960 by Anne Sexton and renewed in 1988 by Linda Sexton. "The Truth The Dead Know" and "Old Dwarf Heart" from *All My Pretty Ones*; copyright 1962 by Anne Sexton, renewed 1990 by Linda G. Sexton. "Lessons in Hunger" from *Complete Poems of Anne Sexton*; copyright 1981 by Linda Gray Sexton and Loring Conant, Jr., executors of the will of Ann Sexton. All reprinted by permission of Houghton Mifflin Harcourt Publishing Company; All rights reserved.

Maurya Simon: "The Bishop of Mysore" from *The Golden Labyrinth*; copyright 1995 by Maurya Simon. "Enough" and "Benediction" from *Ghost Orchid*; copyright 2004 by Maurya Simon. All reprinted with permission of the author, Maurya Simon.

Gary Snyder: "Walking Through Myoshin-ji" from *Axe Handles*; copyright 1983 by Gary Snyder. The above reprinted with permission of Counterpoint Press, LLC. "O Waters" from *Turtle Island*; copyright 1974 by Gary Snyder. Reprinted with permission of New Directions Publishing Corp.

Cathy Song: "The Youngest Daughter" and "Leaving" from *Picture Bride*; copyright 1983 by Cathy Song. Reprinted with permission of the author, Cathy Song, and the publisher, Yale University Press. "School Figures" from *School Figures*; copyright 1994 by Cathy Song. Reprinted with permission of the author, Cathy Song, and the publisher, University of Pittsburgh Press. "The Day Has Come When My Mother" from *Cloud Moving Hands*; copyright 2007 by Cathy Song. Reprinted with permission of the author, Cathy Song, and the publisher, University of Pittsburgh Press.

Gary Soto: "The Tale of Sunlight" and "A Red Palm" from *New and Selected Poems*; copyright 1978 and 1990 by Gary Soto. Reprinted with permission of Chronicle Books, LLC.

Kathleen Spivack: "Now the Slow Creation," "The Eyelid   The Red Tide," "The Insult Sonnet," and "The Moments-of-Past-Happiness Quilt" from *The Beds We Lie In: Selected and New Poems*; copyright 1984 by Kathleen Spivack. All reprinted with permission of the author, Kathleen Spivack.

Derek Walcott: "Love After Love" and "Dark August" from *Collected Poems, 1948–1984*; copyright 1986 by Derek Walcott. Reprinted with permission of Farrar, Straus, and Giroux, LLC.

Mitsuye Yamada: "What Your Mother Tells You," "Evacuation," "Harmony at the Fair Grounds," "Block 4 Barrack 4 Apt C," "Thirty Years Under," "Cincinnati," "Mirror Mirror," and "Drowning in My Own Language" from *Camp Notes and Other Writings*; copyright 1998 by Mitsuye Yamada. All reprinted with permission of Rutgers University Press.

John Yau: "Chinese Villanelle" and "Electric Drills" from *Radiant Silhouette*; copyright 1989 by John Yau. "Avenue of Americans," "Cenotaph," "Red Fountain," "Genghis Chan: Private Eye XXIV," and "Genghis Chan: Private Eye XXVII" from *Forbidden Entries*; copyright 1996 by John Yau. The above reprinted with permission of the author, John Yau. "Borrowed Love Poem 1" from *Borrowed Love Poems*; copyright 2002 by John Yau. Reprinted with permission of Viking Penguin, a division of Penguin Group (USA), Inc.

Ray Young Bear: "Wa ta se Na ka mo ni, Vietnam Memorial" from *The Invisible Musician*; copyright 1990 by Ray A. Young Bear. Reprinted with permission of Holy Cow! Press (www.holycowpress.org).

INDEX